Handbook for
NANNIES

Mary Thompson

Batsford Academic and Educational
London

Acknowledgments

I would like to thank all the nannies, employers, agency proprietors and tutors who have so willingly shared their knowledge and experience. In addition to those mentioned in the book, I am grateful to Sheila Bellamy, the NNEB training officer, and Marie Andrews, the former NNEB Course Tutor at Southwark College, for their advice and encouragement. Both Mrs Pamela Townsend, Principal of Chiltern College, and Mrs Louise Davis, Principal of Norland College, have also been especially helpful. The transparency used to illustrate the cover of this book was kindly supplied by Mrs Davis.

I shall always be indebted to Colin Valdar who gave me the privilege of editing Nursery World, and to Ivy Godfrey who was associated with the magazine for over 50 years. Without the experience of working with them, I would not have been able to write this book.

London 1985   MT

© Mary Thompson 1985
First published 1985

Typeset by Progress Filmsetting Ltd
and printed in Great Britain by
Billings Ltd
Worcester
for the publishers
Batsford Academic and Educational
an imprint of B T Batsford Ltd
4 Fitzhardinge Street
London W1H 0AH

British Library Cataloguing in Publication Data

Thompson, Mary
    Handbook for nannies.
    1. Day care centers—Vocational guidance
    I. Title
    362.7'02341   HV851

ISBN 0 7134 4750 8

Contents

4 Contents

6 *Contents*

Introduction

If you want to be a nannie, or if you are already working as a nannie, this book is meant for you.

You may be still at school; you may have time to fill in before you go to university; you may be an Australian or New Zealander living in the UK and thinking of getting a job as a nannie; you may be a nursery nurse student or already a qualified nursery nurse (NNEB), but at whatever stage of your education the information contained in these pages will be of practical help to all nannies who do a job that can be demanding and lonely, as well as being satisfying, creative – and fun.

Gaining experience

If you are untrained, but keen to work as a nannie, you could try to gain some experience with children so as to make sure it would be the right work for you.

Here are some ideas:

– Spend some time with babies and young children from the families of friends and relations
– Watch children in the park, in the children's library, in shops
– Listen to children on buses and trains
– Visit a nursery school, day nursery or playgroup
– Offer to help with a playgroup, church or mothers' club creche
– Advertise yourself as a babysitter
– Ask organisations such as Toy Libraries, Family Centres, Holiday Play Schemes, Adventure Playgrounds for Handicapped Children, whether they would allow you to observe them, then help.

Being a mother's help

If you feel you would like to make a career of being a nannie, or doing any kind of work with children, it is advisable to take a recognised training, but there may be a delay before you can start a course, you may still be unsure whether this is the type of work you want to do, or you may need to earn some money. In such situations you could take a post as a mother's help.

Look for these jobs in local papers, *The Times*, *The Lady* and *Nursery World*. You could also try agencies. Advertising yourself is another approach. An 18-year-old who advertised in *The Lady* for a mother's help post told me she received over 100 replies.

The looking for a nannie post section of this book also applies to anyone wanting to work as a mother's help.

Training

An information sheet *Work with children and young people* (S9) is available free from the Central Council for Education and Training in Social Work, Information Service, Derbyshire House, St Chad's Street, London WC1H 8AD. (Enclose a stamped addressed label.) This sheet details various courses that prepare people for work with children, and some of them would be suitable for nannies.

The most widely recognised and directly applicable is the Nursery Nurse Examination Board Certificate course. There is a brief description of this and other courses in chapter 24 but full details are available from the NNEB, Argyle House, 29–31 Euston Road, London NW1 2SD. (Enclose a sae.) The three private colleges, Chiltern, Norland and Princess Christian, are also listed on pages 223 and 224.

The NNEB course is open to people of either sex, though at present there are few male NNEBs. In the summer of 1984 there were six male students amongst the 4936 students who qualified as NNEBs.

So far, male nursery nurses seem to go to jobs in day nurseries, schools or residential units. Some may consider caring for young children in private families – in days gone by rich families sometimes employed male tutors rather than governesses so it would not be without precedent.

In these days boys are sometimes employed as baby sitters – perhaps parents feel a boy would be more able to protect a child from intruders – and within a family an older brother often takes his share of baby sitting.

Going to an agency

When you look at the columns of agency advertisements in newspapers and magazines it can be difficult to know which agency to choose.

For a start you could ask the Federation of Personnel Services of Great Britain, 120 Baker Street, London W1M 1LD for their list of member agencies that deal with the placement of nannies and nursery nurses. (Enclose a stamped address envelope.)

To become and remain a member of the Federation agencies must adhere to a code of conduct; they are interviewed by the Federation and their method of operation is carefully checked, so any agency on the Federation's list should be reliable and businesslike. It will also use the Federation's form of contract for employers and nannies.

However, there are some smaller agencies run by ex-nannies who are qualified NNEBs and these offer an understanding, personal service though they may not be Federation members.

When choosing an agency you should bear in mind the following points:

Training and experience
If you are trained or experienced and particularly want a post as a nannie, look for agencies that specialise in jobs for nannies; those that also place housekeepers, au pairs, even gardeners, may not have such a choice of nannie posts.

Equally, if you are looking for a mother's help post, choose an agency that specifically mentions mothers' helps.

Location
If you want to work in a particular area you may find that there is an agency concentrating on that area so look at the agency addresses and make phone calls to those that seem likely. Nannies who want to work in Knightsbridge or Kensington will find that there are many agencies covering those areas.

Personal recommendation
Ask other nannies, friends and college tutors for their advice and experience – negative and positive.

Continuity
Agencies come and go. Although new ones may well be good, those

that have been going for some years have at least proved their ability to function effectively.

Appearance and attitude

When you go for the interview look around. Are the agency premises well equipped, efficient looking? Do you like the manner of the person interviewing you? Is the interview thorough? (If they ask you for references this is generally a good sign that they take trouble.) Are the application forms well drawn up? Do they offer a personal service? Some agencies ask employer and nannie to meet at the office to discuss and sign the contract so that everyone is absolutely clear about the terms and conditions.

Choice of jobs

If the agency has no job that appeals to you there is no need to settle for just anything they offer. Go to a few agencies. If no one has what you want perhaps you are being unrealistic!

Follow up

Some agencies offer an advice service for nannies who have found jobs through them. This can be very helpful – especially in a first job – so ask if they may be contacted if need arises. You could also ask if they could introduce you to other nannies in the area where you will be working.

Registration

Agencies need to be registered in accordance with the Employment Agencies Act 1973; the agency's certificate and licence number is often displayed in the agency office, or it should be available for inspection. The agency's Licence Number should appear on the agency stationery.

1 What sort of job?

Temporary or permanent?

When you first decide to become a nannie – even when you have finished a training – you may be uncertain about what type of work or family would suit you best. One way of finding out is by taking temporary jobs.

Temporary jobs are also useful if you want to fill in time before starting another course, obtaining a permanent job in a particular field, or going abroad to work.

Some nannies feel that they will be bored staying in one place with one family so they prefer a succession of temporary jobs. To do this you really need your home, or friends with a flat, that you can return to and use as a base during any periods of unemployment.

I know one widow who had a pleasant house of her own but liked to take temporary jobs for a month or so at a time. This gave her a change of scene, a chance to meet new people, and some extra income.

A succession of temporary jobs can be fun for a while – even if after a spell of it you feel you want to settle for one family.

Be warned – you may go into a complicated crisis family situation. Perhaps the family want temporary help because of a new baby; so as to go on holiday without the children; because they are moving house; because of illness, bereavement or divorce. It may be a time when children are feeling strange and unsettled and you will be one more new and uncertain factor in their lives. If you can relate to the child quickly and help him or her through a time of upheaval you will be doing something positive and worthwhile.

I once went as nannie to a six-year-old whose mother had to go hundreds of miles away for a divorce hearing. The child was upset that her mother had gone; we were in a large house with just one maid and there was a terrible thunderstorm the first night.

Fortunately the weather improved after that. We went for some lovely country walks. I took her to riding lessons which she loved and, above all, I read to her. With these activities the week passed quickly and quite happily for us both, but I had to put the child absolutely first and concentrate all my time and attention on her.

You may go to a family where the nannie has left suddenly – perhaps even been dismissed for some reason. Again you could be dealing with an unsettled child.

It may also be that the family is not in the habit of employing a nannie and is anxious to get its 'money's worth' from you. 'I have just finished washing the kitchen floor,' said one temporary nannie when I spoke to her on the telephone. But she told me she was enjoying looking after girls aged four and six while the parents were at work – and she was being paid £75 a week all found.

In temporary jobs be prepared to work hard, for long hours and with little free time. Your help is really needed, otherwise they would not have gone to the trouble and expense of employing a temporary nannie. Even if the routine, staff arrangements, room you are given, family set-up is not greatly to your liking, remember that it is only temporary. You can learn from every experience and the end is in sight.

One advantage of temporary jobs is that they enable you to build up a variety of experience in a short time. So many employers want you to have practised with other people's children. After a few temporary jobs your experience will sound more impressive. On the other hand, you ought not to be too much of a nomad: one agency principal told me, 'I am not very keen on people who spend their whole time going from job to job, always living in other people's houses; I consider they are rather peculiar.' So it is wise to have a good reason for taking a succession of temporary jobs.

Note for experienced though unqualified nannies
Nannies Galore told me they especially welcomed nannies with experience who had acquired skills and knowledge through working in jobs where they were gradually given greater responsibilities and the opportunity of caring for babies. They were often able to place such people in 'maternity' (resident) posts for six weeks.

Commitment
If you are doing temporary jobs do be fair to the family and children. Stay for the period you promised – even if something

tempting comes along. I wouldn't want a nannie who ditched the previous employer – would you?

If you are not sure how long you will want to stay with the family, agree initially to stay for one or two weeks – you can always extend it to your mutual advantage.

When you are doing temporary jobs you may need to be registered with more than one agency. Try being with just two for a start. They will soon get to know you, find that you are available at short notice and hear about you from their families. When they know you well and have had enthusiastic reports on you from employers they will send you to the best jobs on their books or try to find you the kind of permanent job you want.

Make sure your passport is always up to date as you may get a sudden opportunity of a job or child escort trip abroad.

Daily or residential?

Before making a decision it is worth thinking about the advantages and disadvantages of both types of posts. If you are fortunate enough to live in an area where there are daily jobs within easy travelling reach, then you have a choice – unless you are committed to living in your own home because you are married, have a stable home-sharing arrangement or parents, brothers and sisters who need you.

Those who live in rural areas, depressed towns or places where there is already an abundance of nannies, may need to go away from home in order to find the type of job they want.

People who are away from their own country often find that a residential post gives them a base and 'someone you can discuss things with when you are 21 and 12,000 miles away from home,' as one New Zealander put it to me.

One agency said: 'Many of our best jobs are with families in the country; they are looking for a live-in nannie to take charge of a nursery suite. The more traditional nannie-employing families tend to want a resident nannie.'

Everyone could draw up their own list of advantages and disadvantages attached to the different types of post.

Here are a few points you should take into account:

Non-resident advantages
– Clear times on and off duty

– Greater possibility of free weekends
– More scope for leading your own life away from the family
– You live in your own home or shared flat.

Non-resident disadvantages
– Time and money spent in travelling
– Hours of duty may be long to accommodate a working mother
– Home where you work may be in an unsocial area
– You may be expected to do a considerable amount of housework.

Mrs O'Reilly, Proprietor of The Harrow Nanny Agency, told me that there were more daily nannies (trained and untrained) wanting Monday to Friday posts than there were posts available. It was then (July 1984) taking her six weeks or so to find a daily post for a nannie of 25+, expecting a weekly salary of £80 to £90.

Possible resident advantages
– Hopefully, living in a comfortable home with bed-sitting room/flat of high standard
– Tax benefits as salary is in addition to keep
– Possible use of facilities in the home, eg telephone, television, video, swimming pool, car, horse, books
– Opportunities for travel with the family
– The chance to live in London if your home is elsewhere
– Time to get to know family and/or other staff and make friends with them
– Large garden/grounds to enjoy
– Nursery suite with independent care of the children.

Possible resident disadvantages
– Homesickness
– Loneliness
– Long hours of duty and limited free time at weekends
– Insufficient variety and stimulation
– Nowhere to entertain friends
– Disturbed sleep (night feeds and wakeful children)
– Being 'On call' in the evenings
– Long and expensive journey from home (under 24 rail card will help overcome this)
– The need to fit into the routine and lifestyle in someone else's home.

You are not, of course, committed to one type of job for your whole nannie career. Circumstances may change for you, making one or the other preferable, or you may like to try each in turn. If you take a residential post and find you are not happy, it is a pity to give up the whole idea of being a nannie. Have a try somewhere else on a daily basis.

What sort of family?

You are now trained or about to finish your course, or you have decided to work as a nannie. Before you start studying advertisements, applying for jobs or going to agencies there are some points to consider. Try to think out which kind of situation would suit you best, but be open minded. An agency may tell you about a post you would never have imagined. One New Zealander, a graduate who had taken temporary nannie posts, was about to go off to Devonshire to 'nannie' two brothers aged 16 and 19 when I spoke to her. The family wanted someone to be with the boys, keep an eye on them and drive them around while the parents went abroad.

Working mother
Do you want sole charge of the child during the day? Would you be happy if the mother was out at work while you cared for her child/children? Many nannies prefer this situation. They are clearly in charge; there is no conflict over the daily programme; the child cannot refer to first one then the other. He knows nannie is looking after him for a given time.

One agency principal said 'It means the nannie has the run of the house all day, she may be expected to do more housework than if she was in a nursery suite but she has more freedom'.

'A working mother with one child is the ideal type of employer – as far as many nannies are concerned,' another agency told me.

Another great advantage of being nannie to a working mother is that parents are quite often perfectly happy to resume the childcare at the weekends; so the nannie has weekends free, as opposed to a traditional nannie-employing family that might allow the nannie only one free weekend each month.

However, it is no use taking a job in this situation if you are going to think: 'How awful of her to be working and leaving the child all day; why did she have children if she isn't prepared to look after them?'

You must accept that for their own good reasons some mothers return to their jobs (they may never get another comparable one if they once give it up) because they cannot, or do not wish to do otherwise. If they didn't return to work there wouldn't be so many jobs for nannies!

If you are going to feel trapped in the childcaring/homemaking role because another woman has what appears to be her freedom, and you resent the mother going out to work, it will not be happy for anyone – least of all for the child. So think it out, get your attitudes clear; regard your work as a nannie as your profession/career.

Many a mother would rather stay at home with her baby. She may feel almost jealous of the nannie at times: 'She takes him for a walk in the park while I stand in front of this class, sit at this desk, work on this ward . . .'. If the mother develops this attitude you may do well to look for a job elsewhere.

Here are some typical working mother advertisements

'Nannie needed for Sarah, 20 months, friendly, non-smoking family with mother working full time. Own room. Most evenings and weekends free.' (North London address)

'Professional couple seek young nannie, weekday, non-resident. Sole charge boy 12 months.'

'Teacher/dentist require non-residential NNEB for Jane aged 6 months; weekdays only.' (Surrey)

Lorraine Thompson, who founded Nannies Need Nannies, thinks there are many advantages for the nannie who goes to working parents. She says: 'Think carefully about accepting a post that requires you to work alongside either of a child's parents for most of the working day. Personal experience and comments from other nannies show that it normally does not work. Sole charge during the day keeps everybody sane. Even the children may suffer from the split discipline. Think about whether you could cope alongside a mother or father'.

One-parent families
According to *Family Matters: Perspectives on the Family and Social Policy* 1983 (Pergamon Press), more than 12% of children in the UK can expect to live in a one parent family at some time. For some of these children it means that a nannie will be a vital person in the

child's life. The nannie will be the sole person who cares for him day by day while the parent is working.

One journalist, divorced, said to me: 'I do not know how I would have managed without the nannies who cared for my daughter. It has made all the difference finding such super girls'.

When you go to care for the child of a lone parent there may be extra problems to face as the child may have suffered the stress of a parent's illness and death – or maybe a sudden death in an accident. Others will have been living in a tense situation preceding a marriage break-up. In such homes you must be prepared and able to help a child who has suffered confusion, insecurity and sadness.

If there has been a divorce you will need plenty of tact and patience for helping the remaining parent and child – and the non-custodial parent to organise access meetings that will not be traumatic for the child.

Whatever happens and however complicated the situation with her/his children, step parents and step or half brothers and sisters, you will need to remain calm, impartial, and non-judgemental; give your employer and the child your complete loyalty. You are the person who must remain emotionally uninvolved while offering the child consistent, kind and understanding care. All this can be very demanding.

In single-parent situations the parent and nannie often become close friends and feel that they are working together for the good of the child. But always remember it is the parent's child not yours. Don't ever let the parent feel left out. Refer to him or her in conversation: 'We will pin up your picture for Mummy to see . . .'. If you, as nannie, become too important to the child he may be devastated once again when you leave. These situations are not easy.

One single mother told me how she had employed a succession of au pair girls to care for her son, but they left her with enormous telephone bills. A parent who goes out to work all day and leaves a nannie in charge at home is very vulnerable. Having a nannie they can trust and rely on is going to be a great relief for such parents. As nannie to a child in a single-parent home you are doing a really worthwhile job. To give you an idea of the scope, here is a one-parent advertisement from a quality newspaper:

'Recently widowed barrister living Chelsea requires live-in nannie for three-year-old daughter. Good salary; driver and dog lover essential.' A magazine advertisement requests: 'Nannie/ mother's help for three children. Single-parent family, working mother. Live-in, most weekends free. Good salary. Must be able to drive.'

One-parent families – first job? Mrs Louise Davis of the Norland College told me that they never sent Norland Nurses to a single parent for a first post. She feels that it would not be advisable for any nannie. 'With a single parent the nannie can become more of a confidante to the employer, but it needs maturity to take on that role.'

Mrs Pamela Townsend, Principal of Chiltern College, felt much the same: 'A single parent may be adjusting to a new situation after divorce or bereavement; he or she may be experimenting with new relationships and this can be hard for a nannie to accept'.

'A nannie could be tempted to be judgemental, or to try and interfere,' added Mrs Davis.

These are the considered opinions of two experienced people. Each nannie will have to decide for herself when she replies to an advertisement and discovers it is for a single-parent family, or when an agency asks if she would like to be put forward for such a post.

The important thing is to have a clear picture of the situation. The employer should be fair and tell you if there is a 'live-in' boy friend or girl friend. You will know whether this makes any difference to you. In the circumstances will you be able to create a caring, loving environment for the child and help give him the security he needs? If you feel confident and happy to tackle the job, you could become a real friend to child and parent.

More than one family
There are all kinds of permutations in the share-a-nannie field.

There are mothers with part-time jobs who want a nannie for just two days a week. The nannie goes to her and then finds a similar family for the other three days.

There are parents who cannot really afford a nannie for just one child so they try to find another parent with one child, ask the nannie to care for both children, then the parents share the cost of the nannie's salary. In such cases the nannie may work in the two homes alternately, or care for both of the children in just one of the homes.

Some mothers start out with the idea of sharing. I saw one advertisement:

> 'Wanted: experienced nannie; non-smoker for Kate (2) and Billy (6 months) + friend Julian (4) for three days of the week. Phone Kate's Mum . . . or Julian's Mum . . .'

One mother told me she had engaged a nannie for one baby of six months but hoped to find another mother who had a baby and wanted a nannie. Then it would be company for the children and more interesting for the nannie – as well as reducing the cost to each mother, but enabling them to pay the nannie more. The nannie was starting at £40 per week all found.

If you are involved in such a nannie-share arrangement it seems reasonable to expect a higher salary because you do have greater responsibility: two employers to satisfy, two or more quite different children to look after.

Three families in one area of London advertised for 'Caring, energetic daily nannie (non-smoker) for three pre-school children on rota basis'. The mother told me they wanted someone 'sensible', a 'person the children would like' who would go to the three houses in turn, cook for the children, play with them and do some housework. They offered £70–£80 a week and the hours were nine to five two days a week, nine to four the other three days. She said they had had 21 replies to the advertisement placed in two magazines; eleven of those seemed suitable and five of them (mostly NNEBs) were asked to come for interview, but only one turned up. (Evidently this is not unusual.) They were hoping to interview others before deciding whether to appoint the one interviewed as she had seemed 'rather young'. The three families had had such an arrangement previously and found it worked well.

'Some people dislike the split loyalty of having more than one family and they are put off by that, but those who like it think it gives them more variety,' one of the mothers explained.

The advertisement may be more subtle: 'My excellent NNEB nannie is now available two days a week . . .'

You could equally well advertise yourself, especially if you want a particular area. I saw an advertisement outside a newsagent. 'NNEB with two-year-old daughter could nannie another child; her home or ours.'

Part-time work
If you are unable to find a full-time post of the type or in the area you want, it is worth considering a part-time job, and doing some other part-time work – not necessarily as a nannie – for the rest of the time. This will at least give you experience.

One mother told me she had only four replies (all unsuitable) to her advertisement for a daily nannie three days a week for one young baby. Through an agency she eventually found a 31 year-old, untrained but experienced nannie who has taken another nannie post for the other two days. The mother chose this nannie from 11 sent by the agency because she seemed to have 'a natural love of children' and, being older, the mother felt she could happily leave her in charge of the house and telephone, and to deal with callers, as well as the baby.

Rich or ordinary?
I once saw two nannie positions advertised side by side in a magazine. One was for a GP's family in South London, the other was for a titled family in a Stately Home. What different lifestyles those two nannies will experience, I reflected. Which would you prefer?

It can be enjoyable to live in a beautiful mansion surrounded by parkland. Life can be comfortable, duties not too onerous – it can also be lonely and rather boring. So much depends on the attitude of the family and other staff – and on the kind of person you are.

If you are going to feel annoyed by the family's wealth and position perhaps it is not the place for you. But, whatever the affluence of the household, the children will need your care and attention. Riches may not bring happiness – as we all know. There may be some qualities only you can provide. You could become a person who means so much to a lonely child, the person who provides consistent care when parents are frequently absent or occupied with their own lives.

As a nannie you need to be able to accept that life is not equal; some children do have an apparently easier time than others. It is your job to give of your best to the child whatever his circumstances. Don't try to be as grand as the family if you are not. Accept yourself as you are; be confident about your own gifts and abilities. There is no need to be over-awed by wealth or position. You are a professional person of integrity to whom the family has entrusted the care of their child or children.

Here is an advertisement from a 'comfortable' home:

'Country-loving nannie with training and experience, aged over 20, to care for 19 month old and two step children (aged 12 and 14) during part of boarding school holidays. Lovely Leicestershire manor house. Own room and tv; car provided for sole use + petrol. Good salary and annual bonus. Non-smoker.' On the other hand you might prefer: 'Super nannie/mother's help wanted for four children. Must love the country, horses, dogs, cats, etc. Chaotic household . . .' or 'Parents who manage a busy pub need nannie/mother's help . . .'

One of the advantages of nannieing is the great variety of households you could join; from cabin to castle. Study the advertisements, contact the agencies and take your pick.

Sheila Bell of Northumbrian Nannies pointed out to me that when a nannie lives with a rich family it is easy for her to become accustomed to a high standard of living. The family may have very good, varied food with plenty of delicacies, she may be given expensive presents and have the opportunity of driving a large, comfortable car. 'But', said Sheila, 'the nannie must keep her feet on the ground. I say to the nannies: "If this is not the lifestyle you are used to, enjoy it while you have the chance, but don't depend on it, don't take advantage of it".'

She went on to give an example: 'A nannie in a wealthy household had many of her meals with the family – they always had good wine with their meals and the nannie enjoyed it. When she went out with her boyfriend they could afford only the cheaper house wine. The nannie couldn't help noticing the difference'.

Those who have trained as NNEBs will know full well that there are deprived children in even the pleasantest town. They will not forget the needs of those children, even though their work is elsewhere for a while. A nannie job is largely what you make it, every different kind of work widens your experience of life, gives you more confidence and enables you to go on and do the next job even better.

Religion
You may decide you would be happiest working in a family that shares your religion – whatever this may be. If you go to a family of a different faith there may be slight problems over the style of food preparation and diet.

You could be expected to take children to an act of worship, or to observe festivals that are unfamiliar to you. The whole outlook on life, values and priorities may be different from your own.

If you are a keen Protestant you may not feel at home with the children's 'Hail Mary' or Guardian Angel prayers. On the other hand, if you are a Roman Catholic you may long to give another dimension to the children's religion.

These are not insuperable problems, but it is wisest to think them out before taking on a job. Try to be open-minded. It could be an educational and enriching experience to stay with a family of a different culture or creed.

The principal of Norland College told me that non-Jewish Norland nurses quite often went to Jewish families. In such cases the mother explained all the dietary regulations to the Norlander and the difference in creed did not seem to cause any problems.

If you go to a family of a different faith try to learn about their religion so you understand their customs and prohibitions.

Politics

If you have strong views or party allegiance it is probably as well not to go to the children of a politician of some conflicting party. Though it is good for children to realise that there are different points of view on most issues, it will not make for harmony in the home if you are violently opposed to the parents' views. Do not go to a situation where you can see you will be resentful or critical.

The same applies to CND and nuclear arms protestors. It is best if you have similar views.

One nannie told me that when she went to an interview the mother told her that the family ate kosher meals. The nannie did not really know what this involved. She liked the family and accepted the post.

It was only when she went to a public library on the way home and looked up 'kosher' that she realised all the restrictions implied. However, she has become used to it and can accept the diet because she likes the family and the job, but some nannies might not adapt to it so easily. This nannie is sensitive and thoughtful; she said to me: 'Of course I would never take a hamburger into the house – I eat it in the restaurant or on the way home'.

What age children?

Perhaps you are open-minded when you pick up the classified page

or call an agency. Baby, three-year-old, five-year-old and toddler
. . . you would be quite happy with any of them.

If you have taken the NNEB or NAMCW course (General
Certificate or Diploma) you will have learnt how to care for a young
baby. Those who trained at Norland or Chiltern are recognised as
being very capable and experienced in this field and they are much
in demand for maternity posts and permanent jobs where they care
for a new baby from birth.

The principal of one agency told me that some nannies were
happiest with young babies and they liked to move on to another
family with a new baby when the first child was about a year old.

On the other hand, another agency said: 'If only the NNEBs
would be more willing to go to young babies they could get splendid
jobs. They are trained to take over from birth to five but so many of
them want jobs with older (four to five year-old) children. Go for
the younger child – that's my advice'.

Those who are untrained and looking for their first nannie job
may, understandably, be nervous of taking on a new baby.
Sometimes you can learn a great deal from the mother; if she is
confident, gives clear instructions, shows you what to do, you may
be able to cope. There are plenty of helpful books and leaflets
available (see *Recommended reading* list) and the health visitor
should be able to offer support. (See notes on Caring for a baby.) If
you are inexperienced it is best to start in a post where the mother is
around for at least some of the time so that you are not left in sole
charge all day.

At one time a 'nursemaid' could start as an assistant to the
nannie in a rich household and learn from her. I did see one
advertisement for a 'second nannie' recently, but the employer
wanted 'Norland/NNEB'.

From talking to employers I find that many are willing to take an
untrained nannie if she has had experience with babies or children
of the relevant age. Several have spoken of 'excellent nannies' who
have 'worked themselves up' from being a mother's help.

So, if you are untrained but want to make a career of being a
nannie, go to jobs that will give you a variety of experience. Learn
by watching, doing, reading.

Three to five year olds
Those who have not worked as a nannie before may well find it
easiest to start with a child of three to five. At this age you can talk

to him, listen to him, enjoy doing activities with him.

He has generally become toilet trained, learnt to feed himself, and to do simple tasks. Hopefully he has outgrown temper tantrums, can understand something of time (eg that mother will be returning this afternoon) and is full of energy, curiosity and imagination. It is an exciting stage; he is fast acquiring knowledge and experience. A nannie who is a companion, ready to play with him, read to him, take him out, can contribute enormously to his development and have a satisfying day.

A child of this age may also be starting to attend a nursery school or playgroup, or the nannie may be invited to take him to another child's home to play, so she sees other children of the same age and meets the teachers, playgroup helpers and other mothers and nannies.

In betweens
A child of six months to three years needs a great deal of physical care. The nannie must be able to cope with everything from nappies to potty training; with bottle feeding, weaning and early meals. During this time the child will be learning to sit, crawl, walk, talk. He will develop rapidly, experiment, explore, get dirty and sticky and need constant attention. You cannot take your eyes off a two-year-old on the loose!

This is a stage that needs all a trained nannie's skill and understanding. It is very demanding, though rewarding.

An untrained nannie who is going to care for a child at this stage needs some experience (see *Gaining experience* section) and willingness to learn from the mother, other people and books. Although all children are so individual, once you have cared for a child at this stage (on placement or in a job) you will have more idea what to expect.

———

If you are wondering what age child would be most suitable for your first job talk it over with your tutor or with an agency principal who is herself a trained nannie (eg The Harrow Nanny Agency; Canonbury Nannies; Northumbrian Nannies or one of the old established agencies that specialises in placing nannies).

Two children or more
You may feel that caring for two children or more is a better use of

your time. It makes the day more varied and interesting and, because you will be busier than with one child, the day passes more quickly. Look at the advertised vacancies, then decide for yourself. You may find that the salary is higher (reflecting the greater responsibility) for two or more children. Also, the more children you care for the less housework you should be expected to do.

Two children are not necessarily more work than one, but three is often twice as much as two – at least that's the way it seems to work. I had three children in three years and two weeks!

Twins and other multiples Almost every expectant mother wonders, 'Is it going to be twins?' For 11 or 12 in every thousand such mothers in Britain the answer is 'Yes'.

Twins are always considered rather special people; there is a fascination and mystery about them. Caring for them appeals to some nannies and these posts are generally advertised specifically as 'nannie for twins aged . . .'.

Anyone who is going to care for twins should be well advised to study *Twins from Conception to Five Years* (see *Recommended reading* list) and get in touch with the Twins Clubs Association (they also have a register of families with triplets and quads) for details of literature, meetings and advice.

When caring for twins try to treat them as individuals – call them by their names, and have a relationship with each one of them not just with the pair. Make sure they both receive plenty of love and attention; be especially considerate to any non-twin brothers or sisters as they can feel left out or jealous when people make a fuss of 'the twins'.

Whether or not they are dressed alike, given identical equipment, presents and outings, is largely up to the mother. It seems hard to expect them to share every toy and there is a good case for giving them some different individual possessions. I think it is also good to take out just one of the pair sometimes, if this can be arranged. A Granny may well feel more able to cope with one at a time while nannie looks after the other.

Nannie to quads Anna, who trained as an NNEB at South Devon Technical College, took a job as nannie to quads. She helped with the babies while they were in a Special Care Baby Unit. When two of the babies reached a suitable weight they came home to Anna and the mother; a week later the other two joined them, then the real hard work began.

Anna and the mother had to have a fairly rigid routine and found that was the easiest way to work. 'Feeding on demand was out of the question – we would have spent all our time feeding'.

Every day 25 nappies were washed – and dried on the line if possible. (Tumble drying for so many is expensive.) The babies were bathed two at a time and taken for walks in two double lie-back buggies.

With all multiples, careful organisation is needed – and stamina on the part of mother and nannie(s). Anna was very conscious that quads were individuals 'who have their own personalities and appearances, just as other siblings would'.

The quads had a four-year-old older brother who 'coped very well with the arrival of the babies'. The mother and Anna were careful to give him some individual attention because, 'inevitably he was jealous at first as all the visitors were interested in the babies'. Nursery nurse students from a local college went to the family for practical work placements; by the end of a week they assured Anna they had learnt a great deal and felt they could cope with any babies after that experience!

Nannie to a handicapped child
A loving, capable nannie can make all the difference to the whole life of a handicapped child. Sometimes nannie and parents share the task of caring for the child and make it possible for him to stay in his own home rather than be placed in an institution.

The parents may find it too difficult to cope alone, and they may also need someone skilled who can accept much of the responsibility for the child and free them to be with other children of the family.

Before accepting a post as a nannie to a handicapped child it probably is essential to have a trial period to make sure nannie and child relate well and that the nannie can cope. There may be problems of temper, incontinence, or little communication.

If you become nannie to a handicapped child try to find out all you can about his particular disability. Those who have trained as nursery nurses will have visited special schools and day care facilities for handicapped children, but those who have not trained should certainly visit such schools and homes. You will learn from talking to the staff and watching their methods.

The Church of England Children's Society, the Steiner Association, the Spastics Society, and Mencap are the sort of organisations who will help you, plus the association for children with that particular disability, eg Down's Syndrome, National Deaf Children's Society. Some of these organisations have been listed in this book, but other addresses and advice can be obtained from the National Children's Bureau, 8 Wakeley Street, EC1. (Always enclose a stamped addressed envelope or label when writing to a society or charity.)

With a handicapped child it is most important that you do not underestimate his ability. 'Parents tend to baby them; they think they are more handicapped than they are,' a residential social worker said when showing me round a Church of England Children's Society home for severely mentally and physically handicapped children. You may have to show the parents how much the child is able to do.

Through a programme of teaching with weekly or fortnightly goals, the Portage Scheme can support parents and nannie, and aid progress.

If you are working with a handicapped child try to arrange to visit or help at a playgroup for non-handicapped children, so that you keep in touch with the norm and meet other childcare workers.

Posts with handicapped children are generally advertised specifically. Look in *The Lady* or *Nursery World*.

2 Working abroad and holiday jobs

Preparations

Going abroad as a nannie has a glamorous image. The jobs overseas section of childcare magazines is keenly read; agencies have a good response when they advertise posts abroad.

'South of France, own room and bathroom for young nannie who can take sole charge of boy five; English spoken.'

'Switzerland. Nannie needed for one year . . .'.

'London and New York. Traditional nannie wanted, six months a year in each place. Full staff kept, car available, childcare duties only . . .'.

Some jobs are with 'foreign' families, others with British families living overseas.

They all sound very attractive, but remember, once the novelty has worn off you can feel lonely, homesick or exploited.

One agency principal told me she had ceased to place nannies abroad because she didn't like not knowing where she was sending them. Another said that before she placed a nannie with a family abroad she took up references concerning the family; in any case she really preferred placing people abroad through her own reliable, personal contacts.

If you are seeking a post abroad it is as well to go to a reputable agency experienced in this field. Even if you do not take a job through them listen to their advice.

Documents
Unless you have a passport already you will be responsible for

obtaining one for yourself. (A form can be obtained from the Post Office.) Please do not embarrass someone who has not known you for the minimum required time by asking him to sign the form for you.

The employer is responsible for obtaining the necessary labour permit/green card, though in some cases the agency will undertake this task: 'It's a lot of rigmarole', one told me. If you need a visa (eg for a holiday in the USA) you should get it yourself from a High Commission or Embassy.

The Lady magazine states: 'Most countries require that foreign workers hold work permits and are properly insured against accident and illness. Before travelling check with the embassy of the country in which you intend to work that your passport, visa and permit are correct. If you have any difficulty in finding the address of an Embassy write to our Classified Advertisement Department, marking the letter (Embassy Enquiry).'

When you are abroad keep your passport yourself (if someone else has it you are to some extent in their power) but do not necessarily carry it around with you as your bag could be snatched or lost.

Money
Before you go obtain appropriate currency from your bank or at the airport. It is a help to arrive with some money in your pocket.

If you possibly can, take travellers' cheques or arrange with your bank some way in which you could find the fare home in an emergency. The least you should do is to have a guarantee from your family or a friend that they will advance the money for your fare home should it be necessary. Knowing that you could go home at any time will make you feel more secure.

Perhaps all this sounds rather gloomy. I have seen many letters from nannies who have had an exciting, highly enjoyable time abroad. It can be an experience that leads to a whole new way of life. You may even find that you marry and settle in the country. By all means be adventurous, prepared to consider something new, but look at the job and yourself realistically.

Do you make new friends easily? Are you prepared to try and learn the language? Are you fit and healthy? Adaptable?

Contract
Try not to commit yourself for too long a period. It is better to have a contract you can renew if all goes well.

All that is said in the previous section, concerning interviews and settling on a job, applies strongly to jobs abroad. In addition to the matters you would clarify about a job in the UK you need to check:

- How much holiday will you have? When can you take it?
- Will there be any help with your fare home for holidays?
- In emergency, eg family bereavement, will you be able to go home at once, even if it is just for a week or two?
- Arrangements for treatment should you become ill or have an accident
- Insurance for your personal possessions
- Driving licence needed and insurance arrangements
- Would a friend/your mother be able to come and stay with you?
- Are inoculations needed? (Consult family doctor) and read DHSS leaflet (SA35 '*Protect your health abroad*' from local DHSS offices and travel agents.)

Before you go
- Make sure you have clothes and shoes suitable for the climate and social life
- Buy an appropriate phrase or *Teach-Yourself* language book
- Pack a few favourite books you could enjoy reading and re-reading. In a foreign country one sometimes longs for an English book to read, but they may be expensive to buy there
- Try to talk to someone who has been to that country recently – to the particular area if you are going to Canada, India, Australia or the United States of America. (In such huge countries as these climate, culture, social life will vary with the region.)
- Try to learn something about the history, geography, politics, social customs, religion of the country in which you will be working. (Embassy information departments; travel and tourist offices and public libraries)
- Contact the Women's Corona Society, Eland House, Stag Place, SW1. They aim to advise and help British people about to live and work abroad. You will find them a friendly source of information
- If you are going to be nannie to British children of three years upwards it is worth contacting the Parents' National Educational Union, Strode House, 44 Osnaburgh Street, London NW1 3NN. They produce teaching handbooks, notes, courses, and tapes for parents to use with children and keep them abreast of the work they

would be doing at school in the UK. A nannie expected to give 'first lessons' would find their material invaluable; it has a structure and plan and prevents you from being vague and unmethodical.

Social contacts
If you are going abroad with a British family, or to join a British family, you will probably meet other British families – and perhaps their nannies. There may be a strong local expatriate community with a good social life. Ask about this at the interview.

If you are not going with a British family – or even if you are – you may want to make some contacts of your own. Find out about the local church of your denomination (London headquarters would be able to give you details or a local address to which to write). If you are Church of England you may also enjoy attending the local American Episcopal Church.

Organisations that promote social clubs and meeting places for British people abroad include the YWCA/YMCA, Girls' Friendly Society, Clubs for those in the Services. If you belong to the Girl Guides Association (or have been a keen Guide) you may be able to make contact with local Guiding.

In places such as Spain, Malta and Majorca there are local weekly or daily English language papers that give details of expatriate groups and activities.

But do not be insular. Try to mix with the people of the country. Make the most of your time there.

Packing
Use the check list on page 57. You may also want to include some of the following:

– One or two story books to give the children, eg Puffins
– A little present from England (Wales or Scotland) for the child, eg tee shirt, model London bus or taxi, small costume doll
– A small present for the mother or family, eg jar of good English marmalade, teatowel with local/London scene or theme, short-bread, packet of tea
– Cosmetics. If you have a favourite foundation and/or moisture cream you may want to take a new jar with you
– Simple remedies – aspirin, laxative
– A few favourite tapes/cassettes
– Pictures/postcards of your home area, photographs of your house

and family (to enjoy yourself and show your host family)
– Bible
– Any items your employer or the Corona Society recommend you to take.

USA posts

The principal of Norland College told me she knew of several nannies who had been sent home from an airport in the USA. Do not go to the States as a nannie unless your employer has obtained a green card for you. It will not be 'all right when you arrive' without it. Being turned back and sent home again is distressing and expensive.

The principal also warned that there are problems about working in the States as a nannie, and mentioned two particular difficulties Norlanders had encountered:

1 Families seemed to have little regard for a nannie's free time. They expected her to give up a weekend off if they offered her an extra 50 dollars.
2 Families with spoilt children imagined an English nannie would immediately transform them into polite, well brought-up young ladies and gentlemen!

Anyone going to work in the States really should be able to drive. Except in New York, Washington and a few other big cities there seems to be little suitable public transport. No wonder Americans call their car a 'third leg'.

Had my husband not been prepared to drive while we were in the States I do not think we would have seen much at all, without relying on the kindness of other people. We managed to borrow an automatic car, but were surprised to find not everyone drove an automatic, as we had expected. It is worth remembering this if you have a licence for an automatic only.

Warning story
One NNEB (trained at Torquay, and with plenty of experience and confidence) replied to an advertisement for a nannie to cruise in the Virgin Islands with an American family who had four children. The advertisement specified 'Childcare duties and early lessons' and stated that the previous nannie had been with the family for four years.

From a shoal of applicants this NNEB was chosen. She was sent her air fare, and off she went, full of excitement and with presents and learning materials for the children. She had worked abroad before, and had spent some time in the USA so she had more idea what to expect than many nannies would have had.

On arrival she found:

She was expected to do the cooking
The previous 'nannie' had in fact been a maid
The children were spoilt
The mother was demanding
She would have very little time off.

Fortunately, the NNEB was mature for her age (26) and sensible. She managed to avoid unpleasantness and simply told the family the job was not what she had expected. They tried to persuade her to stay and even offered more salary, but she refused and came home. She had taken enough money to buy an air ticket home, and the family did volunteer to lend it to her when they saw her mind was made up.

The NNEB had given up her flat and job in London (a coveted hospital play post) to go to the USA, so when she returned she stayed with friends for a few days then took temporary nannie posts. She now has a day nursery post and a share in a flat, so all worked out well. But it could have been more traumatic.

Hotels and holiday camps abroad

A sunny hotel room in seaside Spain can be a pleasant change from a bed-sitting room in Islington. As a qualified and experienced nannie you could find a job working with children on holiday. Hotels, apartment complexes and camp sites in European countries employ nannies/children's nurses/children's hostesses/play leaders to organise activities for children so that parents have some freetime without them.

Duties generally include running 'clubs', sports activities, competitions, trails, rambles, barbecues and craft sessions. You need to be able to cope with children of different nationalities, ages and temperaments. You must make it fun for the children, show that you are enjoying it too and satisfy the parents that you are capable, safety-conscious, and keen to give the children a really enjoyable time.

I watched the 'children's representatives' at work in a Churchill Family Holidays hotel in Majorca. The children were entertained for three-hour sessions every morning and they rejoined their parents for lunch. In the afternoons they rested or went to the beach or enjoyed activities in and around the hotel with their parents; they then had a 'club' session, which included tea, to give the parents another break from about 4.00 pm to 6.00 pm. The representatives were free to enjoy all the facilities of the hotel and they undertook evening baby patrols at the request of parents.

I could see that they needed to be cheerful, outgoing personalities, have plenty of energy, and be well able to cope. Some children can be 'awkward' even on holiday. The representatives had to be able to work well with the hotel staff, the tour operators and the parents. But they all seemed to be enjoying themselves.

An agent who advertised in *The Times* for 'Children's nurses for holiday hotels on the Continent' told me he wanted people who were prepared to throw themselves into the holiday and enjoy it because they would be 'mixing with the guests, eating with them and joining in sports with them as well as organising activities for the children'. He offered six month contracts, all expenses and £30 a week.

If you go to a job like this do take with you plenty of books of games and ideas for activities, some favourite stories to read to the children, and your own list of races, games, trails, crafts, you could organise with the children. Some quiz, joke, rhyme, sketches for acting and puzzle books would also be useful. (Look for these in the Girl Guide and Scout shops as well as ordinary bookshops.)

Find out what sports/games/craft equipment is provided. As a minimum you will need:

- Large and small balls of all types
- Skipping ropes
- Bats, rackets, rounders stick
- Quoits
- Skittles
- Chalk
- Felt-tipped pens (for doing notices)
- Tapes, cassettes (for musical games)
- Paper for posters, games, art
- Dice
- A few 'quiet' games, eg snakes and ladders, ludo, scrabble,

Monopoly (You may be glad to lend these to a parent who has a child unwell or suffering from sun and heat)
- A whistle
- A guitar or recorder
- Balloons
- Badges (for self and children)
- Small prizes
(See also *Garden play* section)

If it is a new venture and the company/hotel does not have this equipment discuss where and how it is to be bought.

UK holiday schemes (residential)

'England Holidays' the English Tourist Board's free holiday guide, available from Tourist Information Centres or by post, lists a number of organisations that provide activity and special interest holidays that accept unaccompanied children. If you study this you will see that some take children from five or six. Telephone or write to see if they have any vacancies suitable for NNEBs or people experienced with children. Dolphin Holiday activities (68 Churchway, London NW1 1LT) told me they like to employ NNEBs.

Working on these holidays is demanding but it can be great fun. You have an opportunity of canoeing, riding, hill walking, swimming, sailing . . . as well as supervising or looking after the children. Salaries are not great: for instance, PGL who take on about 2,000 people each summer, pay £15 a week plus keep (initially), but it is good experience and something an NNEB might like to do after finishing the course, but before starting a permanent job.

Local holiday schemes

Charities, Neighbourhood Associations and Local Authorities sometimes organise school holiday play schemes and need staff: paid on a pocket money basis, or as volunteers. Working on such schemes is rewarding, fun and another way of gaining experience.

Ask your local social services about schemes planned for your area and watch the local paper for announcements or advertisements.

If you are already nannie to a child old enough to join in one of these schemes you might be able to take the child to activities or outings and give a hand with the other children too – just as a mother might take her child and also help with the group. But discuss this with your employer before making arrangements.

Summer camps in America

The delights of a children's holiday camp in America have been immortalised in the song, *Camp Granada*. These camps provide sports and art and craft activities led by students and other young people. Sometimes they advertise in English newspapers and offer fare, board, accommodation and pocket money with time for a short sight-seeing holiday at the end of the camp. They usually ask people to commit themselves for at least six weeks so it is easier to fit in a holiday job like this at the end of a course.

When you reply to one of these advertisements ask to be put in touch with someone in England who has been to the camp and can tell you what to expect.

You could ask Vacation Work International for advice and their USA Summer Employment Directory (enclose large sae). Camp America, 37 Queens Gate, London SW7 5HR advertise for student staff (over 18) and say that they could arrange 'Family Companion' and 'House Guest' positions for nursery nurses. Be sure to check the green card position.

This is how one Norlander described her experience of a summer camp:

'The aim was to enable children who would be coming from the inner city housing projects of Chicago's notorious "Southside" to have a vacation from the city. The rural camp setting was completely different from anything they were used to. Whilst at camp they lived in wooden cabins with an outside unit where showers and lavatories were located.

'I was in charge of a group of seven girls aged seven to nine. Our days were exhausting. Breakfast would be at 8 am. They would then make beds, clean the cabin and the shower house. Activities such as arts and crafts, animal rides, nature hikes, drama and music followed. Swimming, volleyball and softball were popular.

'After lunch there would be similar activities until dinner at 6.30 pm. After dinner there would be more activities until lights out at 9.30 pm. We enjoyed a carnival, talent show, splash parties and movies. Occasionally we would cook and camp out overnight.

'There were many abused and behavioural disordered children amongst them and consequently they were the naughtiest children I have ever come across.

'My resources and patience really were tested to the full. Added to the difficulties of the children were my own personal physical and mental exhaustion which meant that at the end of each 12 day session I would collapse and sleep for two days.

'However, just being able to see the enjoyment the children were gaining, and the pleasure they received from flowers, animals and even just wide open spaces, was really reward enough, and I would say it was worth the feelings of frustration and despair which I experienced at various points.

'After camp I had a chance to travel around visiting friends in three different areas of the States and I met an extremely pleasant family with two young children for whom I then worked . . .' (Leigh Perry writing in *The Norlander.*)

UK holiday camps

The easiest thing is to make enquiries yourself. Holiday centres, camps and villages often offer organised activities for children and baby-listening services, but seasonal staff are mostly expected to be proficient in sports, to be life-guards, or playground supervisers, or to give domestic help.

Butlin's told me they employ some nursing staff, 'they must be NNEB' for creche duties from May to September. Accommodation is provided. Details from: Medical Department, Butlin's Holidays Head Office, Bognor Regis, Sussex.

A list of holiday parks, centres and villages (the term 'camp' is now unpopular) is included in the English Tourist Board's England Holidays brochure (free).

UK Hotels

Some four-star hotels employ nannies as 'children's nurses' who care for guests' children in playroom and paddling pools and play-grounds. They also keep lists of local qualified people available for baby-sitting.

If you want such a job, watch the local papers. The manager of the Highcliff Hotel in Bournemouth told me that was where he advertised for nurses. Or go and ask at a large hotel that advertises 'children welcome', or 'children's facilities'. It could be that they had never considered offering a nannie service, but faced by a presentable, qualified person they might give it a try.

You could also contact the head offices of such large hotel groups as Best Western, Trusthouse Forte, Inter-Hotels and Mount Charlotte Hotels. The last advertises . . . 'Each hotel has a nursery playroom packed with toys and a qualified nannie in attendance'.

If you live in a resort area you could contact the local Hotels Association.

Cruise ships

When I worked for *Nursery World* we received a great many letters saying, 'How can I obtain a job on a cruise ship?' It seemed to be so many nursery nurses' idea of a blissful job.

It is in fact extremely demanding, as one NNEB told me. She had to cope with children who were almost abandoned by their mothers once the cruise got under way; children who were spoilt; disturbed and bewildered. 'It was the hardest work I have ever done'.

We advised the nursery nurses to write direct to shipping companies and ask for information (enclosing a sae) but warned them there were long waiting lists.

One Norland nannie decided she would like to do this work, sat down with a list of shipping companies, made some phone calls and a week later was offered a job as a children's hostess aboard a ship bound for Australia. This is unusual.

She describes her work: 'I devised a daily programme including games and activities. It was usually quite hectic as I was working alone, but great fun. If the children did not feel seasick they were often ill on the playroom roundabout! Making sure that each age group, from toddlers to teenagers, had a good holiday was quite a responsibility. . . . You just had to be versatile but all nursery nurses know that. It was a lovely job'.

If you take such a post do check what status you will be given. One NNEB was dismayed when she found that, unlike the teachers on board, she was not allowed to use the officers' facilities.

3 Finding the right job

Having thought out carefully what type of job would suit you best, you have to set about finding it. There are various ways:

Through your college

In some areas local families apply to the nearest NNEB course when they want a nannie. Such vacancies may be posted up in the college or announced by the tutors. Most colleges have their own system for informing and advising students about jobs.

At Norland the college requires students to obtain their first post through the Norland Registry; the Norland Diploma and badge is not awarded until students have completed nine months of satisfactory service in a private residential post approved by the Principal. Employers must supply references before they are accepted for the Norland Registry.

At Chiltern many people telephone and ask for a nannie, but the college tells them to write in setting out briefly requirements and terms offered. These letters are then placed in a file that students can study. The Principal is always ready to advise the students and warn them about possible disadvantages.

The Isle College, Wisbech, has a useful handout for prospective employers of nannies. It describes the aim and content of the course and the final examination taken. Girls who take this course often find posts with local professional families.

Many of the nannie employment agencies send representatives to visit colleges, speak about employment prospects and give advice on job-seeking.

Through agencies

Study the advertisements in papers and magazines and make a short list of agencies that appeal to you. Telephone them and ask if they have jobs of the type you would like. It is not worth spending time and money travelling to an agency that may not have anything to suit you 'at present'. You stand a better chance at a large, old-established, well known agency.

Papers and magazines in which you will see agencies advertising include *The Times, Nursery World, The Lady,* and *NZ News UK*; look also in provincial and local daily or weekly papers.

When you telephone the agency they will probably ask you to come for an interview or they will offer to send you a registration form. It is never necessary for an employee to pay fees to an agency. They charge the employer. Most of them state specifically 'No charge to staff'. If you are in any doubt ask first; if they want to charge you go elsewhere!

You could send for the application form/prospectus from several agencies. You may find some specialise in particular types of post or areas in which you would like to work.

Remember, as a trained and or experienced nannie you are precious to an agency. They depend on people like you. Every agency has jobs. There are plenty of residential jobs – some good, others full of problems. Agencies pass on their jobs to each other, but they do not pass on their 'girls'. It is their aim to place you with an employer who will be delighted with you and spread the word that she found an excellent nannie through. . . . A good agency is equally concerned to place a nannie happily.

'I could put a girl into a post where she could be terribly unhappy,' said Sheila Bell, proprietor of Northumbrian Nannies, 25 Swallow Avenue, Skellingthorpe, Lincoln LN6 0XJ. 'It is a great responsibility placing nannies'.

Like some other agencies, Sheila offers good follow-up. Her nannies meet together occasionally; but they can always refer to her if problems arise.

As a nannie, you are working without other professionals around to guide you. It is quite different from being one of a team in a nursery. You may not know where to turn for professional advice unless the agency is friendly, realistic and headed by someone who has been a nannie.

Do not resent being given a very thorough interview by the agency. That is a good sign. Not all agencies take up the nannie's references before putting her forward for a job – sometimes there is not time if a mother wants help urgently – but if they do take them up it indicates that they are professional and competent.

As a nannie sent by an agency you have a responsibility to them. They have taken time and trouble over finding you a suitable job. Treat them with consideration. Let them know the result when you have been for an interview. Tell them when you actually take up the job. Be a credit to them.

Summary of what an agency can be expected to do for you
– Interview you carefully and discover your special qualities, interests, qualifications, experience, type of post you hope to obtain.
– Tell you about posts they have available.
– Arrange the interview and see that your travelling expenses are paid.
– Tell the prospective employer something about you and whether they have taken up references.
– Advise you on salary and conditions, and supply contract form.
– Negotiate with the employer if there are points about which you are uncertain, eg weekends off, uniform provision.
– Put you in touch with other nannies in the area.
– Be available for help and advice after you have taken up the job and when you want to change jobs.

'We can ask questions girls don't think to ask,' said Mrs O'Reilly NNEB, proprietor The Harrow Nanny Agency, 42a Roxborough Park, Harrow-on-the-Hill Mx HA1 2A. 'We can help to get all arrangements clear to nannie and employer'.

Through advertisements

From all that has been mentioned it will be clear that there is much to be said for finding a job – especially a first job – through an agency. This seems to give protection to the employee and means there is someone to whom she can refer in case of problems. However, many employers prefer to place their own advertisements and draw up their own short list, so it is well worth looking through the situations vacant column of newspapers and magazines. The columns of *Nursery World* and *The Lady* are traditional places for advertising.

Local papers (paid and free), evening papers and quality nationals are other sources. Some religious papers, eg *The Universe* and *Church Times*, occasionally carry such advertisements; and they are useful for nannies wanting to go to a family of their own religious persuasion.

Another paper, not in general circulation, but well supplied with individual and agency nannie posts, is *New Zealand News UK*. It is a weekly primarily intended for New Zealanders in the UK and can be collected from the NZ News UK office in the arcade behind New Zealand House, or send for a copy. In a typical recent issue there were jobs offering 'Horse riding'; 'Use of house in London at weekends'; 'Sailing'.

When replying to advertisements placed by employers the advice given under *Through agencies* applies equally. If an employer asks you to come for an interview she should pay the fares involved.

Advertising yourself If you are going to advertise yourself, study similar advertisements. Training/experience, your age, type of post sought, should be stated. Giving a box number rather than your telephone number or address has much to commend it. (There will be a small extra charge for this service.)

I know one girl, Rosie, who was waiting to go to a nursing training school. She advertised herself in *The Lady*: 'Capable girl aged 19 seeks post as mother's help for three months.' She received over 100 replies! The first came from a mother who had just had her seventh son. After one week Rosie and her mother narrowed it down to five families who lived in or near London.

They drove round, starting at 8.30 am, and visited them all in one day. Rosie's own mother – herself a former sister tutor – was amazed at the people who were ready to entrust a baby to her daughter's sole charge. One mother did not want Rosie, the other four offered her a job.

Rosie chose the mother who offered least money but whom she liked the best. For three months she looked after a nine-month-old baby and did jobs in the house while the mother was working.

She told me afterwards that she enjoyed the experience, but found it slightly boring. Another time she would go to a family with a toddler, or toddler and baby.

By contrast, Rosie's sister, a university student who had the same idea but only three weeks available, went to a family with four children while they were packing up and preparing to move to Hong Kong. She was kept busy every moment of the time, was well-paid and thoroughly enjoyed it, but was quite exhausted by the end.

Rosie's mother told me that replies to her daughter's advertisement continued coming for some weeks and she was offered 'some wonderful jobs' at home and abroad. She felt that by advertising herself Rosie was more in a position of interviewing the employer rather than being interviewed.

Newsagents It is very cheap to advertise outside a newsagent's shop. You are not limited to a certain number of words, and you are likely to obtain replies from the area where you would like to work.

Even if you do not live in such areas you could go to them to put up advertisements. In London the following areas might be fruitful: Chelsea; Kensington; Holland Park; Hampstead; Highgate; Islington; Richmond; Dulwich; Wimbledon.

Some shops will arrange to forward letters or keep them for you to collect – otherwise give them your telephone number.

Personal contacts

'The nannies sent to me from agencies were useless; the one I have now was a friend of a friend's nannie – she is splendid.' So said a mother of two who lived in a comfortable Hampshire home. It just shows there are no rigid rules. You may well find the right job through a friend.

Keep your eyes and ears open; ask around. Let people know the kind of post you want. But do not allow yourself to be 'poached' by a friend or neighbour of your employer, or the child's nursery school teacher. It is both unfair and unwise!

4 A nannie – what have you to offer?

Qualities

Over and over again nannies have used the words 'adaptable' and 'flexible' when I have asked them what kind of person a nannie should be. Employers have generally mentioned, 'she must like children'. Agencies have asked for reliability and sensitivity to the family's need to be alone.

The Scottish NNEB looks for qualities including: 'courtesy, co-operation, dependability, resourcefulness'.

Everyone could probably draw up their own list. I think that a warm, friendly personality is necessary, and a sense of humour certainly helps.

'I chose her because she seemed a nice person'; 'I thought the children would like her'; 'She seemed as if she would fit into the family'; 'I liked the way she picked up the baby.' 'I didn't take the one who seemed as if she would be "stroppy",' added another employer. In the end it is usually the pleasant personalities who carry the day.

If you are applying for a nannie post, presumably you feel you could look after a child responsibly and keep him happy. You need to be able to make quick contact with the child and let him feel that you are in sympathy with him and do care about him.

Children are very quick to sense an adult's feelings towards them. If you are not genuinely concerned for the well-being of the child, prepared to treat him as an individual, and capable of making a good relationship with him, that post is not the one for you.

Practical gifts

Being a nannie means caring for the whole child – many practical skills come into it. Often you will be expected to see to the child's washing, ironing and mending. You should be able to sew on buttons and name tapes, iron a 'party' frock and make a dress for a doll. It is helpful if you can put a new zip into jeans as well.

Many nannies enjoy knitting for the baby or children, and the mother gladly supplies the wool. (Double knit wool is satisfying to handle and results are achieved quickly.) You could ask the child to choose the colour.

Being handy at making things and doing crafts of all kinds is an asset for a nannie (see section on *Creative play*).

Cooking
You should be prepared to do simple cooking. Where the parents are out all day you will be responsible for the child's and your own lunch and tea.

Even if it is a household with staff, the nannie should not rely on the cook. One agency principal told me, 'The nannie may have a nursery suite where she does everything for the child including preparing and cooking his meals.'

If you live in as family you may be expected to help the mother with the meals. 'She is splendid,' said one employer 'she just joins in with us – helps set the table, load the dishwasher – whatever needs doing'. This was in a set-up that seemed to be working very well for everyone: parents, children (baby plus a 10-year-old girl) and nannie.

Driving

Over and over again agencies and nannies said to me 'You must be able to drive; it is essential for so many posts'. It can also make all the difference to life for the nannie herself.

In many country areas, buses are few; in towns, public transport or walking home alone may be unsafe.

Some families advertise 'use of car', others provide the nannie with her own car.

Employers may want the nannie to drive children to school, playgroup, dancing classes, parties. . . . This is an enormous responsibility. Make sure you are fully covered by insurance.

Never take other people's children in your car without their parents' permission. Insist on the children behaving well when they are in the car with you. (See section on *Travel*.)

Driving lessons

While taking a childcare course it should be possible to fit in driving lessons. You could babysit or take a Saturday job to pay for them.

If you have not learnt to drive before starting a job, discuss this with your prospective employers at the interview. They may agree to you having time off for lessons – some employers even offer to pay for them.

'It's very restrictive if you can't drive,' said one nannie. 'Girls who can't drive lose out on good jobs,' emphasised an agency. 'Learning to drive is the next most important skill in life after learning to read,' lamented a non-driver BBC producer while waiting with me for a bus.

Riding

Some nannie advertisements state 'keen rider preferred' and it certainly is an asset to be able to ride a horse. The child may have a pony of her own, or the nannie may be expected to take her to riding lessons. If you can share the child's enthusiasm, ride with her, or at least feel at home with the vocabulary of riding, you will enjoy the job all the more.

Don't feel that riding is only for the privileged child. Riding for the Disabled brings happiness to hundreds of handicapped children each year. Someone who is able to ride and is also trained and experienced with children would be most welcome as a voluntary helper. Contact Riding for the Disabled Association for the address of your nearest branch. Their office is at Avenue R, National Agricultural Centre, Kenilworth, Warwickshire CV8 2LY.

To find a riding school consult 'Where to Ride', a list of riding schools approved or recognised by The British Horse Society, British Equestrian Centre, Stoneleigh, Kenilworth, Warwickshire CV8 2LR (published by Granada). *Riding* in the *Illustrated Teach Yourself* series published by Knight Books is a useful introduction to the skills of riding and horse management.

Riding seems very much cheaper outside London and large cities so it is worth doing some exploring.

Riding holidays

The 'Ponies of Britain' produces a list of Trekking and Riding Holiday Centres in the UK and abroad. Telephone to check current price of the list.

The English Tourist Board's 'England Holidays' (free) lists a number of activity and special interest holiday centres that offer riding; more are included in 'Activity and Hobby Holidays England', also produced by the ETB and obtainable from Tourist Information Centres.

Swimming

It is most important for a nannie to be able to swim. Many local authorities offer free or subsidised lessons. Enquire at local swimming baths (listed in Yellow Pages) or write to the Amateur Swimming Association for booklist and information on courses. (Enclose a sae.) Harold Fern House, Derby Square, Loughborough, Leicestershire, LE11 0AL.

Any nannie who is teaching a child to swim will find My Learn to Swim Book published by Hamlyn and written by Ray Cayless (National Technical Officer, Amateur Swimming Association) a most helpful and attractive book to use with the child.

It may be possible to take the child to mother and toddler sessions at your local swimming pool. You may have more time than the parents have for teaching the child to swim. If you manage to teach the child to swim you are making a real contribution to his health and safety and are giving him an asset for life.

Languages

Being familiar with another language obviously widens the scope for employment abroad or with a European family resident in the UK. Even a groundwork and basic knowledge on which you can build can make all the difference: 'Prefer German speaking . . .'; '. . . basic French'; '. . . some French', were requirements mentioned in advertisements for nannies overseas in a recent issue of The Lady.

One offered paid French classes. Others stated 'young professional English speaking family' (Sweden), 'Parents and children speak English,' (Paris), 'English speaking family' (Italy), but even so a language would be a help for the nannie's own social life.

You could look around for local authority evening classes, private courses and tutors, and borrow or buy cassette courses.

5 The interview

Before you go

Think out beforehand and jot down the relevant facts and dates about your education and training. You will then be prepared for questions or able to fill in a form quickly.

Decide who you would like to give as referees; make a quick phone call to check that they are willing.

If you have written references or testimonials take photo copies with you. (You may be asked to produce the originals subsequently.)

Be open-minded and ready to consider any vacancy the agency thinks suitable for you. If it really does not appeal (eg on grounds of location, age of child/children, circumstances of family or salary) say so – there is no point in wasting everyone's time. It is worse still to agree to go for an interview then not turn up!

Whether you are being interviewed by an agency or an employer you will, of course, dress in a way that gives you confidence and is natural to you. You want to show you are the kind of person to whom an employer would be happy to entrust her children.

If you are given an address and told to write a letter of application make sure you include the following points: Age, education, training, experience, background (eg younger brothers or sisters), interests and why you think this particular job is one you could do well and enjoy.

When you are told to telephone the prospective employer, think out what you are going to say before you pick up the phone.

Going to an interview

Allow yourself plenty of time when you are going for an interview. Write down the directions and check them with a map or a local street guide. It may be clear to the employer that Acacia Grove is the third on the right – not counting the cul-de-sac – but it may not be so obvious to you. The walk from the station can take longer than you expected; the number you want may be at the far end of the road.

At an interview

– Look at the person
– Speak clearly and don't answer just in monosyllables
– Show that you can make quick, friendly contact without being 'pushy'
– Do not be afraid to ask questions
– Take an interest in the child; look at him, speak to him naturally, but don't 'rush' at him
– Never criticise your previous employer. ('The girl said the previous family had "exploited" her,' one mother told me. 'I didn't take her because I thought she might say the same sort of thing about us – although, of course, one doesn't like to think of anyone having been exploited.')
– Be courteous
– Show you are practical – if the child spills his milk offer to wipe it up.

'Get everything clear at the interview' is the message from nannie after nannie. 'Once you have made friends with them it is more difficult to ask about your holiday,' as one put it. 'If only she had told me in the beginning what she wanted me to do each day it would have been so much easier,' said another.

Do they really want a nannie?

Think carefully – does this employer want a nannie or a mother's help? A good agency will have sorted this out with the employer and asked her to be precise about her requirements, but a mother who has never had a nannie before may have advertised for one without really considering what she wants.

If you are young and have not had a nannie job before it could be better to take a mother's help post to gain experience without having to assume 'sole charge'. After a year in such a post you could go as a nannie more confidently. Several agencies told me they were glad to place nannies who had 'worked their way up' from being a mother's help to being a nannie capable of sole charge.

Even if you go as a nannie do accept that you will have to do a certain amount of housework – just as most mothers do. When the child spills milk/paint, makes the highchair sticky, splashes on the bathroom floor, you are the one who will have to clear it up, even if you are in a nursery suite that is cleaned by someone else. Because you have to do a certain amount of cleaning and tidying up, do not think of your work as being a lowly job: it is all part of the skilled, responsible care you are giving to a young child.

Do not agree to conditions and duties you are not prepared to fulfil. It is unfair to accept them so as to get the job, then be discontent.

See all the household

Make sure you meet all the people in the family; this is why a weekend there is a good idea. There may be a Granny living in a top floor flat. Is she going to interfere while mother is out? Will she expect the nannie to do shopping and other jobs for her?

There may also be other children around, perhaps older children from a previous marriage of one of the parents. Do you like those children? Will you be expected to take responsibility for them in the holidays or supervise their homework?

You could be quite happy with these factors and think that it will enrich life with the family. But is it best to know about them beforehand.

Be observant, perceptive. Try to get the feel of the household. Consider whether you would fit in there.

Contract

Under the Contracts of Employment Act 1973 the Employer is bound to provide the nannie with a written statement setting out the terms of her employment. Some agencies have their own contract, others use the model contract drawn up by the Federation of Personnel Services (copies obtainable from FPS, 120 Baker Street, London W1M 1LD) for the guidance of member agencies that place nannies. A list of these agencies can be supplied with the contract sample. (Enclose sae.)

The Harrow Nanny Agency often suggests that employer and

nannie meet at the agency offices to sign the contract. This agency principal, like the principal of Canonbury Nannies, suggests that employers and nannies keep in touch with the agencies and consult them should any problems arise. 'I encourage the girls to come back to me and, if necessary, we all meet here to discuss the position and sort things out.'

According to the agencies the things that can cause problems are sick leave, duties, non-payment of national insurance contributions by the employer, and employers (especially lecturers and teachers) wanting to 'put the nannie off' during holiday periods.

Whatever contract form you use there will probably be other detailed points you have discussed. It is most important that these are written into the contract, then there need be no dispute about what time you are to return from a weekend off or whether you have days/afternoons off on fixed days or to suit the family and by prior arrangement.

This is not an occasion for vagueness. If you like the mother and children it may be hard to raise so many points and have everything in writing, but now is the time to do it. You will, of course, cooperate, be flexible and considerate once you are in the job, but you need to have everything written down so that the family is aware of its obligations to you, and does not take it for granted that you will just meekly fit in with their plans.

Some people I have spoken to – agencies, lecturers, and nannies – have stressed the importance of putting everything in writing. Employers have not always been so definite; they have talked about 'give and take' and 'working it out once she is here', but on reflection they have seen that a written contract is best for both sides. Employers too need to know what they can fairly expect.

Make sure the following points are clear to you both:

Salary and method of payment
Salaries seem to vary greatly; I have had figures from £29 to £75 (July 1984) quoted for resident nannies; £70 to £120 non-resident. This is something you need to discuss with the agency beforehand.

How salary is to be paid: weekly, monthly, cash, cheque, banker's order?

Tax and National Insurance arrangements
The Federation of Personnel Services of Great Britain states:

'Nannies should never accept being self-employed. This is bound to cause problems when they need to claim government benefits. The nannie must insist that the family deducts her tax and national insurance and gives her a weekly or monthly salary statement showing deductions.'

Hours of work and holidays
Agree on hours of work, and days and weekends off. NB You are entitled to Bank Holidays or days off in lieu.

Accommodation
Ask to see your room and the bathroom you will be expected to use.

Living arrangements
Where will meals be taken? (One employer I spoke to seemed very vague: 'We wouldn't want her eating with us every evening, just once a week perhaps to discuss how things are going. She could cook for herself or go out.' – On £40 a week!)

If you are expected to cook your own evening meal, who provides the food? Where do you cook it? Ask.

Duties
How far are these entirely concerned with the children? Will you be expected to see to their clothes? cook for them? clean the nursery/playroom? Do they want you to do some light housework? (This is quite usual in homes where the mother works.) Will you be expected to baby-sit? If so how often? Will this mean extra payment? (In residential work the nannie is generally regarded as being 'off-duty' after 7 pm but where there is a young baby she may be expected to give a 10 pm feed.) If the baby wakes in the night who will be responsible the nannie or mother?

Trial period and notice required
Normally in the first few weeks of employment one week's notice (or salary in lieu of notice) is required on either side. After four week's employment it is generally four weeks on either side.

Sick pay
Most agencies recommend one month at full pay (less National Insurance benefits).

Car

Will you be allowed use of the car? A chance to learn to drive? Will you be expected to drive the children to playgroup, parties, outings or school?

Any allowance of petrol for your private motoring?

Uniform

Nannies from private colleges are often expected to wear uniform on occasions, if not every day. Some nannies like to wear it because they feel it makes them more clearly 'professional' and distinguishes them from au pairs or other staff.

If your old college has no specific uniform you can buy a simple nursing type uniform from E and R Garrould Ltd, 104 Edgware Road, London W2. They have a catalogue, which is obtainable free (shop and mail order service). One style of dress they frequently sell to nannies is cotton, zip fronted with two patch pockets, in white, mid-blue or pink. Alternatively, you could buy a simple cotton shirt waister style dress in Marks and Spencer – or some other chain store – and keep it as a uniform dress.

Harrods are the sole stockists of Norland uniform. Purchasers must produce proof of elegibility to wear it.

Chiltern regulation caps are very beautiful, but at one hospital the authorities told the nursery nurses to stop wearing them. The Chiltern nurses were being mistaken for Sisters!

The NNEB badge could be worn on the nannie's uniform. Any NNEB who does not have a badge can obtain one from the Board if she quotes her NNEB registration number. Telephone to enquire the current price plus postage.

When an employer requires a nannie to wear uniform the employer should provide it.

Entertaining and social life

Unless you are a mother's help under 18, I do not think an employer should stipulate by what time the nannie must be in at night. You are, presumably, a responsible person and able to decide this for yourself, so long as you do not stay out so late you are too tired to get up for the children in the morning.

Normal courtesies apply, as in any family. You would not expect to worry your employer by being unusually late without warning her; you would not entertain friends, or play loud music late at night. You will be expected to conform with their routine for locking up at night. You will respect their attitude and conventions about smoking, and show consideration in your use of the telephone. (Check that reasonable use of the telephone will be allowed.)

If you wish to attend church on Sunday mention this at the interview.

It may seem pernickety to consider and discuss all these points at the interview, but it is better for everyone if the employer thinks out what she is offering and the nannie knows what to expect. Of course there will be give and take on both sides; the nannie must be flexible and willing to set the good of the child against her personal plans, when there is some crisis or emergency.

Before you say 'yes'

Apart from all the formal points mentioned, there are some more things you need to consider before you accept a job. These include:

– Do I like the family? Shall I be able to form a good working relationship with the mother?
– Did I take to the children? Do they seem spoilt, aggressive?
– Will I be able to look after them sympathetically?
– Can I fit in with the household? Is it too formal or too chaotic for me? (One NZ nannie said to me: 'I didn't realise I was driving her crazy by not putting things back in the right place in the kitchen.')
– What about the house and room? Is it warm enough? (You don't want to go to someone who is too mean about heating.)
– Is the room they have offered very noisy? dark?
– What about pets? If you hate dogs, and they have a dog that jumped up at you it may not be the place to choose.
– Is there plenty of space and scope for the child to play? The Harrow agency pointed out: 'The girls are taught to encourage "messy play" then they find the family does not like it and there are no facilities for it'.
– Is the family vegetarian? Are they health food fanatics?
– If you have queries and uncertainties about these points now is the time to discuss them.

It isn't fair to a family to move in, then leave after a few months. If you have gone to them through an agency they will probably have paid a considerable fee for you! (Some agencies do not charge a further fee if they send a second nannie to replace one who has left within six months.) It is usual to think in terms of staying at least nine months or a year (except for maternity posts). If you want to stay for less it is better to take temporary posts.

You can tell for yourself whether you think it is likely to work; whether you will be able and happy to bring up the child in the way the parents wish.

You need to be able to talk to the parents at the interview, and to feel that you will be able to talk to them once you are in the post. 'If you can't talk to the family, don't take the job,' says Sheila Bell.

Try to look at it from the family's point of view. Will they find you adaptable, cheerful? Will they like having you living in their home? Above all, are you prepared to care for their child in a responsible, kind and capable way?

Having accepted the job make up your mind to do the best you possibly can for the child and his family.

Before you start the job

If it is at all possible see if you can spend some time with the family before you move in as the nannie. Spending a weekend with them, using the room they have offered you, seeing their day to day routine and attitude to the upbringing of the children will give you far more idea of the situation to which you will be going. It will also give the family a clearer picture of you. After such a weekend you might mutually agree that it would not work very well.

On the other hand, if you are going to take the job it will allow the child a chance to get to know you and you will be less of a stranger when you move in and take charge.

Those who find a job while they are still at college may be able to arrange to spend part of the vacation with the family.

Those who are going to a family as a daily nannie could offer to babysit a few times, or perhaps they could take the child out one afternoon.

Meeting the previous nannie

Where you are taking over from a nannie who has had a happy relationship with the family and is leaving for a good reason it could be a help to spend some time with her – perhaps a day or two working together. Hopefully, you will at least meet her when you go for the interview and she will be able to show you round and tell you about the routine.

With families where the previous nannie has not been a success there may be less chance of meeting her. If that is the case, don't worry. You have decided you like the family enough to accept the job. Go with an open mind; make your own judgements without accepting other people's labels. The child your predecessor found 'spoilt and difficult' may respond to you. If the family expected too much of the previous nannie they may have learnt from the experience; perhaps they will be more considerate to you.

6 Starting work

So you have been offered a job and accepted it. Everything has been arranged in a clear, straightforward manner. The day when you are to start work and the time of your arrival has been fixed. If you are going to a residential post the employer should pay your fare to come and take up the post. (It is well worth buying an under-24 rail card if you are likely to travel to and from home by train.)

Luggage

Do not take too much with you for a start. If your home is in the UK you can always collect some more clothes when you go home.

Suggested initial list
– Dressing gown or housecoat
– Slippers
– Hot water bottle?
– Nightwear
– Underwear
– Clothes for on and off duty
– Dress or skirt and blouse for evening wear (the family may invite you to join in their parties)
– Tights
– One or two of your own towels
– Toiletries
– Radio/clock radio/cassette player
– Favourite story books to read to the children
– First Aid manual
– Scissors
– Game or puzzle you can introduce to the children
– Aprons
– Stationery and stamps
– Bible

When you arrive

Call the employer and her husband Mr and Mrs . . . . You can be
less formal when you get to know them. 'I always wait until they say
call me Suzanne or whatever,' said one New Zealand nannie.' (She
was a graduate who had enjoyed a number of temporary nannie
assignments while waiting to start a post-graduate course.)

They will probably call you by your Christian name, or Nannie
followed by your Christian or surname – just "Nannie" in
traditional households. Norlanders are usually called Nurse followed by Christian or surname, or just by the Christian name.

What should they call you?

You may decide that being called Nannie (followed by your
Christian or surname) will make your role clearer to the whole
household. If so, say this when you begin working with the family,
everyone will then do this naturally. Once they have started calling
you 'Fiona' or whatever, they will not find it easy to change to
'Nannie Fiona'.

Safety check

On your first or second day in the home look for any danger points
that need remedying or special vigilance. Mention them to your
employer tactfully – after all it is her child you are concerned about.

Features to check include:
– Gas appliances
– Unguarded fires
– Accessible electric plugs
– Temporary connections on any electric appliance (a child could
try to remove black tape on flex)
– Damaged electrical plugs and fittings
– Fuse box in cupboard under stairs or elsewhere that child could
reach in unsupervised moment. (I once sent for the electricity
board because 'All the electricity has failed'. The electrician found
it had been switched off at the fuse box under the stairs. It was an
expensive way of discovering that two-year-old Samuel could reach
this!)
– Flex that is of the condemned type or could cause a child (or

adult) to trip
- Upper storey windows that are easily opened
- Balconies
- Sharp knives and tools
- Tablets in bathroom or on mother's dressing table
- Glass doors (one of my children once threw himself against one in temper: 20 years later the scar on his leg remains)
- Bookcases and cupboards with glass fronts
- Accessible household cleaners/bleach (kitchen, bathroom and lavatory)
- Swimming pools, paddling pools, garden ponds (a child can drown in 5 cm – 2 in. of water)
- Stairs (is there a sharp bend where a child holding on to bannisters could easily miss his footing?)
- Stair gates – are they needed, adequate, too easily opened?
- Bannisters – are the supports horizontal so that a child could fall through, climb through, or up and over? If vertical are they widely spaced so that a child could fall through?
- Playpen – width of slats; easy for child to drag/push across the room and into danger; catches strong enough?
- Front door that could easily be opened by child
- Gates (When we lived in a Devon village and had an adventurous three-year-old the front gate was a constant worry – outside was a tempting lane that led to the village school with its sandpit, but milk lorries just hurtled down that lane)
- If the child goes riding make sure his hat fits properly.

The child's safety will be in your hands. You need to be watchful and alert at all times. So many tragedies could have been avoided. One to four years is a high-risk age group for accidents. They are one of the major causes of death in pre-school children.

Things you need to know

Especially if both the parents are going to be out leaving you in charge of the children you need to have the following information in your mind or clearly written and accessible, kept within easy reach of the telephone:

- Numbers where parents can be reached
- Family doctor's telephone number and note of surgery hours

– Whereabouts of nearest hospital casualty department
– Nearest neighbour you can call on in emergency or if telephone should be out of order. (You want someone likely to be at home during the day)
– Nearest relative of parents (Just suppose both parents were killed or injured in some tragedy)
– Dental surgery telephone number
– Taxi rank or mini-cab office.

Find out where the following are:
– Gas meter
– Electricity meter
– Spare fuses; make sure you know how to replace
– Tap for turning off water at mains
– Central heating switches
– Burglar alarm switches
– First Aid box
– Instruction booklet for washing machine/other appliances (Ask to be shown how to use appliances)

You should give the family a note of the name, address and telephone number of your own nearest relative.

First day

Don't 'overpower' the children. There is plenty of time for them to get to know you. Be calm; remain unimpressed if they try to show off.

Be friendly and courteous, but firm. Watch and listen to the mother. Does she give way to the children? If so it is going to be harder for you!

Talk to the children, not down, of course. (Did you notice how Prince Charles taught Prince William 'microphone', 'camera'? No baby talk to that two-year-old at his birthday photo call.)

Ask the children to do simple things. Move at their pace. If they seem slow to do things for themselves go along with them at first. There will be plenty of time for encouraging independence. You can start teaching them to fasten shoes and do up buttons when they have become accustomed to you.

Don't make an issue over meals and feeding. Check up with the mother privately. Does he really never drink milk? Or was he trying it on?

Let the child see it is going to be fun having you around. Ask him to show you his toys and books. Play with him or sit quietly beside him as he plays. You could have in mind one or two simple games and activities to start playing if the child seems bored.

Follow the family's usual routine (checked out with the mother beforehand). Bath then supper? Supper, bath then bedtime drink and story? Try to keep things familiar and normal.

Don't try washing hair or cutting toenails on the first evening.

Be generous with praise and encouragement. The child will want you to approve of him.

Don't appear to be in a rush, even if it is the end of the first day, you feel tired and are longing to go to your room or home. He will soon sense hurriedness.

On the other hand, be firm about settling him down. 'One story then I am going home/going to tidy my room. . . .' If he gets up again, put him back to bed immediately as he may be trying you out.

Homesickness

Being 'sick for home' is no new affliction. Before Ruth ever stood 'in tears amid the alien corn' it must have struck at the hearts of soldiers, sailors and brides in a foreign land.

It can be deep anguish sweeping over a child at boarding school, a student at college, a young serviceman, even a holidaymaker. Small wonder it affects nannies too.

Mrs O'Reilly considers it to be the 'number one problem' for nannies who take up resident posts.

What can you do to overcome it?
– Keep busy and occupied in mind
– Have a telephone chat with parents or friends at home, if that will make you feel better
– Work out how soon you can go home for a weekend. Often, once you have been home it is easier to settle in new surroundings
– Remember, you will get over it. Think of the crofters driven from their homes in the Clearances; settlers, explorers, refugees – they do settle though their leaving home was more traumatic than simply coming to London (or some other strange city) to take a good job – a job you want to do.
– Try and make new friends and develop a fulfilling, interesting life

while you have the opportunities the job gives you.

– If you are trained, ask the National Association of Certificated Nursery Nurses, c/o 63a Niton Street, London SW6, for details of the nearest branch.

– Remind yourself, it is probably only for a time that you are away.

– You could probably go back home for your next job, but you may not want to by then.

– Think to yourself, 'If I give up and go home again, what will it really be like? Is it so very exciting there? Will I get another job? Surely I have the confidence and courage to give this a fair trial.'

Sheila Bell tells me she often places nannies from the north of England with families in London. To help overcome any homesickness she puts nannies new to London in touch with another nannie from their home area. Sheila runs a particularly caring agency, but this is the kind of service other good agencies will provide.

7 A nannie's opportunities

Nannies are fortunate in that generally they have to relate to only one child, or two or three – seldom more than four – children. It is not like having to get to know a whole nursery class, family group in day care, or a roomful of babies in a day nursery.

The child who has a nannie is fortunate too. He has the comfort and security of being in his own home for much of the day – something he will lose at five anyway – and he has the companionship of a person whose main task it is to care for him and any brothers and sisters or friends who share the nannie.

If the nannie is prepared to talk to the child, listen to him, play with him, stimulate his thinking, look after him physically and provide a calm environment in which he feels happy and appreciated she is giving the child a splendid start in life. Next to the child whose mother or father really enjoys being at home with him and is prepared to give him time and attention, the child with a nannie has many advantages.

The importance of the interaction of children and adults through play was recently emphasised by Professor John Newsom (co-founder of the Child Development Research Unit at Nottingham). He said that research had not proved that children who had an early nursery school education did any better than those who started school at five.

'In nursery schools children enjoy themselves and play with each other, but they are not interacting with those who have skills which they will need later. . . . They talk to an adult for only two per cent of the time they are at nursery school.

'Babies, on the other hand, are very active learners and develop their learning skills through their relationship with an older person.' (*The Times* 16 June 1984)

As a nannie you have a wonderful opportunity of aiding a child's development. Those who have taken an NNEB or similar course will have studied the stages of development through the ages 0 to 7,

factors affecting development, and 'the ways in which parents and
other adults can contribute positively throughout the child's
development'.

Those who have not taken a course will find it fascinating and
helpful to read about child development, follow radio and
television programmes on the subject, or perhaps send for a
correspondence course.

Day to day coping

As a nannie how are you going to provide the safe, stimulating
environment in which the child can develop happily? What will be
your attitude to the child? How will you create a good relationship
with him?

Everyone will use their own personality, have their own ideas,
know the things they think important in the daily upbringing of a
child. These are some of the guidelines I would suggest for thought
and discussion:

Relating to the child

Courtesy

Treat a child as courteously as you would any adult – respect his
dignity. If a child is valued as an individual he will develop the right
kind of self-esteem.

A child who mixes with other adults who are courteous to each
other and to him is more likely to treat others in the same way. Like
so many other qualities, good manners are caught as well as taught.

Never have an argument with a parent or another member of
staff in front of the child. Even if he doesn't appear to be listening
he probably is. In any case he will sense the atmosphere.

You should not discuss the child (or his parents or brothers and
sisters) in his presence. He may not understand what you are
saying, not realise that you are perhaps exaggerating, or are only
semi-serious. You could be sowing doubts and fears and it just isn't
fair to do that.

Names

Use the child's name when you talk to him. Encourage him to call
other people by their names. It always makes a contact warmer and
more personal if you use a person's name. (Salesmen know this
well.)

Conversation
When the child is talking to you, do look at him and listen. It is
very frustrating to a child when an adult only half listens. Put down
the newspaper, give him all your attention for a while. (Giving a
child full attention for a fixed period of time – as in the Children's
Hour method pioneered by Dr Rachel Pinney – is a richly rewarding
exercise for both adult and child.)

If you interrupt the child while he is talking, don't be surprised
when he interrupts you!

Always be sincere. Condescension and flattery are transparent to
child and adult. Lies and deceits lead to lack of trust.

Continuity
As a nannie you are dealing with other people's children. You will
soon be aware of the parents' attitudes, prohibitions and the things
they think important. Try to uphold the same standards. If you
think they are over-strict try to compensate by being kind and
loving, but do not allow the child to break rules set by parents, or to
behave generally in a way you know the parents would not accept.

If you consider that the parents are too lax you will have to go
gently. In time the child will understand that you do not expect
him to be rude to you, do not approve of some unfortunate table
manners. He will learn that you consider certain things dangerous,
and feel more strongly than his parents do about some points, eg
clearing up after messy play.

Never express criticism of the parents, even if you think they are
unwise to allow something. Simply take the line: 'Your mother may
let you . . . it is different for her, she is your mother. I am here to
look after you; its my job to keep you safe/see that you are kind to
the cat/take care of your toys . . .'

Realise that you may have more opportunities than the parents
have of helping the child to behave well. As a nannie you can give
the child your undivided attention; you do not come home feeling
tired after doing a day's demanding work or after a hectic
programme of social life.

The parent may be sad or feel guilty at having been away from
the child all day and so be more likely to be indulgent.

You may have to cope with a 'spoilt' child whose parents give
him material things instead of proper attention. A nannie has much
to offer such a child; he is deprived and really needs to feel nannie
cares about him as a person and has time for him: time for a game,

time for a story, time to sit there while he paints or builds with bricks.

Consideration

Remember to make allowances for the child's over-tiredness, disruption in routine, or any trauma taking place in the home.

If there have been parental arguments, if parents have separated, or been separated, eg through father's posting overseas, taken new partners, been ill, depressed, worried about money, or if a close relative has died, the child is bound to be affected and this may well show itself in his behaviour. (There is a separate section on a *New baby in the family*).

As a skilled, caring person you are likely to be able to help the child come through such disturbances.

Should you feel a child is severely affected and has some problem that time does not seem to be overcoming, talk it over with the family. You may be able to suggest that help is sought from a health visitor or the family doctor.

Obviously, you would approach such a situation tactfully; choose a good moment when the parent is relaxed and has time to talk. Don't discuss it with the father alone (unless he is the single parent) as you could appear to be criticising the mother. Though you may feel the mother is 'hopeless' and the father 'fine' you will only alienate the mother if you discuss the child with the father alone.

Do not discuss the family's or child's problems with other nannies or other parents; be careful what you say to nursery school teachers, playgroup staff and health professionals. It is all too easy for a mother to imagine that you are gossiping about her, though you know you are only concerned for the child. It may be easier to talk things over with one of your former college tutors.

In any case you are of course bound by confidentiality. The Federation of Personnel Services contract form states: 'It is a condition of employment that now and at all times in the future, the employee keeps secret the affairs and concerns of the household and its transactions and business.'

An exception would be where you believed a child was being abused. In such a case seek advice from the Health Visitor.

Encouragement

It may be a temptation to think you will make a child over-confident or conceited if you give too much praise but, as long as you are sincere, a child will thrive on praise and approval. Aim to help him develop the right kind of self-esteem and try to give him confidence in his own capabilities. (Isn't it true for adults too: when someone entrusts you with a task believing that you are able to do it, aren't you more likely to succeed?)

Try to be positive and find something commendable about what the child has done or how he has behaved. Be careful how you use the word 'good'; if you mean he has been helpful, skilful, thorough, then say so.

Consistency

It is so easy to give way to the child who persists, who 'keeps on' until he wears you out and you feel you would agree to almost anything to make him stop pestering you and arguing. Most parents and nannies have felt like that sometimes.

Some mothers and nannies who are already finding it difficult to cope, make it worse for themselves by giving way and buying the thing the child wants, allowing him to go where he wants, or do what he wants because they haven't the energy, will-power or courage to keep saying 'no'.

Think quickly before you say 'no' the first time. Do not take up a position or give a negative answer unless you mean it and are prepared to stick to it. Remember, if it is 'no' today, it should be 'no' tomorrow, and 'no' next week.

If you want to give yourself time to decide say, 'I'll think about it' or 'Let's see how we get on with this . . . first,' – or some such delaying tactic.

When you do say 'no', you yourself must be convinced that you mean it. You will not be able to find an easy way round every problem, but avoid confrontations when you can. Try to be positive: 'Put on your slippers now,' rather than, 'Take those boots off'. 'Let's find some newspaper for the floor before you paint,' instead of 'Don't make a mess'.

Sometimes a child must do as he is told; you must be firm. He will respect you for it in the end.

Audrey Bilski, head teacher and author of books on the young child, says: 'Knowing that certain behaviour always brings a firm 'no' helps create a sense of security. If you are inconsistent and fail to impose any kind of discipline you are being unfair to the child and storing future trouble. A child needs to learn that he cannot have everything and do everything he wants.'

Disobedience

Dr Rachel Pinney, child therapist and author of Creative Listening, has made a strong distinction between 'No, naughty' and 'No, dangerous'. It is a distinction that needs to be borne in mind by anyone dealing with children. Both you and the child should know the difference.

If he is about to dash into a busy road the child must recognise that the tone of your voice means 'Stop; instant obedience is imperative'. If he spits out his food it may be naughty, but if he rams it down his baby brother's throat it could be fatal. It is your responsibility to make the difference clear.

Temper tantrums

Try to avoid temper tantrums occurring. Look and plan ahead. When tantrums do occur, think about them afterwards; try to identify what caused them, consider how to avoid them in future.

So often tantrums are caused by over-tiredness; heat, lack of attention from an adult. How often have you seen a hot, tired child being dragged round a super-market or departmental store by a fraught mother and eventually flying into a temper? Frustration – when, for instance, a toy or piece of equipment does not perform as he wishes, is another cause. Being unable to do what he wants because he cannot achieve it (my oldest son was angrily frustrated by a pedal car he could not work one Christmas – it was our fault because we over-estimated his ability to manipulate it), or because an adult prevents him doing it (eg going upstairs on the bus), are prime tantrum raisers.

Hints for coping

– Never get annoyed or worked up yourself. Take some deep breaths; do something energetic and physical, eg pull up some weeds; polish the furniture.
– If you are indoors suggest taking the child out.
– Offer an alternative toy or way of doing something which he is finding difficult.
– Whispering to a child will sometimes calm him. He stops yelling to hear what you are saying.
– Give the child the attention he is craving for; alternatively, ignore him temporarily to show you disapprove of the behaviour. (You will know which is appropriate in his case.)
– Enter into the child's emotion. 'Yes, I know you feel disappointed

because you can't . . .' At least you will be showing that you understand how he is feeling.
– When the child has recovered, be reassuring. He may feel frightened or ashamed.
– If you became angry tell the child why and say you are sorry.
– It is very easy to lose your own temper, but do not shout, do not smack him. Remember, you are supposed to be the mature adult; you need efficient self control if you are going to 'control' a child.
– Watch that the child does not hurt himself physically, eg by banging his head on the floor.
– If you give way and allow him to do what he wanted or have what he wanted – whatever caused the tantrum – he will think that tantrums pay off. Be warned.

Smacking
The Norland Registry brochure specifically states: 'As the Norland College does not recognise the necessity of smacking in the upbringing of children, employers are earnestly requested not to ask any Norland Nurse to use such form of punishment.'

This is a wise request and one that all nannies could bring to the attention of employers. It is as well to discuss this question at the initial interview. Make your position clear: you do not intend to smack the child.

If the parent smacks the child on some rare occasion it is probably best not to comment – the parent may feel ashamed anyway. However, if it becomes a regular habit, tell them (privately) that you do not agree with such a form of punishment. Suggest an alternative such as deduction of pocket money, loss of privileges.

Though you may be tempted to do so – who isn't sometimes? – do not smack the child – ever. He is not your child. Parents have an inbuilt safety valve, normally they will not damage their child but you just might smack him harder than you intended. Don't risk it. You will find other ways of letting the child know you disapprove of his conduct.

The Isle College Nannies' Course suggests another good reason for not smacking: 'Remember, any unexplained bruises, however innocently acquired can in some circumstances be interpreted as having been inflicted by nannie.'

8   Daily routine

As the days go by you will work out a routine of activities, meals, outings, bath and bed so that the days have a pattern that makes the child feel settled and secure.

Within this routine be flexible, imaginative, consider the child's moods, wishes, and circumstances. The weather will make a difference to your programme, and sometimes to the child's behaviour: high winds can make him restless or nervous; snow can make him excited.

Try to do something new and interesting every day. Do not grow stale and bored yourself: the child will feel bored if you do.

When mother leaves

Helen, an NNEB from Barnet, worked for a year as a daily nannie to a boy of two and a half and a baby. She enjoyed the job – especially in the summer when she could take the children out to the parks. In the winter she used to take them to her own friends, to friends of the mother, and to her own parental home, because she found it a long day with just the children in their own home.

She did some housework, the children's washing, gave the children lunch and tea and had them ready for bed when the mother got home from her work at the BBC.

But there was one thing that used to upset Helen. The children would make a fuss when mother went off to work and left them.

Every nannie will have her own method of dealing with this situation. Mrs Townsend suggests that the mother stays with the nannie and child for the first few days at least, and allows the child to get used to the nannie.

Most nursery nurses and nannies can tell stories of children who make a great fuss and shed tears when mother is going, then five minutes after mother has left the tears have gone.

Mrs Davis says it is best to try and distract the child, play some games, tidy up the toy cupboard and avoid long farewells.

The nannie will have to be firm and honest. It is no use saying: 'Mummy will be back soon,' if she has gone for the day.

'Recap with the child,' says Dr Rachel Pinney. 'Accept their sadness; say "I know you're sad . .."'. Don't pretend the child doesn't feel it; realise he does, and let him know you do. Help him to accept the situation and live through it.'

If you sit down and start playing calmly with some bricks or some creative toy, the child will probably come and play with you of his own accord and gradually recover. The skill is in manoeuvering mother's departure so that the child does not make a fuss. It must be undramatic. Get the mother to kiss the child, say goodbye and GO.

The nannie needs to remember that the mother too may be feeling sad and wishing she could stay at home with her child. She should be reassuring and understanding if the mother telephones from the office to 'make sure he is all right'. The mother probably does not doubt the nannie's capability; the nannie should not see it as a lack of confidence in her, but realise it is the mother's own distress, guilt feeling or anxiety.

Dr Rachel Pinney thinks there is an exception to the foregoing advice: 'If the child shows real, acute terror and distress when the mother is about to leave, it may be necessary for her to stay. She should try to find the reason for this strong reaction'.

'The experienced nannie will be able to distinguish between terror, and just general dislike of mother going with "blackmail tears", or tears shed to please Mum'. Especially when a child first starts school, some mothers can be quite disappointed to find that the child does not cry for them.

Fortunately, in time, most children adjust to the mother being out all day, and they are happy to be with the nannie. She can make the day pleasant for the child and provide a safe, secure, stimulating environment where he can develop, and prepare to move into the world outside his home, smoothly and confidently.

Food and mealtimes

Diet
In consultation with the parents, you will try to see that the children have a sensible, suitable, well-balanced diet. You may be responsible for preparing their meals in nursery or family kitchen

and for serving the meals. You will probably have lunch and tea (and breakfast if resident) with the children each day.

Set a good example by eating plenty of fresh, whole foods, fruit and vegetables. If the meals are prepared by mother or staff try to discuss the menu with whoever is responsible for it. Use the foods that are in season and at their best. The children are bound to have familiar, favourite dishes, but be adventurous as well. When you offer something new, don't draw a great deal of attention to it.

Once we were invited to take our four children to lunch with a friend who had just been to Iceland on holiday. She told us at length about this 'delicious' yoghurt type pudding she had eaten there, and obviously gone to a great deal of trouble to prepare for us. Unfortunately, our four children were suspicious of this pudding after hearing so much about it; to my embarrassment it became clear they did not like it and did not want to eat it. Kindly, the hostess told them to leave it and cleared it away producing ice cream instead.

Discussing the incident after the children had gone into the garden to play we all realised we had said too much about this wonderful pudding. If it had just been produced and put in front of them the outcome might have been different.

Likes and dislikes
Avoid expressing your own dislikes or reservations about food. 'I never eat eggs,' will scarcely encourage the child to do so. You are old enough to decide for yourself, without prejudice, whether you like or dislike things – he may not be. When a particular food is rejected you could always try it again another day – without comment.

Don't encourage a child to eat to please you. Don't press food on him. Never offer a reward such as a chocolate biscuit, 'When you have finished your first course'. That is storing up trouble for him in the future, and does nothing for his teeth.

Refusal to eat
When a child who normally eats happily and healthily refuses food unexpectedly, think why this has happened. He may be suffering from an infection and be feeling unwell, or perhaps he is upset and unhappy about something. Maybe the food is just unappetising. As you get to know the child you will quickly recognise when he is unwell or distressed.

If you think he is just being awkward, or trying to gain attention, treat it calmly, be matter of fact. Trying to force a child to eat only creates more problems. Playing games to get him to eat only prolongs the meal and wearies everyone. By and large a child will eat according to his needs.

When a child refuses a meal, then says he is hungry and asks for a biscuit half an hour later, it is probably wisest, though sometimes hard, not to give it. You don't want the child to start nibbling all the time, or having frequent snacks; it is better for him to get into the habit of eating at regular meal times.

Try to come to a common mind with the parents over this so that you are not in a situation where mother gives the child the biscuit the nannie has just refused him.

On the other hand, if the parents want to insist on the child finishing what is on his plate, tell them, privately, that you do not agree. One nannie told me how she hated watching a mother trying to force food into her child's mouth. She felt so upset about it she told the mother (a powerful lady) that she would not stay with the family if that was to continue.

The mother accepted what the nannie said, and agreed to stop trying to force the child to eat. (Sometimes it pays for a nannie to be firm and clear about her principles. Possibly this mother had not realised she was creating problems and was just repeating treatment she herself had received as a child, or that she believed to be correct.)

Parents will soon notice that the nannie does not coax the child to eat, nor does she have confrontations over finishing what is on the plate.

Spitting out food
Sometimes children start spitting out food – perhaps they just enjoy doing it, or maybe it is to gain attention. Try not to let the child see that this annoys you: just tell him clearly and firmly not to do it because it looks and is messy, and other people do not like seeing it. If he persists, take the plate of food away. If he is really hungry he will not spit it out. For a few days you could avoid giving him soft, pappy food at family meal times. It is not as easy to make rusk or apple into a mush to spit out.

Mealtimes with nannie
Try to serve food attractively. The children can help set the table

and enjoy arranging it well (good for dexterity and number sense as well as style). Make the children sit down at the table and eat properly; tv snacks are not a good idea. A mother may be rushed and tired and glad to give the children something on a tray, but a nannie has more time to sit and enjoy meals with the children.

Make meal times a happy part of the day; try to draw all the children into any conversation. Let the baby sit with you round the table and have his bottle/food. (See *Family meal times*.) Never allow a child to wander round drinking from a bottle or sucker cup.

Let the children use 'children's cutlery', non-breakable plates and bowls, or ordinary china, as they seem happiest and you and the mother see fit. Beware of smoked glass (it shatters) and thin glasses with young children.

Some Children like to take their own mug and plate when they go visiting or on holiday, but I think it is better to get the children accustomed to eating and drinking from what is available. Those who become attached to one cup can feel upset if it is lost or left behind at a friend's house.

Saying grace
Where the family are in the habit of saying grace, follow their custom when you give the children meals.

If they do not say grace, but you do, you could say your own silently; don't force it on the children. They may notice you saying yours and ask for explanation. This could lead to saying a simple sentence of thanksgiving together (just address it to 'God' if the family is Jewish, or ask the children to teach you their grace). It is good for children to learn thankfulness from an early age.

Self-feeding

Once a baby is six or seven months old he can begin to feed himself with dry toast, rusks (make your own from bread baked in the oven, then you will not be giving extra sugar), chunks of apple and carrot. But never leave him with food within reach while he is unattended. If you have to go and answer the telephone or see to a toddler in another room, take the food away from the baby. Never leave a baby unattended when wearing a bib.

Should a baby choke on anything, hold him upside down and pat him firmly between the shoulder blades. Choking needs speedy action; a child can become short of oxygen when his breathing is obstructed. Be re-assuring after you have dealt with the choking. The baby will probably have been frightened.

You will probably introduce some kind of baby cup or sucking beaker at about six months, though the baby will still enjoy a bottle in the evening or during the night.

Have several cups (they get thrown on the floor or left at friend's houses) and boil frequently. Babyboots do an attractive polypropylene range. For a start, I prefer the little one with a lid, but no handles.

Bring the baby to the table in his high chair so that he can join in the meal time and be with the family. When he first starts to feed himself it is bound to be messy. If you have family meals you may find this annoys parents who are not used to babies so just keep a damp flannel handy and try to keep things unsticky. Wipe down the high chair after every meal and clear up any bits dropped on the floor. Try to seat the baby so that anything he spills does not go over the parents' clothing.

Watch out for tablecloths he can pull, anything sharp he can grab, and glasses. Don't put the baby where hot foods could be spilled on him, or the carving knife dropped on him.

Family meals

Sometimes the parents, children and nannie may all sit down to a meal together. Check that the children are sitting comfortably before the meal starts.

Bibs save washing but they hardly add to a child's dignity; change to table napkins as soon as possible.

When all are having a meal together, who corrects the children? It is probably wisest to leave it to the parents to take the initiative. Sometimes a look from you will suffice.

Children are quite capable of 'trying it on' and behaving in a way you do not allow when you and the children are having meals without the parents. You will have to play it by ear and be tactful. It may be easiest to say to the parents afterwards: 'Jamie generally sits at the table until his sister has finished when we are having lunch together in the nursery/on weekdays. . . .'

Whatever standard of behaviour the parents teach and expect from the children you will, of course, try to maintain when you and the children are eating alone. They will learn from your own conduct as much as from your instructions.

The parents may have few opportunities for enjoying meals with the children, so it may be a good idea for the nannie to withdraw for a little while and leave them as a family. You could always take your coffee into another room, or go off with the baby and leave other children with the parents.

A mother who has cooked a good meal for all the family would probably be grateful for a hand with the clearing up/washing up/dishwasher loading, even if this is not part of the nannie's duties.

One parent could look after the children while nannie and the other parent clear away; or nannie could offer to wash up while both parents play a game with the children. The nannie will know the family and what it is best to suggest.

Remember to say when you enjoy a dish mother – or father – has cooked for you all. It can be disheartening preparing food for people who never comment or show appreciation.

Do everything you can to make the family meal a really happy occasion when parents and children can talk and listen to each other. To the question: 'When do you feel most that you are a family?' Many would reply: 'When gathered round a meal table'. Family meal times are precious and memorable. The nannie's training of the children, attitude and co-operation, can help to make them a success.

When guests come

When you are in the habit of eating a meal with the family – or perhaps specific meals such as Sunday lunch – and they have guests, it is tactful to suggest you will make your own meal/have it with the children/eat it in your room, whatever seems appropriate.

Your employer's friends are not necessarily your friends; their age, interests, lifestyle may be quite different from yours. If relatives are coming the family may want to talk to them in privacy, exchange family news, discuss plans. . . . Be sensitive. It is far better to err on the side of absenting yourself (by prior arrangement) than to feel or even worse, be made to feel, that you are an intruder.

Do not be hurt because they do not include you in a dinner party. Remember they have their own life and you have yours. It is not that they do not like you but, however friendly you are, basically it is an employer/employee relationship.

Out of good nature, or because you quite enjoy cooking for parties, you may find yourself helping the parents to prepare for a party. It is hard to refuse to help, and it will not improve relationships if you do refuse, but the employer ought to be fair and give you time off in compensation. Flexibility is all very well, but it should be two-sided. Don't be 'put upon' by a greedy employer, or allow yourself to be so caught up in their lives you are not living your own life to the full.

Enough to eat?

A nannie who has some particular dietary requirement, for instance religious, to do with allergies, likes and dislikes, or vegetarianism, should have made this clear at the interview.

However, when you move in with the family you may find there is some aspect of their catering that is unsatisfactory for you. (This is why a preliminary stay is a good idea, though all may not be revealed even then.)

The parents could turn out to be faddy, irrational, or just plain mean about food. Perhaps it will be the cooking (by family or staff) that is poor and boring.

This is something the nannie will have to be brave and speak up about. Because the mother is sticking to a cottage cheese and lettuce diet she cannot expect the nannie to do the same. It is not right that the resident nannie who is being provided with meals as part of her renumeration should then have to go out and buy herself food because she is hungry – the apples she fancies, a tin of coke to keep in her room perhaps, but not basic food.

It is no use feeling discontent, or grumbling to someone else about the inadequate food; you must mention it to the person who can remedy the situation. As with all problems, or potential problems in the nannie/employer situation, it is far better to talk about them. It may be that the mother has just not stopped to think that you are younger, active, working hard looking after her child/children and you need sufficient, interesting food. It ought to be possible to sort it out amicably.

Equally, the nannie should be fair to the employers; it is not fair to help yourself to their sherry; tuck into the home made jam they were given; or finish up the last of the coffee, and not tell them or go out for any more.

Sweets
Try not to let the child see you eating sweets if, like me, you are

fond of sweets yourself. I find the best way to avoid eating them is to avoid the sweetshop.

When a child is given sweets let him enjoy one or two after a meal, don't let him get in the habit of eating them while playing or watching television. We all know that it is not a good idea to give sweets as a reward, pacifier, or distraction. It is easy to grow up turning to sweets for comfort.

Some people are very anti-sweets. Parents magazine has a house-style rule: 'Never mention sweets or chocolates! Substitute wholefood alternatives, fruit – fresh or dried, carob not chocolate, and nuts (but not for babies who may choke)'.

I know parents who try to keep sweets from their children entirely. That may not be a good idea. One of my sons often says to me reproachfully: 'I never knew what coca-cola was until I was ten'. He still likes it!

Training the child

Tidiness

I have one friend who often complains about her husband's untidiness. 'The trouble is' she says, 'he was brought up by a nannie who ran round after him and never taught him to put things away.' It may be easier to bring a child up like that, but it is hardly kind.

As a nannie, without being too authoritarian, you have a chance of encouraging a child to be organised, reasonably tidy and considerate. I know it can be an effort, but in the long run it is better for the child to hang up his towel, pick up his dirty socks, put something back in the place where it lives, rather than having you do these jobs for him.

If you encourage him to be self-reliant, tidy and careful, his parents will notice and perhaps let him know that they also expect him to hang up his coat.

There's no need to be bossy – praise and encouragement go a long way.

Also make sure the child has plenty of hooks to hang things on, storage space for clothes and toys, a place to keep his boots, tricycle, etc. 'A place for everything and everything in its place,' as some old fashioned nannies used to say. Ample storage space makes tidiness easier. Mention the need for more when there is an appropriate moment.

In time, the child himself may prefer order to mess and muddle.

Example helps. If you kick your shoes off and leave them on the floor don't be surprised if he does the same.

Avoiding waste
Waste is another area where a nannie can help a child develop thoughtful habits.
    Get in the habit of:

– Switching off lights when you leave a room empty.
– Giving portions of food and drinks of the appropriate size. You can always offer more, but it is a pity to get in the habit of wasting food and milk.
– Putting in the plug, and turning off the tap when you have enough hot water.

    Other saving measures will occur to you. Parents will appreciate your being careful, but not skimpy.

Pets

At the interview you will have discovered whether the family has pets, something of their attitude to animals and what will be your duties or opportunities concerning them.

Health and safety rules
Where the family has a dog, be watchful on the following points:

– See that pet and child have mutual respect and do not damage one another
– Watch the child when he is playing with a dog (especially friends' and relations' dogs when they are visiting the home or you their home). A dog who has seemed a faithful friend can sometimes turn on an adult or child quite inexplicably
– Make sure the children always wash their hands after playing with cats and dogs, and handling their blankets, baskets and dishes. (Toxocara worms that may be on animals or in their bedding produce eggs that can hatch inside the human body and damage the lungs, eyes, or liver.) Where there are children regular worming of dogs is essential.
– You also need to take care that children do not play in parks on grass where people have exercised their dogs, or in your own or friends' gardens where the family's or neighbours' dogs may have

fouled it. Sandpits should be covered if the family or neighbours have a dog
– Do not allow a dog to lick a baby's face, hands, or toys
– Make sure the child knows he must not kiss a dog or cat, however dear
– Do not allow a child to handle a dog's toys, eg rubber bone
– Hoover or carpet sweep all loose hairs shed on floor or upholstery. (Special precautions are needed to prevent crawling babies picking up hairs and putting them in their mouths)
– Remove dishes of unfinished animal food before the baby gets to them
– Don't expect an under-five to be responsible for a rabbit, guinea pig or hamster; you will have to clean it out and see that it is fed and watered regularly
– Be scrupulous about your own hygiene if you are caring for pets and children
– An ordinary cold water gold fish is one of the easiest pets to care for, and children seem to like them.

If the family had a cat or dog before they had a baby, watch the animal for signs of aggression or jealousy. Continue to give the pet attention, otherwise he may feel neglected and become vicious towards the baby. Remember, a baby or small child left alone with an animal is defenceless.

Cat nets are mentioned in the garden hazards section. Watch for the cat trying to snuggle into a baby's warm cot when the baby is in it. During the day keep bedroom doors closed – cats like jumping onto beds for a snooze, but you do not want hairs, fleas or mites on a child's bedding or on your own.

9 Physical care

Achieving control

You will have learnt from your course or experience that children vary greatly in the age at which they achieve control of bowels and bladder. About half way through the second year most children can begin to recognise when the bladder is full, and when they are about to have a bowel movement. Until they have this awareness potty training is a matter of timing and catching in a regular routine. You will work out a schedule for offering a child his potty or suggesting a visit to the loo. I am sure it is important not to be too anxious; training should be treated in a matter-of-fact way.

Many books and articles stress 'give praise and encouragement', but I don't think one should overdo this. Play it cool; don't give the impression that you mind particularly whether he uses the pot or not. After all, he is the one who will benefit if he does; wet, soiled nappies or pants must be miserable to wear.

My own view is that many people keep children in nappies far too long. I see them in supermarkets with great bundles of disposables and think what a waste of money and natural resources. I prefer to have plenty of pants readily available, and to give the floor a quick mop if necessary. But every nannie will have her own views.

At night, and when you are going out, it is different, of course.

Families have their own vocabulary for lavatory functions; you could adopt the family's usage initially, but the child will need to use terms widely understood when he goes to school or playgroup.

When a child has gained control and is apparently 'trained', infections, colds, tummy upsets and stress can cause reversion. Treat this calmly, but try to think out why it has happened.

Night time control

Children who are dry by day, may continue to need nappies at night until they are three or even older. You could progress to leaving a nappy spread out on the sheet beneath him before dispensing with nappies altogether. You can continue using a waterproof sheet (fitted, large enough to tuck well under the mattress, or fastened with tapes for comfort) as well as the waterproof mattress cover. You will need at least three waterproof sheets to allow for frequent washing and drying.

Some nannies and mothers like to 'lift' a child before they go to bed themselves. This can give the child a dry and more comfortable night and cut down on washing, but it does disturb him, or get him into the habit of passing water when half asleep. You will have to decide what is best in your situation.

Even if it seems delayed, night time control will come as the child matures. There is no need to worry him about it.

Potties and lavatories

Although a child may have his own potty and be accustomed to using it, it is as well if he learns to use any potty or lavatory, otherwise you could have problems when away or out for the day.

Watch that children do not shut themselves in strange lavatories and bathrooms, then find they cannot undo the door. (One of our sons shut himself in the bathroom in the house a friend lent us for a holiday the first night we were there. My husband had to go and borrow tools from a neighbour and take the lock off the door to get him out.)

In the child's home check that the bathroom and lavatory doors are easy to unfasten and teach him how to undo them. You could discourage him from locking himself in anyway: it isn't necessary in a family home.

You will help the child to be independent and cope with pants and trousers as soon as possible. (Watch the zips on little boy's jeans – never let him wear jeans without wearing pants!)

Show the child how to use toilet paper and teach him to wash his hands after every visit to the loo.

Bedwetting

Most children will gradually develop sufficient control and a strong enough bladder to remain dry all through the night. You can help them by seeing they use the potty or lavatory before settling for the night, making sure they are warm enough in bed, and by drawing back the curtains or leaving on a landing light so that there is just enough light for them to see to use a potty or go to the lavatory in the night.

If a child seems slow to become dry at night you probably need patience and suitable bedding, but if it continues after he is four the parents may want to seek advice and ask the GP to check that there is nothing wrong physically.

Charts, calendars, buzzers and medicines seem more appropriate for an over-five. Most children grow out of the bed-wetting habit quite naturally; it is best treated calmly.

The child who has appeared to be in control, but then reverts to bed-wetting may be experiencing some stress or disturbance; if you think this is the case try to work out what could be the cause of the unhappiness and how you can help him overcome this. The arrival of a new baby, parental strife, the prospect of starting playgroup or school, moving house, or a change of nannie may be unsettling him. Re-assurance will be needed.

If there are no apparent emotional causes, it may be necessary to check that all is well physically. Illness and infection can, of course, cause the odd accidents; it is best to make no fuss about these and simply change the bedding unobtrusively.

The Health Education Council has produced an excellent leaflet, *Bedwetting*. It should be available in your local clinic and Community Health Council Office; if not write to the Council at 78 New Oxford Street, London WC1A 1AH and ask for a copy.

Bathtime routine

Warn the child beforehand. You will know that it is unwise, and unkind, to take him away from an absorbing game or tv programme, without allowing him time to finish off the game, or see the end of a programme he is enjoying. Any ensuing confrontation can be more exhausting than allowing him a little longer play.

– Get everything ready for the bath before the child starts undressing. (Don't leave his clean night clothes where he can splash them!)
– Check that water is not too hot.

– Never, never leave a child alone in the bath. If you must answer the telephone or front door, or see to the baby, scoop the child out of the bath, wrap him in a towel and leave him on the floor (make sure he can't turn on hot taps) or take him with you. Hoicked under your arm may not be as comfortable as the bath, but it is safer.

– A few toys make bathtime fun, but do not introduce a confusion of boats, ducks, fish, divers: one or two at a time are enough. Funnels, pipes, tubes and sieves are good bath playthings too.

– A little bubble bath makes it all more pleasant. Watch that the child's skin does not react to it. Try to keep soap out of the child's eyes.

– I always found hairwashing unpopular. It must have been my lack of technique. As a nannie you will have your own method of doing it painlessly. Ask another nannie for her hints. Always rinse hair thoroughly. There is now a children's hair conditioner on the market; this seems to be a great help for washing little girls' long hair. I wish it had been around when our daughter was small.

– Make sure all lavatory cleaners, bleaches, etc, are well out of reach. See that no pills or medicines have been left around; medicine cabinets should be locked if the parents must keep one in the bathroom the children use. When other people use the children's bathroom watch out for razor blades and scissors; remember any guest who comes to stay may not be as child safety conscious as you and the parents are. Talcum powder can cause children to choke.

– Do not leave buckets of soaking nappies where a toddler can dabble in them.

– Get in the habit of wiping the bath with a clean, damp cloth as soon as it has emptied (you can go back and clean it with powder or fluid when the children are in bed). This preliminary clean teaches the children to be considerate, and they may enjoy the job anyway. Mop up floor if necessary (wet floors can cause damage as well as falls).

– A nannie who is methodical and organised will encourage the children to pick up clothes and put shoes together neatly.

If you are not very tidy yourself, you could change your ways and train the children at the same time. We have all found it seems quicker to do the tidying up oneself at the end of a tiring day, but if you can get the children into the habit of doing it you will all benefit.

– Talk (or sing) to the children while you bath them. When they

are little you can name the parts of the child's body as you wash him – or he washes himself. With an older child you can extend his vocabulary as you introduce terms such as: depth, temperature, submerge, swirl . . .
– Have a regular routine for nail care.
– Let the child enjoy the bath, relax and slowly unwind after the day.
– Don't let the water play get too vigorous – it is surprising how soon walls can be made dripping wet.

Bedtime and sleep

A daily nannie may go off duty before the toddler's bedtime, and leave the mother to enjoy giving him a bath, story, goodnight chat and kiss. Some nannies get the child ready for bed by the time the parents return home, but the parents settle the child into bed for the night. Yet other nannies do not leave until the child is in bed and asleep. Practice varies from home to home. It seems best if the parents and nannie work out a norm, but all remain flexible to suit each other's commitments.

Resident nannies generally put the child to bed except on the nannie's day off. Where there is more than one child, nannie and parent may each put one to bed. There are many permutations.

Sometimes nannie could offer to give a hand with preparing the adults' evening meal, while a parent reads the bedtime story. Most nannies respect parents' wishes; without being told, they sense when parents would like to be left alone with a child and they slip away to do something else.

When you put the child to bed check for any hazards (see *Baby bedtime* section) and tell the child where you or the responsible adult will be.

See that the child has a familiar cuddly toy. (I think it is better for children to have several bedtime favourites. If they become especially attached to only one and it is lost or left behind after a holiday it will be harder to console the child.)

After you have read or told a story (see *Story* section), check that the child is comfortable (visit to lavatory or drink of water as required) and warm or cool enough.

You could chat for a few minutes and recall some of the enjoyable events of the day – seeing a puppy in the park, painting a pattern, visiting a friend . . . Say prayers if that is the custom of the family;

give a kiss and cuddle if that comes natural to you, say goodnight and leave the child, or settle comfortably in a chair until he drops off to sleep. Night lights, or landing light left on and door ajar, are a matter of preference.

The important thing is that the child should feel secure, comfortable and relaxed. Always try to leave the child in a contented, happy state.

When you want to get ready to go out, or are anxious to go to your room and relax, try not to appear hurried and rushed. The child will sense this, just as he will if you put him to bed to be free of him; he could end up taking even longer to settle. Be firm about being called back. Don't encourage, 'Nannie I want . . .'

Wakeful toddlers

When the toddler you look after constantly wakes in the night, you will, naturally, try to think out why this happens. Are you putting him to bed too early? Is he hot/cold, hungry/thirsty, insecure/unhappy, not getting enough loving attention by day? Your own perception, training and experience should help you sort this out in discussion with the parents. You could also ask the health visitor's advice.

In the night
After you have checked that the child is comfortable you could offer him a drink of water, make sure he has a favourite cuddly toy, tuck him in cosily, then say goodnight firmly. You could say something like: 'Your parents are asleep, I want to go back to sleep; if you have another sleep you will feel ready for playgroup or a walk in the park . . .'

It may help if you suggest something for the child to think about. For instance:

- All the different people who are working while he is in bed
- The children he knows, and how they are in their beds
- His parents, aunts and uncles, grandparents . . . all asleep
- He could go for an imaginary walk – picture the road, houses, trees . . .
- He could recite nursery rhymes to himself
- He could imagine he is in a toyshop.

You will have plenty of other ideas of your own. I think it is important not to let the child be worried or frightened about anything. Let him keep a soft light on if he wishes. Tell him if he can't sleep, he can just lie still and quiet and he will still be resting.

Be imaginative, put yourself in the child's place; try not to be annoyed at being woken – on the other hand make it clear this is not a time when you are going to play with him. You will have your own views, but I would not allow the child to get into bed with me – I think that privilege should be reserved for parents and grannies.

Early morning waking

I think that one of the most exhausting things about caring for children is the way they wake you early, morning after morning. With hindsight, I should have been much much firmer about making our children go back to their own rooms to play quietly, instead of allowing them to waken us and keep us awake so early.

You can't force children to go on sleeping when they have had enough sleep, and it seems unkind to insist on them staying in bed or cot, if they are awake, full of energy and keen to get on with their day. To prevent yourself being woken too early, you could consider putting the child to bed a little later (you may have to consult parents; if they are adamant about early nights, perhaps they could share the early mornings). Try to prevent yourself being woken so early you feel frazzled and less patient with the child as a result. Of course, you may be an early riser and enjoy having extra time in the morning to get ahead.

When the child is old enough, explain to him that you do not want to be woken so early (unless he needs you urgently), or before a given time. Encourage him to go to the lavatory by himself, then to play quietly until you appear.

Children's clothes and shoes

Buying new clothes for children can be a pleasant task; shoes are a bit more trying – sometimes you have to chase around to find the right size and fitting.

When buying clothes for children, these are the kind of points you will probably have in mind:

– Is it within the budget? If you really cannot find anything acceptable within the price the parents have suggested, you could

go back to them and explain the situation – maybe they have not bought children's clothes lately.
– Does the child like it? (I once bought my daughter a dress she didn't really like – she wore it once!)
– Does it suit the child?
– Is it comfortable? Beware tight armholes, frills that tickle, fabrics that chafe
– Will it be easy to wash and iron, and will it withstand frequent washing?
– Does it fit, but allow a little room for growth?
– Is it well made and finished?
– Is it easy to put on and off – or does it have fiddly buttons?
– Will the shop change it if the parents do not approve?

Clothing care
Looking after the children's clothes is often one of a nannie's duties. Try to do any repairs as soon as they are needed. Check for loose buttons, etc, when you put clean clothes away – they could be dangerous when bitten off the garment.

Ironing damp clothes is so much easier than ironing dry, crumpled items that have been in the ironing basket for weeks. Spray starch makes ironing easier, but do not use it close to a baby or child, and try not to breathe it in yourself. Soaking grubby or stained items in a pre-wash powder does seem to improve the look of them.

Use enough soap powder – my children often used to grumble that their shirts were greyer than most of their friends' shirts – I realised in time that I was just not using enough powder.

Shoes
There are plenty of leaflets and guides to choosing children's shoes; many are prepared by the shoe companies. Those given the task of choosing children's shoes will bear in mind the following points:

– It is worth buying well-known makes (eg Startrite and Clarks) that produce a whole range of fittings.
– Go to a shop with a large stock and helpful, trained assistants.
– Go at non-busy times when the assistant can give you plenty of attention.
– Ask for the child's foot to be measured with him standing.
– Buy the colour and style that the child likes and will enjoy

wearing (it is not much fun for anyone to wear shoes they dislike or find uncomfortable).
– If you can't find what you want, leave it until another day when you can set out fresh. (Have you ever seen tired, irritable children and impatient parents in shoe shops?)
– Don't be rushed or persuaded into a purchase. If there is cause for complaint go back to the shop first; if no satisfaction, contact the makers or local consumer advice bureau.

Spring into Step is a useful leaflet available free (enclose sae) from Cuxson-Gerrard and Co Ltd, Fountain Lane, Oldbury, Warley, West Midlands, B69 3BB.

10 Caring for a young baby

Many trained or experienced nannies specialise in looking after new babies. Often they move into the home before the mother has the baby as this enables them to get to know the family and the house, and to establish a relationship with the mother.

Others meet the mother before the birth, then join the family when the baby comes home from hospital. They may have the pleasure of going to the hospital to bring the mother and baby home. Nurses from the maternity unit generally carry the baby out to the car and then hand him to mother or nannie in the back seat.

It is likely that the mother will have bought the basic equipment and layette, or she may have it already if this is her second or subsequent child. You could just make sure that she has the main items:

– Cot or crib and bedding (check that cot bars are not less than 7 cm (2¾ in.) and not more than 9 cm (3½ in.) apart; that the mattress is 'safety' type, ie it has air spaces allowing baby to breathe freely even when lying face down, and that the gap between mattress and cot interior is not more than 5 cm (2 in.). Sheets should be of absorbent cotton
– Sling in which mother or nannie can carry baby and have arms free. A padded version will be more comfortable for the baby, eg Babyboots Easy Rider Baby Carrier
– Pram/carrycot and transporter/lie-back pushchair, to suit the family's lifestyle
– Buckets with lids, for soaking nappies
– Bath and stand and jug for filling bath,
– Baby soap, lotion, powder
– Brush and comb
– Towels and bath mat

Layette
- Vests   Envelope neck style are easiest to put on and off
- Nappies and pins   You and the mother will have to discuss terry or disposable and decide which to use regularly. It is probably as well to have some of each type initially. Norland nurseries use only terry nappies and no plastic pants in the first year. Leaflet on advantages of disposables and samples obtainable from Disposable Nappy Bureau. With terry nappies it is well worth buying the best quality
- Plastic pants
- Gowns or stretch suits
- Bootees and mittens
- Bonnets
- Cardigans
- Knitted jacket and trousers or suits for outerwear
- Shawls
- Nightdresses or bodysuit/coverall
- A sheepskin is warm and comforting and can be used in cot, buggy, playpen and as a kicking/changing mat. Most Australian mothers find them indispensable.

Especially with a first baby, encourage the mother to buy only the minimum. She is bound to have gifts and you can always go and buy anything else that is needed. Most large towns now have Babyboots branches that stock everything needed.

In time you will need to add the following to the equipment:

- Full size cot, if you have only a crib at the beginning
- Bouncing cradle/reclining chair – being in one of these enables the young baby to see what is going on and feel part of the family. Never use on any raised work top, chest, table, bed, etc. On the floor, out of draughts, is safest.
- Highchair and safety harness
- Playpen
- Car seat
- Safety gate for stairs
- Potty.

When you are buying baby equipment it is worth looking around. Department stores usually have a wide selection of all makes. The better the shop, the better the variety generally. You don't have to buy there, just look and compare.

The following factors are worth bearing in mind when you buy equipment for a nursery:

- Space available
- Budget
- Long term usefulness
- Conformity with safety standards.

Branches of organisations such as the National Childbirth Trust and Twins Clubs often organise a second-hand selling system, and items are also advertised in local papers. However, especially for a first baby, many mothers prefer to buy new equipment.

Expectant mothers

One nannie told me she thought it was 'especially difficult' working with an expectant mother. She had found such mothers worried, 'Will the baby be normal?'. 'Will the first child accept the new baby?', and about their own pregnancy. All this could cause strain: a nannie therefore needs to be tolerant and understanding.

'I worked for one expectant mother who used to cry at the slightest thing,' she said. 'I just used to walk away, get busy with the other child, and pretend it was not happening'.

This nannie found that once the baby arrived it was easier, partly because they were both so busy that the mother had less time to sit and worry. Where there is a new baby and another child it is a great help if mother or nannie takes the child out and gives the other person a quiet time with the baby.

Mother, nannie and new baby

Looking after a new baby is exciting and demanding. The nannie who is engaged for a new baby must win the mother's trust and confidence, yet not be bossy or too quick to take over.

When a nannie is trained and/or experienced, and the mother has never had a baby before, the mother can feel inadequate and almost threatened by the nannie. The nannie must be very tactful when she makes suggestions and shows the mother how to do things for the baby.

Nannies who have spent part of their training working in a baby unit will already have had experience of teaching new mothers, but as a nannie in a family it is on a more personal one-to-one basis.

A woman who has just had a baby is always extra sensitive. She may imagine criticism where none has been meant, she may be demanding, irritable, rather overwhelmed by all that has happened to her in the last few months, and the responsibility she now has. Her body and emotions are having to adjust to her new role; when she has engaged a nannie there is the added factor of another woman in the home. She may have had little contact with nannies; perhaps she has never previously employed any help in the home.

Where the baby and nannie are safely in a nursery suite and the nannie is clearly in charge of the baby it may be easier for the nannie. However, most nannies will be in ordinary homes where mother and nannie will be coping together – at least initially – getting accustomed to each other and the baby.

A nannie helping a new mother must be understanding, patient, and slow to take offence. In a first job it is not easy, especially if the nannie is only 18 or so. Those from Norland and Chiltern have the advantage of being older (20 when they qualify). Sheila Bell of Northumbrian Nannies said to me: 'We expect a tremendous amount of these young girls when they go to first babies'.

Don't be daunted. Once you have looked after one new baby it should be easier next time. The chances are that you and the mother will make good friends: after all, you both have the same basic concern – the welfare of the baby. You can enjoy sharing the tasks and getting to know the baby together. Many mothers have told me that they were 'extremely grateful' to the nannies who helped them with their first baby.

Taking charge of a baby

When you go to take charge of a baby so that his mother is free to return to work or other commitments, it is best if you can spend some time with mother and baby before being left alone with the baby. This will give you a chance to become familiar with the household routine and to get to know them both. They will have settled into a relationship and timetable (write out the timetable with the mother if this seems a good idea) and you will want to disturb the baby as little as possible.

Watch how the mother feeds, winds and changes the baby; the bath and settling down in cot or pram routine; whether the mother is noisy or quiet and how much she talks to the baby. Then, when you are left alone, try to handle and treat him in the same way – so long as you feel comfortable treating him in that way, and it is natural to you. You must be relaxed in yourself. A baby soon senses tension and unhappiness. If at any time you are feeling cross (perhaps with another child) or upset about anything, try to regain your composure before picking up the baby.

As an NNEB you will have learnt to 'organise daily routine care of the child from birth to seven years'. There is no need to give a full description of daily baby care here as there are plenty of books on the subject.

Here are just a few reminders:

– From the earliest days talk to the baby in normal 'grown-up' language
– Give him (safe) toys to touch, watch (mobiles over the cot, but not a confusing number), suck and explore
– Check constantly that the baby is warm/cool enough and away from draughts
– Look out for pets (see separate section) and toddlers who may not understand how to treat a baby. Pinches and 'pats' are quickly given by little brothers and sisters!
– Remember a baby needs friendly attention; don't just leave him in another part of the room or alone in the nursery or garden
– When he is awake, let him be with you and any other children – he can hear you, watch you, and enjoy being drawn into the circle
– Don't get into the habit of 'tip-toeing' when the baby is asleep; it is far better for him to get accustomed to ordinary household noise. We have all met people obsessed about being quiet because the baby is asleep – there is no need to accept such tyranny.
– Babies like a vertical position. Hold a baby up to your shoulder; when you need to place him horizontally put him on his tummy on a blanket on the floor – this will increase comfort and make him feel more secure and confident.

Nappies
You and the mother will already have discussed the advantages and disadvantages of traditional or disposable nappies. You will work out your own combination of nappies, nappy roll, liners, pants, to suit the baby and household conditions. The most important thing is to prevent the baby developing nappy rash and inflamed skin which can be caused by too tight elastic in pants.

Here are a few reminders:

– At the first sign of nappy rash take positive action.
– Change nappies more frequently. (Nappy rash is caused by skin staying in contact with wet/soiled nappies.)
– Clean and dry the baby thoroughly after every nappy change.
– Leave the baby lying on towelling, but without a nappy on, for a little while each day. Fresh air and gentle sunlight will help to heal the skin, and the baby will enjoy the lack of restriction.
– Use a nappy cream – but do not rely on this to solve the problem.
– Check that nappies are being washed and rinsed thoroughly.
– If the rash persists consult the doctor or health visitor.

NB   Do not leave the baby on a bed or working top when you are changing him, he can surprise you and hurt himself by rolling off. The floor is safer.

Bathing the baby
Just about the most popular lesson in Mothercraft courses is bathing the baby. Giving the baby his bath can be one of the greatest pleasures for a nannie. Make it a happy, relaxed, unhurried time for the baby too.

Some reminders   Where there are older children settle them happily or invite them to help you. If you care for an older child inclined to jealousy, you could perhaps bath the baby while that child is having a nap, out with parent, playing with a friend, or at playgroup. It can be hard for an older child to see a baby getting so much attention. In time you may be able to bath the children together and that can be fun for both.

– Collect together all the things you need before taking the baby out of his cot
– Check that water in taps will not come out scalding hot if the other child turns the tap on while you are busy. (You may have to ask the family to adjust a central hot water system.)
– Warn older child if towel rail is very hot and keep baby well away from rail, pipes or radiator that may also be very hot
– If you leave him on the floor while you run off to fetch something you have forgotten, he could roll over and touch these
– Talk to the baby – or sing to him – while you bath him
– Make sure you dry him thoroughly
– Never leave a baby, or any child, in the bath alone. (Tragedies happen in seconds.)

If you are caring for just one baby you will probably be able to establish a routine and give him a bath about the same time every day. Find a time that suits you and the baby, a time when you are likely to be undisturbed; before a 10 am feed suits some babies.

Crying baby
Check list for reasons

– Hunger/thirst
– Pain or discomfort – too hot/cold (feel the baby's chest as well as hands and feet). Wet/dirty nappy, clothing too tight
– Fear: sudden noise, bright lights, rough movement
– Fatigue
– Loneliness
– Boredom.

Every baby is an individual; you will soon become sensitive to his particular needs, likes and dislikes.

Remember that babies also like a little peace. The other day I was with some cousins and a one-year-old baby. They would not give that poor baby any peace; they picked him up, fiddled with him, tossed him in the air, rocked him about . . . It was all done lovingly, but it was quite exhausting to watch. By contrast some other people at the party had a baby much the same age, but they fed him, changed him, talked to him a little, then gave him a chance to have a little doze.

Hint: when a baby is crying (and you have checked that the cause is not one of the first three suggested above) try humming or singing to him. Often he will stop crying out of sheer surprise. Perhaps there was good sense in earth mothers crooning to their babies and singing them lullabies.

Baby and bedtime
Mother and nannie will need to discuss where baby is to sleep (in parents' room/nannie's room/alone in nursery?) and what kind of bedtime routine would suit the family best. Work out which one of you is to attend to the baby in the evenings and settle him for the night. A mother who has been out at work all day may want to keep the baby in his carrycot in the living room for part of the evening.

Where a nannie has sole charge of a baby in a nursery suite she will be responsible for settling him in his cot and listening for him in the evenings (except on her evenings off). Some parents are thankful to have a peaceful evening alone without the baby. Patterns vary, and so do the babies in their habits and sleep requirements. But as a nannie you will probably aim to develop or maintain an established bedtime routine.

When you are settling a baby or young child in his cot for the night check the following:

- Dropside securely fastened
- No pillow for a baby under 12 months
- No toys or mobiles, with small parts that could be pulled loose, sucked and swallowed, within reach; no toys on strings
- Crib or cot is stable and cannot be tipped
- No loosely knitted clothing or ribbon fastenings that could come loose and be sucked and swallowed, or catch on any part of the cot
- Sheets are absorbent and firmly tucked over the mattress so that the child cannot wriggle them free and be left lying on plastic (dangerous if he regurgitates milk)
- Child who can stand does not have toy he could step on to climb over bars
- Children at the stage when they could climb out are safer with the side left down. (I learnt this when one of our sons went up and over and lost a tooth)
- A child who will not stay tucked up can be put in a sleeping bag. It is more difficult to stand in this and it will keep him warm
- Make sure the room temperature is right for the baby. No matter how many blankets he has, a baby can die of hypothermia if the room temperature is too low.

Routine
You may decide to change to giving an evening instead of a morning bath when the baby is about six months old. In any case, you will wash and change him, have a little play with him, feed him and then try to settle him down. You can put him in his cot, but you can't make him sleep. If he persistently refuses to settle, review your routine.

Wrap him snugly, tuck him in firmly and neatly, subdue the light and sit with him for a little while. Touch him if this seems to make him feel happier and more secure. Don't leave him alone and unhappy. You want to make bedtime a peaceful, comfortable end to the baby's day.

Where you are looking after a toddler as well as a baby, one of the parents could read the toddler a story or play with him while you put the baby to bed. You could always alternate with mother, putting the baby to bed while you play with the toddler. When parents are not available at this time you will probably decide to leave the toddler to play quietly while you attend to the baby. After the baby is settled you could give the toddler a spell of individual attention and gently help him to unwind after the day. Avoid over-exciting games just before bedtime. Unfortunately, some parents like to give children a bedtime romp, then they expect nannie to soothe the children.

Bedtime is a lovely time for story telling and reading. (See separate section on *Stories*.)

Night waking
Resident nannies will need to discuss with the parents who is to go to the baby or toddler who wakes in the night. If the parents have the child in their room then nannie is the fortunate one who will get unbroken sleep.

Where the child sleeps with nannie in her room or in a nursery suite, it will be the nannie's task to see to him when he wakes. If a child is very wakeful you could reasonably expect the parents to have him sometimes. Discuss with the parents what is to happen about this when it is your day/weekend off, but you are still sleeping in the house. There is much to be said for getting right away for 24 or 48 hours on your weekend off duty.

Working parents with a wakeful baby will probably find it a strain being disturbed at night then going off to do a demanding day's work. A nannie who has a broken night could more easily take a compensatory nap when the baby is asleep during the day.

Talk this over with the parents and work it out together. Remember, a mother who has recently had a baby and then returned to full time work may be feeling tired and be finding it hard to cope. A nannie can reassure her that the wakeful nights do not go on for ever.

Night feeds When a baby cries in the night it is better to see to him quickly. You will probably have to get up for him in the end, so the sooner you go to him the less distressed he will become.

A quick nappy change, a check that he is warm enough and the cot is dry, a re-assuring cuddle, and perhaps a feed, will be necessary. This is where the breast-feeding mother with baby beside her at night has such an advantage.

Nannie will have her own training and experience to guide her about night feeds. She will also discuss them with the mother and health visitor. A full milk feed may be necessary; otherwise fruit juice – gradually diluted with more water – or just plain, boiled water may suffice. (Fruit juice given in the night can damage teeth.)

When milk feeds seem to be needed, leave everything ready before you go to bed. Don't get into the habit of making the night wakening into a social interlude. Move quietly, use soft lights, don't start playing with the baby in the night. Try to give him the idea it is sleep time.

Breast-feeding

The mother will probably have made up her own mind about breast-feeding and will have discussed it with staff at the ante-natal unit and with the doctors, nurses and midwives who looked after her before, during and after the birth.

When she comes home from the hospital with the new baby she will expect you to be understanding and knowledgeable about breast-feeding. There are plenty of books and articles on the subject and you can easily make yourself well-informed.

The main points to bear in mind are:

– The comfort, pleasure and re-assurance that the baby obtains from the breast
– The inter-action between mother and baby that it creates
– The more the baby sucks at the breast the more he will stimulate the flow
– Breast-milk is so easily digested it is absorbed more quickly than formula milk and thus the breast-fed baby requires more frequent feeds than the bottle-fed baby
– It is more convenient for the mother – especially in the night
– It can give the mother great pleasure and satisfaction at the time, and when she looks back on her child's babyhood. (A child often likes to be told that his mother fed him – it is a way of assuring him how much he was loved.)
– It is cheaper than buying baby milks!

Having said all this, it is most important that the mother should not be left feeling a failure because she has been unable to breast-feed. (Even if she was unsuccessful in hospital, it may still be possible to establish it – ask the health visitor for advice.) Some mothers just do not like the idea and prefer not to breast-feed. That is their choice; do not make them feel guilty about it.

If the mother was able to feed the baby for only a short time, she can be re-assured that she gave the baby a good start.

A mother who is disappointed that she could not breast-feed can be extra loving and affectionate towards the baby to compensate.

Privacy

The nannie must be sensitive and think whether the mother wishes to breast-feed the baby in front of her, or in privacy. The mother may be shy at first, but as she gradually becomes more used to the nannie she may quite naturally put the baby to the breast while the nannie is there. Some mothers are happy to breast-feed in public. It is entirely a personal matter.

Where the nannie wears uniform she may seem more professional and the mother accepts her presence in the same way as she would that of a student nurse (who may have much less experience).

Help the mother to settle comfortably in chair or bed, offer to answer the telephone and deal with callers so that she is not disturbed. Leave other children in the room, or take them off to play, as the mother wishes.

Working mother breast-feeding

The mother may wish to continue breast-feeding although she has returned to work or an active social life. In this case she will express her milk. (It takes patience, practice and time.) Once expressed it should be stored in a fridge. Scrupulous hygiene is essential; bottles and teats used for giving the mother's milk need the same care as those used for powdered milks. (See *Bottle-feeding* section.)

If you are left with a breast-fed baby remember he will need feeding frequently. When a mother is going off for the day discuss with her what alternatives you should give if the supply she has left proves insufficient.

Bottle-feeding

When caring for a bottle-fed baby you will use your own knowledge/training/experience and follow the mother and health visitor's instructions. Most of the baby milk manufacturers produce useful free booklets (see list at end of the book). You will, of course, be scrupulous about cleanliness and following instructions about measuring and mixing. Accurate measuring is essential.

Sterilise (by chemicals or boiling) bottle and teats, screw ring and cap between every feed. Bacteria thrives on any residue of milk. Sterilisation is necessary until baby is at least six months old. (Consult health visitor.)

The baby has probably built up resistance to any germs the mother has on her skin, but he may not have the same resistance to his nannie's germs so be very thorough about cleaning your hands and nails. Keep one towel (clean daily) especially for when you are going to prepare feeds and equipment.

All babies are individuals, but gradually they each establish a feeding pattern and you will get to know when he needs a feed. If he seems hungry there is no point in letting him cry until it is the scheduled time for a feed. Within reason, babies are generally fed 'on demand' these days.

When you are going to give the baby a bottle, settle any other children into a game or some activity, sit where you are comfortable, give the feed lovingly. Feeding a baby with a bottle is a special pleasure and privilege, so enjoy it. You will not force him to take it all if he does not seem to want it. Most babies seem to prefer warm milk (test on inside of wrist). You can take the chill off a feed by standing the bottle in hot water or an electric bottle warmer. Do not keep warm milk for another feed as germs grow rapidly in warm milk.

Make sure the hole in the teat is the right size.

Never leave a baby alone sucking from a bottle. If you have to go and see to another child, take the bottle out of the baby's mouth while you are away.

Winding

Much of the rubbing, patting, jogging and slapping that babies endure is quite unnecessary. Simple sit baby up for a few minutes two or three times in the course of a feed and don't expect a burp every time. Air is lighter than milk so the air that he has swallowed should come up as his tummy fills with milk.

If a baby cries between feeds he may be thirsty. Tepid boiled water could be offered as a soothing drink.

Weaning

You will use your knowledge and experience, and introduce foods other than milk in consultation with the mother and health visitor. Here again there are plenty of books and leaflets on the subject.

It is now thought that introducing mixed feeding too young will encourage too much fat. Four or five months is often suggested as the right time. Some advisers suggest six months.

General advice includes:
– Keep the diet low-fat
– Do not add extra sugar and salt
– Introduce new foods gradually and slowly – be imaginative and consider how the baby's system is having to adjust to these new foods after milk and fruit juice only
– Be patient and loving when giving new foods (you may prefer to hold him on your lap when giving him first tastes)
– Never be upset or cross if he refuses food – he isn't doing it to spite you!
– If you use commercially prepared baby foods, read the ingredients and the directions carefully. Buy those with least additives.
– Use simple meals and straightforward foods before progressing to 'dinners'
– Follow the manfacturer's instructions on storage. It is better to throw away the remainder rather than risk a tummy upset.
– As the child has less milk and more solids make sure he still has sufficient liquid. Plain water (boiled for those under ten months) is a good drink and far better than highly coloured and sweetened squashes and fizzy drinks (real fruit juice diluted with water is better). Offer with or after meals.

Preparing baby foods
It is not difficult to prepare the baby's foods; if you are cooking for yourself and the children you can give the baby small portions of some of your foods (liquidised if necessary).

If you are in a large household it is best not to rely on the cook to prepare the baby's food. You may have a nursery suite kitchen in which you can do this, otherwise you will have to arrange to do it in the kitchen. In the latter case it is wise to ask the mother to buy (or give you the money to buy) the utensils you need and will keep especially for the baby foods.

Prepare food in the normal way, but omit salt, spices, herbs, and other seasonings from the baby's portion.

Good kitchen hygiene is essential:
– Wash fruit and vegetables thoroughly
– Be scrupulous about washing baby's cutlery and dishes and keep a separate tea towel for these. Store these and utensils (mixers, blenders, sieve, wooden spoons, etc) in a clean dry place and keep covered to prevent contact with flies and dust
– Allow hot food to cool before you put it in a fridge
– Make sure poultry is cooked at a high temperature; if frozen *thaw completely* and rinse thoroughly before cooking.

Vegetarian families
When a family is strictly vegetarian and wishes the baby to have such a diet you have little option. Advice leaflets are obtainable from the Vegetarian Society.

Make sure the baby has sufficient variety of protein and iron. Discuss with health visitor.

Goat's milk
If the mother wishes the child to have goat's milk, or if goat's milk has been prescribed for the baby, the family will, presumably, have checked the reliability of the source and the suitability for the baby. Watch for any allergy to the goat's milk. Follow the mother's, doctor's or health visitor's instructions for feeds; any problems could be discussed with the health visitor.

Allergies/chemical reactions
If anyone in the baby's family has an allergy to certain foods, or suffers from hayfever, eczema or asthma, be extra cautious when introducing new foods; beware especially of eggs, shellfish, tomatoes, strawberries and chocolate.

Where a baby appears to be allergic to cow's milk, a doctor will suggest suitable alternatives. Follow instructions precisely.

Baby and toddler

With just one child, a mother may have managed to continue her job or other commitments with the help of relations, baby sitters, friends, but when the second baby comes she finds she needs a nannie.

A nannie can thus find herself going to a family where having a nannie, as well as having a baby brother or sister, is a new experience for the child.

In such a situation it is a great help if the nannie can join the family before the baby comes. This will give her a chance to get to know the child and the way the household runs, before the mother goes off to have the baby and she is left to cope with the child/other children.

When a child is about to have a new brother or sister, here are some things you could do together:

– Notice other babies – let the child see them close to, hear them cry
– Help him to realise that the new baby will be very small (some children are understandably misled by people who tell him he is going to have a 'playmate')
– Talk to him about the care you and the mother will have to give to the baby
– Help the child to understand that he will not be loved any less because there is a baby in the family
– Ask the mother or child to show you photographs of the child when he was a baby, look at them together, talk about when he was a baby and how he has grown, etc.

You will think of plenty more.

When the new baby is born
You could take the child to buy a present for the baby. When people come with presents for the baby it is a great help if they bring something for the older child too. Discuss this with the parents. Perhaps they would allow you to buy a few small surprise presents for the child, to be given at appropriate moments. When my third and fourth babies were born they 'brought presents' for the other children.

Be reassuring and extra loving, giving plenty of attention to the first child.

Be understanding. Help the child to know that there is nothing strange, unusual or naughty about feeling jealous. If.he is old enough, tell him most people feel like that when a brother or sister is born – maybe you have an experience of your own to describe. Talk to him and think together about happy families you know and people who are obviously great friends with their brothers and sisters.

Try to attend to the baby when the toddler is not present. It is hard to watch someone else receiving loving attention. After you have fed, bathed and changed the baby, spend a few minutes giving the toddler your undivided attention – a game, story, conversation, watching a favourite programme together.

Allow the older child to do as much, or as little, for the baby as he wishes. Let him hold him when he asks to do so; don't fuss round him once you have shown him how to hold the baby comfortably – he is unlikely to drop him. Tell him not to lift the baby out of pram, recliner or cot without asking you or parent first.

If the older child wants to get in the buggy, cot or pram when it is not occupied by the baby let him. Don't call him 'a baby' or laugh at him. It may be a way of showing you and the parents that he is crying out (silently) for more love. I would give him a bottle or even let him wear a nappie if he wants to. The stage will soon pass.

Do see that the toddler has his share of mother's lap and attention. You could offer to take the baby out, or look after him in the nursery while parent(s) do something with the older child alone.

See that the physical, emotional, developmental needs of both (or all) the children are fulfilled. The baby needs the cuddling and conversation the first child received, but this first child does not grow up suddenly when the next appears, he still needs comfort, security and stimulation. Don't let the baby deprive the toddler of some of his childhood experience.

Clinics

Well–baby clinics, child health clinics or whatever they are called in your area, offer the following services:

– Baby weighing and check on progress
– Advice service on any aspect of the well baby's welfare. A sick baby or child should not be taken to the clinic; it is intended for children who are well
– Developmental checks at regular intervals
– Immunisations (in some areas these are given by the GP) and a card recording them.

Where a mother is working, or does not wish to take the child to the clinic herself, the nannie could do this, with the mother's agreement.

A nannie will find it useful to make friends with the health visitor she meets at the clinic. She can be consulted on any aspect of baby or young child care, at almost any time. In some areas there is a 24 hour telephone advice service. It can be reassuring for a nannie to feel she can turn to the health visitor for skilled advice.

The health visitor may know of several nannies in the area and be willing to put them in touch with each other. Going to the clinic will help the nannie to get to know mothers and young children in the neighbourhood; there are mother and toddler clubs attached to some clinics, and talks, films, slide sessions may be arranged for the mothers. Attending these could be a help to an untrained nannie, and it could give her charge an opportunity to meet and play with other children.

Do be kind to other children; if your child has a rash or is unwell, stay at home from clinic that week.

On the move

Indoors
Most babies go through a crawling stage at around ten months. Some go on hands and knees, some shuffle on their bottoms, a few go straight into pulling themselves up on to their feet, then walking.

Whatever style of movement the baby chooses, once he is mobile, look out. This is a stage when a nannie needs to be extremely watchful; much damage to child – and home – can be avoided with forethought.

Precautions and hints
– Gates may be needed on stairs
– Ornaments, precious books, etc, need to be put away, or high out of reach
– Drawers and cupboards may need bolts
– Bits and pieces, eg needles, string must not be left lying around
– Floors and carpets must be swept or hoovered frequently. Bits of fluff soon go into a baby's mouth
– Loose flexes from lamps and other appliances must be lifted off the floor – watch the telephone flex too
– Crawling babies get very dirty so you need plenty of easily washable clothes
– Bulky nappies between the legs make walking more awkward so it

may be better to use neat disposables, even though you may prefer terries for night time
- Taking care of cleaning substances, animal feeding bowls, sharp objects, etc, is mentioned in other lists
- Watching a baby take his first few steps is a special delight
- Make sure you keep the parents well aware of the baby's progress; tell them about his first crawling movements and early steps. If they are at home but not in the same room as you and the children you could call them to come and see those exciting first tottering steps.

Outdoors
For walking in the street, or for outings where you may take the child out of the car and into a shop, or any place where he could run away from you, reins can ease the problem. (Also see *Holiday* section.) Babyboots sell harness with walking reins.

Pushchairs and prams
- Always use a correctly adjusted safety harness
- Beware of toddler seats on prams - they upset the balance
- Shopping bags clipped to pram or buggy can also cause the pram to tip - baskets and trays are safer
- Prams and pushchairs that can be taken apart for travelling must be re-assembled carefully - check before use
- Brakes must be efficient - check and go back to shop or manufacturer if there are any faults

High chairs
Babies enjoy sitting in high chairs and seeing and hearing the family life going on around them - the tray is also useful for toys. See that his safety harness is always fastened securely and that there is a strap or bar between his legs.

All equipment
Cots, swinging cribs, baby walkers, push chairs, car harness . . . all such equipment needs constant checking for efficiency, maintenance (nuts loosen; stitches come undone; straps weaken), and suitability as the child grows larger and stronger.

A nannie may well be using such equipment far more frequently than the parents do, and she may be more familiar with it and the safety standards to which it should comply. It is up to the nannie to see that equipment is in good order, and to tell the parents when something needs repair or replacement.

11 Play

A nannie who has taken the NNEB or a similar course will be aware of the vital importance of providing stimulating, varied play. The Scottish NNEB syllabus lists the following types of play: active, creative, constructive, experimental, exploratory, imaginative, manipulative.

Those who have not taken a course can learn much from books (see list), tv programmes and from watching children in playgrounds, parks, nursery schools, playgroups, and the home.

Suggestions for creative activities

Materials and equipment
- Water and sand, and all kinds of funnels, bowls, sieves, spoons, jugs and tubes
- Large wooden bricks (the smaller the child the larger the brick)
- Cardboard boxes of various sizes
- Things to look at, eg mobiles, friezes (don't confuse baby with too many)
- Sound toys: rattles, chimes, shakers, drums, musical instruments (Bontempi have a large range)
- Balls, beanbags, skittles
- Skipping ropes
- Odds and ends box: cotton reels, empty containers, little boxes, little tins (check for sharp edges)
- Feely toys to squeeze, stroke, bend . . . A feely book and scraps of different fabrics, eg velvet, cotton, wool, leather, silk to handle
- Play mirror (unbreakable)
- Mobility toys to push, pull, sit on and supply support for new walkers. Trucks to fill with bricks, etc
- Wheeled toys: tricycles, scooters, dolls' prams
- Paint

– Dressing-up clothes: hats are especially popular
– Home corners, with make believe stoves, fridges made from cardboard boxes
– Puppets of all types (glove, finger, marionette – home-made and bought): send to Pelham Puppets, Marlborough, Wilts for catalogue)
– Scissors and paste – magazines, cards, coloured paper . . .
– Dough, plasticine, clay
– Thick crayons (Crayola offer good value), chalks, (thin crayons, coloured pencils, and felt-tip pens for older children)
– Manipulative toys, eg beads for threading, laced cards and sewing cards
– Nesting, stacking, hammering and other 'educational' toys
– Puzzles (wooden are best for young children)
– Games, eg Ludo, snakes and ladders, junior scrabble, draughts, dominoes, picture dominoes and other matching card games
– Magnifying glass, microscope
– Scales and all kinds of objects for weighing games
– Torch
– Constructional toys, eg Lego (large or standard size components as appropriate) and Brio Mec (Builder and Constructor sets in wood)
– Pattern and design making toys – mosaics
– Planks, boxes, stilts, for practising balance and jumping
– TV for watching Play School and other programmes together
– Radio/record player to sit and listen together
– Musical activities, eg singing, dancing, clapping rhythm when you listen to a piece of music together or nannie plays
– Climbing frame
– Sets such as farm, village, and trains and track in wood (Wooden toys are very satisfying to touch and hold, they are durable, feel right in weight, and offer great scope for imaginative play. See the Brio catalogue for details of a wide selection of wooden toys)
– Shop (it is not necessary to buy little sets – make your own collection of packets).

Toys

Looking after the toys
A famous actress said to me: 'I like the nannies who come with rolls of sticking tape and plaster in their bags – the ones who can mend

toys, put the card games together in rubber bands, stick the boxes that are falling apart . . . NNEBs are generally very good about that sort of thing'.

She made a second important point: 'I also like those who will come and ask you before they throw away old, broken toys that may be precious to the family. I know you need to keep the toys in order and not have masses that are useless crammed into cupboards, but the nannie should make sure the family are ready to part with them'.

Caring for toys and encouraging the child to play with them creatively is an important part of a nannie's job.

Storing toys
It is worth taking trouble over storing toys and keeping them in order. A messy, muddled, overcrowded toy cupboard does not encourage a child to get the best from his toys, enjoy choosing a new one to play with, or to take care of them.

Discuss it with the parents if you need more shelves – these are better than drawers which could be pulled out and dropped on feet, while cupboards and boxes soon look jumbly. Toys can look attractive on shelves and it is fun, for child and nannie, to arrange and re-arrange them.

The following can also be used for toy storage: plastic bowls, cheap waste paper bins, ice cream containers (which can be stacked), bags, nets, shoe-tidy style bags, cardboard boxes, tins (check for sharp edges), wooden boxes.

Maintenance
Keep the original box for as long as possible (you may be able to prolong its life with sticky tape) and try to put back all the pieces in a game or puzzle every time. Find the first piece that goes missing – otherwise it is easy to think the game is incomplete anyway and cease to trouble. (I can remember teachers who would not allow the class to leave until every pair of the counted scissors had been found and returned to the box.)

Try to mend a toy as soon as it breaks. If it is fairly new and it seems to have had only fair wear and tear consult the toyshop or manufacturer.

Labelling the boxes and jars (felt-tip, lower case letters) will help the child become familiar with a few words – beads, dominoes, Lego, etc – and encourage orderliness.

Do be gentle and careful with the toys yourself. It is distressing for a child when an adult steps or handles carelessly causing damage, and parents/grandparents may be annoyed if an expensive toy does not receive reasonable care.

Sharing toys

Help older children to keep their toys and games safe from younger brothers and sisters who may damage them, or interfere with the game. (Sometimes the older child can go in the playpen to keep out of the small child's reach.)

Though most toys may be shared in a family, a child may have had an individual present and feel that a particular plaything is his. Respect this – don't allow another child to use it without asking first. One prime cause of family quarrels can be: 'He took my . . .'

When other children come to play, be watchful. Don't let them go home with your charge's toy car in a pocket. 'I think that is William's . . .'; remove it gently but firmly.

Don't insist that your charge must allow a friend to play with a certain precious toy. It is better to learn to share willingly rather than be forced to share grudgingly.

Choosing toys

A friend or relative might ask you to buy a suitable present for the child. The parent may give you some money to spend on toys, or you may want to give the child a Birthday or Christmas present.

Here are some points to consider:

– Does the toy DO anything?
– Does it give possibilities of creative, imaginative play?
– Remember you are buying a toy to please the child not the adult (though the adult will want to feel it is good value)
– Is the toy safe? Beware sharp edges; unsuitable fillings; loose pieces that can be pulled off and swallowed. Is it flameproof? Can it be sucked safely?
– Is it suitable for the age and ability of the child? Does it offer scope for future play? (labels indicating age suitability can be useful, but they often suggest a very large range, eg 'for children of five to eleven' – hardly flattering for the 11-year-old!)

By and large, the younger the child, the bigger the toy needs to be. Large, chunky bricks, a sturdy wooden engine to push and pull for the two-year-old. Small interlocking bricks and scale model cars

and trains can be given later
– Is it sexist or racist?
– Is it well designed? Will it withstand use? Is it strong enough?
– Be on your guard with boxed craft sets and games. So often the contents of the box do not match the expectations raised by the picture on the lid
– Avoid battery toys – they are expensive to keep going and they can be rather boring

There are so many good guides and catalogues describing toys suitable for children at different stages there is no need to give a detailed list in this book. Creative play material is suggested in the *Development* section.

Send for catalogues from some of the toy manufacturers listed at the back of this book, or write to Inter-Action Inprint for their *Good Toy Guide* (updated each year). The Design Council also issues a Guide to Play Equipment for young children (available from the Council) and you can see some of the newest well designed toys at the Design Centre.

As with so much else in life, it really is worth buying quality toys rather than the cheaper and inferior copies you see on market stalls and in some shops.

Toy libraries
In some areas toy libraries are open to handicapped and deprived children only; in others the organisers are keen for more local families to use them so that those who belong are not stigmatised as 'problem families'. Find out from the health visitor, or by contacting the Toy Libraries Association (enclose sae), where the nearest branch can be found.

Toy libraries allow scope for finding out if a particular toy is suitable and has sufficient play value for the child – before a family makes an expensive purchase. Such libraries are also fun to use as they allow time for play as well as exchange.

Buying toys
– Go to a proper toy shop or toy department in a large store. You want to see a wide range – not just the special offers bought in by a supermarket – often in conjunction with a television advertising campaign
– Talk to assistants who are knowledgeable

– Buy the products of well-established, reliable manufacturers
– Check if there is replacement in case of manufacturers' faults
(You should always be able to obtain this, and local Consumer
Advice Centres will be able to advise you, but it is as well to
discover the shopkeeper's attitude)
– Leave the child at home. Toyshops can be bewildering; a child
may be beguiled by a toy that does not satisfy your criteria, he will
be disappointed if he cannot have what he wants, and the whole
visit can be frustrating. 'Toyshops are not for children,' a
shopkeeper told me once. I think he was right. You may disagree. I
never return to shops that try to sell through the child: 'Do you
want anything else? Have you seen these . . .?', send me out of the
shop fast.

Playing with toys

There is no 'right way' to play with a toy. 'The right way to play
with a toy is the way the child wants to play with it,' said Susan
Isaacs, a pioneer in understanding young children.

This is why a toy needs to be versatile and give scope for
imagination. Never push a child into using an educational toy
'correctly'. If he wants to build with the pieces from the posting box
or use the nesting beakers for water play – let him.

If a child asks for help give it, talking about what you are doing.
Don't be 'bossy', let him experiment and find his own way round a
problem. There is no need to take over.

Quantity   The other day I went to see the home of a two-year-old.
'This is where he plays,' said the mother. It looked utterly
confusing. A large quantity of expensive toys were spread out and in
heaps on a carpet. Individual toys were attractive, full of scope and
well chosen, but there were just too many for one child to cope with
at once.

It is far better for a child to have a few of his toys at a time. The
nannie can always get out others when he seems bored and in need
of a change. Putting a child in a playpen or play area with a mass of
toys is no way of giving him a happy playtime. He wants company,
conversation and scope for creativity – not clutter.

Clearing toys away

A mother who comes from work feeling tired, or one who comes
into the nursery suite at bedtime, may reasonably expect the place

to be fairly tidy. But it is unkind suddenly to say to the child: 'Put your toys away now'. Give a warning: 'We shall have to pack up at four o'clock,' or 'When the big hand is on the four . . .', or whatever he can understand.

It is disheartening for a child to be left alone with a great pile of toys to put away by himself. Help him do it. Make a game of it if you like. 'Let's pick up all the soft/red/wheeled . . . toys first,' or 'Let's start with the cars . . .' how ever you both care to group them in sets.

You could put away ten things, and then another ten, or see how many you can put away neatly in a given number of minutes. Every nannie will have her own ideas. Make it fun as well as a discipline.

Having a good system of storage will pay dividends when it comes to clearing up time.

Of course, you will treasure the child's paintings/models/brick constructions and keep them carefully for him to show his parents.

Games

Playing a game can diffuse a situation, distract a child from pain or disappointment, help pass a time of waiting. You will have plenty of ideas of your own for simple games you could play together anywhere – while waiting for a bus or train, when you have tidied away all the toys and it is nearly time for mother to come home, when nannie has to do some chore such as washing the bathroom floor or ironing.

Oral games
– I spy type
– Jokes, riddles, puzzles
– Simple spelling quizzes
– Number questions and easy mental arithmetic (the child could count with any handy objects)
– Singing games (take it in turns to hum a nursery rhyme while the other guesses which it is)
– Opposites
– Lists of fruits, flowers, birds, etc
– Let's pretend games acting out familiar situations (one as shopkeeper, one as customer; a person lost asking the way; pretending to be well-known personalities. At mealtimes our children sometimes liked to pretend they were in a restaurant –

Mummy seemed to end up as the waitress most times!)

Use the situation you are in – at a bus stop count the cars, look for cars of specific colours; at the clinic guess the baby's ages.

In a surgery waiting room you could play simple consequence type drawing games. (Whenever you take the child out it is a good idea to have paper and pencil in your bag – you can always think of some diversion using these.)

Don't make games all one way. Encourage the child to think out new ones, take the initiative, be the questioner, not always the respondent.

Board games
Snakes and ladders, Ludo, dominoes (spot or picture), all manner of dice and objects along a route games, simple card games and others (you could send for Waddington's catalogue for more ideas), can be a learning experience as well as being fun and a diversion.

When a child is bored and restless, when he is looking at the television without really watching it, when you feel it is time to sit down together quietly you could play a game. It is often easier to get out one of your choice, set it up and start playing, rather than having a long discussion on which game to play. The child can always choose the next one to be played.

While playing a game together, give the game your total attention – unless the baby is sitting beside you, in which case you will want to talk to him and give him something to shake so that he does not feel left out. It is better to play with enthusiasm for 15 minutes, rather than half-heartedly for 30. Leave off before the child has had enough; that way he will be keener to play again another day.

Playing games can help a child learn to share, and to accept defeat. (Though it is disheartening if you always lose. My husband and I had a craze for Chinese Chequers, but once he could win easily every single time I lost interest and would not accept any advantage.)

Games help develop speech, number recognition and under-standing, reasoning ability and concentration. They can help to bring a child and adult closer.

When a grandparent or other relation comes to visit the child it can relax the situation if you all play a game together. Once the child and visitor are happily involved the nannie can slip away to do something else and leave the others together without her.

Nannie and child might be playing a game together when the mother comes home. Never let the mother feel an intruder. Nannie could say, 'Would you like to play while I make you a cup of tea?', or some such. If the parent has come into the nursery suite to be with the child, nannie can easily find something else to do and leave child and parent together in peace to go on playing or do as they wish.

Playing a game with a child is a way of giving him individual attention. One of our friends makes a point of playing a game of chess with each of our children when she comes to visit us. She adjusts her game according to the child's skill but somehow does not allow them to feel she is 'playing down'.

Cooking together

You may have a nursery suite with cooking facilities, or the use of the family kitchen. The children will probably enjoy being with you, watching you and helping you while you are cooking – perhaps lunch or high tea for you and the children, or the evening meal for the family.

A child in a high chair can be given plastic bowls, wooden and plastic spoons – whatever you can find that will be safe for him to handle or suck. Try to give him different shapes, textures, weights, and maybe a bowl of water as well.

With an older child there will be opportunities for weighing, measuring, judging and guessing then checking. You can enlarge his vocabulary with such terms as halves/quarters, full/empty, spread/mix/crumble/beat, boiled/baked/steamed/simmered . . . you can introduce concepts and degrees of temperature, talk about tastes and smells, compare ingredients crunchy/smooth, soft/hard, moist/wet . . . There is no need to go on – you will have your own ideas; new things will keep occurring to you.

By your example you can teach the child:
– The importance of cleanliness in a kitchen and that hands must be scrupulously clean when preparing food
– To be methodical about assembling ingredients and equipment
– The need to weigh and measure carefully and follow instructions
– The importance of clearing up thoroughly.

Kitchen safety

A *few simple rules:*
– Wipe up all spills immediately so that there are no slippery patches on the floor
– Keep all sharp, pointed implements out of reach or under strict supervision
– Warn child about any hot surfaces, pans, kettles, etc
– Turn saucepan handles to the side of the stove (a safety guard round the cooker is a good investment)
– Keep all cleaning fluids, bleach etc well out of reach
– Check safety of plugs, sockets, flexes
– Teach a child how to use apparatus; emphasise never put a fork or other object into a toaster to hook out the toast (can be fatal)
– Never use a chip pan while there are children in the kitchen. (Make sure you know how to deal with a chip pan fire: exclude air from the pan with fire blanket, lid or metal plate. Never douse with water)
– Make sure flexes from kettles, mixers, electric cooking and coffee pots do not dangle dangerously
– See that a baby or small child in a chair is not in a position where hot foods/liquids could be spilled on him.

Play in the garden
Many of the toys and activities already listed can be enjoyed in the garden as well as indoors.

Ideas
Here are a few suggestions for making time in the garden creative and fun:

– Digging (in designated area)
– Mud play
– Sowing quick growing seeds (eg Nasturtium, Love-in-a-mist, Clarkia, Hollyhock, Larkspur, Stocks – for others consult *The Flower Expert* by Dr D G Hessayon) and putting in little plants
– Hopping, skipping, jumping, balancing
– Hide and seek with people or objects
– Ball games
– Quoits and frisbys
– Skittles

– Paddling, splashing, swimming
– Clothes washing
– Balloon games
– Blowing bubbles
– Painting pictures/patterns (take out easle or table) foot and finger painting
– Water painting of steps, fence etc
– Water play with buckets, bowls etc (coloured water is more fun – use culinary colourings)
– Finding and observing insects (set free afterwards)
– Looking at leaves, flowers, insects under microscope or with magnifying glass
– Tents and home corners (a few rugs can give plenty of scope for imagination)
– Shadow games
– Stories can be read or told by nannie sitting in garden chair or on a rug.

Hazards
Even the family back garden has hazards for young children. *Watch out for these danger points*

– Tools left around – prongs of gardening forks and rakes can cause nasty injuries
– Sheds and garages – make sure these are locked so that weedkillers, turps etc are not accessible to children (**Never, never** store in lemonade bottles)
– Electrical appliances – mowers, trimmers etc and all sharp tools should be stored sensibly
– Poisonous plants and berries – Laburnum seeds can be fatal. Teach the children never to put any berry/fruit/seed/nut/leaf into the mouth without showing it to an adult first. Write to the Publicity Department, Sterling House, The Priory, 1 Onslow Street, Guildford, Surrey, GU1 4YS, for free illustrated chart.
– Gates and doors should be securely fastened. Check for holes in fences and hedges – a small toddler can vanish through one in a moment!
– Make sure that no puppy or dog mess is around (the neighbour's dog may have visited your garden!)
– Ponds can lead to frightening, unpleasant dips – if not worse. A child can drown in 50 cm (2 in.) of water

– Paddling pools – children in paddling pools must be supervised all the time

– Sandpits – cover needed to exclude cats and dogs when no one is playing there

– Swings, climbing frames, etc – make sure safe and secure and nothing has been left lying around to injure child should he fall off. Grass or sand are the safest surfaces underneath apparatus

– Babies in prams – cat net needed when young baby left alone; insect net may also be necessary

– Bare feet – it is fun to run and play on the grass in bare feet – check no sharp stones or objects left around

– Insects – teach children to respect them and that bite/sting is insect's defence. Watch but do not touch

– Deckchairs – it is best if the children do not handle them until they are old enough to be shown how to avoid pinching their fingers.

12 Playing and learning

Although a nannie is not normally expected to give a child any formal lessons, she has many opportunities for stimulating the child's development, arousing his curiosity, and extending his knowledge. She can encourage him to be creative, to think and reason for himself. Educationalists say: 'Every mother is a teacher'. Every nannie is a teacher too.

Number sense

There are many fun games and activities that will encourage a child's number sense. Most parents will automatically count 'one, two, three . . .' when a child learns to climb the stairs. This is exactly on the right lines. Whenever young children are taught to count they should have objects to handle or touch, things to see and do.

Any bricks, construction apparatus or small toys can be used for sorting, matching and counting games. You can talk about numbers, names and shapes, without pushing or overdoing it, as they occur in day-to-day activities. 'We shall need . . . plates'; 'How many crayons in the box?' 'How many people at the bus stop?' 'Here are . . . clean nappies'.

As the child grows older you can play card games and make simple counting apparatus for him. You can also introduce games such as 'Tell me three round things in this room'. You can sort objects into hard and soft, into colours, shapes, and sizes.

You could sort the cutlery into knives (remove sharp ones), forks and spoons; the socks into pairs; the pile of ironing into fabrics. The possibilities are endless once you start thinking them out.

Those who are interested in figures and would like to enjoy some new maths games with children should obtain *Let's Play Maths* by Michael Holt and Zoltan Dienes published by Penguin; Michael

Holt's books of games *Fun With Numbers* (Piccolo); and the books of puzzles (Longman Young Books) compiled by Michael Holt and Ronald Ridout. They are full of fun and ideas. *Let's Play Maths* has sound advice on play with children in general and how to introduce fun games that will 'encourage an alert open-minded attitude in youngsters and help them develop their potential for clear thinking'.

Language development

Those who have trained as NNEBs, or taken similar courses, will have studied the normal stages of speech and language development from 0 to 7 years, and how such development can be stimulated and encouraged. I always think that the way children acquire speech is almost miraculous. For an adult it seems almost impossible to learn a language just through hearing it spoken all around you. Listening to small children chattering away in their language which is foreign to you is fascinating. When you think how many words a child of three knows it is just amazing. But such achievement depends on hearing speech. A child learns to talk if people talk to him.

A nannie who has charge of a child must talk, talk, talk to him. When you start caring for a tiny baby, talk to him, sing to him, let him hear other children and adults talking.

All the time you are with a child you can help him develop by talking to him.

– Talk to him about what you are both doing (washing, dressing, eating, playing . . .)
– Name the objects you handle, the furniture in the room, the people you meet
– Talk about the things you see on the television, out of the window, in pictures, books and magazines
– When you are outdoors chat about what you can see
– Encourage the child to talk to you
– Play games that encourage the use of language
– Read and tell him rhymes and stories (see separate sections)
– Tell him jokes and ask him simple riddles
– Read labels on packages, names and addresses on letters
– Record the child on cassette then play it back to him
– Talk to a child naturally as to a friend
– Gradually introduce new words and phrases

– Try to speak clearly and grammatically yourself, using apt descriptive words.

Where there are two or more children, check that one does not rely on others or another to do his talking for him.

If you help a child develop fluent, confident speech, you are making him a gift for life and helping forward his whole future development.

Never talk down to a child; he will soon detect it. Far better to use a word that is new to him and allow him to grow familiar with it.

When you are with children all day it is quite natural to long for a few minutes of peace and quiet. With a younger child there will be the times when he is sleeping, or at least having a short nap. With an older child his talking can be almost non-stop. Rather than annoying the child by answering half-heartedly and not giving full attention, I think it is better to say something like: 'I am going to sit here quietly and read the paper until a given time or until the big hand is (as appropriate)' or 'We want to listen to the news, so please keep quiet . . .'.

Children have to learn not to interrupt, that sometimes they must be quiet, eg when an adult is talking on the telephone, when another child is listening to a story. If children are encouraged to talk for much of the time they can reasonably be asked to keep quiet at given times. Sometimes they will want to be quiet themselves when they are concentrating on a game or activity.

Speech and accent

It seems only fair to the parents that a nannie should try to encourage a child to speak in a way that is acceptable to them. A nannie with a regional accent may notice it reflected in the child's speech, but there is no need to worry about this. Children seem to adjust their speech according to their companions. Prunella Scales, who helped me with advice about nannies, told me her children could 'speak Battersea or BBC'.

When I was a child I spoke like an Aberdonian because I went to school in Aberdeen, but when we moved back to London I soon lost the accent – rather to my regret.

I don't think a nannie needs to alter her speech to sound like the family, if they speak differently. Artificiality of any kind soon comes through. They chose you as nannie to their children speaking the way you did at the interview. Be true to yourself, speak in the way that is comfortable and natural to you.

Retarded speech
When a child seems unusually late or slow in making sounds and saying a few words it is worth thinking about the causes.

Maybe he has been cared for by a nannie, au pair or childminder who did not talk to him sufficiently. Perhaps he has brothers and sisters close in age – or he is one of multiples – and they do the talking for him. He may not have had enough one-to-one contact with an adult. He could have attended a nursery where he was one of a group and his lack of speech went unnoticed. If these are the causes, a nannie can soon put it right through patient, gentle conversation, frequent repetition of everyday words and names. If the child does not respond, and by the age of two he is saying little, it would be as well to have the causes checked.

Suggest the mother mentions it to the health visitor or doctor. The child could be mentally slow, deaf, autistic or have some other problem. There is no need to be alarmist – it will probably turn out that there is nothing seriously wrong – but it is as well to make sure.

Should any problem be diagnosed, contact the Association for All Speech Impaired Children. They offer helpful literature and advice.

Stammering
Stammering and stuttering often occur because a child's mind races ahead of his words. Nervousness or over-excitement may cause the child to stumble over particular sounds or words. Drawing attention to it and correcting it, may only make the child self-conscious and exacerbate the problem. Just listen patiently and give him plenty of praise and encouragement to improve his confidence.

If the child has no apparent problems and seems happy in himself the stammering is probably only a temporary phase best ignored. When the stammering is allied with other problems or unhappiness, and persists after the age of six or seven, the parents will need to seek advice from the family or school doctor.

Seasons and festivals

When you are looking after a pre-school child day by day, you want to make life varied and stimulating for you both. You can use the seasons of the year to introduce new activities and widen the child's experience.

Activity books, magazine articles, television programmes, displays in the library, playgroup, nursery school, and your own inventiveness and creativity should produce plenty of ideas. Perhaps your employer would be willing to order *Child Education* for you. This contains large colourful pictures that would be useful for the playroom, and ideas for crafts, music, nature study to suit the seasons.

Spring, summer, autumn and winter are themes that can easily be explored on walks, nature tables, charts, scrap books. You could try always to have some plants, bulbs or seeds growing indoors, or in the child's own garden patch or window box. Herbs are fun to grow; bean sprouts give quick results (don't plant too many at once); vegetable tops of all sorts are old favourites; crystals (of alum, iron sulphate, copper sulphate) grown in water produce fascinating strings of colour; pre-soaked acorns and conkers develop shoots; barley, wheat and grasses can be dried. A little thought will produce plenty of ideas. Bottles and jars can be used for planting and sowing as well as pots; cress will grow on sliced potato; seeds of little flowers, eg Virginia Stocks, can be sown to spell out a child's name.

Seeds such as nasturtium could be planted in a pot and given as a present when in bloom, eg for Granny's birthday. Nowadays there is much more awareness that wild flowers should be left to bloom where they are, not to wilt in fishpaste jars on a nature table, but it probably would do no harm to pick a few daisies; a child could take pleasure in arranging these artistically. When flowers are cheap, ask the parents if you can buy a few for the playroom, or maybe you can pick some from the garden, let the child enjoy having flowers around, arranging them and looking after them.

As different foods come into season you will use them and find out more about them. Some children are very vague about which vegetables grow under the ground, which above. They are not alone; the other day a middle-aged woman looked at some redcurrants on a stall and asked me what they were and how you used them; you could talk about the different fruits and vegetables and collect pictures of them growing, as well as finding varied ways of cooking them.

The religious festivals give scope for ceremonies, making models, gifts and cards, drawing pictures and exploring the theme in stories and poems. Think of an Advent candle ring, Christmas friezes, model cribs, acting Nativity plays, learning carols, making cards and presents, decorating a tree and all the colourful, cheerful things you can make and do at Christmas time.

Mothering Sunday gives further scope for presents and cards; then it will be Easter gardens, chicks, rabbits and decorating eggs.

Harvest Festivals are fun to attend – even if you don't go to a service you could walk round a church or cathedral decorated for harvest and talk about what you see.

Jewish festivals
Judaism has many festivals celebrated in the home with rituals, family meals and reminders of historic events. Children in Jewish families share in these special days and they can help with the preparations and learn about the significance of the festival. Even if the nannie is not of the Jewish faith, and so does not take part in the celebrations, she can learn about the festival so that she understands and is sympathetic and interested in what the children will be doing.

Creative listening

Dr Rachel Pinney, physician and therapist, pioneered 'Creative listening', a new way of listening to children, and now she teaches this method in workshops for playgroup workers, nursery nurses and student teachers. It is very simple.

The adult agrees to give a child a specified period of total attention. During that time the adult is with the child one-to-one, and does whatever the child wishes: within the bounds of safety and propriety. Often it takes the form of watching the child play, build with bricks, paint, climb, dress up. The key thing is that the adult watches attentively. She does not pick up the paper, watch the television, or chat to a friend; it is the child's time.

Sometimes the adult recaps what the child is doing, saying, for instance, 'You are building with the red bricks now . . .' but does not make suggestions.

Children seem to benefit from these periods of complete attention. When Dr Rachel sits with them I have seen them relax and look happy. With our own youngest son I found he wanted me to listen with him to his pop records. We both enjoyed the time.

A 'Children's Hour', as these times are often called, is like a gift to a child. It is a gift a nannie is well placed to offer.

To learn more about the method send for the booklet, *Creative Listening*, from Dr Rachel Pinney, 28 Wallace House, Caledonian Estate, London N7.

13 Books, stories and poetry

Reading to a child

Reading to a child, or telling him stories, is one of the great pleasures of the nannie's job. However awkward, restless, demanding a child has been, listening to a story can restore him so that he relaxes, becomes more friendly and amenable.

When you read a story to a child you feel close to him as you share tension and excitement, ponder a mystery, laugh, or feel sad together. An adult can forget cares and worries when she puts her arm round a child, lifts him on to her lap, or sits beside him and becomes absorbed in a story with him.

By reading a child stories, as well as giving delight, you are laying foundations for speech, language and reading. You are helping the child to recognise that books are a source of joy, amusement and information. With a book in our hands we can all – even a young child – find relief from tensions, grow in sympathy and understanding, and have our imagination aroused.

Reading or telling a child stories can give him a feel and fascination for words, enjoyment in rhythm, and practice in listening and concentration.

Choosing stories
You will have your own favourite stories for children. If you do not find a story appealing when you read it to them, neither will they. Those who have taken the NNEB course will have studied children's books, and probably made books for children.

Anyone who does not have a knowledge of books for young children could spend a happy hour or two browsing in bookshops and children's libraries. (Ask librarians for lists of suggested books, authors, illustrators. Many prepare such lists for parents and others.)

There are many books about children and reading, but I would bring to your notice *Supertot: A Parents' Guide to Toddlers* by Jean Marzollo (Unwin Paperbacks) which gives a helpful, basic list of 43 accepted children's favourites. Everyone's list would be different, but there are certain 'classics' such as *The Very Hungry Caterpillar* by Eric Carle (Hamish Hamilton), *Rosie's Walk* by Pat Hutchins (Picture Puffin), *The Little Red Engine* books by Diana Ross (Faber), that would appear on most nannies' lists.

I would especially recommend, the Dr Seuss *Beginner Books* (Collins); *Bedtime for Frances* and *Bread and Jam for Frances* by Russell Hoban (Faber); *Jim and the Beanstalk* by James Briggs (Picture Puffin); *The Tiger who came to Tea* by Judith Kerr (Picture Lions); and *The Little Babar Books* (Methuen).

Keep introducing new stories and authors as well as returning again and again to old favourites. (You and the child could take it in turn to suggest which story to read – then you can ensure a variety.)

The National Book League, 45 East Hill, SW19, has a reference collection of children's books and occasional special displays of outstanding books for children.

Buying books
A friend or relation may ask you to buy or suggest a book that would be a suitable present for the child. When going to buy a book for a child allow yourself plenty of time; do not take the child with you. If you do you will not be able to concentrate on the choice. Go to a large bookshop or store with a book department; better still find a specialist children's bookshop.

Points to consider Though they often seem horrendously expensive, a really attractive hardback version of a worthwhile story will be an investment. There is something satisfying about handling a well produced book, and it is good to introduce children to this pleasure.

Children are likely to be given paperbacks – and very attractive so many of them are too, especially Picture Puffins, Picture Lions and those produced by Methuen – but it is good to take the chance of buying them an occasional hardback. It is often possible to buy children's books in charity shops, at fêtes, and at playgroup or school jumble sales.

– Look for sharp, clear, bold designs and pictures. Dick Bruna's *Miffy* series and the *Kate and Sam* series (Methuen) are admirable examples.

– Avoid books with pictures overprinted with text – this tends to be confusing for a young child.

– Look for an attractive, clear typeface; notice how well it is laid out to relate to the illustrations.

– Choose a book with paper that has an appealing, friendly feel.

– Consider whether the story is about an everyday situation, a fairy tale, a fable, a story with a model, or is it basically an information book. (eg *The butterfly* and *The Seed* – both excellent publications by Macmillan)

– Given the price of children's books, does it seem fair value?

– Is it a story the child is likely to want to hear (or later read for himself) again and again? Will he soon outgrow it?

– Will the relative/friend who has asked you to choose the book think it is a good, attractive, suitable buy?

– Is it an investment?

– Will you be happy reading the book to the child?

– Check that the condition is perfect. Ask for an unhandled copy. (Unless it is being remaindered, publishers' agreements prevent the book being sold at a reduction even if it is slightly battered.)

– Avoid gimmicky books. I believe a book is a book – records, crayons, paper models, puppets . . . detract from the book as a joy in itself. A really good story book does not need such additions to make it sell.

Admittedly, 'pop-up' books are liked by children. If you buy one of these make sure it is strong enough to withstand use, and that it does not have any parts that are too complicated to manipulate.

Baby books Quite a small baby can hold a little board or rag book and be stimulated by it. By giving him a book you are helping to convey the message, books bring pleasure, books are important. The child from the home where books are familiar objects has a great advantage.

Care of books
The way the nannie treats books will do most to show the child that they are precious and need to be handled with care. If you set a good example, hopefully, the children will treat them as you do.

Adequate, convenient storage is essential for preservation and ready accessibility. The parents probably will provide the child with a bookcase or shelving for books – if not you could ask them to do so. Arranging and re-arranging books, keeping them neat and straight, and knowing exactly where to find the one you want, is part of the joy of owning books. You may be able to cover some of the child's books so as to preserve the dust jackets.

The way the nannie keeps her own books will also be a lesson to the child. You will, of course, teach such habits as turning pages carefully, never leaving a book face down. Do not let a younger child get to an older child's books and damage them. (I remember being upset when my little brother scribbled over one of my favourite books.)

Books and learning to read

For under-fives books are not primarily tools for teaching a child to read, they are to give pleasure as well as the other benefits already mentioned, but there are some mechanics of reading that a child can acquire with little, or without any, deliberate teaching from the nannie.

He will gradually realise that a story starts at the front and progresses to the back of the book, and that English is read from left to right. As nannie points to a word or runs her finger along a line of text he will realise that the story is being communicated by these shapes and symbols.

In time he will perceive that words and letters have different shapes, and he will come to recognise particular words. Never push him to read the text with you. You may find that he has learnt the story by heart and appears to be reading it with you, but this is memory not early reading ability.

Children vary in their readiness for learning to read. There is no point in worrying them, trying to push them on and destroying their delight in books, by trying to teach them before they are ready. When they are keen to read they will learn fast.

Hear him read when he asks you to listen to him reading, before that read with him. Give him plenty of experience of books so that he knows that books are for pleasure and is never confined to those in school reading schemes.

Telling stories

Most children enjoy hearing a story told to them, a story that is special, individual, perhaps about them.

When I was a magazine editor we had a great many children's stories submitted. Almost invariably the author said: 'I told my own children this story and they loved it . . .'. Occasionally the story in question was suitable for publication, but more frequently it did not have enough substance, action, or plot, for other readers to use it with success.

This is not to say that the author's child had not enjoyed the story. The way the mother told it, her familiar voice and vocabulary, and the fact that it was re-capping things the child had done, seen and experienced, made the story intimate and exciting for the child who featured in it.

Any nannie could make up simple stories for her charge. As a start, just recount the incidents in a child's day in story form. You could go on to create a favourite character, or whole family of characters with distinctive names, and weave stories about their doings. I found my own children liked to laugh at a story. We had a slap-dash cheery mother character (not too far removed from their experience), and she had all sorts of adventures and mishaps with her children, though all turned out well in the end every time.

Creating a story character who is real to you both can make a bond between you. When I was a student I cared for a boy of four. He was rather disturbed by the arrival of a new baby, but what could have been difficult for me was made easier by telling him stories.

He seemed to love the simple tales I recounted as we walked along the street going shopping, sat in the garden or nursery while his mother attended to the baby, and as I put him to bed. This experience gave me confidence to make up and tell stories for other children. As a nannie you so often find that as well as you giving to them, children give to you, and help you develop your gifts and capabilities.

Rhymes and poetry

Children can respond to the fun, rhythm, language and thought communicated by poems and rhymes. Make sure you include poetry and verse in your reading times, and at odd moments during the day.

Nursery rhymes
These are part of a child's heritage. New collections of the old

favourites are constantly being produced. It is worth having one really comprehensive, hardback collection you can keep handy. Before you suggest which the parents should buy study some in children's libraries and bookshops. When you are reading nursery rhymes to children and teaching them, just leave out those you find horrific, eg *Three Blind Mice*.

Finger play and action rhymes

What child has not laughed at such rhymes as *Round and round the garden . . .*? You will probably have a repertoire of favourites you have used with children. Such rhymes can while away odd moments of waiting, they help language development, and they are fun to share. Ladybird publish a useful series of rhymes for mother and child; *This Little Puffin* is another standby.

Poetry
You can introduce children to poetry when they are young and help them discover delight that could remain with them for life. Keep a favourite anthology at hand – stowed away behind glass doors it can easily stay pristine but unappreciated. When you have a quiet moment together, read the children one or two poems that appeal to you but, of course, you will not want to bore them. If you can find delight and wonder in a poem, you may be able to impart this to a child.

Include poems that will make them laugh: some of Spike Milligan's, Edward Lear's, Hilaire Belloc's; those that are descriptive, eg by R L Stevenson, James Reeves'; some that ask questions, eg *What does Little Birdie say?* by Alfred, Lord Tennyson or *Morning* by Emily Dickinson.

Browse around to find a collection of verse to appeal to you and the child. I use *The Illustrated Treasury of Poetry for Children* published by Collins.

Making books with the children

There are all kinds of books you can make for the children (you may have done this as part of your course) and enjoy using with them.

Here are just a few ideas – you will have many more of your own:

Birthday card books. Make sure the parents agree to you using the cards like this. Paste in a book made by you from sugar paper, punched and fastened, or in a bought scrap book with plain pages or plastic pockets. Write under each card the name of the person who sent it. This will be a useful record for the family, and as the child grows up and his collection of birthday card books grows it will help him to remember people he has known and how they have cared about him.

Theme books – cut pictures out of colour supplements and magazines. The child could choose, you could cut, he could paste in the book.

Photograph book – for instamatic or other pictures of the child on outings. You could also take a number of photographs in one day, and use them to make a picture book of the child's day. A 'People I know' book would also be fun. You could include the postman, crossing keeper, stallholders, hairdresser, shop keepers, etc, as well as family and household.

Picture and pattern collection – keep some of the child's work and note the date he did each piece. Mount or insert in a book.

14 Out and about

When children seem bored with their toys, full of energy, restless, or quarrelsome, it is often easier to leave any job you are trying to do and take them out.

A walk can relieve tension for you all, get you away from the house and problems, and give you new things to think about, as well as being in the fresh air.

Find places where people do not exercise their dogs; let the children run, jump, play ball and enjoy plenty of space for freedom, noise, movement.

Walks in the rain can be fun; let them splash in puddles in their Wellies, feel the raindrops on face and hands, be exhilarated by the wind.

Library

Many local authorities allow children to join public libraries when they are three years old. Going to change the library books may be a convenient objective for a walk and nannie could change her own book while she is there. Seeing an adult reading, handling books carefully and appreciating them conveys the message that books are important.

For the child, seeing books in the children's library will make him more familiar with books, give him a chance to discover new authors and illustrators, and provide scope for exercising choice. (Check that the parents approve before you enrol the child in the library.)

Of course, you will not risk leaving a baby outside the library in his pram. Some librarians are reluctant to allow prams/push chairs inside the library so you may have to scoop the child out and carry him around while you change your book, however awkward it is!

Some children's libraries have story sessions. Look in the local Yellow Pages and ring up for details.

Walks

Taking the baby or young children for a walk in the park is a traditional nannie activity and it can be fun too.

Here are some hints for making it an enjoyable and learning occasion:
– Talk about what you see
– Stop to admire flowers, birds, grass, views, buildings of beauty (look up so as to notice architectural details (eg mouldings round windows, unusual chimney pots) sky and clouds)
– You can help a child to be aware of his environment by asking him questions: 'Which front door colour do you prefer?' 'Which shaped window do you like best?'
– Visit swings/slides/roundabouts (you will, of course, keep alert – accidents happen so quickly, especially where there are hard surfaces below play apparatus – equipment set on grass is much safer)
– As you walk and talk bring new terms into the conversation, eg road, street, lane; speak about left and right, or mention north, south, east and west. Young children can absorb such information without realising how much they are learning
– Every outing should be a lesson in road safety. You may not give deliberate teaching, but simply say, 'We must wait for the lights . . .' 'Look that way . . .'
– Always use proper crossings even when it means walking further. Now is the chance to instil good habits
– Wheeled toys can add to the fun of the outing; you are responsible for the child's safety with them, and also for seeing that they do not inconvenience other pedestrians.
– Your walk in the park may be a chance to meet other nannies and children. In London and some big cities there are afternoon groups for mothers/childminders, nannies and toddlers in many parks and open spaces. These 'one o'clock clubs' generally provide toys and activities in a safe, fenced off space – or in a hut for rainy days; story and rhyme sessions may be organised by the leaders.

The child may be interested in cars, and before you know where you are he will be testing you on different makes!

We all have our own interests and if you are keen about something yourself such as gardening, architecture, transport, you can soon communicate your own enthusiasm and awaken some in the child.

Playground safety

– Observe any age regulations, eg 'for children over five only'
– Stay close to the child and watch him all the time
– *Slides* Climb up the steps behind him the first few times. If he suddenly changes his mind, don't force him on, lift or help him down.

If there is no other adult standing by the slide, run round to catch or steady him as he slides down. (My youngest son fell off a slide and broke a finger.)

Watch that the steps are not slippery after rain and that the child is wearing shoes without anything loose to catch on steps or slide
– Look out for over-boisterous older children who may intimidate your child
– If you have a baby in a pram as well as a toddler, park the pram where you can see it all the time
– *Roundabouts* Make sure the child understands he should not try to jump off while it is revolving
– *Climbing frames* If the child should get stuck, be calm and re-assuring – guide or lift him down
– *See-saws* Make sure children do not run underneath a raised end. Show them how to use their feet to prevent hard bumps
– *Swings* Watch out for other children and empty, moving swings. Common sense will dictate size and height to be safely enjoyed.

As many as 15,000 children a year suffer injuries in playgrounds in Britain, according to a Consumers' Association survey. In Deptford, one of the areas studied, young children who went to a playground every day were found to have a one in eight chance of suffering a serious accident in a year.

About 85% of the injuries resulted from falls, most of them onto hard surfaces such as concrete, tarmac or hard-packed earth. On tarmac and concrete any fall can give a child severe head injuries.

Country walk safety

– Keep well into the side and, if there is no pavement, always walk on the right facing oncoming traffic. In a Court Case quoted in *Home and School*, the magazine of the National Confederation of Parent–Teacher Associations, 'a father of a child of four years was held to be guilty of negligence, jointly with a motorist, when the child was injured, since the father had failed to look after the child properly, by allowing him to walk on the left hand side of the road . . . .'.
– Respect notices about bulls.
– Try to prevent children from falling into stagnant ponds and ditches. The water in these can contain harmful bacteria (especially after a storm when the water has been disturbed); any child who has swallowed such water or any water that may have been polluted should be taken without delay to a doctor or hospital casualty department.
– Observe rules about berries, fruits etc, as described in *Garden* section.

Museums and art galleries

As the child grows older you may like to take him into a local museum or art gallery. Don't overdo it. Just look at a few things and talk about them. Help him to think of a museum as an exciting place he wants to visit again.

A postcard picture will remind him of the visit and give him something to show his parents.

Outings
In time you will want to go further afield by bus, train, coach or car. As a nannie you will, of course, take good care of the child. Hold his hand on busy streets or use reins.

Watch his fingers do not get trapped in doors and lifts. Keep him away from the edge of the platform on railways and underground.

Be vigilant on escalators: trailing clothing can be dangerous and there have been cases of children getting a foot caught in the side of the escalator. Obey regulations about folding push chairs.

Teach the child to recite his name and address and telephone number: see that he has this information somewhere on his person.

Avoid supermarkets and departmental stores. How often have

you heard lost child announcements in big stores? Have you ever seen cross, disobedient or ever-excited children in stores? My nephew once crawled into the centre of a huge carpet on top of a pile in an up-market store. He stayed there tantalisingly out of my sister-in-law's grasp, and refused to return to her for a while.

I always think that babies and very young children seem at risk in super-markets. A tin or bottle could so easily be dropped or fall on them.

You and the parents will of course have taught the child:

Never walk off with a stranger

Never get into a stranger's car

Never accept sweets or gifts from a stranger.

Places of interest

When you take a child to a museum, country house, castle, or exhibition, talk to him about what you are seeing; do not rush round too quickly, above all, do not bore him. You do not want to put him off museums for life! Wait until he is ready for them.

Most large museums have a wide selection of models, colouring books, posters, little gifts, simple books. Children will enjoy choosing something to take home, it will be a reminder of the visit and a talking point for the family.

At a castle, or other ancient building, constant vigilance is needed. For instance, it is tempting to climb or jump up to look over battlements, but the drop below may be steep. I remember being worried when we took our four adventurous children to Stirling Castle; not long afterwards I read that a child had fallen while climbing on the walls. I once heard of a boy of seven who slipped on a stone staircase in an Irish castle and fell (fatally) through an arrow slit in the wall.

Zoos, wildlife parks, city farms

In these places it is important to observe regulations about car windows, feeding and touching animals.

It is fun to see feeding times at a zoo so judge your visit accordingly. Do include an animal ride, if this is available and the child wants one. Riding on a camel or in a llama trap could be an incident that lives in the memories of happy childhood. (Photographs help too.)

City farms give young children an opportunity to see chickens, pigs, goats, calves, ponies and other small animals close at hand; sometimes they are allowed to touch them. Admission is free or cheap, so if there is such a farm near you visits can be made frequently. (Addresses from City Farms Advisory Service, Old Vicarage, 66 Fraser St, Bedminster, Bristol BS3 4L7.)

In the country local Tourist Boards will tell you about farms that are willing to show visitors round. Farm Open Days are becoming increasingly popular and they give townspeople a chance to learn about the countryside and how it should be treated.

Animals and birds in parks

Many London and provincial parks have small aviaries (Dulwich), deer enclosures, or roaming deer (Richmond and Battersea), tame squirrels and other animal and bird life for children to watch and enjoy. Even seeing just a few guinea pigs, rabbits, peacocks or baby deer, will add to the pleasure of an outing.

The GLC have children's zoos in Battersea Park and Crystal Palace, and a mobile zoo that is taken to other parks. Phone for details.

Not exactly wild life, but well worth seeing are the huge models of dinosaurs (made for the Great Exhibition of 1851) on islands and banks of the lake at Crystal Palace Park. (Telephone for opening times and transport details.)

Churches and cathedrals

In a church or cathedral don't bother the child with architectural details. Let him get the feel of the place and look around at his own pace. Sit quietly yourself enjoying the beauty. Say a prayer together if that is appropriate.

There is no need to be prohibitive; the way you walk around, look, and speak quietly will show the child how to behave. Help him to think, 'What is this building for?' That is more important than 'when' and the names of special pieces of church furniture.

Often there is a children's trail guide that will be useful for an older child. Again, a postcard or present will be a reminder of the visit and help the child to share the experience with his parents. (Some cathedrals do not allow push chairs or prams to be wheeled around inside.)

Events in London

When there is a State Visit, the Opening of Parliament, or other big royal event, you may want to take the children to see it. Discuss this with the parents first. Plan carefully. If possible ask another adult and child to go with you.

Sometimes there is a rehearsal parade that is quite spectacular but attracts fewer spectators.

Changing the Guard at Buckingham Palace and at Horse Guards Parade are colourful, free, not too long-drawn-out events. To check the times of these ceremonies, and for details of other events, telephone the recorded Teletourist service. You will, of course, find these spectacles less crowded if you go in the winter when fewer tourists are about.

Entertainments: theatres, films

Even under-fives can enjoy live entertainment and become involved in what is happening on the stage, whether it is replying to a pantomime comedian, 'Oh Yes it is . . .' type of response, telling the hero to 'look-out' when the baddy is behind him, laughing at antics, or cheering on the 'goodies'.

Look around at a child audience and notice how much they are concentrating on the action. Going to the theatre can be a really memorable experience for a child. Think back to your own childhood. Most of us can remember films and plays we saw when we were young, the first time we went to the ballet, or saw *Peter Pan*.

Parents may provide the money to take children to a live show; grandparents may ask you to accompany them when they give the child a theatre outing; or you could offer to take the child to a suitable entertainment. You might prefer to go with another nannie and child.

Watch local papers for news of entertainments such as puppet and magic shows, concerts, pantomimes and plays for the pre-school child. There is increasing provision of local authority sponsored entertainment for pre-school children, and a growing number of children's theatres and touring groups are presenting performances especially designed for young children. Information about children's events in London can be obtained by telephoning

01 246 8007 and listening to the recorded announcement of shows, sports, festivals.

Activities

Movement, music and dance
Taking the children to dancing classes may be one of the nannie's duties. Perhaps the parents had not enrolled the children in dancing classes because escorting them there would be one more chore. However, a nannie could have more time and opportunity for taking a child to a weekly session. Dancing schools are listed in the Yellow Pages. Some schools take children from three upwards. These include The Antonia Dugdale Schools of Dancing and the eurhythmy sessions (music and movement) at Rudolph Steiner House in London.

Community Centres, Further Education Colleges, and Polytechnics sometimes run family or children's music clubs and classes. Find out what there is in your locality. The music adviser or inspector for the local education authority may be able to help you.

Sports and gymnastics
'Tiny Tots' Tumble Time', 'Baby Bounce' sessions, or straightforward gymnastic lessons for under-fives are becoming increasingly popular. Again the child needs accompanying, and often the adult is expected to supervise the child throughout the session, so it is time-consuming for an adult and yet another activity a nannie may be able to organise more easily than a parent. Sports Centres, Leisure Centres, Recreational Centres are the places where you will find gymnastics for pre-schoolers; look for addresses in Yellow Pages or write to the British Amateur Gymnastics Association.

Swimming
The importance of a nannie being able to swim has already been mentioned. An outing to a warm 'learner' pool can be fun and also help the child to feel at home in the water and at swimming baths from an early age. If he is given pleasure and confidence he will learn to swim more easily. There are 'mother/parent and toddler' lessons at many public swimming pools and at such places as Crystal Palace Sports' Centre and the central YMCA in London. (The YMCA also offers Keep Fit for parents and children under five.)

Don't let the child get cold or frightened. Be reassuring and enjoy it yourself. It is important that small children are not put off by noise, splashing and roughness from older children, or by over enthusiastic teachers. Pick the uncrowded times; let the session end *before* the child has had enough.

Eating out

You may not approve of hamburgers and chips, but for eating out with children the fast food restaurants have much to offer. Children can see what they are ordering, they will not be forced to sit and wait for a long time, the food is easy to eat – and they like it. Pizza, Hamburger, Little Chef, McDonald-type places generally have high chairs and they are sympathetic towards children. Eating in places like this saves carrying too much food around for a picnic, and it gives you somewhere to sit and rest. The children will think it is a treat.

The Peadouce *Family Welcome Guide* lists facilities in hotels and restaurants that cater well for children (Sphere). Some public houses have gardens where children are welcome, but it is best to ask first.

Responsibility

Wherever you take children on an outing remember you are responsible for their safety and their behaviour. Obedience is essential. It is up to you to manage the outing so that the child enjoys it, is not a nuisance to other people, and returns in one piece to tell his parents about his exciting outing with nannie.

A nannie is fortunate. Isn't it much more fun taking a child to the Zoo or a park, upstairs on a bus, in a boat on the lake, or to see the Changing of the Guard, rather than looking after a roomful of children, or sitting at a desk?

On any outing don't let the child get too hot/cold, tired/thirsty/ hungry. You want it to be a pleasure for you both. Let him stay and watch whatever he is really enjoying, don't drag him on to the next thing. Be sympathetic to his interests, go at his speed. The outing is meant to be for his benefit.

To find places suitable for young children check with local Tourist Boards. They all issue 'Where to go' type guides to their region and these will give you many ideas and descriptions of places you might never have considered visiting. You can always telephone to ask if it really is suitable and would be enjoyable for young children.

As a nannie looking after children every day, you will be able to take the children out on weekdays, and so have the advantage of being able to visit attractions when they are uncrowded. Small children find crowds bewildering, and it is easier for a child to become separated and lost in a large crowd. So pick the off-peak days and times.

Always carry enough money to take the children home by taxi should need arise. You could ask the parents to give you 'a float' for outing expenses.

15 Companionship

Friends to play

It is part of a nannie's responsibility to see that her charge has
playmates of his own age and older. The mother's friends, other
nannies, mothers you meet at clinics, parks or the library, may have
children with whom your charge can make friends. Of course,
though you and the other mother/nannie become friends the
children may not hit it off together, but it is worth trying.

Before inviting another mother or nannie to visit the house with
a child you must obtain the employer's agreement. She may be
afraid of the other child having some infectious disease, or may,
naturally, wonder who is going to come into her home in her
absence. It is understandable that she wants to know something
about the person. If possible, she should meet the person first, or at
least speak to her on the telephone.

When another mother or nannie comes to visit you in your
employer's home, do not show her all round the house, do not give
her the freedom of the place; stay together where you can both see
the children playing. Where both parents are at work and there are
no other adults or staff at home, you are 'in charge' of the house and
the family's possessions so you must act responsibly. Just suppose
that mother you asked back for coffee is light-fingered? Sadly, one
cannot take everyone's honesty for granted.

When the visit has been approved and arranged, think about
how you will spend the time. Help your child to get some toys out
ready. (Not any that are very fragile or precious.) He could arrange
cups, beakers, biscuits so that you can serve coffee and juice with
minimum fuss.

Be welcoming when the visitors arrive. Sit peacefully with the
other adult; be watchful but not obtrusive. The children may not
want to play together at first; children under three may not play

together at all. Each may pursue his own activity, yet be aware of the other child. Babies are often fascinated by other children so if there is a baby in the family draw him into the occasion. Let him sit in his little chair, watch and be given toys by the other children. After the age of three children are more likely to play together, but don't push them, or make more than the occasional suggestion. It will be revealing for you to watch how 'your child' interacts with another, to listen as they chat together, to observe as they play unselfconsciously.

Don't talk about the children with the other nannie/mother. Children take in much more than most of us realise; they will be half-listening to your conversation, perhaps misunderstand what you are saying and be hurt, puzzled or distressed by some comment. As a nannie you must be loyal to your child and his parents.

Mixing with other children is an important part of a child's development; it can also bring him great pleasure and prepare him for playgroup or school. Being with another child can stimulate speech development, help a child learn to co-operate, take turns and share. Do not expect too much of him at first, he will gradually learn how to play with another child. Introduce distractions if squabbles or disputes arise.

It will be useful for you and the other nannie/mother to watch the children playing. You may be able to exchange ideas for activities and discover new ways of using your child's toys and apparatus.

If you are the visitor do not over-stay; if you are the hostess you can say gently, 'I think . . . is getting tired, ready for his lunch . . .'. You can easily increase the length of visits as the children grow more accustomed to playing with each other. It may lead to the nannies/mothers taking it in turn to leave the other in charge so as to do some shopping or give another child in the family more individual attention.

Watch that the children do not pocket each other's toys. Just ask firmly but kindly for the little car or whatever has been taken: 'That is Peter's, he will want it later on, you can play with it next time you come here . . .' or whatever you feel comfortable saying.

Playgroups

By the time your charge is three or so, you may well feel he needs regular contact with other children. With the parents' agreement you could look around for a playgroup for him. You could short list it to just two or three and let the parents make the final choice. Of course, in a rural area there may not be much choice. Some groups have waiting lists, so you will have to start looking in good time.

Choosing a group
Qualities and points to consider when selecting a playgroup:

– Location and convenience of access from the child's home
– Charges
– Suitability of premises. Is it attractive, does it have enough space?
– Are the premises warm/cool enough? Well-lit? Without obvious danger points, eg glass doors; unfenced garden?
– Staffing. Are there plenty of friendly helpers? Do they seem happy at the group?
– Do you like the person in charge? Are you in sympathy with her attitudes and methods?
– Is the environment stimulating for the children?
– Equipment: Is it varied, well-maintained, plentiful?
– Were the children relaxed, happy looking? Controlled, or too boisterous?
– Were the children active, creative and well occupied? (Avoid groups where children seem to spend a lot of time just waiting for turns.)

Try to visit the playgroup more than once; be observant when you go there. Talk to mothers and other nannies; find out what they feel about different playgroups in the area, but make up your own mind in the light of factors mentioned above.

When you and/or the parents have settled on a group, take the child to see it. Talk to him about the playgroup and what he will do there. Mark his coat, boots, apron, etc, and show him where his name is in them. Teach him generally accepted words, eg 'lavatory', that all helpers will understand.

Settling in
– When he first starts, stay with him until he seems happy settled
– When you are going to leave him, say goodbye and GO
– Leave him for gradually lengthening times until he is staying for the whole session
– Be on time to collect him at the end
– Don't send him if he seems unwell

Do not be surprised that the child is tired after the playgroup session. Go straight home to lunch or tea; do not drag him round shops. Let him have a quiet play, story time (or nap after a morning session) until his energy is restored.

Take an interest in what he did at playgroup, and treasure any model/picture he brings home, but do not pester him with questions about the session. He may just not want to talk, or be feeling too tired. If he tells you all about it, he may not want to repeat it all for his mother when she comes home, so save the questions for her, so long as you are attentive and listen to what he wants to share with you.

Try to make friends with at least one mother and child.

Disliking playgroup
When a child does not seem to enjoy a playgroup and does not want to go to it, he may not be ready for it (or there may be something wrong with the group), so I do not think you should insist on him going. After all, that will come soon enough when he starts school. Talk it over with the mother. One of the child's advantages is that he has a nannie prepared to give him time and attention. If he is happy with you, and he can play with other children on reciprocal visits, that may be enough for the time being.

If mothers normally take turns helping at the playgroup join the rota (with your employer's agreement). It will add to your experience and may aid your chances of a job in nursery school, playgroup or creche. If you are asked to serve on a playgroup committee, try to accept. This too will increase your experience. It will also be a way of getting to know some mothers or other nannies.

Mother and toddler groups

Health visitors, churches, family centres, women's organisations often sponsor mother and toddler clubs. Going to one of these with the child you care for could give you both the chance to make new friends, and be an activity to look forward to each week.

At some groups the children play in one part of the meeting room while the mothers and nannies sit and chat, or listen to a speaker in another part.

You could think you will feel a bit out of it because you are not a mother, but you may find other nannies have joined or are willing to join with you. In a club I visited the health visitor introduced me to two nannies and they seemed to have made easy contact with the mothers.

Look on church notice boards, in libraries, doctors' surgeries, clinics and local papers to find such clubs.

Children's parties

Giving a party
Organising the children's birthday parties may be a task that falls to nannie. A few families engage professional party organisers. It can be made a happy, fun experience for all, provided it is carefully and imaginatively planned.

A few hints
– Make sure invitations clearly state beginning and end times
– Don't ask too many children, and keep to approximately the same age group as the birthday child, plus one or two older ones to help
– Ask the child which friends he would like to invite
– Ensure that you have enough help (maybe you could recruit a nannie friend)
– You could tie some balloons to gate or front door (have you ever searched for the house where the party is being held?)
– When the children arrive show them where their coats/boots are being placed
– Make a list of any presents received, or write name of donor on box, etc. (It is embarrassing when someone is thanked for the wrong present)
– Have plenty of games prepared; you want far more than you think you could possibly need – then you can move on quickly if one is soon exhausted or not a success. There are plenty of books listing games, eg *Giving a Children's Party* by Cornelia and George Kay, (Fontana).
– Prepare a mixture of active and sitting still games.
– An attractive, colourful tea table adds to the success of the party. If the children are old enough they could help you make some decorations for the table. (See *Let's Have a Party* by Maureen Roffey, for a selection of ideas); also decorate the room and give it a party feel
– Make the play area as clear as possible; ideally have the tea in a separate room so the children can play then go in and see the table

when it is time to eat. If you are using the family's dining room, you will, of course, put away precious ornaments, dishes, rugs. It is best not to give anything to eat until you all sit down for the tea.

Food
– Do not mix food on dishes; keep sandwiches of the same type together
– You could bring in fruit salad, ice cream, jellies, etc, when savouries have been eaten
– Remove things that seem unpopular; replenish supplies of those that disappear fast
– Watch that the slow and shy get their fair share
– Have plenty of drinks available (including a good supply of cold milk)
– Use sturdy and pretty paper or plastic beakers. There is no need to pour too much into the beaker – this invites spills – you can always offer more
– If there are other nannies or mothers there see that they are well supplied with tea and sandwiches. Perhaps one of them could take charge of this while you look after the children
– Keep all food items small and neat, eg cocktail sausages; little sandwiches (crusts off) and cakes; small savoury items, eg cheese straws
– Little cakes iced with the children's names would be popular
– The birthday cake can be a simple sponge decorated with icing and candles, and perhaps made in some interesting shape, to look like a boat, etc. Really elaborate cakes are appreciated by the adults more than by the children
– An entertainment (hired professional conjurer, ventriloquist, puppeteer, clown, etc) generally comes after tea or you could just let the children watch a favourite tv programme (maybe on video), to recover before the next few games. (Make the entertainer feel welcome, give him/her some tea. If they get the feel of the children and the party it will help them.) Dressing up is popular so have some easily put on clothes ready (hats, cloaks, skirts, etc) if the children are old enough for this
– Going-home-presents need not be expensive, but they should be fun. Two or three little things attractively wrapped could give more pleasure than one bigger present. You could make it a lucky dip and have the same gifts, eg plastic toys, squeaker, bubble blowing kit, model animal, wax crayons, transfers, for each child – say 'one of

each shaped present' or have two or three dips according to the number of little presents for each child. If they wish to take them home unopened, let them
– Try to relish the party fully yourself. As a nannie it will be easier for you than it is for most mothers; throw yourself into it – with zest. Make it a real success so that the children thoroughly enjoy themselves. That will please you, the child and his parents too
– Suggest the parents take some photographs while the party is in full swing. It will be fun for the child to see these subsequently and they will be a souvenir of a happy occasion.

Taking a child to a party
– Talk to the child about the party beforehand, explain what is likely to happen
– Let him choose (within reason) what he will wear. If you buy something new, make sure it is comfortable and he really likes it
– Let him suggest a present for the child and, if possible, go to buy it together
– If he is old enough let him write his own acceptance of the invitation. (You could print it faintly on a card and he could go over your letters.) Let him write on the wrapping and birthday card too, if feasible
– Get to the party at the specified time
– If you are invited to stay with the other nannies/mothers sit with them. The child may be re-assured if he can see you – even if you are not right beside him. If the nannies are obviously not expected to stay for the whole party, wait until he is happily settled, say a brief goodbye and go
– Don't worry him with instructions about saying 'please' and 'thank you', just hope that the training and example you and the parents have given him will help him to be naturally polite.
– Collect him punctually!
– At home the next day you could perhaps write a letter of thanks together. He could dictate a message for you to write below a drawing, or you could write the message for him to copy. You will know the easiest method to suit the child

If the party-givers have been hospitable to you, you could include your own note of thanks, or simply write and say how much the child enjoyed the party.
If there were any games, activities, or teatime treats that seemed

especially popular it could be worth making a note of them for when you are next planning a party.

Preparation for school

Much that has been said about preparing for playgroup also applies to preparing for school.

– Teach the child to tie laces (buy or make lacing toy) or do up buckles
– Teach him how to manage zips (again you could make or buy a toy or let him practice on one of his mother's garments
– Write 'R' and 'L' on insteps of gym shoes, etc, and teach him which is which and how to put them on and off (how to put on socks too if they will be removed for physical education)
– Mark shoes and clothing as instructed by school, or as seems sensible to you. (When ordering name tapes go for large letters)
– Teach him to use scissors. (Beware if there is a younger child around: I know a young man in his thirties who has a glass eye as a result of a childhood accident with scissors). Let him practise using a brush, pencil, crayons, paste
– Make sure he can ask to go to the lavatory and can manage alone
– Walk or drive past the school, watch the children coming out, talk to any of the children you know already. Help it to become a familiar place.
– Go to the school on visits, or for short sessions as the school suggests.
– Look at picture books about going to school (make sure they are realistic and related to the type of school the child will be attending).
– Help him to gain self-confidence and assurance; encourage him to talk to different people, do little jobs, remember messages
– Make sure he can cut up his own food; wipe his nose; put his coat on and off and hang it up
– Make sure he can say his own name clearly and recognise it in lower case letters. He should also be able to recite address and telephone number
– Talk to him (positively) about your own school days
– *Never, never* treat school as a threat, or with foreboding
– If it is a uniformed school, suggest the parents order or buy in good time. Seeing the new blazer/shorts/skirt ready in the wardrobe

can create pleasant anticipation.

– If you are leaving the family because he is starting school, assure the child you will not forget him and will come and see him to hear how he is getting on (if feasible and permissible) or will write to him.

16 Family holidays

A holiday for your employers

Sometimes advertisements for nannies mention: 'Holidays abroad'; 'Holiday house in Cornwall'; 'French holiday home'; and such inducements.

It is fun to go abroad with the family, but remember, on the trip to Disneyland, in the Cornish cottage, or the Spanish villa, you are still a nannie. It is not a holiday for you. You need your own holiday right away from the family and small children. Don't expect the family's holiday to be a holiday for you too, and don't allow them to count it as your holiday.

You may enjoy the change of scene and the excitement of travelling and seeing new places, but you will probably find you are working extra hard. I think it is best to throw yourself into the holiday, and do everything you can to make it an enjoyable, relaxing time for the family.

– Give the parents opportunities for going out together without the children, or perhaps with just one child, while you care for others. The father (or mother) may not be accustomed to spending so much time with the children so a break from them could be welcome
– Take a full share of the chores when you are self-catering
– Organise the children's packing so that the parents have as little rush of preparation as possible
– When the parents want to sit on the beach and play with their children, be ready to go off and leave them as a family without you. As in all your life with the family, you need to be sensitive, aware of their needs, moods and feelings
– On a holiday, don't worry about your 'rights', off duties, own social life. It is their holiday; try and make it a really good holiday for them. No one else can do that for them; you are the person who

can make all the difference
– Appear to be enjoying yourself; appreciate the scenery, food, comfort of the hotel. After all it has probably cost them quite a lot (fare and accommodation) to take you too; make them feel it was worth it.

Holiday planning

When planning a holiday for a family with young children, try to avoid:
– Long car or coach trip from airport to hotel
– Night flights (either way)
– Hotels a long way from the beach
– Self-catering cottages that are too small for the family (says sleeps six, but it turns out that includes living room put-you-up)
– A holiday that will tire parents and be a strain, eg a lot of driving
– Overdoing the culture. Children can become bored by museums and cathedrals; it is a pity to put them off these by over exposure when young, it seems better to wait until it can be a treat. (The other day a seven-year-old told me how she had seen the dinosaurs at the Natural History Museum. She was thrilled by them and wanted her mother to take her there. She had been with a school party and a teacher had obviously found the right moment for the visit.)

Useful reading
– The DHSS produce a leaflet *Medical Treatment Overseas*; you or the parents should send for a copy, or collect one from a clinic or Community Health Council office, before the holiday
– Maws produce a Holiday booklet, *Around the year Travelling and Holidaying with an Infant* available from their Baby Care Bureau, Ashe Laboratories Ltd, Ashetree Works, Kingston Road, Leather-head, Surrey KT22 7JZ
– *Holiday Healthcare* by May and Baker is available free from CMS PR 19–21 Great Portland Street, London W1 (enclose a stamped addressed label)

Inoculations
Check with airline/travel agent/doctor/health visitor whether any inoculations are necessary for the children going to the countries you will be visiting. Have these done in good time before the

holiday. Make sure the child is up to date with routine immunisations.

Preparing for the holiday
If the children are old enough, talk to them about your destination. Show them maps, pictures, point out route. Teach them to give a greeting in the appropriate language.

Packing for the children
In hot countries you will need fewer clothes as you can wash and dry overnight.

Include from these items as appropriate:
– Cotton tee shirts and long-sleeved shirts
– Shorts and jeans. For a hotel take two or three 'smart' outfits
– Swimsuits
– Sun hat, clip on sunshade for buggy
– Nightwear
– Underwear: socks, sandals (flipflops could be bought there) shoes, Wellingtons?
– Enough disposable nappies to keep you going for two or three days plus two or three terries as spares
– Plastic pants
– Plastic sheet and spare cot sheet
– Towels for beach
– Sterilising kit for bottle-feeding
– Formula milk and baby foods (for abroad you may need whole holiday's supply; at home enough for two or three days should suffice)
– Tin opener
– Nappy rash ointment and toiletries
– Potty
– Paper tissues
– Bibs
– Favourite soft toy or other comforter
– Basic first aid kit
– Torch
– A few familiar favourite biscuits or sweets (for abroad)
– Cup, plate spoon, mat
– Warm jersey
– Books, games, puzzles, crayons etc as space allows

– Beach toys if you have favourites and space in the luggage – if not suggest you buy on arrival.
– Coat, anorak, one piece suits – as will be needed
– Sun protection cream, insect repellent, soothing cream

Let the children share in the excitement and anticipation. They could help you gradually assemble all the items to be packed.

Ask the children if there is anything (clothing, book, toy) they would specially like to take.

Holiday First Aid kit
Discuss with the parents; decide whether you or they are to be responsible for assembling, packing, keeping handy for all the party.

Suggested contents as may be appropriate for location

– Insect repellent (long sleeves, trousers, socks will help protect after dark)
– Calamine lotion or ointment for stings and bites
– Soluble aspirin
– Antiseptic ointment
– Laxative
– Water purifying tablets
– Sunburn lotion
– Plasters
– Bandages
– Crepe bandage
– Scissors, tweezers (for splinters and thorns).

Nannies own luggage
Apart from the obvious clothing and toiletries, remember your own swimsuit, beach towel, sandals, sunburn protection and lotion, hair drier. (all sorts of adaptable/travel models now available), something you feel happy to wear for evenings, address book (if you have time to write cards), sun glasses. In hot countries you will probably buy a hat and sandals when there.

Remember to tell your own parents where you are going and how to contact you there.

Travelling with children

Clothing
For travelling make sure children are wearing comfortable shoes and

socks and loose clothing. This applies to you too. You could wear shirt, or frock, and jersey for easy adjustment to temperature where you arrive (coat if you expect it to be chilly).

By air
Bottle-fed babies   On short flights staff are unlikely to have time to heat bottle feeds; take ready prepared bottle(s) as necessary plus extra bottle of diluted fruit juice in case of delay. Feed the baby at the airport before you board the plane if this fits the baby's schedule.

Push chairs and cots   Sky cots must be ordered when flight bookings are made. Make sure the parents know this.
     On the day of flight book in early to obtain the most suitable seats for children and/or adult with cari-cot.
     Airlines have varied regulations. If the buggy has to go in the hold, you (or you and the parents in turn) will have to carry the baby (in arms, sling or cari-cot) to the plane, so keep your hand luggage light. When you are allowed to keep the buggy with you it is a great advantage.
     With a toddler, insist that he holds your hand, or is on reins, when you are going out to the plane on bus or satellite, and walking across tarmac.

Flight   Pack a few cheap, surprise toys for the journey. Don't worry if you lose them down the sides of the seat. Include colouring book and pencils too.
     Sweets to suck
     Change of pants/nappies
     Damp flannel, small towel in plastic bag.

Toilet and changing   It is awkward changing a baby on a plane so change before you board if necessary and possible, and when you land (this saves keeping the passengers waiting for the loo).
     See that small children go to the loo before boarding; try to prevent them going on the plane, especially when gangways are blocked by trolleys.

By train
You will need diversions for a long train journey (don't produce them all at once), but also let children who are old enough enjoy

the experience of being on a train. Don't while away the journey, make the most of it. Talk about what you see, notice the speed, gradients, features of stations, changing terrain, etc.

The other day I went to Bath by train; further down the gangway a nannie was reading Grimm's *Fairy Tales* to the children she was taking to visit Granny. The children could have heard the fairy stories any time; most children are rarely on a train. The children did not seem to appreciate the stories, and neither did the passengers trying to read *The Times*, and it seemed an opportunity wasted.

As a child I was frequently taken on long train journeys (my mother allowed me to take my large baby doll; other passengers thought it was a baby so we had the compartment to ourselves for the 500 miles!), and I thoroughly enjoyed the sensation of being on a train. It was an essential part of the holiday excitement.

Choose seats in non-smoking sections, as far as possible from the smoking parts. Put the children by the window, of course. Do not let them go to the lavatory alone. (As with air travel, suggest they go *before* boarding.)

Going to the buffet car can be part of the fun of the journey, on the other hand, it can be a long walk down the train and it is better not to rely entirely on there being a buffet service – even on long journeys it can be 'unavailable'. It is wisest to have some simple snacks with you – or bring with you all that you will need for a long journey. I find cartons of milk, juice (drunk with straw if children old enough) are easy. Small, varied sandwiches; little packets of biscuits; a yoghurt; crisps; an apple; these are the kind of thing most children will appreciate (chocolate makes them thirsty and messy).

A meal can be an event on a long train journey. You could say, 'we will have lunch', 'a snack', at a given time or place. This will help to break the journey into sections and the children can look forward to the 'picnic' rather than nibbling constantly.

For long journeys at busy seasons it is worth booking seats; otherwise get to the station early for the train.

Train travel is very safe (think how often you read of a child killed in a motorway crash, but hardly ever of one killed on a train); I have yet to meet a child who is train sick; with a family rail card there are great savings in fares. Of course, the disadvantage is being without a car when you arrive.

There may be occasions when parents decide to drive to the holiday cottage, while nannie takes the children most of the way by train. For children who are fidgety, prone to car sickness or are a trial to the driver, train travel could be the answer.

By boat
Whether you are going on a river ferry, across the channel, or on a Rhine cruise, the rule is the same. Keep your eyes, and probably hands too, on the children all the time they are on deck, at the top of stairways, in the hold returning to your car. Don't let them wander off to another part of the boat. Impress on them they must stay with you or their parents.

There is much to be said for finding a quiet seat on cross channel ferries and staying there, with perhaps an escorted trip for refreshments and loo. (*Note* On cross-channel ferries it is wise to visit the loo before going ashore in France where public ones seem scarce, or crowded.)

On a night crossing you will be likely to have cabins; if the children stay flat and have a sleep they will be less likely to suffer sea malady, (or see other people suffering from it) and they will be fresher (possibly for a long drive) the next day.

The boat travel can be an exciting part of the holiday. Present it as an adventure, not as a hazard. Don't even discuss seasickness.

By car
Children are safer in the back of the car (even though the law allows them to sit in the front in an approved restraint or seat belt).

Up to about nine months they can travel in a firm sided cari-cot secured to the back seat. Place the cot facing the front of the car, and tuck child in firmly (to reduce the chance of child being hurled out after an impact).

The child who can sit up by himself will need an approved car safety seat designed for a child of his age.

If you are sent to buy the safety seat, look carefully at several models; find one with crutch strap, side wings and quick release button. It should conform to British Standards Institution BS 3254.

The child may enjoy the feel of a furry cover, when it is not too warm. Mothercare sell a washable type.

When a car has been standing in hot sun, check that the seat has not become too hot to the touch – before you put the child into it.

As soon as he is old enough, teach the child to do up and undo fastening.

Use the harness every time.

After the age of about four, the child will probably want to sit on the ordinary back seat; he will need a special harness designed for children, or an adult harness adjusted to fit him when on a proper booster seat, NOT any old cushion.

Babyboots stock a wide range of car safety systems, sold complete with anchorage bolts.

When you join a family as nannie, it is as well to check the car for the points mentioned above.

If you are driving the children, never allow them to sit in the back unrestrained – it isn't fair to them or you. You can't rely on any child sitting still all the time you are driving. If the family has not provided a back seat restraint system, do not agree to drive the children. Be firm about this from the start.

Do not tolerate distracting behaviour; stop as soon as you can with safety; refuse to go on until they are quiet.

Nannie and children as passengers   On holidays and outings you may be required to sit in the back of the car with the children while the parents sit at the front. Do your part to keep the children quiet and undistracting.

Play quiet games of the I-spy type, but do not encourage reading/drawing games as they can induce muzziness or sickness. Keep door safety locks fastened.

Ask the parents to stop frequently.

Make sure the child or baby is warm/cool enough, has sufficient air, but is not in a draught. A child is more likely to be irritable if too hot; miserable if cold.

Never leave a baby or child alone in a car, even while you make a quick call in a shop.

In hot weather make sure the car is not too hot after standing parked in the sun. Plastic seats can become extremely hot to the touch; the temperature inside a stationary car in the sun can soar.

The passenger in the back with children has a duty to control the children so that the driver can concentrate on driving; all your lives depend on it. Do not allow sharp edged or noisy toys, quarrels, silliness, or over-excitement.

If the children tend towards car sickness and they seem drowsy let them sleep – don't worry them to play games. Constant looking out of the window can add to the travel sick sensation.

By coach
More coach companies now provide airline style service on coaches, but if you are going on a journey without stops for meals it does mean a long period sitting still. Such journeys are not ideal for children. When the novelty of being on a coach has worn off, let them drop off to sleep. Though there are loos on modern coaches, you may need to take a folding type potty – in that case let the child 'practice' at home with it before the holiday.

Boating holidays

Quite young children are taken on canal and Norfolk Broads holidays with success. Presumably the parents will not entertain this idea unless they are capable of managing the boat (and locks) and the children. If the boat hired is large enough they may take nannie to be another responsible adult in charge of the children.

Such holidays can be great fun, but you do need to take good care of toddlers – babies immobile in a cari-cot are far easier.

Make children wear life jackets at all times, apart from in bunks and when sitting down to meals in the cabin or salon. Jackets must be efficient, capable of supporting a child, and in good order. Check that they are approved BSI models, and the right size.

If the family are planning such a holiday and you really do not want to go on it, it is better to say so. But be adventurous, you may enjoy it more than you expect. Perhaps you or they have friends who have taken such a holiday, and they could tell you useful things to take, any possible snags, and the bonus points.

I enjoyed a trip on the Calder Valley canal, it was very peaceful, but small children might have been bored. Take books and games for wet days when you cannot get off the boat for walks – or walk in the rain and feel exhilarated by it.

Self-catering holidays

Cottages/chalets/caravans
A family taking furnished accommodation in the UK should seriously consider viewing it before booking. You want to be sure that size, location, equipment, facilities are suitable – one so often hears of families being disappointed. 'Near beach' may not tell you there is a steep path to the sands, or that the car park is full by 10 am.

There is much to be said for going to one registered with the local Tourist Board, eg Thames and Chilterns Tourist Board have more than 100 individual properties under their supervision.

Check that towels and bedding are supplied (take extra cot sheets in any case)
– Choose accommodation with a washing machine and spin drier in addition to basic equipment
– Pack toys/games/books/activity materials for a wet day
– It is an advantage to have heating available, even if it will be charged extra
– A colour television helps make the holiday a success for all.

Hotel holidays

When you go to a hotel with a family, look out for danger spots such as:

– Unfenced gardens and access to road
– Swimming pools – even when there is a lifeguard on duty you still need to be watchful
– Play apparatus, eg climbing bars that are intended for older children
– Balconies with low walls or horizontal guard rails
– Lifts, especially the type without internal doors (children have had terrible accidents in these)
– Glass doors and windows (are catches firm?)
– Plugs and electrical appliances
– Scalding water in taps. (Warn child where you cannot control temperature)
– If cot provided – check carefully
– Remember, other countries do not always have such stringent safety regulations as the UK enforces

Some hotels advertise 'baby-listening', but all it amounts to is leaving the telephone off the hook and the receptionist listens for the baby crying. Consider whether this is adequate?

The first night
Before you go to bed:

– Make sure you know the whereabouts of fire stairs and exits; check that emergency doors will open
– Think which way you would go, and how you would escape with

the children should there be a fire
– Leave a torch handy by your bed
– If the children are not sharing a room with you or parents see that they know how to get to you or parents
– If the children are old enough and likely to go to the lavatory in the night, make sure they can manage all locks and fastenings if they do not have a lavatory en suite.

At the end of the holiday Search room thoroughly for bits and pieces left in drawers, behind cot, etc. Children can be distressed at losing things.

Eating and drinking while travelling and on holiday

– Give children light, non-fatty foods before and during a journey; cut out those that are fried, fatty and spicy
– Squash, (dilute with bottled water if abroad), plain water (boiled if necessary), and fruit juice (can be diluted) are better than fizzy drinks
– Plain biscuits, such as cream crackers, may help ward off travel sickness. They are far better (and less messy) than chocolate biscuits
– Avoid sticky, creamy cakes
– Give varied food the child will enjoy – small pieces of cheese, raisins, neat sandwiches, any of their favourite foods you consider suitable
– Adults may enjoy Kendal Mint Cake. Let children try it, but emphasise it should be sucked
– Apples, oranges, tangerines will help to quench thirst
– Take plenty of 'cleaning-up' aids. A kitchen roll may be useful on a car journey
– When pouring drinks for children while travelling or on a picnic, pour out just half a cupful at a time. This will be less of a catastrophe if spilt.

Overseas especially
– Beware of bottled water which is unsealed
– Stay away from cafés and food shops that look (or smell) unhygenic or have flies buzzing round inside them
– Buy ice cream that is wrapped and refrigerated and made by well-known manufacturers

– Avoid 'hot dogs' and similar snacks from stalls (as well to avoid in the UK too)
– Make sure all salad has been thoroughly washed in clean water; if in doubt don't order, and don't eat lettuce garnish. Don't eat water cress. Peel tomatoes.
– Fruit that can be peeled is safest for children
– Buy branded bottled drinks and water in supermarkets as this is far cheaper than from hotel bar
– If tea, coffee, milk are *ad lib* at breakfast, encourage the children to drink plenty while they have the chance.

Holiday ills

Diarrhoea and stomach upsets

These upsets tend to inflict travellers of any age. Travelling, excitement, exotic and unaccustomed foods and drink, tropical sun and the change in time zones can all help to bring them on.

Diarrhoea is generally caused by an infection, picked up from food and water, or through low standards of hygiene. The condition can be distressing for anyone, but for young children it can be dangerous. The great risk is dehydration – loss of body fluid and salts through the diarrhoea.

When a child is suffering from diarrhoea, give him plenty of fluid – mineral water, very weak tea and barley water are best; do not offer highly sweetened or acidic drinks. When the child is a little better, generally after 24 hours, he could have clear soup or Bovril. Milk is more likely to make him feel sick.

Do not give a child diarrhoea tablets or mixture unless it has been prescribed for that child by a doctor.

It is probably best if the child stays quietly in hotel room, or on a shaded balcony or terrace. Make sure he washes his hands scrupulously after every visit to the lavatory.

Be specially careful with a baby suffering from diarrhoea; breast-feeds should continue; bottle fed babies need extra boiled water. All adults handling the child should be meticulous about hygiene. If the baby's diarrhoea is severe you will need to seek medical help.

Bites and stings

These can be alarming for a child. Try to calm him; apply a soothing cream when appropriate and available. Should any swelling arise round the mouth or throat after a bee or wasp sting take the child to a hospital casualty department.

On a beach in Maryland one of our sons was stung by a jellyfish; it looked red and painful, but we were told the only handy remedy was to splash on cold water from the showers. Some doctors suggest calamine lotion. If you are warned that there are jellyfish (or worse still Portuguese man-o' war) about avoid that beach. Even if there is no particular warning, tell the children to keep away from any such creatures that they see.

Coping in the heat

Sunburn

Take thought; prevent it. Painful sunburn can blight a holiday for adult or child. Babies and young children are sensitive to bright sunshine. You must think for them.

Here are some precautions:
– Realise it may be brighter than you thought. Sunlight is reflected from the sea. (We took one-year-old Christopher to the beach at Southbourne on a day that was not apparently sunny; that night he developed awful blisters on his shoulders. We should have let him acclimatise slowly)
– Don't let the child play in the sun for more than a few minutes the first day; keep him in shade, under a parasol, or those little thatched sun shelters you see on beaches in Spain and Majorca. The children can gradually spend more time in the sun as they get used to it
– Keep their shoulders covered with a cotton shirt, and try to insist on them wearing cotton sun hats (take with you or buy locally). Be especially cautious with fair or auburn haired children
– Use sun screening cream and re-apply after the child gets wet in the sea
– Remember, a cari-cot or pram lined with plastic will become very hot to the touch
– Make sure a baby or young child has plenty to drink when it is hot. The body loses fluid through perspiration. (If the child's urine is very strong and yellow he is short of fluid)
– In hot climates it is a good idea for everyone to have an afternoon rest or nap. You can always let the children stay up a little later to compensate.

Home again Should any of the party become ill soon after returning from a holiday abroad, seek medical advice and tell the doctor which countries you have visited.

Fun on the beach

Before the holiday think out some games and activities for the beach. Consult books of games and activities, eg *The Beaver Book of the Seaside* by Jean Richardson, and make a list of ideas that you think might appeal to the children.

The parents may want to go off and leave you in charge of the children for a while. You must not doze off in the sunshine, you need to watch the children all the time. If you paddle with them, or play games with them it will be easier to keep them with you.

Games
- Ball games: throwing and catching
  throwing at an object
  rolling and jumping over ball
  scoop out holes and roll ball into them
  throwing ball into bucket
- Skittles
- Drawing games: make faces, pictures, patterns using marks made by a stick, shells, seaweed, pebbles
- Building walls, forts, boats, as well as traditional castles
- Balancing. You could make a plastic bucket or flower pot version of the old flower pot game
- Colouring. Take some chalk to colour pebbles or pieces of driftwood
- Creatures. Collect little creatures in a bucket of sea water; handle gently and return to sea or pool when you go home
- Sand toys. Take a variety of little containers, moulds, tubes, sieves, cartons, spoons.

Safety
- Dinghies, airbeds, floating toys can be fun, but they can also be lethal
- Keep the children near the edge, where you can see them all the time
- Do not let them depend on water wings, etc, for support out of their depth

- 'Up to your middle only' is a good rule
- Remember that beaches sometimes shelve suddenly, currents can be powerful
- Keep where other people are in the water
- Stay away from rocks
- Do not let children run along breakwaters
- Never ignore red flags
- Make sure you know how to perform mouth-to-mouth resuscitation.

When several adults are on the beach with the children, don't all think one of the others is watching them. At least one of you must watch them all the time.

If you give your child a distinctive piece of clothing (we gave one of ours a red woolly hat on a chilly day in Cornwall) you can spot him more easily on a crowded beach.

In some resorts, areas of beach are prohibited to dogs. Those are good areas for people with young children!

When taking children to the beach by car, try to minimise the walk back to the car when they are tired, you are laden with wet costumes, shells, etc. One person could stay with the children while another collects the car then picks you up. Children can get tired and cross at the end of a day on the beach, but it is a pity to let this happen after a happy day.

If the family are all enjoying being on the beach, nannie could suggest she goes for a walk and leaves them for a while – it will be a break for her as well as giving them time without her.

When the family is self-catering nannie and mother may be able to take it in turns (or father too) to go back to the cottage first and get the tea ready for the children.

17 Left in charge

Parents sometimes feel they need a break right away from home and children, so they go off for a weekend, week or fortnight, leaving the nannie in charge.

For some nannies this can be rather daunting. One told me she was worried about being left with two lively little girls, aged six and three, while their parents went abroad for two weeks. However, the employers agreed to the nannie's own mother coming to stay in the house to keep nannie and the children company, and all went well.

Other nannies have told me that when employers went away for a weekend they were allowed to have a friend to stay and to invite friends in for meals. You are trusted not take advantage of the situation and have a great party in your employer's absence!

Points to watch

– Make sure parents leave address and phone numbers where they can be contacted
– See that they tell the children they are going, and when they will be back
– Ask them for the name, address and telephone number of nearest relative to contact in case of emergency
– Be highly responsible about locking up house, turning off gas, etc, when you go out with the children
– Check that the parents have left you adequate food and/or housekeeping money
– Ask for some extra money to take the children on plenty of outings so you can try to make it a pleasant holiday time for them
– Consider taking the children to stay in your own home for a day or two (discuss with parents before they leave)
– If there are other staff, eg cook, housekeeper, see that they know what they are expected to do for you and the children. (One nannie

told me that when she was left in charge while the parents were away the housekeeper was most awkward and wouldn't do any of the nursery chores she did when the employer was around)
– If there is a daily cleaner check days she has been asked to come, etc. You may be responsible for letting her into the house
– Try to treat this as an opportunity for getting to know the children better, for encouraging good habits, for doing positive, interesting activities so that the children have things to tell parents and show them when they return.

Children who are close to their parents will be bound to miss them, but a kind, caring nannie can help them keep cheerful and busy if they are that sort of age. With a little child or baby you will need to be extra loving and comforting.

Talk to the children about the parents, mention them frequently, explain that postcards take a long time to come from the Continent (how many have you had after friends are home again?), leave the housework and ironing and give the children plenty of attention and stimulation. Allow them to invite friends for a picnic (in the garden or park), let them have a little party, plan some outings. Perhaps you could change round the nursery together, or re-arrange the playroom.

Before the parents go you may be able to sit down with them and plan a programme for the children. Maybe they will leave some little presents – a new book, game, art materials, puzzle you can all enjoy together.

Parent in hospital

Much of the material on looking after children while parents go away on holiday, also applies when a parent is in hospital, though you will probably need to be extra re-assuring.

Do not talk in whispers and discuss the patient's progress with staff, friends, the other parent, in front of the children. If they only half hear or misunderstand they could become secretly – or openly – worried. It is better to give a simple, clear explanation that is true, but not, perhaps, the whole story.

The nannie will probably be called upon for extra baby-sitting or child minding. Try to do this cheerfully without getting too tired or stale. When the patient has recovered it would be reasonable to give you compensatory time off.

When one parent is ill, the other may also be more demanding on you, wanting your company, re-assurance, sympathy. If the mother is away don't get too involved with the father. Keep the relationship professional. You are there to care for the children, not to be a nursemaid to him.

Child visiting parent in hospital

Many hospitals now allow children to visit at specified times.

If the children have never been in a hospital before show them a book with pictures of a hospital, people in bed, nurses in uniform, so that they will know what to expect.

– Think together what you can take to the patient. Arrange a little jar of flowers – garden or wild; a little basket of fruit, take one of the child's drawings or models, perhaps a photograph; something that smells nice; buy a magazine for the patient on the way to the hospital
– Let the child choose what to wear for the visit
– Do not stay too long; it can be irksome for the child and tiring for the patient
– Make the child wash thoroughly when you get home
– If you are going to hospital or nursing home to see mother with a new baby, try and go into the mother when she is not nursing the baby and can give the child her full attention
– Tell the child when mother and baby will probably be coming home so that he can count up the days and nights and realise it will not be long
– Let the child help prepare the bedroom for mother's homecoming. Flowers, a present, her familiar things ready, will help to re-assure the child she really will be coming.

18 Special circumstances

A bereaved child

When you go to a family that has experienced a recent bereavement, or if someone who is very close to the family or a member of it dies while you are with them, you will have to think out your own attitudes and feelings.

As someone who is probably not directly involved emotionally you will want to help and strengthen the child and try to make life seem safe and normal. You will need to be gently honest. It is no use giving the child false hopes, but you can present the truth in a way that will help the child to understand that all life on earth comes to an end in the natural course of things. We go on to the next stage which we believe will be wonderful, happy – however you feel able to describe it. Children can understand that there is mystery about it, but nothing to fear. If that is your own conviction you will be able to assure the child of God's continuing love for him and for the person who has moved on into the next life. It is not much help to talk about angels, or 'going to be with Jesus' if these are concepts unfamiliar to the child.

Unless it causes great distress, I think it is better to talk about the person who has died. They are not forgotten, you can, perhaps, remember happy times spent together and be grateful for the person's kindness, abilities, courage. Never let the child feel he cannot or must not mention the person who has died.

When a child of the family has died there will be special demands on the nannie. She will be conscious of the family's grief, perhaps find them over-protective to remaining children, she may well be sad herself. Somehow she has to help the family recover. She must try to give the child a peaceful, ordered life. She should be sympathetic, but not sentimental.

A hospital nurse has to accept that a patient has died, then put

171

grief aside and get on with the next task. A nannie will have to get on with the task of helping the family recover and the child to feel secure, loved, and hopeful about the future. She does not need to minimise their grief, or give false comfort, but while understanding their feelings – and saying that she does – she must try to be positive and creative, just as with the child suffering after divorce.

Access visits

A nannie who cares for a child whose parents have divorced or separated recently will need to give extra tender care and plenty of attention. She will understand the child's feelings and may have to tolerate resultant behaviour.

The nannie will not be surprised, or hurt, if he displays anger towards her, his parents, brothers and sisters (or step brothers and sisters), or playthings. It is better that he should express some of his anger rather than having it contained and repressed.

His distress at the marital situation, or before or after access visits, may cause him to be quiet and withdrawn, wild and boisterous, sick, liable to injure himself, or to regress in toilet training. A nannie must be watchful, patient, and try to help him through the trauma.

– Let him know that you understand his stress and know something of his feelings; absorb some of his emotion
– Never be judgemental. Try not to take sides, even in your own mind. You probably do not know the full circumstances. Things are not always as they seem
– Try to think of some new game, toy, outing, activity as a diversion. Perhaps it is a time when a child could acquire a pet. Even a goldfish can be a healing interest
– After an access visit do not be inquisitive. Just listen if the child wants to tell you about the outing
– When the child returns from an access visit with an expensive present he has been given by the non-custodial parent, admire it, but, of course, do not make a great fuss of it in front of the parent who has custody and employs you. He/she will be sensitive about it and may feel annoyed, see it as a bribe, or be critical. Don't forget the parent with custody may be upset about the child seeing the other parent and feel threatened, jealous, or just sad
– Be gentle and sympathetic towards the parent, but do not be

drawn into the situation. Be discrete in what you say to either parent
– Utter confidentiality is essential. As a nannie you are in a privileged position and close relationship with the family, but you must not gossip about their affairs. It can be tempting when a well-known personage is involved, but for the sake of the child, out of loyalty to the parents, and for your own self-respect – resist such temptation.

19 Illness and First Aid

Those who have taken the NNEB course will have studied: 'Modes of transmission, incubation, onset, symptoms and causes of common childhood illnesses and ailments, together with the treatment likely to be prescribed and the complications which may arise'.

Nursery nurses are also expected to 'competently carry out the activities involved in the care of the affected child in the home, including actions to minimise the possibility of complications'.

Nannies who have not taken the course could learn the basic facts about childhood illnesses by studying a reliable household dictionary or health guide, eg Collin's *Practical Dictionary of Household Hints*, or Macmillan's *Family Health Guide*.

Recognising illness

As you get to know the child better day by day you will quickly be able to spot when he is unwell.

Signs to warn you include:
- Sickness
- Lack of appetite or refusal to feed
- Coughing and wheezing
- Feverishness
- Severe and persistent pain, eg ear or abdominal
- Rashes
- Diarrhoea
- Running nose and eyes
- Swollen glands
- Flushed appearance
- Breathlessness
- Unaccustomed drowsiness
- Sore throat.

When a child has any of these symptoms you should alert the mother (telephone her at work if necessary) and allow her to decide about consulting a doctor.

If the parents have gone away and left you in charge, or are otherwise uncontactable, you will have to decide.

Obviously, it is better to telephone for the doctor early in the day. The family's own GP is more likely to visit in that case. Sometimes children seem to deteriorate in the early evening, or they seem no better. With night approaching you feel concerned and worry what to do. When in doubt, phone the doctor.

Give the doctor a full, clear picture of the child's symptoms and condition. Before you pick up the telephone make a note of the points you wish to mention – it is easy to omit something significant. You could also note the advice the doctor gives you. Keep the notes and show them to the parents.

When a child has any of these following conditions medical advice is needed:

– Complete refusal to feed accompanied by weak crying, unaccustomed quietness and apathy
– Convulsions
– Severe and persistent pain
– Severe diarrhoea and vomiting
– Breathlessness
– Severe injuries, burns, bleeding, swallowing a solid object, pills or poisons
– Abnormally high or low temperature (average is 98.6°F; 37°C) (Keep unshaken thermometer for mother/doctor to see)
– Seems hot, lifeless and whining without obvious cause.

In an emergency, when you cannot find a doctor who will come, wrap the baby or child in a blanket and take him to the nearest hospital with a casualty department.

If you suspect that the child has an infectious illness consult the receptionist before taking him to a surgery waiting room, as if a child has German measles he could endanger an expectant mother.

Support for the mother

It can be frightening and worrying when children are ill. Sometimes they seem desperately ill, but they recover remarkably quickly. You and the mother need to try to hide your anxiety as you don't want to make the child worried.

A nannie may have to be calm and re-assuring towards the mother too. You will have to show her sympathy and give her support. A working mother can feel guilty and blame herself for the child's illness, then be a bit bad tempered with the nannie. Try to be understanding and imagine how you would feel in her place.

Caring for the sick child

– Ensure that the child has plenty to drink (unless instructed otherwise). Give him plain water, lemonade, barley drinks, or any favourite cold drink. Pour out a little at a time. Encourage him to drink it. Hold the glass or mug for him if necessary. Sometimes a pretty cup (eg a coffee cup) will make the child take the drink with enjoyment; a straw may be a novelty and help. A different and attractive plate helps too
– Keep the room warm/cool enough and well ventilated
– A new toy can be appreciated, or you could get out an old favourite he has not played with lately. Do not suggest any toy/puzzle/construction set that is likely to be fiddly and frustrating. Children often like a younger age toy when they are not feeling well. It is wise to encourage a child to play because this will distract him from pain and discomfort
– Sit with the child for a while. Read to him if he seems to want that
– It can be lonely left in bed while life goes on for the rest of the family. A couch in the playroom may be better and warmer for the child who is not seriously ill, or who is recovering. When he returns to his bedroom at night he should settle more easily than if he stays in the bedroom all day.

Medicines and tablets
– Never give the children any medicine without seeking medical advice first
– Measure dose accurately and stick to stipulated time intervals
– Give in a matter-of-fact way, but as casually as you can, so that (hopefully) the child will just accept medicine
– Have some water close at hand and offer immediately to wash down any medicine lingering in the mouth. (Ensures complete dose, washes away taste, removes stickiness from teeth)
– Make sure the child is properly awake when you give the

medicine, and that he has swallowed it all before lying down
– Keep the medicines locked up, in another room, or on a high
shelf so that a younger child cannot get to them
– Always give the full course as prescribed
– If the child says: 'I want Mummy to give it to me,' it is easiest to
assent, if mother is available. You do not want a confrontation with
a sick child.

High temperatures
When a child has a high fever you may be directed to sponge him
with tepid water to reduce his temperature. Give him plenty of
water to drink; aspirin as recommended by doctor; dress him in
loose, cool clothing. Remember, a child's temperature can go up
quickly, but return to normal very soon. Raised temperature is not
the only indication of something wrong; do not ignore an obvious
'unwellness' just because the temperature is not abnormally high.

Diarrhoea
Make it as easy and convenient as possible for the child to use potty
or lavatory. Keep him clean and fresh; comfort him if distressed.
See that he has plenty to drink.

Clothing
When a child is ill and possibly perspiring more than normally, his
clothes will need changing extra often. A jersey over pyjamas is
better than close fitting underwear underneath the pyjamas. Allow
the child to choose a jersey he likes wearing and you can wash
easily.

Mother and child
If the mother obviously wants to sit with the child and look after
him herself, make it easy for her. Do some of the jobs she normally
does so as to free her.

Other children may be feeling rather neglected if one child is ill,
so be especially patient with them; give them an extra cuddle and
time with you. They may secretly be worried so explain simply what
is wrong with the brother or sister, so be re-assuring.

Should one child be so ill he has to be admitted to hospital, the
mother may go and stay there with him. This will put an extra
burden on a nannie caring for other children; though you will
probably accept the responsibility willingly, the family should

recognise that you have lost free time/worked extra hard, and make some compensation to show their gratitude.

First aid

What you need to know
Those who have taken an NNEB course will be familiar with the aims and principles of first aid. It is advisable for all nannies to know how to give mouth-to-mouth resuscitation, and first aid for the following:

- Bleeding from external injuries
- Nose bleeding
- Shock
- Electric shock
- Fainting
- Concussion
- Burns and scalds
- Poisoning
- Stings and bites
- Foreign bodies in the eye
- Swallowed foreign body
- Choking
- Cuts and bruises and grazes.

With serious accidents and injuries, suspected fractures, loss of consciousness, severe bleeding, poisoning, swallowing of foreign body, severe burns and scalds, seek immediate professional help. Always remember, First Aid means just that. It is the immediate response to an accident or injury. Sometimes at moments of crisis knowledge deserts one, so have a first aid chart or information card handy with the first aid box. You could make your own simple card using a recognised First Aid Manual. (Ask health visitor to check it.)

The aims are:

To keep the injured person alive
To relieve suffering and prevent further injury
To obtain skilled help.

The priorities are:

Restore breathing

Stop bleeding
Send for help.

When a child has been injured, stay calm, try to be reassuring. Do not leave him alone, unless you cannot or dare not move him, and must go to the telephone, eg if you and the child are in the house alone.

Electric shock
Switch off the supply at the wall or main. Don't touch the child until power has been cut off from the appliance or wire that has caused the shock. Give mouth-to-mouth resuscitation if necessary.

First aid box
Many books and manuals give lists of suggested contents and you can buy commercially packed kits. See what the family has available, consider whether it is adequate, discuss with parents and bring it up to standard. Remember to keep it renewed. Make sure you all (including children) know where the box is kept.

Mouth-to-mouth resuscitation
The procedure for 'the kiss of life' should be memorised by anyone in contact with children. Applying it can literally be life-saving. It may be effective after choking, drowning, gassing, smothering, suffocation, poisoning or electric shock. Anyone can attempt it in an emergency; do not be deterred if you have not done it before, but be prepared and learn how. Basically it means blowing air into a casualty's lungs in order to re-start breathing. Never breathe into a child who is breathing on his own.

Casualty visits
When a child is injured and you take him to a casualty department do not be annoyed if you are closely questioned about how an injury occurred. Hospital staff must always bear in mind the possibility of non-accidental injury. Only by questioning everyone can they discover neglect and cruelty which isn't always immediately apparent.

Learning more

Those who have not taken a course that includes first aid could consider attending local First Aid classes. You should be able to obtain information about these from the local Red Cross or St John's Ambulance. Some evening institutes offer courses.

A sensible employer will be only too glad for her nannie to take such a course, and is likely to co-operate so that the nannie can attend regularly and pass an examination at the end of the course.

The health visitor may also be able to tell you about courses. Perhaps a local clinic offers one for mothers.

Taking a child to doctor or hospital

A mother who is working, caring for a baby, or otherwise busy, may ask the nannie to take her child to the doctor, or for a hospital appointment.

– Tell the child why you are going to the surgery/hospital, and what is likely to happen. You could warn that you may have to wait, so take a book or activity, or pop something new into your bag, eg a dot-to-dot book if the child is old enough for one, and produce it when waiting
– Ask the mother exactly what you should say to the doctor. The mother could write it down
– When you first go into the consulting room tell the doctor you are nannie, not mother. He may treat you more professionally and ask for your observations
– If the child has to have an examination/injection or some procedure, treat it all in a matter of fact, calm way; explain simply. Be warm, re-assuring; hold the child firmly if necessary. Should you feel any squeamishness about injections, do not impart this to the child; help him to accept it; look at the child eye-to-eye, rather than at the needle
– At the first possible opportunity make a note of what the doctor said; give this to the mother
– You could try to make the journey home specially enjoyable. Stop to feed the ducks; have a ride on a machine outside a shop; buy a comic . . .
– If you had a tedious wait/unpleasant treatment, tell the mother in front of the child, how 'well-behaved', 'grown-up' he was. Children thrive on praise and encouragement
– When a child has to be admitted to hospital the mother may be unable or unwilling to stay there with him, even though this is

encouraged by the hospital. In such a case it may be possible for a nannie, who is well-known and loved by the child, to stay with him instead. Discuss this with the mother and the hospital: if necessary ask the National Association for the Welfare of Children in Hospital for advice.

20 Being a Nannie – the nannie herself

'A happy nannie makes a happy child', a nannie said to me once. What can you do to make the most of your time as a nannie and be a happy person?

Here are some guidelines I venture to suggest:
– Do your job as capably, conscientiously and imaginatively as you can
– Keep plenty of interest and contacts. Your own life must be satisfying
– Stay in close touch with friends and family
– Do something interesting on your day off. (See list of suggestions)
– Try to make some new friends
– Acquire some new skill.

Day off suggestions

– Take a day trip to France
– Go by train (or car) to visit some historical/famous city you have never seen before. It is surprising how far you can go from London on an Awayday: Bath, Norwich, Lincoln, Birmingham, South coast resorts, for instance. While you are young enough to have an under-24 rail card, make the most of it.
   There are also many day trips from London by coach, eg on the Green Line and Oxford South Midland.
   Out of London you could buy a day road or rail rover ticket and explore the local area.
– Skating (ice rinks listed in Yellow Pages)
– Riding (see earlier section)
– Art galleries and exhibitions

– Museums
– Conducted walks round London (see daily papers)
– Walk the Wall route from The Tower to the Museum of London, marked out with blue and cream tiles (1¾ miles)
– Telephone Teletourist for the day's events
– Go to see the Changing of the Guard
– Visit Harrods
– Explore street markets, eg Caledonian Market, Portobello Road, which you have never visited before
– Take a Regents Canal boat trip, or walk the towpath
– Go on a river trip to see the Thames Barrier
– Go to Greenwich (museums, park, Royal Naval College, interesting shops)
– Climb to the Whispering Gallery in St Paul's and stay for Evensong sung by the choir
– Walk on Hampstead Heath
– Go for a sauna
– Visit the English Tourist Board shop at Victoria, or your local Travel Information Centre, for leaflets, guide books, and advice on days out
– Buy a reduced unsold ticket for a concert or play that night
– See The London Butterfly House at Syon Park
– Browse around the shops and stalls in Covent Garden (Free map from Visitors' Centre, 1–4 King Street, London, WC2)
– Have your hair re-styled (Look in *Miss London* and other give-away magazines for money off coupons and offers)
– Spend a day at the National Theatre – tour, talk, exhibitions (not available Wednesdays and Saturdays)
– Contact the BBC Ticket Unit for information on free seats for recordings of popular programmes
– Take a dancing lesson (see Yellow Pages for list).

Making new friends

Loneliness is one of the greatest problems encountered by a nannie. You are not working with a group of people with whom you can make friends, you are no longer in a student crowd, you may be far from home and your own natural circle of friends. Those who are non-resident nannies and live at home or in a flat with or near friends, will not have the same problems; it is the resident nannie who tends to be lonely on her day/weekend off.

Ideas
– Look out for other nannies when you take the children to clinics, mother and toddler clubs, sports session, school, parties, playgroups
– Ask the health visitor to put you in touch with another nannie working nearby
– Contact Lorraine Thompson of Nannies Need Nannies, 28 May Street, South Shields, Tyne and Wear NR33 3AU; she will give you names and telephone numbers of other nannies in your area. Although, obviously, you will not want to spend all your off-duty with other nannies, two of you together may have more confidence to join local organisations or go to functions advertised in the local paper
– Whatever church you belong to there is likely to be some youth organisation attached, eg *Methodist* Youth Clubs
  Roman Catholic Guilds and Clubs
  Anglican – All Souls, Langham Place (beside Broadcasting House) has a number of organisations and groups, and a flourishing church life with plenty of younger members
  St Martin-in-the-Fields (Trafalgar Square) has a club for young professional people. Nannies are made welcome at this
  St James's, Piccadilly has a varied programme of lectures, and social gatherings
  Church of Scotland, St Columba's, Pont Street, and Crown Court Church Covent Garden have organisations and clubs.
– Helping hand. It isn't fair to offer to help with some organisation just so as to make social contacts yourself, but none-the-less, helping out of genuine concern and with a common interest does bring people together. Follow your own special interests and do some research to find where you can offer your time and skills. You could contact the Volunteer Centre, 129 Lower King's Road, Berkhamstead, Herts HP4 2AB
– The Central YMCA and YWCA have sports and leisure facilities
– If you have been, or still are, a Guide member consult Guide Headquarters for news of central London activities and local contacts
– Speak to Capital Radio's Helpline (Telephone 01 388 7575 from 9.30 am to 5.30 pm Monday to Friday)
– Go roller skating
– Take part in an activity at a Leisure Centre, eg Michael Sobell Sports' Centre, Hornsey Road, N7
– Those within reach of Morley College, 61 Westminster Bridge

Road, SE1 7HT, could send for the prospectus to discover the great variety of courses on offer in this purpose-built adult education centre which has a library, refectory and bar, in addition to well-equipped lecture rooms. Courses include social and community studies, eg Developing Creche Work Skills, Human Relations – towards a better understanding of the self and others, and all sorts of Art, Dance, Drama, Music, Languages and others. Classes are held morning, afternoon and evening, and there is a creche and playgroup. There are also Saturday morning Family Activities for adults and accompanying children.

In a village Some ideas from the previous lists will be applicable but here are some for the country:
– Ask the family where you can meet some local young people. Perhaps there will be a Young Farmers' Club, Church Youth Club, Community/village hall with activities in which you can join
– Look in the local paper for news of local organisations, eg Scottish Societies, Choirs, Drama, Sports clubs and centres, Keep Fit classes, young political groups, anything that appeals to you and will give you a chance to mix with other young people. Once you make a few contacts and get introduced to a group it is easier
– Ask your employer if any of her friends have nannies to whom they can introduce you
– Look out for other people of your own age when you take the child out to the village shop, post office.

Health and beauty

For the sake of your own self-esteem and confidence wear the clothes you enjoy wearing. Don't slop around in things which feel uncomfortable or dowdy. If you don't like it, accept that the buy was a mistake and allow the next jumble sale, or charity shop you pass to benefit. Life is too short to wear things that do not please you.

Children will notice your clothes and they will be happier if nannie 'looks pretty'. Your employers and other staff will notice too. If you look 'professional' they will be more inclined to treat you as a professional person.

Those who wear uniform daily have no problems. Others may decide on a neat skirt, dungarees or jeans (check this is acceptable to the employer), shirts and jerseys. You want outfits that are attractive, comfortable, practicable and easy to launder.

Especially where there is a young baby you will be carrying around, perhaps up and down stairs, do make sure your shoes are not the type liable to make you slip or stumble.

Obviously, you will not go in for elaborate make-up during the day. A nannie is likely to have her hands in water often so you will need handcream kept within easy reach (spare jar in kitchen or children's bathroom if necessary).

Jewellery that could scratch or tear, and heavy bracelets that could knock a baby, are out while on duty. Watch that you do not wear beads or pearls a baby could grab and break. Earrings in pierced ears also carry a slight risk; a small child could snatch at them unintentionally.

A reliable watch is important. If you wear rings take care you do not lose them in the nappie pail!

When you move in ask the employer for the name and address of the family's GP. It is probably easiest to register with the same doctor. They may have opted for private medical care and be willing to pay for this for you too, but it is probably best to register with a National Health doctor to be on the safe side.

Using leisure in the home

A nannie will often have periods when she is 'on call' without having any work to do, yet she is not free to go out. Try to make use of the time.

Here are some ideas:
– Invite a friend to come for coffee. (At the interview ask if you may have occasional visitors. Always introduce them to one of your employers)
– Listen to radio or cassettes. (It is really worthwhile for a nannie to have a good radio/cassette player)
– Relax and enjoy television (hopefully one will be provided in your own room)
– Read one of those books you have always meant to read
– Consider embarking on a cassette language course
– Keep up to date with child welfare. (You could buy one different magazine each week, eg *Mother, Mother and Baby, Nursery World, Living, Parents, New Society*)
– Make yourself a skirt, start to knit a sweater, do some embroidery

– Perhaps you will just be thankful to have a 'beauty evening'
– Write a letter to a friend; to a magazine that pays for those they publish. (Study style used first; don't duplicate letter – never send to more than one)
– Plan your holiday or read about where you have booked to go
– Tidy through all your clothes and sort them out
– Make your Birthday Book up to date
– Write out recipes you want to keep, and begin your own cookery book
– Borrow one of your employer's books/dictionaries and look up some of the facts/quotations/meanings you have often meant to check
– Don't overdo the phone calls, it isn't fair to your employer, but if you are left to baby-sit all evening, one brief chat to a friend should be permissible
– Think of anything you would have added to this *Handbook* and be so kind as to send it to me for the next edition
– Begin writing your own life story (make list of dates and facts you need to check with your parents when you see them).

Acquiring new skills

Some of the day off and evening activities already suggested will give a nannie new knowledge and skills. Anyone who is looking after a young child will be learning about child development and behaviour all the time, but apart from these experiences, some nannies will be keen to gain specific knowledge, skills and qualifications. Here are some things you may want to consider doing.

– Attending a local evening institute/college of further education/ community college for one afternoon or evening each week. It seems reasonable to ask an employer to agree to this
– Taking a playgroup leaders' course at a college, or based on a playgroup
– Studying by correspondence. (Make sure the course is well organised and leads to a recognised qualification)
– Buying a typewriter and 'teach yourself' manual or cassettes
– Taking any opportunities presented for learning a second language, eg conversing in French with a French au pair, or with the parents in their language if that is not English

– Learning Welsh while working in Wales
– Driving, riding, swimming lessons have already been mentioned, but a driver could prepare for the Advanced Motorists test
– Developing skills in needlework (and other crafts) already at basic or even advanced stage
– Learning by watching mother or cook at work in the kitchen
– Seizing chances of intelligent conversation with visitors, and listening carefully
– Practising piano playing (or any instrument) by arrangement with employer
– Joining a professional association, eg Association of Certificated Nursery Nurses and attending their seminars, meeting other people working in childcare and keeping up to date. (Non-members are often welcome at seminars; ask local branch for details)
– Borrowing from the library and reading books on child development, educational methods and pioneers, activities with children.

Business matters

The importance of a proper contract with the employers has already been emphasised.

As well as having a contract signed by both sides you need to assure yourself that the employers are business like and are operating PAYE efficiently. One nannie told me she paid twice as much income tax as she should have done because the employers filled in a form incorrectly, implying she had received the salary for six months, not spread over a year as was the case. Fortunately, the next employer was an accountant and he discovered the mistake. If you are in any doubt consult the local income tax office.

You also need to be sure that the employer is deducting the correct national insurance contribution and stamping your card faithfully. In case of problems consult the local Department of Health and Social Security office.

Insurance
There is an insurance scheme especially designed to give complete cover to qualified NNEBs, and those who are unqualified but working as nannies.

Professional negligence can be proved in apparently trivial matters. For instance, a child's untied shoe lace resulted in the child being injured. The parents sued the nannie.

Even a professional can make a mistake. For about £12.50 per annum an NNEB is provided with cover for £100,000; unqualified nannies pay about £17.50 per annum. In order to maintain this low price the scheme needs the support of nannies. It would be worthwhile for any nannie to send to Lyall, Eason and Dudley, 4 Pickers Green, Lindfield, West Sussex RH16 2BS, for details of this policy. The company's message is 'If you are looking after children you will need looking after too'. The NNEB asked them to look into the question of insurance for nannies, particularly from the point of view of professional negligence. They are also able to supply details of policies insuring nannies' personal belongings and providing cover for medical expenses while working abroad.

An employer might well be prepared to pay the premium for a nannie to be insured against negligence. You could mention this at the interview.

The owner of The Harrow Nanny Agency, who kindly told me about the policy, strongly advises the nannies she places to take up such insurance; it certainly seems a wise precaution for every nannie.

Hambro Life Assurance Company have introduced a pension and life assurance scheme for nannies. Details from them at 7 Old Park Lane, London W1.

21 Relating to the family

Being the 'third adult'

Living in a household as the 'third adult', or as one of the staff, but as a person with a close relationship with the family, can have problems.

You may like the children's father very much (better than you like the mother), but remember, he is their father. You haven't come to the family to upset a marriage (or firm commitment) and family life. You have come to care for the children. Their best interests must be put first. Most nannies are not stupid; they recognise danger signs and the difference between a warm, friendly relationship and one that will only cause sadness all round.

Enjoy your own friends; stop yourself from becoming emotionally involved with the child's father. You can easily make it clear that you are not interested.

If the father pays too much attention to you, there is probably something wrong with the marriage anyway so don't make it worse. The man who makes advances to his children's nannie is scarcely a good bet.

Where the father is widowed or divorced and not re-married the position is different, but don't make hurried decisions, or think of marrying him for the children's sake or because it would all fit together neatly. Play it cool; take a long hard look at the situation. Perhaps you should have a break away from the family before you decide? In other circumstances would this have seemed the right person for you?

If you do feel really happy about it, then good luck. I know one former nannie who went to the village GP to care for his children after his wife died. When they announced they were marrying and the children were to be bridesmaids and pageboys at the wedding, people re-acted with mixed feelings. But the couple were sure, they went ahead and it has worked out happily.

Making friends with the family

Hopefully, you will make friends with both parents. It has been heartening to hear so many employers saying: 'She has been a very good nannie'; 'She is a lovely girl'; 'She really loves the children'. A good nannie can make such a difference to life for parents and children.

Many nannies have told me how they have become firm friends with employers. Others have said appreciatively: 'They treated me like another daughter'. Where it works well nannie and parents can have a very happy relationship.

Some parents do not want to be too friendly. They would rather keep a professional, more distant relationship. You will have to take the cue from them. From the initial interview you will probably get a fair idea of the type of relationship you will have.

In a traditional, royal, aristocratic, or very wealthy set-up, the nannie will probably not be treated as one of the family. 'They wouldn't have dreamed of asking me to any of their dinner parties,' said one Norland Nurse.

'Where there are other staff, the nannie can just be a cog in the wheel and fall between family and servants,' explained Mrs Townsend of Chiltern.

It is really a matter of choice; some nannies are happier in the traditional household where they have a nursery suite in which they are in charge, other staff do all the domestic work and cooking, and the parents see the children for a short time each day, and not always every day.

One Norland Nurse told me of going to such a family (where she was in fact very happy) and how one day she said to the mother: 'Would you like to give the baby her bottle?' 'Why? I thought that was what I paid you to do.' was the reply. However, the nannie was not put off: 'Eventually I got her "trained", and she quite enjoyed giving it.'

From Norland about 20% of the 'graduates' go to big houses and the classic nannie post; the rest go to professional working parents as they 'seem to prefer to live as part of a family'. This is for first jobs. Mrs Davis explained that many then bought their own flats and became daily nannies.

From Chiltern there is 'tremendous variation'. 'Those who are not "high fliers" are happiest in ordinary families,' said Mrs Townsend. Many of the newly qualified Chiltern nannies go straight to jobs abroad; Canada is popular; and a number go to Service families in Cyprus.

I know of one Sussex mansion where two nannies and three children lead a fairly separate life in nursery accommodation on the two top floors. One nannie is trained, the other untrained. They each have a car and both live near enough to go home for days off, if they wish. From the house they have magnificent views of the surrounding park where they sometimes take the children for walks and picnics, regardless of the National Trust visitors. There are still jobs of this type available. It may be work a nannie could enjoy doing just for a while, as a different experience.

Living in harmony

Whenever people live together as a household – in marriage, flatshare, family, community or institution – there are always minor irritations and matters that niggle.

A nannie could try to be on her guard and see that she does not annoy her employers, perhaps without realising it. As a guide you might aim to show the employers the same consideration as you would expect someone to show you or your parents.

Some of the potential causes of annoyance:
– Wasting hot water
– Monopolising telephone (incoming as well as outgoing calls)
– Loud music
– Untidy bedroom
– General untidiness in the house
– Taking too long in the bathroom (when shared with parents)
– Leaving only dregs of petrol in the car
– Forgetting to give messages.

It will be easy to think of the habits and shortcomings that could make you feel irritated with your employer! Just accept that all households have their idiosyncrasies. Try never to be petty; look the other way, ignore it, forget the irritation. Life is too short and full of positive opportunities to make it worth worrying about trivial matters.

If you like the job and the children accept that nothing is perfect and think of all the good points. If you are not happy there anyway, start studying the situations vacant columns!

When a job doesn't work out, try to think why and when things went wrong. Could you have done anything to improve matters? Were you inconsiderate? unreliable? awkward? We can all learn from every experience.

Mrs Davis, Principal of Norland College, advises the Norland Nurses: 'Absorb the emotion in a family. Try to diffuse the situation, rather than reacting. When the mother comes home and yells at the nannie, accept that she has had a hard day at the office'.

To avoid a clash of engagements she suggests that family and nurse keep a diary in which they all enter special events such as parental engagements that affect the nurse and children, events for the children, eg parties and playgroup puppet shows, and the nurse's own commitments, eg a special dance to which she has been invited. When an employer knows a nannie has made firm engagements she will probably stick to the off-duty arrangements and not suddenly expect the nannie to baby-sit on her day off.

Mrs Townsend, Principal of Chiltern College, has equally down to earth advice: 'Try to remember what you were taught at college, be adaptable – respect the parents' wishes and be diplomatic, not dogmatic.

'Put the child first at all times. If there is any misunderstanding with the parents, don't let it fester. Talk about it with them'.

A mother who found 'a marvellous nannie, devoted to the children and hardworking', had this to say: 'Perhaps the most difficult task has been to establish a delicate balance between making a nannie feel part of the family, and yet maintaining essential privacy on both sides. There is no one formula for this except to establish a good, honest working relationship and to encourage as much activity away from the home as is reasonably possible'.

Nannie's own room

Most nannies seem to have their own room; few employers now expect a nannie to share with a child, although a nannie who has complete charge of a young baby may find it simpler to have the baby in with her, or in an adjoining nursery.

At Norland the students working in the residential nurseries have complete 24 hour charge of the babies and small children. I saw the pleasant, comfortable, simple bedrooms equipped with bed and cot, and storage space for the child's clothes. All the nurses I spoke to seemed very happy to be able to give a child individual attention (under the close supervision of the trained staff) and they took a delight in having 'their' baby with them.

For a nannie in a residential post her room will be her refuge, somewhere to relax and just be herself. If you smoke (strongly discouraged by colleges, and many employers stipulate 'non-smoking') it may be the only place in the home where you can do so.

Make up your mind about the children's use of your room. There is much to be said for making them respect that it is your room. They should be asked to knock before entering.

In many households you will be expected to keep your own room clean.

If you do not like the arrangement of the room, ask if you may change it; if you need a stronger bulb ask for one. If you want to use your electric sewing machine just ask the employer's first.

Those who use heated rollers or tongs will see that they are well out of the children's reach when hot, and not left out where a child could turn the heat on and experiment alone.

There is no point in putting up with feeling cold. If the room is chilly (some people keep central heating rather low), ask for some supplementary heating.

You will have seen the room at the interview so you will have known what to expect, but you may not have realised it would be so noisy – perhaps it is at the front of a house on a main road. There is not a great deal you can do about this; except ask for thicker curtains. It doesn't seem realistic to expect the family to install double glazing for you.

Nannie's visitors
Unless it is a rather grand and formal household where you have little personal contact with the employers, it should be easy to introduce your visitors to the family. It seems only courteous to let them know who is in their house.

Nannie's own life

It is probably best to go slow on discussing your private life, as you would with any employer. Remember you have to live with them therefore it is generally better to talk over any personal problems with your own friends.

If you have a difference of opinion with your employers, don't sulk or brood about it. Forget it as you would a disagreement with your mother or sister. Make allowances for a mother who has a demanding job and may be tired.

Be fair to the family, but not 'put upon'. One of the problems is that the nicer the family and the more you get on well with them, the more you may do for them; they can forget you have your own life – apart from being their nannie.

Discretion

A nannie often has a close and intimate relationship with her employers. She knows about their lifestyle, habits, and perhaps their finances. She sees the people they entertain. The guests, or the employers themselves, may be well-known personalities in theatre, television, politics . . . The nannie is in a privileged position. It can be a temptation to gossip and comment to friends. But most nannies will resist this. It doesn't help your own self-esteem, if you feel you say or repeat things best not mentioned, and it is unfair to your employer.

Remember that The Federation of Personnel Services' model contract states: 'It is a condition of employment that now and at all times in the future the employee keeps secret the affairs and concerns of the household and its transactions and business'.

A nannie could reasonably feel that an employer should display the same confidentiality towards her.

The family's friends and relations

As time goes on you will get to know some of the family's friends and relations, especially if you live very much as family. It seems best to call them Mr, Mrs, Dr, at first. Because the employer calls her 'Hetty' there is no need for you to do so.

When the family are entertaining, be feeling. A mother who has come to see her daughter and grandchildren may not want the nannie sitting in on the visit. Take the opportunity to go out on your own, or spend some time peacefully in your room.

If you offer to make coffee or tea for an unexpected family caller it will probably be appreciated, and give the employer and visitor a chance to chat together.

Grandparents

Grandparents can be very important people in children's lives. Try to build up a good relationship with them. Make sure they do not feel 'pushed out' because nannie means so much to the children and is always with them. Again, give them time together without you.

You could talk to the child about 'Granny' and bring her into his thoughts, suggest he draws a picture for her, speaks to her on the telephone occasionally – or whatever seems appropriate.

Sometimes a nannie is expected to take the children to visit grandparents, or even to stay with them with the children while parents are on holiday. You will, of course, be considerate to the grandparents and do your best to make the visit a success.

Take the children out of the house, let them run and jump in parks or garden; be tactful about mealtimes and help the child out if grandparents expect him to clear his plate. Explain what kind of food and routine he usually follows and maintain that routine as far as you can in order to keep the child feeling secure.

Try to enjoy the visit and make it fun for the children. If grandma seems a bit critical, fussy, forgetful of what young children are like, just do your best in the situation. Listen to what she says; for the sake of peace do not argue with her on minor issues, even if you do not agree with her.

It may well be that you will get on extremely well with the grandparents and enjoy visits to or from them. If not, remember it is only a passing interlude. The important thing is to keep the children happy.

Complications

With the increase in the divorce rate, 'step grandparents' figure in more and more families. There are also grandparents who are afraid they will lose touch with their grandchildren after their parents divorce and re-marry. In all such situations a nannie has to be sensitive to the feelings of the people – and children – concerned, and be tactful to all. She may well be a person grandparents feel they can contact to ask about the welfare of children. Whatever happens, the nannie should avoid being drawn into wrangles and disputes. 'Never take sides,' says an agency proprietor.

Keeping the children secure and serene should be the nannie's aim. You will have to trust your own commonsense to guide you. Whatever the complications of the family's life 'Children first' must be your motto.

22 Leaving a post

When you go to a post and it doesn't seem to be working out, there often seems no good reason to stay, provided you have somewhere else to go. If parents and nannie are not in harmony, or the nannie is disgruntled, it will not be pleasant for the children.

Recently, I heard of one nannie who left a post after three days. When she arrived she found that, contrary to what she had been led to expect, the family wanted her to do all the housework.

If you find you really do not like the children or the parents – or if they do not seem to like you – it is better to go. One mother told me that she engaged a nannie who had a child of her own. Her children took a dislike to the nannie and child, and one day they bolted the doors so they could not get into the house. When the mother got home from her rounds (she was a GP) her children were leaning out of the upstairs window shouting at the nannie and child: 'Go away; we don't like you'.

Problems can arise when the mother feels guilty about leaving her children, for work, social service or pleasure, and then spoils them to compensate.

Mothers who keep constant tabs on a nannie, asking her if she has done things, taking an undue interest in her private life, or generally interfering in her management of the children, are unlikely to keep a nannie for long. Mutual respect is needed.

Rows between husband and wife are another cause of nannie unhappiness. 'In a modern house you can't help hearing,' one nannie said. Even worse are the couples that try to involve the nannie in their disputes. 'Never be drawn into an argument,' says Sheila Bell of Northumbrian Nannies. 'Don't be used as a go-between in husband and wife relationships,' says Mrs Davis. 'Never pass judgement just LISTEN'.

When, basically, you like the family and the job, try to think how things can be put right. You should be able to talk to the parents and see their point of view. Remember, they are asking you to care for their most precious possession – their child. The amazing thing is that so many employers are willing to entrust them to young, inexperienced nannies!

It is a pity to leave quickly, if things can be straightened out. Presumably, you all liked each other at the interview, otherwise you would not have been offered and would not have accepted the job. 'Give it at least a month,' said nannie Donna. She had been with her family for two years, but knew other nannies who had come down to London from the north, felt homesick, found some problems, and left without giving it a fair trial.

There are situations when all has worked out well, but the nannie feels it is time for her to make a move. Perhaps to gain different experience, perhaps because she feels she is getting stale and would like a change; maybe she prefers babies and feels the children are getting too old for her.

Telling the adults

For those who have firmly decided to leave, Mrs Davis, Principal of Norland College, has some sound advice.

'It is difficult to resign when you have become part of a family. When you have finally made up your mind, do not use it for pay rise bargaining. Pick the right moment when the wife and husband are together. Discuss it with them, but have a written note of your resignation ready to give them.

'If you just go and talk about it, an employer may persuade you to stay on when you really would rather leave.'

It is usual to give one month's notice on either side, but the length of time should be written into the contract.

Nannies may feel that one year is long enough with one family; some families decide they want a nannie for one year only as if the nannie stays longer the children will become too attached to her. The length of time the employer would expect you to stay should be discussed at the interview.

A nannie who wants to stay in a post for less than nine months or one year should go for temporary work. It is hard on the children if the nannies change too often, and it can be expensive for an employer who has to keep paying agencies fees.

For posts abroad most agencies ask nannies to stay a minimum of one year.

Telling the children

When you decide to leave you will try to give the family adequate notice for the child's sake. 'Every child who has a nannie is at risk of nannie going away – try not to leave suddenly,' is Dr Rachel Pinney's advice.

It is best if you can explain why you are leaving: 'I want to be nearer my mother,' or 'your mother is going to stay at home so you will not need me'. If you are leaving because you are getting married that is easier for the children to understand. One former nannie told me that her two little charges were bridesmaids at her wedding.

If a replacement nannie is coming, see if you can overlap for a day or two so that the child's routine is not too disturbed.

When you have left send the child a postcard occasionally and remember his birthday. It helps a child if he feels the nannie really cares about him and still likes him, even if she is not his nannie any more.

Children brought up in a vicarage sometimes suffer because people make a fuss of them, give them presents, want to take them out, because they are the vicar's children. When they leave the parish this generally ceases – a new vicar with children comes along and these children receive the shower of Easter eggs, Christmas presents and treats.

It is important that in such, and similar circumstances, the child should not feel rejected himself. It can be hard for him to understand that circumstances have changed. As far as he is concerned he is still the same person. The child whose nannie has moved on is still the same child – don't let him feel, 'she doesn't love me any more'.

Much the same applies for those working with handicapped youngsters. The youngsters are encouraged to be independent and do things for themselves, then they feel that the house mothers and staff have rejected them because they no longer do physical tasks for them. They need re-assurance and friendship from other young people and volunteers, as well as from the staff.

Attachment to the children

Any nannie who stays with a family for longer than six months is likely to get attached to the children, and to receive love from them. The nannie should not allow herself to become too fond of the child. She must remember she is not his mother; while responding to his affection she should not allow him to become too attached to her.

If the mother is absent all day, nannie should mention her frequently, and make it clear mother is number one person for the child. A nannie should not 'take over' the children as Mrs Davis put it. She should 'use her intuition, allow families private time and respect employers' wishes'. Sensitivity and concern for the child's true welfare are the qualities needed.

Going to a new nannie post

When you are going to a second or subsequent nannie post you are in a better position to know what would suit you. You will know the aspects that you enjoyed in your previous jobs, and the disadvantages to watch for. You could draw up your own list of favourable and unfavourable points just to remind yourself.

You will now have experience to offer, and references from an employer. You can be selective. If she goes to a successful agency a good nannie will be offered a choice of jobs.

This may be a stage in a nannie's life when she wants to experiment. If you live in the north, be prepared to go south; 'try the country for a change from town', says Christine of Jamie Turner Ltd.

As with applying for first jobs, you will probably go to agencies, follow up advertisements or advertise yourself. Norland Nurses will use the Norland Registry which has permanent and short-term posts.

23 What next after being a nannie?

'Some people simply get to the stage when they have been a nannie for long enough,' said Sheila Bell of Northumbrian Nannies. Perhaps you feel like that, have decided you want to live in your own flat, go home to live with parents, get married, advance your career prospects, earn more money, work more sociable hours. There are many reasons for taking a temporary or permanent break from being a nannie. What else can you do? Here are some suggestions for work or study in related fields.

Social work

The professional training for all social work is the Certificate of Qualification in Social work. There are two year courses for non-graduates aged 20 to 24 (five O levels or equivalent are the minimum requirement for this) and also three year courses designed for non-graduates with family commitments. This course further qualifies NNEBs for senior posts in day care centres undertaking intensive work with families.

For details of Social Work courses and application procedure write for leaflet 2.1 available from the Central Council for Education and Training in Social Work.

The Certificate in Social Services (CSS) provides training for work in residential homes, residential special schools and day care services. It can be taken with Child Care options and is required for some more senior posts in day nurseries, eg deputy officer in charge Grade 4.

There are no formal entry requirements for two year courses leading to this qualification; they are offered in further education colleges. Sometimes those already in posts are given an opportunity of taking such courses.

Leaflet 7.3 from CCETSW fully describes the training; leaflet 7.1 lists colleges offering courses.

Teaching

To become a teacher in a local authority school it is necessary to gain either a B Ed degree, or Post Graduate Certificate in Education. The Education Information Department can provide leaflets on entrance requirements for colleges and education courses. Apply direct to the college of your choice.

Roehampton Institute, formed from four teacher training colleges (Digby Stuart, Froebel, Southlands, and Whitelands), offers good professional training for teaching in nursery schools upwards. Ask for their current entry qualifications.

Montessori courses
Montessori courses are widely advertised, but the qualification by itself is not recognised for teaching in UK State schools. Some independent schools do accept it as a teaching qualification.

Teaching mentally handicapped children
The Education Information Department has leaflets detailing courses specially intended for people wishing to teach mentally handicapped children.

Nursing

Those who wish to consider training as a nurse (SRN, SEN or RSCN) should contact the Nursing and Hospital Careers Information Centre.

The Registered Sick Children's Nurse course lasts four years for those who are not already SRN. NNEBs are often attracted to this work and, according to a spokeswoman from Great Ormond Street Hospital, applications from them would be 'particularly welcome'.

Those wanting to take a shorter course (18 months) might consider Dental Nursing. Experience with children would be a great advantage for this type of nursing; after qualification as a Dental Surgery Assistant it may be possible to obtain a post with a dentist who has many child patients, or with a Schoolchildren's Dental Health Service.

Training schools include the Royal Dental Hospital in London, the Eastman Dental Hospital, Guy's Hospital, University College Hospital, King's College Hospital and the Liverpool Dental Hospital. Some have two intakes of students each year, others only one; places are in great demand. A salary is paid during training.

Play leadership

The importance of play for a child's development, happiness and creativity is increasingly being recognised. There are courses for those who want to learn more about children's play and how to apply the knowledge in particular settings.

Courses

Diploma in Play Leadership

A one year full-time course leading to this diploma is available at Thurrock Technical College. The minimum age of entry is 18 years; candidates under the age of 23 must have four GCE passes, one of which should be at A level.

Hospital Play Specialist

Southwark College run a Hospital Play Specialist course designed for those who already hold a nursing or teaching qualification, or NNEB.

Play, Drama and Art Therapy

Courses on these subjects are organised by Playspace and held at the Polytechnic of Central London. Details from Playspace Administrator, Short Courses Unit.

Adventure Playground organisation and supervision

The London Adventure Playground Association organise courses.

Employment in play activities

Local authorities, community associations, churches and charities often sponsor after school and school holiday play schemes, and advertise for temporary, seasonal and permanent staff. NNEBs would be well qualified for work with schemes for younger children. Watch local papers for advertisements; do some research, find schemes and see if they would consider employing you so that they could offer more for younger children.

Employment in hospitals

Qualified nursery nurses are sometimes appointed to children's wards, and given responsibility for play activities, on the strength of their NNEB. At a large London hospital I met Carol from Cornwall. She lived in the nurses' home, wore a distinctive nursery nurse uniform and worked on a children's ward. Her duties were:

Teaching student nurses how to prepare and give feeds to sick babies and babies in special care

Distributing toys to the patients (she kept the key of the toy cupboard), changing the toys and finding and organising new things for the children to do, eg painting and water play, collecting up the toys and keeping them in good order

Assisting the teacher who came daily to give the older children lessons (some were there many weeks on traction).

Another NNEB I met was appointed to a children's ward that was mainly occupied by short-stay ear, nose and throat patients. She assisted the play specialist, helped serve the breakfast, set out the playroom toys and equipment, took toys and games to the children in bed, talked to the children and played with them.

NNEBs are also employed on maternity wards and the Special Care Baby Units.

It is worth contacting local hospitals to find out if such vacancies are likely to arise. The National Association for the Welfare of Children in Hospital (now housed in the same block as the NNEB) is committed 'to raise the level of professional and public awareness of the psycho-social needs of sick children'. It continues to develop work on all aspects of children in hospital – including play. Their news letter would be of interest to anyone considering work in this field.

Advanced Nursery Nurse Courses

NNEBs have long felt there was a need for an advanced course and qualification. One course started at North Lindsey College of Technology in April 1984. It is of two-year duration and covers such topics as Student supervision; Physical and Mental Handicap in Children; The Nursery Nurse and Family Deprivation; Role of Technology in Education. Further details can be obtained from the Principal, North Lindsey College of Technology, Kingsway,

Scunthorpe, South Humberside.

The ILEA now offers an NNEB Certificate in Post Qualifying Training. Topics covered include Student Supervision; Child Observation; Early Learning; Children's Thinking; Interpersonal Skills. The course aims to provide 'in depth examination of the multi-cultural needs of children in an inner city, and to foster the caring and organising skills of those working with children'. For entry to the course the NNEB certificate and two years practical full-time experience with children are required. Details are available from the ILEA Staff Training Centre, Copperfield Street, London SE1.

It is likely that other similar courses will be started by local authorities in different parts of the UK. Ask the NNEB for the latest information (enclose sae).

Open University

Many of the Open University courses would be relevant for those wishing to learn more about child development and education. It is worth writing for the prospectus and considering following a course in one subject, eg Special Needs in Education, even if you are not at present in a position to tackle a degree course. The Open University, PO Box 188, Milton Keynes 3 6NW. You could also ask for details of 'The First Years of Life' course. (Enclose sae.)

Working in a day nursery

A nannie who decides to change to day nursery work can find it difficult (as can a newly qualified NNEB) to obtain a post because she lacks experience, apart from student placements.

To overcome this problem consider taking a temporary nursery post through an agency. Those who have the NNEB and live within reach of central London may well be able to obtain work through the Marylebone Agency which specialises in finding temporary staff for nurseries run by Local Authorities, privately, and by large companies.

'They have to take the risk of being unemployed between jobs, but if they are good workers I can generally keep NNEBs in work and let them have the opportunity of gaining that vital experience', explained the agency Principal. Some of the nursery nurses she places are subsequently offered permanent post in nurseries where they have worked temporarily.

Permanent and maternity leave day nursery posts are advertised in *Nursery World* and local papers.

Childminding

Nannies who have children of their own, and those who would like to work in their own homes, could consider becoming childminders. A good childminder can easily find enough children to mind. Many working parents prefer their child to be cared for solely, or in a small group in a private home, rather than in a nursery. Someone who is an experienced nannie or NNEB would be welcomed as a childminder by parents and the local authority.

– Discover the Local Authority regulations concerning numbers, premises
– Prepare your home carefully. Be willing to invest some money in having suitable equipment; toys; stair gates and other safety features; spare nappies and pants (you may decide to dress the children in your nappies and pants (clearly marked) all day to save confusion
– Try to find someone who can come to your aid, or stand in for you in an emergency
– Advertise yourself, reply to advertisements or spread the news by word of mouth
– Spend time with the parents and children who apply to you. If you think you will find the mother 'difficult', unreliable (about collecting the child at the specified time), or too hard to please, or if for any reason you do not feel in tune with the child and mother, it is probably wisest to refuse (tactfully) to take on that child. You could stick to one age range, or have a family group, as you prefer
– Fix your fees (in consultation with local social services if necessary) and stipulate method and day of payment. You probably cannot afford to be soft-hearted; the fees will be your income instead of a salary, so approach it in a business like way. It is better to offer a good service and charge properly, than do it on the cheap and feel underpaid
– Once you have taken the children into your care give them your whole-hearted attention, as you would if you were a nannie to them. Make the day stimulating, cheerful, well organised so that mother, child and you, are all happy about it.

Advice on registration and insurance for childminders can be obtained from National Childminding Association, 204/206 High Street, Bromley BR1 1PP. (Enclose sae.)

Some local authorities are now employing visitors and local organisers for childminders. An NNEB who has also been a childminder may stand a good chance of obtaining such a post.

There are also clubs and groups for childminders; attending these can benefit both childminder and child. Ask your local Social Services for details.

A leaflet, *So you want to be a Childminder* is available from The Health Education Council, 78 New Oxford Street, London WC1A 1AH (enclose sae) or look for it in Community Health Council centres.

Running a private nursery

Some people qualify as NNEBs with the express purpose of starting a nursery of their own. Others gain experience in various childcare fields, including nannieing, then decide to open their own day nursery or nursery school.

When you are considering such a project, you will need to think carefully.

Here are some factors you should take into account:
– Is there local need for such a nursery?
– Are there enough families who could afford to pay fees?
– Would the local Social Services/planning authorities/other local authorities involved allow me to open a nursery in the premises I have in mind?
– How many children would they permit me to take? Would this be enough to make the nursery viable?
– Have I the capital to purchase/lease premises/pay rent/pay rates and buy equipment?
– Can I obtain (and pay for) adequate help?
– Remember you will need cash flow to pay for insurance (essential), advertising, and fees for surveyor, architect, accountant etc.
– You will need to consider toilet, parking and access for dropping and collecting children, and outdoor play facilities, and whether these will be approved by the Local Authority.

One way of overcoming the initial difficulties and being able to get going quickly is to buy a 'going concern'. Sometimes a trained nurse/teacher/nursery nurse starts such a nursery when her own children are small, but when they grow older she loses interest, or is freer to take a job. Such a person might be open to an offer. Search for all the actual and potential snags first, and have proper legal agreements drawn up. You don't want her to sell to you, then start up again half a mile away and take your potential pupils/nursery children!

An NNEB cannot run a private nursery school on her own, or with other nursery nurses only, she needs to employ a qualified teacher too.

If you are thinking of starting such a nursery it would be wise to try and visit similar projects so as to see the standard of provision, and find out about snags.

NB Numbers, ratio of staff to children, facilities, are strictly regulated by local authorities. It is as well to develop a good relationship with local officials.

Fostering

When you marry and give up a residential post, have children of your own, or find your own children are grown up and you want to return to some kind of childcare work, fostering may be the answer.

Local authorities and charities (such as Be My Parent) are often anxious to find homes for 'hard to place' children. Someone with training and/or experience as a nannie could be well suited to such fostering, as well as for short term fostering of children who go into care for a variety of reasons.

Contact your local Social Services Foster Care department and discuss the possibilities with them. You may see particular needs advertised in your local paper.

There is also private fostering of children of West African parents studying or working in the UK. Such parents advertise in *Nursery World* and seek 'loving, friendly' foster parents. Many people are unhappy that such a system should still be legally allowed, and these parents tend to offer low payments, but as it exists it seems only fair to mention it.

Most nannies will know that, 'before a child is placed in a foster home, the local authority must by law be notified of this arrangement by the foster parents, and it is essential for 14 days written notice to be given to the authority'.

Save the Children Fund's Overseas Children's Project is ready to give advice about such fostering, and is building up a register of suitable foster parents. (Contact them at Mary Datchelor House, 17 Grove Lane, London SE5.)

Running an agency

Someone who has been a nannie herself has many advantages if she decides to open an employment agency. A number of nannies have done this successfully, other have tried and been overcome by the problems!

To operate as an agency you need to be licensed as an Employment Agency, and that entails a registration fee. You need printed stationery, a telephone, office accommodation – you can use your own home but watch your income tax and rating position – and a budget for advertising.

To become established some nannies take baby-sitting and weekend bookings and do these themselves, or perhaps they mind one or two children for short periods on an hourly basis. If you are qualified it is easy to supplement your income in this way. On the other hand, if you are out being a nannie you are not available for speaking to employers who telephone, interviewing prospective nannies, and administering your business.

You can have an answer phone machine but sometimes people want to make an immediate personal contact, they are put off by the recording machine and simply telephone the next agency in the newspaper column. None-the-less I spoke to a Norland Nannie who was very happy running her own agency and assured me she made an adequate living from it.

As a nannie you have the advantage of knowing the job, the snags, the expectations of employers and girls, and the kind of conditions/contract that will be fair and workable.

Agencies such as Canonbury Nannies and The Harrow Nanny Agency, both run by NNEBs, produce their own application forms, guidelines and contracts. They know what is important for both sides.

Some agencies run by NNEBs, eg Clifton Nannies, have expanded as they discovered different needs – they also place housekeepers, elderly helps and au pairs. Obviously, the more people you can place the more profitable the enterprise.

Sheila Bell of Northumbrian Nannies takes great pastoral care of the nannies she places, and she is always willing to give advice to girls she has sent to posts. The postcards from happily placed nannies in various parts of the world testify to her friendly, personal care.

It seems that anyone running an agency must be really concerned for the individuals she places and feel a sense of responsibility. Understandably, one agency proprietor told me she had given up placing nannies, 'because I don't like sending girls off to families I know nothing about'.

If you are thinking of starting a nannie agency, you should ask yourself:

– Have I sufficient capital to get going?
– Can I overcome cash flow problems? (Sometimes employers are slow to pay, or a placement may not be a success and they need a second nannie without being charged a further fee)
– Can I keep my accounts carefully, or find someone to help me do this?
– Am I good judge of people?
– Am I prepared to take trouble over individuals and families?
– Do I have the confidence to speak up for a nannie who is being unfairly treated?
– Have I enough contacts, or can I establish them? eg with local colleges
– Is there a local area, or some 'gap in the market' that I can fill?
– Am I prepared to work at becoming established and being the kind of agency employers and nannies will recommend to their friends?

To make an agency a success there seems much to be said for having a distinctive name and logo. Be imaginative; search around for new and varied places to advertise. If you stick to the traditional magazines you need to have something special and different to offer to make you stand out from all the others. In a recent issue of *The Lady* 48 different agencies were advertising.

If the idea appeals to you, and you are able to make a success of running an agency, it is a satisfying, worthwhile job. Entrusting your children to a nannie and taking someone into your household is a serious business; finding a job where you are happy and fulfilled can transform life. Child, employer and nannie benefit when a skilled, caring agency brings them together. Running such an agency is an important way of helping children and nannies.

Some people have started by organising a baby-sitting agency. A nursery nurse could run such an agency in a university city, recruiting students and giving them basic training for baby-sitting duties, before sending them on assignments.

Other occupations a nannie could enjoy

– Working as a house matron/house mistress in an independent boarding school. Some advertisements state SRN or SEN, but not all. (Study them in *The Lady*.)
– Care assistant/residential social worker in home or school for handicapped children or young people
– Housemother/warden in residential accommodation or sheltered housing for the elderly
– Dining hall supervisor in school, university, residential home
– Prison Officer (Home Office P7 Division, 89 Eccleston Square, London SW1V 1PU)
– Children's bookshop assistant
– Children's party organiser (you offer to organise games, prizes, entertainment, parting gifts and sometimes the tea too)
– Maternity clothing hire scheme organiser
– Organiser of creches and play schemes for children of parents attending trade shows, conferences, exhibitions, etc.
– Shopkeeper – setting up, or buying and developing a shop specialising in children's clothes, baby accessories, toys, maternity wear. (Chose location carefully)
– Handicapped children's travel escort (employed by local authorities)
– Playground attendant
– Housemother/group leader in children's holiday home, including holiday centres for handicapped children
– Shared care worker for families with handicapped children (giving regular daily or residential care to a handicapped child to enable parents to have some respite, eg Barnardo's Southwark Project, 283 Tooley Street, London SE1)
– Multi-ethnic care worker (child care workers speaking Bengali, Hindi, Mandarin or Cantonese, are often needed for special projects with women and young children. Contact Social Services in areas of multi-ethnic population.)

Training as a nursery nurse or working as a nannie is also a good preparation for motherhood! I met one NNEB who has nine children (no multiples) aged 26 to 11; all are healthy, attractive and intelligent.

24 Training to be a nannie

Nursery Nurse Examination Board (NNEB) Certificate

The most widely recognised training for work with children under seven is the NNEB course. Many of those who read this book will be following it or have completed it successfully.

The course is offered at about 145 local authority colleges in England and Wales, one in the Isle of Man, one in Jersey, two in Northern Ireland and about 18 in Scotland. The full list can be obtained from the National Nursery Examination Board or the Scottish Nursery Nurses' Examination Board. (Enclose a large sae or label.)

Apply as soon as possible as demand for places is heavy. You must show that you are able to benefit from the course and have the ability to complete it, but there are no rigid entry qualifications. Each college has different entry requirements and some ask for a few 'O' levels or good CSEs. The minimum age for starting the course is 16, but there is no upper limit. Some people take the course after having worked with children in an unqualified capacity, others after they have had children of their own. Tuition is free for under-18s. Local authority grants are sometimes available to mature students.

The two year full-time course covers the physical, intellectual, emotional and social development of the child from 0 to seven years. it includes child health, nutrition and baby care, and there is strong emphasis on the importance of play. Social policy and the rights and responsibilities of families are also studied.

The personal development of each student is encouraged and the colleges offer a variety of general studies and such subjects as art, craft, woodwork and needlework.

Two-fifths of the course time is spent in practical work with children in nurseries, hospitals, schools and families.

The private colleges

At present there are three private colleges in England: Chiltern, Norland (founded 1892) and Princess Christian. These colleges are residential and fees are payable but local authorities will sometimes give discretionary awards to students who have special reasons for wanting to study at one of the private colleges.

Private colleges require 'O' levels and 18 is the minimum age for entry. The prospectus of each college gives details of regulations, syllabus and fees. Students at the private colleges take the NNEB, the Royal Society of Health Diploma for Nursery Nurses and the college certificate or diploma. Places at these colleges are in great demand. In February 1983 the earliest vacancy at Norland was for a course beginning in January 1986.

Other useful courses
The Preliminary Certificate in Social Care (PCSC)

A two year full-time course leading to this certificate can be taken by 16 to 18-year olds. 'O' levels are not essential for it.

This certificate is not a social work qualification but gives an introduction to careers in the social services, child care and community work. Some who take this course use it to obtain work as a nursery assistant in a school or children's residential home, or as a foundation for other courses. It is recognised by people who employ nannies.

The course is offered at further education colleges; a list of these (ask for leaflet 6.1) is obtainable from Central Council for Education and Training in Social Work. *Cut out for a Caring Career?* (leaflet 6) describes the course fully and is also obtainable from the Council. Enclose a large sae with requests for these leaflets. For notes on other social work courses see the previous chapter.

National Association for Maternal and Child Welfare courses

This Association aims 'to promote understanding of the total needs of the family in the community, especially in the early days of childhood, and to foster the self development of students and contribute to their understanding of personal relationships as well as the needs of children'.

Basic Certificate
This course in human development and family life covers:

- The family
- The adolescent
- Preparation for parenthood
- Growth and development of the unborn child
- The development of the child from birth to five years
- Safety of the child and family
- Children with special needs
- The child and his school.

Examination is by continuous assessment, oral test, written or practical test. Certificates are awarded grades A to F. The course is offered in schools and taken by young people of both sexes and varying academic ability.

NAMCW General Certificate

This course includes the subjects listed previously, plus General Care of the Baby and Young Child, First Aid, and other topics important for nannies. It is taken in schools and colleges of further education and marked by the NAMCW. Passes at Grade A or B are recognised by the General Nursing Council as an alternative to 'O' level or CSE Grade 1 for entry to student nurse training.

NAMCW Diploma

Students gaining good grades in this course in Human Development, Child Care and Social Responsibility 'should have attained a standard of knowledge and practical experience to equip them to accept individual responsibility for other people's children . . .'. This Diploma course is offered in colleges and schools and it follows the subjects already mentioned, but in greater depth. It is most useful for anyone who wishes to work as a nannie.

The professional mother of a 12-month-old daughter told me she had successfully engaged a local non-resident nannie who took this course in school.

Details of all NAMCW courses are available from the General Secretary of the Association (enclose sae) and will be sent with order forms for the Syllabus Booklets.

The City and Guilds of London Institute

Many colleges of further education and technical colleges offer the Institute's part- or full-time courses. Ask about them at your local college. Toy making and Basketry in the Home Economics and Creative Studies section would be useful for those who want to work with children.

In the Institute's Foundation Courses for secondary schools and colleges there is a Community Care section. A list of publications and further information is obtainable from the Institute, 76 Portland Place, London W1N 4AA.

Isle College, Wisbech

At this college there is a nannie's course which aims to 'provide the necessary theoretical knowledge and practical skills to enable young ladies to obtain employment as nannies in private homes'. This is a residential, one year course, with strong emphasis on practical skills as well as academic work, leading to the National Association for Maternal and Child Welfare Certificate and other external certificates in addition to the College Certificate. Some local authorities will give awards for residential fees and parents in the Services and living abroad can obtain allowances for daughters attending the course. Full details of the course are obtainable from the Department of Community and Creative Studies, Isle College, Wisbech, Cambridgeshire.

London Academy of Pre-School Education

A full-time 15 month (four term) course leading to the NAMCW Diploma in Child Care is being offered by this private non-residential college. Both school leavers and mature women are accepted; the fees can be paid in instalments and the Academy is in touch with nannie agencies that may be able to arrange vacation or part-time work for students. Details from London Academy of Pre-School Education, 178 High Street, London W3 9NN. When this book was written the Academy course had not begun so it has not been possible to assess it. Those thinking of studying at the Academy could contact the NAMCW for advice.

Recommended reading

in addition to books mentioned in main text

The Baby and Child Book, Drs Andrew and Penny Stanway, Pan Books 1983
From abdominal pain to learning to write, this handbook of baby and childcare seems to cover every topic in its 806 pages of information and encouraging advice. A nannie would find the book invaluable for emergencies and day to day coping.

Can I Speak to the Doctor?, Dr Bill Dolman, Cassell, 1981
Your questions answered. Whether your problems is earache – should I call the doctor?; a sleepwalking child, or the toddler who chews everything he can reach; Dr Dolman has an explanation and advice. His book teaches about illness and general health as well as children's ailments, and it is written in an easy, friendly style.

Baby and Child, Penelope Leach, Penguin 1980
NNEBs will have studied this handbook already. Those who are not familiar with it are advised to obtain a copy because it gives a clear account of child development in the first five years of life, practical hints and useful information.

Understanding the Under-fives, Donand Baker, Evans Brothers 1975
As this book is now out of print you will need to look for it in college and public libraries; it is well worth making an effort to find a copy. The late Donald Baker had a wonderful understanding of children and the ways in which they develop and learn. His book emphasises the importance of play and suggests stimulating activities, apparatus and experiences.

Twins from Conception to Five Years, Averil Clegg and Anne Woollett, Century 1983
Anyone looking after twins would appreciate this practical guide with its delightful and illuminating drawings and photographs.

Community Care Helping Others, Gordon Sturrock, Sampson Low 1983

Although primarily intended for young people training for the Duke of Edinburgh's Award, I have included this book because it contains so much useful information about voluntary work and organisations. It would be helpful for a nannie who wants to find out about organisations working in particular fields, or for someone looking for opportunities for voluntary work and gaining experience.

———

The following companies and organisations produce helpful free leaflets. You could write and ask for a list. Enclose a stamped addressed envelope.

Robinsons of Chesterfield
Wheat Bridge, Chesterfield, Derbyshire S40 2AD
Play Safe specially recommended

Persil Educational Leaflets
50 Upper Brook Street, London W1Y 1PG
Taking Care of Baby's Clothes and *Play Ideas for the Under Fives*

Robinson's Baby Foods
Carrow, Norwich NR1 2DD
Feeding Your Baby

Farley Health Products
Plymouth, Devon

Pelham Puppets
Marlborough, Wiltshire
The Puppet Show, a booklet to help you use puppets and put on little plays.

Sterling Health
Surbiton, Surrey KT6 4PH
Children's Infections, specially recommended.

Health Education Council
78 New Oxford Street, London WC1A 1AH
They produce a host of informative, free booklets and guides. Browse through them in the Oxford Street offices, look for them in clinics, surgeries and Mothers' clubs or ask the Health Visitor to suggest titles you could send for.

Examples: *Bed wetting*; *Play and Things to Play With, Your Children's Teeth*

Cow and Gate Ltd
PO Box 99, Bythesea Road, Trowbridge, Wiltshire

Holidays and Outings
Go to Local Tourist Information Centres to see the range of free and reasonably priced publications giving ideas for where to go and what to see.

Heritage Publications, Merchants House, Barley Market Street, Tavistock, Devon, publish comprehensive guides to the South and South West of England; they would be worth buying when planning to take the children out and about in those areas.

Local authorities
Some authorities publish their own guides to services and facilities for under fives in particular areas. For instance Lambeth has seven guides showing where and how to contact the Playbus, local Toy Library, Playgroups, Adventure Playgrounds, etc.

The Early Learning Centre
Hawksworth, Swindon, Wiltshire SN2 1TT
Their catalogue can be used for mail order or for studying the range of sound educational materials to be seen in their show rooms.

Montrose Products
28–34 Fortress Road, London NW5
The catalogue shows the firm's great variety of large apparatus, such as swings and climbing frames, available for individuals or groups.

The Optical Information Council
Walter House, 418 Strand, London WC2
Produces an important free leaflet (reference number 0112) *Children's Eyecare*.

Child Safety Information Service
Tufty Club, Rospa, Cannon House, The Priory, Queensway, Birmingham B4 6BV

The Disposable Baby Napkin Bureau
28 Newman Street, London W1P 3HA
Free samples as well as a leaflet, *Getting the best from Disposables*

Brio UK Ltd
Belton Road West, Loughborough, Leicestershire LE11 0TR
Colourful catalogue, wallsheet and booklets

British Medical Association, Family Doctor Publications
BMA House, Tavistock Square, London WC1H 9JP

You and your baby: stage 2, Birth to Infancy.
This informative, well illustrated 80 page booklet is designed for
new mothers but it would be most valuable for any nannie.

Useful addresses

in addition to those given in the text

When writing for information always enclose a stamped addressed envelope or label

Association for All Speech Impaired Children
347 Central Market, Smithfield Market, London EC1A 9NH

Church of England Children's Society
Old Town Hall, Kennington Road, London SE11 4QD

Central Council for Education and Training in Social Work
(*England*)   Derbyshire House, St Chad's Street, London WC1 8AD
(*Scotland*)   9 South Street, David Street, Edinburgh EH2 2BW
(*Wales*)   West Wing, St David's House, Wood Street, Cardiff CF1 1ES
(*Northern Ireland*)   14 Malone Road, Belfast BT9 5BN

Chiltern Nursery College
20 and 32 Peppard Road, Caversham, Reading, Berkshire

Down's Children's Association
Quinborne Community Centre, Ridgeacre Road, Birmingham B32 2TW

Invalid Children' Aid Association
126 Buckingham Palace Road, London SW1W 9SB

National Association for Maternal and Child Welfare
1 South Audley Street, London W1Y 6JS

National Association for the Welfare of Children in Hospital
Argyle House, Euston Road, London NW1 2SD

National Association of Certificated Nursery Nurses
c/o Miss Jenny Curtis, 63a Niton Street, London SW6

National Children's Bureau
8 Wakeley Street, London EC1V 7QE

National Deaf Children's Society
45 Hereford Road, London W2

National Nursery Examination Board
Argyle House (3rd Floor), 29–31 Euston Road, London NW1 2DS

Norland Nursery Training College
Denford Park, Hungerford, Berkshire

Open University
Walton Hall, Walton, Milton Keynes, MK67 6AB

Pre-School Playgroups Association
Alford House, Aveline Street, London SE11 5DJ

Princess Christian College
26 Wilbraham Road, Fallowfield, Manchester 14

Scottish NNEB
38 Queen Street, Glasgow G1 3DY

Scottish Pre-School Playgroups Association
7 Royal Terrace, Glasgow G37 NT

Toy Libraries Association
Seabrook House, Wyllots Manor, Drakes Lane, Potters Bar,
    Hertfordshire EN6 2HL

Twins' Club Association
Pooh corner, 2 Steel Road, Chiswich, London W4

Vegetarian Society
53 Marloes Road, London W8

Index

THE GHOSTS OF MILLER'S CROSSING

David Clark

1

"Stop!"

"Get out of the way!" The exclamation was followed by the large thump of something slamming into a wall, and woke the sleeping seven-year-old Edward Meyer. When he went to bed under a sea of stars painted on the ceiling of his bedroom by the nightlight his mother gave him for his fifth birthday, it was quiet, and all was right with the world. The world that startled him awake was loud, and the air was soaked in fear. A war had been waged downstairs.

"No!" Edward heard his father scream woefully. "No! No! No!" His voice repeated. Each word was more pained than the first.

Edward sat up and swung his feet around, letting them hang off the bed. He sat and listened as things bumped and slammed around in the room below him, the kitchen. A deep growl sent him crawling across the bed to the corner of his room. He sat and shivered in the corner while the house around him shook and shuttered. There were more bumps and slams below him and other voices yelling, but Edward was too scared to hear them. He just sat and shook, waiting for the world around him to return to the place of tranquil peace that it was when he went to sleep.

It took several minutes, but the sounds downstairs disappeared and everything, including Edward, stopped trembling. He slid across the bed and his feet landed on the floor, where he took several tentative steps to the door. Out in the hall he asked, "Mom? Dad?" But no voice answered the scared seven-year-old. He asked again, just outside the door of their bedroom. "Mom? Dad?" Again, there was no response, and Edward peered around the doorframe and found no one in the room. Behind him, downstairs, he heard footsteps running across their hardwood floor. It sounded like whoever it was ran from the front door to the kitchen.

From the top of the stairs, Edward saw the front door was wide open. Flashes of red and blue lights cast eerie shadows against the walls. In the distance he heard talking, not the screaming he heard before. He crept down the stairs and around toward the kitchen door.

Light shone through the cracks around the door, and Edward reached out and pushed it open. In a flash, his world would never be the same. Two pools of crimson on the kitchen floor. The bodies of his mother and father laid still inside them. His father's body was twisted into an unnatural shape. His head laid feet from the rest and stared at Edward with a blank expression. A warm liquid ran down the inside of Edward's legs. The world shook and twisted around him again.

"Lewis! Grab Eddie. Get him out of here," a familiar voice commanded from across the kitchen. In an instant, Edward felt himself swept up and pulled close against the chest of a large man wearing the uniform of a sheriff's deputy. The man rushed him out the front door and placed him in the passenger seat of his police cruiser. Then he whisked Edward away. His eyes watched the image of his childhood home disappear behind him in the mirror.

2

"Doctor Law will be with you shortly."

"Thanks," Edward said and took the seat Nurse Rymer walked him to. Then he sat and waited for her to leave the room. That had been a normal routine for many of his meetings with Doctor Law throughout his years here. A nurse, usually the almost retired head nurse Sally Rymer who had the bedside manner of a bedpan, would bring him to this room, or any of the others setup identical to this one, and then leave him to wait for the doctor, alone. Or so he assumed.

"This room needs some color," Edward Meyer said to himself. The old leak stains on the white drop ceiling and scuffs on the floor were the only signs of character. The simple plastic white chair Edward sat on resembled one you might find on an outdoor patio. They sat around a stainless-steel table bolted to the floor.

He mumbled with a chuckle, "Looks slightly institutional to me," then remembered he needed to be careful. The two-way mirror on the wall never gave away the secret of who was on the other side.

Today was his eighteenth birthday, and he sat alone in a green cotton shirt, drawstring pants, and slippers. This was no birthday celebration. He was there for an important discussion with his doctor. In truth, it was more of an evaluation; one he had high hopes for.

He thought about the first time he waited, alone, in that room. The table and chair were the same, but his attire and reason for being there were different. He wore jeans and an Iron Maiden t-shirt and sat there confused as to why he was there. He was only fourteen, and things had been rough with his foster parents. OK, "rough" might not be the best word. "Horrendous," yeah, that's the correct term. He wasn't beaten or neglected. Food, care, clothes, etc... nothing was withheld. In fact, to those looking in from the outside, he'd had a great childhood with supportive foster parents that gave him all they could to make sure he had a loving home.

When he turned nine, they encouraged him to sign up for little league, which he jumped at. He loved baseball. They traveled around to every practice and game, ensuring he always saw two parents supporting him. The same for every school event. To some extent, he felt they were trying to overcompensate for him having lost both parents in a horrible tragedy at age seven.

The door clicked and Edward saw the tall, slender forty-something frame of Doctor Law enter. His nose buried in papers as always.

"Good morning, Edward." Doctor Law said. His name was always the source of a few jokes among Edward and the other patients. *With a name like that, he should be a lawyer.* But Edward's favorite was *he was the "Law" around this place.* He liked that one, because it was true, and it was his joke.

Doctor Law pulled a chair away from the table and then stopped with a bewildered look on his face. He frantically studied the folder in his hands. Without looking up, he said, "I will be right back. I have the wrong folder." He walked back out the door, flipping through the pages with the look of confusion growing the whole time.

Edward always wondered if these types of mistakes were legitimate or some kind of experiment, with someone observing the subject's reactions through the two-way portal in the wall. He played it cool, sat, and waited for the doctor to return.

The two-way mirror grabbed his attention during his first visit as well. They didn't hide what it was, just who was behind it. He remembered sitting there, focusing as hard as he could to see through it; hoping his foster parents were on the other side and would be in soon to take him home. That was not the case. Instead, only Doctor Law entered the room.

They talked for hours about many topics. He asked about his relationship with his foster mom, and then about his foster father. To both questions, Edward gave glowing answers about how close he felt to them and how great his life was going.

The conversation moved to school and friends. He wanted to know if Edward was being bullied or harassed at school. He suggested that kids sometimes single out a child who has been in a foster home or has had a traumatic past. Well, the answer to that was most definitely not. Edward had lots of friends, both in and away from school. Other than the normal ribbing you give each other during a baseball game or in the schoolyard, he remembered nothing like bullying. He couldn't think of any time he may have bullied anyone else, either.

Doctor Law asked him if any of his friends tried to get him to take or experiment with any drugs. That answer was a very loud, "Absolutely not!" His foster parents asked him about drugs once before. They even took him to the doctor for testing. Edward tried everything he could to convince them. Two days later, the results were in, and his foster parents were apologetic. They explained they heard rumors from other parents about drug use among his friends, and wanted to be sure. Doctor Law listened to his answer while consulting a file laid out on the table before him. He didn't challenge Edward's answer, or ask him any more questions about it.

Next, he asked about his real parents. Edward thought for a minute about how to answer, since he was still unsure why he was there. He could have said he never thought about them or what happened to them anymore, but that would have been a lie. He thought about it daily. Sometimes hourly. He told Doctor Law how he felt and how badly he missed them. Edward then felt the need to explain. He loved his foster parents, but he missed his real parents. Doctor Law interrupted his explanation to tell him that was normal, and they understood that. Hearing that made Edward feel less guilty, though it was not really bothering him much.

Doctor Law asked delicately about the moment he found them. Edward shifted in his seat and explained, "Something woke me up. I laid there for a few moments and heard several loud crashes coming from the kitchen. I called for my mom, and she never answered. I heard another crash, and she screamed. I walked downstairs and pushed open the door. That's when... I saw both lying on the floor." Edward sighed heavily. "Shortly after that, a police officer came in and rushed me out of the house."

That was a memory Edward wished he could lose. For months, he woke up screaming as the image of his dead parents invaded his sleep. His foster mother would storm in and hold him for hours, trying with all her might to protect him from the memory, but nothing drove it away.

Moments after Edward walked in, Officer Tillingsly grabbed and rushed him out to his patrol car. He left him there for the longest minute or two of his life. When he returned, he took Edward to the police station. The officer was a friend of Edward's father, and was always around. He could tell Officer Tillingsly was in as much shock as Edward was. He sat Edward in the chair behind his desk and gave him a soda to drink. Sitting in a chair beside him, they talked about anything and everything, including a fishing trip he'd taken with Edward and his father over the summer.

They'd been out there for hours with no bites if you didn't count the bugs. Officer Tillingsly thought he had a bite on his line once. He reeled it in close to the boat, but when he looked, he leaned over the side a little too far. Flapping his arms like a back-pedaling turkey, he hung there for a few seconds until gravity won and he entered the water with a splash. Edward remember hearing his father laughing while saying, 'Well, Lewis, if we weren't going to catch anything before, we won't now. You scared them all off."

When they got home, Edward's mother asked if they had caught anything. Edward told her, "We caught Officer Tillingsly." She looked at them like they had lost their minds. All three busted out in hysterical laughter. There was no laughter between them now. His attempt to distract Edward—both of them really—failed.

The station itself was a hive of activity. Everyone moved around from one room to another in a blur. All talking, and all giving Edward the same heartbroken look as they walked past. Some even had tears in their eyes. Everyone, and I mean everyone, knew his family in this typical small town with only one elementary, junior, and senior high school. On top of that, his father was a local legend. He was a high school All-American Quarterback. Sportswriters and scouts came from all over to meet him during his senior year. He had the pick of prime offers from the best schools, and I mean the best schools. Alabama, Penn State, and Notre Dame were at the top of a lengthy list. Even with all those great offers, he bypassed college to stay and work on the family farm.

After high school, he married his high school sweetheart. They were both active in the community, helping to run the fall festival each year, things at church, town council meetings, and the school board. With all of that, Edward's house was always full of the sounds of laughter and conversation. Most memories were happy ones, but there were a few that were not so joyous. Once or twice a month, a group of men would show up late at night and talk to his father for a few minutes before leaving. Edward would hear a car door close when he came home the next morning just before sunrise. His parents never discussed his comings and goings in front of him; all he knew was that his father kept to himself and seemed different for the next couple of days.

A click from the door gave Edward the sense of déjà vu, as Doctor Law opened the door carrying a file like he did about ten minutes ago. He hoped it was the right file that time. He sat back in his chair and watched the doctor circle around to the only other chair in the room. Edward cleared his mind; it was now time for his Oscar-worthy   performance.

3

"Sorry about that, Edward. I had the wrong file," Doctor Law announced with an obvious lack of emotion while sitting down. His bedside manner always lacked warmth. "Happy birthday. Have you already put in your meal request?" he asked without looking at Edward.

The annual birthday meal was one of the few attempts to make you feel as normal as possible. In each of the previous years, Edward ordered the same thing, and this year was no different. "Thank you. Yes, I have. I am simple. No steak or lobster for me. I want three slices of deep dish six cheese pizza and a cola."

"Let me talk to them and see if we can order you a real pizza. None of that stuff the cafeteria makes. You only turn eighteen once, right?"

What the doctor said was true. You turn eighteen only once, but the pizza was not what he was after. He wanted the gift that could happen if this meeting went well.

"Shall we get started?" Doctor Law settled into his seat, opened the folder, and grabbed a pen from the chest pocket in his white coat. "How are things going for you lately? It has been what... three months since we last spoke?"

Has it been that long? Edward had lost track of the time since he and Doctor Law sat down and talked in a true evaluation setting. It was easy to do, since Doctor Law and the rest of the staff interacted with all the patients daily to check on them and observe their conditions, but he played along. "Has it been that long? I am good. How are you?"

"That is great to hear. I am well. Thank you for asking," Doctor Law said while still looking down at the folder. He examined each page before flipping to the next. "So, I see you are completely off of your medications. Feeling any side effects or relapses?"

Edward remembered when they weaned him off of his various daily medications over a year ago. At first, he felt more screwed up in the head than he did on the pills, but the staff reassured him that was natural. His body chemistry needed to readjust to life without them. They were right! It took him several weeks to feel "normal," which, to his realization, was better than he had ever felt since he walked in here. He always thought it was odd that you come to a place like this for "help," but are immediately put into an unstable situation of shock and medication. He had no clue during his first meeting with Doctor Law that his foster parents had already left, not until a nursing administrator came in to help show him to his room. When he heard that phrase and realized his family had abandoned him, he fell into a dark and frenzied panic. He tried to run down the hallway toward the door he came in through, but there was no handle on his side of it. He was trapped.

After the administrator dragged him to his room, he entered a semi-catatonic depressive state. The next week was full of random explosions of emotions, followed by a dormant withdrawn state. The only reason it didn't last longer was the medication they forced him to take. After the first week, it took hold and altered his mental state to the point of not caring about anything anymore. He became what he overheard the staff call a "neutral." Someone not happy nor sad, existing somewhere in the middle. After a few years, Edward determined the entire pattern of care depended on everyone being a neutral. Neutrals were easier to control; they accepted the treatment. Most did not know they were ill and were so emotionally disconnected from the world, they were not aware of anything going on around them. Edward differed from the others.

Unlike most of the patients in the facility, Edward was not mentally or emotionally ill. Nor was he disturbed or suffering from anything. In reality, he was highly intelligent. Just misunderstood. His intelligence allowed him to see through the treatments even while on the medications. Medications that didn't address any of the reasons he was there. The more he studied the treatment method they were using on him, the more he started understanding the game. A game he had to master to make them think he had recovered from whatever they thought was wrong with him.

"No, sir, no side effects in over a year. To be honest, Doctor Law, I have never felt better."

"What about relapses? Last time we talked, you said it had been months since you had seen any images."

It was time for Edward to submit his performance for a Best Actor nomination. In a very controlled, confident, yet casual tone, he said, "I can't remember the last time I saw the image of someone that was not there."

Edward made sure to not look up at the audience of five blue and white semi-translucent individuals gathered behind Doctor Law. They were in the room roaming around and exploring when Edward sat down. The two-way mirror was a spot of extreme fascination for all but one of them. That one stood in the corner, swaying from side to side. As they moved, they floated through each other instead of bumping into one another. Their interaction, or lack thereof, made it appear as though they were unaware of each other or anyone else in the room. Some of the figures were familiar to Edward. He saw them often, but the one in the corner was a rare visitor. She only showed up for special occasions.

The first time he saw one of his "special friends" he was nine and scared shitless. It was late at night, and he got out of bed to go to the bathroom. Before he even opened the bedroom door, he felt something. It was sitting at the end of the hallway, surrounded by a glowing fog. It had the form of an old man and was fading in and out, allowing Edward to see right through him. The sight caused Edward to freeze in his tracks as a cold prickly sweat broke out all over his body. His pulse quickened to the pace of a machine gun, which he could hear in his own ears. The feeling of an immense weight fell over him, dulling the remaining senses. A feeling he still felt every time. Sometimes it was stronger, but it did not paralyze him anymore. Over the years, he learned to control it.

Edward tried to scream, but nothing came out, like in a nightmare. But that was no nightmare. That was real. He felt a warm trickle of liquid drizzle down the inside of his thigh. He tried to scream again, and that time the sound came out full volume, summoning his foster parents, who ran into the hall to his side. Edward attempted to point out the man to them, but they could not see him. Thinking it was another one of his night-terrors, they took him to the bathroom to clean him up. He pulled against them and fought every step as they moved closer to the haunting vision. Once inside the bathroom, Edward would not take his eyes off the door the whole time he was in there. He feared that the man would come in there after them, but he didn't.

The next night, one floated over his bed as he laid down to sleep. He thought about screaming, but to what end? They would run in, but not believe him. Instead, he pulled his covers up as high as he could to hide from the image and fight the chill consuming his shaking body. He squeezed his eyes shut, trying to force himself to fall asleep, which had the opposite effect. Eventually it vanished, leading to several apprehensive moments while Edward laid there waiting to see if it would return.

That continued every night. Sometimes it was one presence; other nights groups would encircle his bed. They never moved or made any sounds. They stood, or floated, there as if they were on guard duty, or just enjoyed watching him sleep.

It took a few years before the fear subsided. He noticed he felt their presence before they showed up, which cut down on the surprise. He tried to talk to them, but they never responded. He tried to walk toward them and around them, but they never acknowledged him. It was as if they had no awareness that Edward was even there. A fact that Edward enjoyed. Over time, he noticed a few regulars, so he gave them names, and when no one was around, he would greet them. "What's up, Bob?" and "I like you, Bob. You never hide anything from me. You are completely transparent." His all-time favorite joke that his twelve-year-old sense of humor loved was, "You look boo-tiful today."

"And you understand now that what you were seeing was not real. They were not real people, or 'ghosts', as you once called them. It was all in your mind, caused by the traumatic loss of your parents, right?" Without lifting his head, Doctor Law studied Edward's reaction over the edge of his wire-framed glasses.

"Oh, yes sir. Absolutely. I was just a child when my parents died. When I walked in and saw them lying there on the floor like that, I was torn to pieces. It was that 'emotional distress,' as you call it, that caused me to see people who are not really there. As we discussed in our many conversations, the images I saw were because of my desire to see my parents again. Once I realized that, I stopped seeing them and knew how silly my outbursts were. I feel horrible about how I treated my foster parents." Edward hoped he didn't spread it on too thick. He spent years perfecting the art of the game.

"Very good. You have been very well adjusted for the last few years. It is so seldom we have such a successful breakthrough, but I am happy to see it." Doctor Law made a few notes. "With today being your eighteenth birthday, and with the great progress you have made, I believe we might have some very good news for you."

With a feigned surprised look: "Really? What is it?" In reality, Edward knew exactly what it was. He had been working toward this day for several years.

4

A frustrated father pounded on the closed door of the hotel room bathroom containing his sixteen-year-old daughter. "Come on Sarah, let's go." They had been on the road for two days, make that two long days, cooped up together in the cab of a moving truck. They had only another three hours to drive to reach their destination. The original plan was to get an early start. That plan did not include her hour-long shower and two hours of make-up artistry. Edward and his seven-year-old son, Jacob, were packed and ready to leave over an hour ago. Instead, they waited and mindlessly flipped through the few TV channels available.

After he left the facility on his eighteenth birthday, he reunited with his foster parents. Everything was great the second time around. They felt bad for leaving him there and worked hard to be the family he had needed for the last four years. He put in the effort too, and suppressed his "quirks" as much as he could. Four years later, he walked across the stage and received a Bachelor of Arts in Education with a minor in English. It still brings a smile to his face every time he thinks of how proud they were of him.

His foster father was surprised by the choice of English. Before he went away, Edward was obsessed with computers and technology. In the hospital, Edward found comfort in escaping into a good story as a buffer against what he was surrounded by day in and day out. During his years of institutionalization, he read a shocking three hundred and thirty-one books. His reading material covered every genre imaginable, but anytime he could get his hands on one of the American Masters, like Melville or Hemingway, it was heaven on earth. He found an appreciation for those works. Before that, the only reading he did was for school assignments, and even then, he waited until the last minute and tried to skim it to learn what he needed to take a test or write a report. A few times, he even just rented the movie version of the book to cram for a test. All he really crammed during those sessions was popcorn and soda. His grade on the test showed him how different the movies were from the actual books.

During the many nights he passed reading, he saw the story as a movie playing in his head, letting his imagination run wild and take him to a place far away from the clinical walls that surrounded him.

After college, he moved to Portland, Oregon to take a High School English teaching job. He had other offers that were more local, but his foster mother grew up in the Pacific Northwest and after all the years of hearing her talk about it and showing him pictures, he felt a yearning inside him that he needed to explore.

It did not disappoint. The serenity of the various nature trails surrounding the area, combined with the small-town environment with big city luxuries, felt like the perfect fit. He never thought he could be happier. That was, of course, until his third year of teaching when he saw Karen Lynwood, the new history teacher, walking down the hallway. She was a vision that took his breath away: long flowing raven hair, piercing blue eyes, a smile that would not just light up the room, but the entire skyline. Edward, never one to wait, was slightly forward, and during lunch on the first day of school, he walked right up to her in the teacher's lounge and asked her out. Edward was not socially awkward. Quite the opposite. He was outgoing, and, he had encouragement from his special friends. After she said yes, Edward asked her for her name, and then introduced himself. That became a joke they would share on every anniversary together, then at their wedding, and then every wedding anniversary after that. One their children would mock at each retelling.

A few years ago, his wife complained of feeling constantly exhausted. She was never one to slow down and take care of herself. Between all the children's activities, her teaching, and the strict fitness regimen she had followed since college, Edward was convinced she had run herself ragged. He encouraged her day after day to take a break, but she resisted. Knowing there was only one way to help, Edward stepped in and took on many of Karen's daily responsibilities with the hope she would use the time off to rest.

For the first few days, Karen resisted. She would find other ways to fill her newly freed time. Each time, Edward would intercede. It turned into a game between them that produced a laugh from time to time. But the humor soon died as the fatigue became too much for Karen to deal with. She needed to stay in bed most weekends to regain her strength for the following week.

After a few weeks, she finally gave in and went to see the doctor. Edward thought the most horrific sight he would see in his life was the bodies of his dead parents, but he was wrong. Very wrong. That didn't even come close to the sight of the look on Karen's face when she told him she had aggressive breast cancer. She had just returned from the doctors, seated in the corner of the teacher's lounge waiting for Edward, all the color gone from her face along with her sparkling blue eyes. In their place sat lifeless dark orbs that resembled pieces of expressionless coal. To say it was unexpected would be an understatement. She was so young, every prior medical exam missed it. Her family had no history of cancer or any illness. Edward kept thinking about all the plans they had for the future, all the plans they would never be able to see come true.

The next eighteen months became the source of nightmares. Endless doctor visits, surgeries, treatments promising a fraction of a hope, and disappointment after disappointment. She declined quickly. It started out with fatigue. Then she was bedridden. She eventually needed a specialized hospital bed and in-home care. Then hospice after just a matter of months. Everything in Edward and the kids' lives ceased to exist during that time.

The worse she got, the more effort Edward put into searching for a cure, but it was all for naught. On a sunny Wednesday morning, surrounded by her family and friends, the body that once contained Karen's soul took its last breath. The soul had left weeks ago; the body was just a shell of who she used to be. Edward was not sure which was harder, walking out of that facility for the last time knowing he would never be back to visit her, or walking back into their home knowing she would never be there again.

He spent the next eight months teaching and doing anything he could to keep him and the kids out of the house. He found it unbearable to be there without her. He felt guilty just sitting there, always thinking he needed to help her, even though he knew she was gone. At night, he would swear he could hear her voice whispering through the halls. Every time he jumped up and went running through the house hoping to catch a glimpse of her. Only twice he saw her walking down the hallway. It seemed very real. She was there, interacting with objects in the house, so real he thought he could reach out and touch her. She was always alone. He never saw any others when he saw her. He also never felt the normal cold shivers or tingling in the spine. She looked healthier than she had in months, exactly how he wanted to remember her. Every time he moved toward her; she would disappear before he could reach her.

When the school year ended, Edward knew he and the kids had to leave if they were ever going to feel normal again. He searched online for teaching jobs in neighboring cities, but found nothing. He widened his search nationally and came across one in his old hometown of Miller's Crossing. He applied and heard back from Principal Rob Stephens in just a few days. The interview went so well he hired him right on the spot. Edward felt relieved and hopeful. It could not have worked out any better. He had a job in his old hometown, and they even had a place to live. He would just have to face the demons he'd left that night on his family's old farm.

They packed up their lives and memories, and with just a week before the new school year began, the three of them headed out on what Edward called "A New Adventure." The drive took a few days. They took their time and saw some sights. While he tried to make the move as enjoyable as he could for his children, the anxiety inside him ramped up with every passing mile. He had not been back in his old house since the day he found his parents. Each time he tried to picture what it would look like; he only saw the image of his parents on the kitchen floor.

"OK, Dad, I'm ready."

Edward thought to himself, *thank God,* Jacob expressed the sentiment out loud. His exclamation drew a look of disgust and a light slap to the back of the head from his sister as she walked by. Jacob followed her out and tried to get a revenge shot at her before they loaded up. Edward sat there for just a second before turning off the TV and letting out a little sigh before he followed them to begin the last three hours of their trip.

5

After an uneventful three hours' drive through the scenic mountainous countryside, they reached a sign indicating their cross-country trek was just about complete.

Now Entering Miller's Crossing
Population 12,379

"Do they change the sign every time someone is born or dies?" sniped the teenager, still distraught about leaving the big-city life behind.

"Oh, stop it, Sarah." It is a good question that Edward had never considered. Did they reduce it by three when his parents died, and he left?

As they drove into town, the woods and hills gave way to sporadic houses on large lots. There were no fences separating each yard, which Sarah and Jacob had never seen. He explained things are different out here.

The houses were all different styles; no subdivisions or sprawling apartment complexes, with their resort style pools and entertainment areas. Just house after house, unchanged for generations. The only thing they had in common was a mailbox out by the street with their family's name on it.

Absent were the expansive galleria or malls, instead having just a few strips of locally owned stores in the center of the city. The closest thing to name brand stores were Walt's Hardware and Lucy's Bakery.

As they passed through the center of the town, the scene returned to cozy homes nestled back in the woods. Sounding somewhat panicked, Sarah asked, "Dad, where is the Walmart?"

"Oh honey, there isn't one here. I think there is one a few towns over."

Sarah whipped her head around with a stunned expression. "What? There isn't one? Is there a movie theater? An organic store? What about a Macy's?"

Edward thought, *there goes Sarah's weekend mall-scapades.*

While the culture shock set in on his daughter, Edward sensed a comfortable familiarity setting in. "When I grew up here, there was a movie theater out on Route 22 just before you got to Sterling, maybe a forty-minute drive away, but it only had two screens."

Just the thought of only two screens left Sarah's mouth agape.

Edward added a little more fuel to the fire. "Oh, just wait until you see the high school. It's coming up in just a few minutes down the road."

The sight of the elementary school nearly brought a tear to Edward's eye. It looked like it did when he was a student there. The playground in the front with the swings made of metal chains and rubber seats, the metal monkey bars, the slide. The flagpole with the American flag flying proudly out front. He doubted anyone here protested its display or asked to have it taken down; something that was common in the larger cities. The trees looked bigger. His mind drifted back to memories of running in through those doors trying to beat the bell, playing baseball on the simple clay diamond during the spring, and the school fall festival.

The screams of his daughter and hysterical laughter of his son interrupted his trip down memory lane. "DAD! What the hell is that? Is that Rydell High from Grease? This is not the fifties."

Just like the elementary school, Miller's Crossing High School looked like the school time forgot. The building was not modern, in any sense of the word. A large, long, two-story, red-brick, window-lined building with a simple roof over it. A large central staircase wound up the hill in the front, right up to the main doors. The sign out front underneath its own flagpole proudly flying old glory announced the start of school in four days. Behind the parking lot on the side was a large football field with metal bleachers on either side and two small scoreboards at either end, with the Coca-Cola sign in the middle of it. Of course, his parents took him to every home game; everyone in town attended them. The homecoming games were special nights that were among his fondest memories. His father dressed Edward in his old jersey and his mom wore his dad's old letter jacket. At halftime, the band formed an arch around midfield as they called out one by one the former players that were in attendance. One by one, they walked out to midfield amid the cheers of those in the stands and oh, how they cheered for his father. Edward and his mom clapped and screamed when they called his name.

"Sarah, it's a great school. You'll love it there. Plus, I'll be teaching there."

That thought hit her right between the eyes. "Ewww, you're teaching at the same school? Why aren't you at the other high school, like back home?"

"This is the only high school."

Sarah's sigh announced her disappointment at the appeal of attending the same school where her father would be teaching. That had never happened before.

A few roads past the high school, Edward took the familiar left down the grass driveway toward the old family farm. As many times as he thought about selling this place, he never could. He reached out to a local realtor once about selling, but changed his mind. The realtor put him in touch with someone who could help take care of the property until he finally made the decision. From how things looked, the thirty dollars every three months was money well spent. The mown yard and old farmland to either side of the driveway were a welcome surprise.

His anticipation grew as he maneuvered the van up over a modest hill and around the corner, giving him the first look in decades at his home. Oh yes, the caretaker's services were well worth the price. The house looked great. The screen on the wraparound front porch was still intact, none of the bushes around it overgrown. The storm shutters were off and stored, probably in the shed, like he requested a few weeks back.

He pulled to a stop next to the front door, got out, and walked to the door. There was an envelope stuck in the door jamb. Edward pulled it out and opened it.

Welcome home, Edward.

- Jim Morris

That note was one of the little pleasures of living in a small town that Edward had missed so much. When they moved to the Portland area, the neighbors watched them through the window. None of them said anything for weeks.

Edward fished the front door key out of his pocket and looked up, pausing at the image of his mother standing at the door with her arms extended as if to hug him. He stood there and talked to himself. "Steady now. You didn't see that. It's just the stress of coming back here. Come on." Her vision, now and at this place, was almost too much for Edward to handle. The encounter did not have the same eerie feeling he sometimes experienced. Instead, a warm and welcoming feeling overcame him. It invoked memories of her welcoming him home from school like she did so many days. He forced himself to hold it together, but couldn't resist quietly saying, "Hi, Mom. I'm home."

"Dad, are you OK?" Jacob asked as he walked up next to his father.

Edward steadied himself. "Yep, just thinking. Let's go in." With that, he pushed the key in, and it opened right up. There was no evidence of the lock sticking like Jim Morris mentioned. He must have squirted some lubricant into it.

When he opened the door, only a hint of stale air escaped, which came as a relief to Edward. He walked in and looked around, half expecting to see boxes all over the place. Instead, it was just as he last remembered it: the sofa with the eighties floral print, books still left on the bookshelf, the console TV that he was sure his kids won't know how to operate, the loop rug on the dark hardwood floor. All the things from his childhood were where he left them. But the one area that grabbed his attention most was the table full of family photos, all framed and sitting on display. How he wished someone had packed up even one of those and sent them with him when he left that night. He took nothing with him, just the clothes on his back. Something as simple as a family photo would have meant the world to him.

"Well, guys, this is where your dad lived when he was a little boy," he announced.

Sarah and Jacob explored the family room, inspecting everything. While Edward couldn't get over how everything was as he remembered it, his kids struggled to see past the layers and layers of dust that had built up over the years. Edward saw Sarah drawing a very distinct line in the layer while running her finger along one of the shelves.

"So, it needs a little cleaning. This will be great, guys. Some of my happiest memories happened right here on this farm." Edward ignored the customary teenage rolling of the eyes. "Let me show you guys around."

6

It was a long day of cleaning and unloading the van for Edward and his children, but finally, it was done and time for everyone to settle down and relax before falling to sleep. Edward had a feeling the sleep part would come much faster than they expected. When they stopped to eat some dinner, Jacob nearly fell asleep at the table. Edward wanted to make sure the kids were all set before the end of the day. Something about living out of a box always felt unsettling to him, and he didn't want them to have to feel that way, even for a night. To his satisfaction, he achieved his goal. Sarah was set up in his father's old office, which was larger than his old bedroom. Jacob jumped at the chance to take his dad's old room. It had what he called a "neat window" in it. The neat window was a tiny alcove created by a dormer on the front side of the house. Edward always liked that spot too. As a kid he sat on that ledge and watched for his dad to come home from work.

Edward's back felt the strain of unloading all the kids' furniture and boxes. He rubbed it as he walked up the stairs to his room for some much-needed rest. It seemed simple enough, but entering his parents' room proved more difficult than he expected. He had stacked a few boxes of his belongings in the hallway, but nothing had made it inside yet. He stood at the door for a few moments and tried to gather up the nerve to even open it, something he had not done yet. The room was their sanctuary. His mind struggled with accepting his role as head of the household in this home. With a mind too tired to battle psychological ghosts, he conceded there was always tomorrow and headed downstairs to the old comfy sofa in the family room. The same one he spent many a Saturday morning lounging on while watching cartoons.

He attempted to get comfortable but faced a realization: either the sofa has gotten smaller, or he was bigger. He used to be able to lay the entire length of his body on the sofa with room to spare; now his feet hung off unless he laid on his side in a partial fetal position. He grabbed the remote off the table next to the sofa and turned on the flat screen TV they'd placed on top of the old console model. He fiddled through the channels for a few moments. Unable to find anything, he finally just let it land on whatever channel it was on when he grew tired of changing it. It didn't matter, though. He watched it for only a few moments before falling asleep like he did so many times as a child. Unlike when he was a child, three shimmering figures loomed over him. Edward was too tired to notice. He pulled the blanket up in response to the chill.

When he woke up, there was an infomercial grinding in the background. He reached blindly toward the floor searching for the remote, which he found, and clicked it off. He had every intention of falling back to sleep in the silence, but he didn't find the silence he hoped for. At first, he thought the sound came from one of the kids' televisions. He pulled the blanket up and rolled over, but after a few minutes he sat up and listened intently. His ears were hearing something real and close by. It was the unmistakable sound of a human voice, and not just one, but several of them, and they were outside.

He reached to the table beside him and disconnected his cell phone from the charger. A quick glance at the time revealed it was only two a.m. Now the sounds of people outside might be odd, but not unheard of in the city. But not here, and not on the old family farm out in the middle of nowhere. The thought of kids using their vacant lot for an innocent adolescent late-night hangout made some sense to Edward. The house had been vacant for so long and no one knew they have moved in. A simple warning and request that they move along should end the party.

He opened the door expecting to see a few pickups and cars on the property, but he saw nothing. The voices sounded distant, but Edward couldn't tell from which direction. He stepped off the porch and walked around the house and looked out at the empty pastures. It was a cool night, a touch of fog hanging above the ground. It felt rather refreshing compared to the oppressive heat of the summer day. A chill shot down the back of his neck, followed by the appearance of a few drops of cold sweat and tingly nerves. Edward recognized the feeling and thought, *not now please* as he continued to search for the source of the sounds.

He searched for several minutes, but still saw nothing, Edward was about to give up when he noticed a quick glint of light flash toward him from the southeast corner of his property. He walked toward that area, not taking his eyes off that spot the entire way. He thought about running in that direction to scare whoever it was away, but decided to be cautious until he saw who was there.

It took Edward several minutes to get close enough to see anything. With each flash of light he saw, Edward stopped to observe for a few seconds before he started creeping forward again. Soon, though, he saw the source of the light, as multiple forms holding flashlights came into view. It appeared to be several people in a line. They walked at a casual but determined pace with their lights focused on something straight in front of them. Edward froze dead in his tracks. About fifty feet in front of the line of people, he saw *them*. They were there but not at the same time. They had a human shape and form, but solid black, lifeless eyes. They never touched the ground. The scene was all too familiar to Edward. He crouched down among the tall grass and watched.

They stayed well in front of the line of people behind them. The line yelled at them like cowboys driving cattle on a ranch. Only a few of the pursuers yelled. Each exclamation put down the protests of the two ghastly floating creatures, who complied and moved forward toward the tree line at the edge of his property.

They faded in and out as they moved through the empty field. Both appeared to be male and dressed in pants and a shirt of some type. One appeared to be holding something. He occasionally brandished it like a weapon above his head. Each time he did, one from the line behind them stepped forward, held up something small in his hands, and admonished him.

The pace of the two glowing creatures slowed down. That allowed those following to close the gap, but from Edward's vantage point that appeared to be intentional. They slowed and turned slightly, instead of heading straight forward, and eventually stopped altogether. They held their position, flickering in and out of visibility inside a light patch of fog. The largest vision glared back over his shoulder at the individuals following them, and let out a protest that sent a chill through Edward's essence. The sound was not a scream or a yell, more primal and otherworldly, and created a tremble of fear in Edward's hands to go along with the chill.

The line of pursuers stopped, which appeared to only embolden both creatures. The second one turned around completely, pointed at them, and bellowed an inhuman scream. Edward's pulse quickened as he felt a terror grow in him. A terror similar to what he felt that first time in the hallway so many years ago.

The man stepped forward again. This time in the moonlight, Edward saw he was an older man, dressed in all black. Edward leaned forward slightly to see what he held, but the distance was too great, and he didn't dare to move any closer. The mysterious man in black spoke to the creatures in a voice that pierced the cool night air. "Let God arise and let His enemies be scattered, and let them that hate Him flee from before His Face!"

Both wailed wildly again, louder than before. The man in black was unfazed and continued to preach at them. "O' Most Glorious Prince of the Heavenly Armies, St. Michael the Archangel, defend us in the battle and in our wrestling against principalities and powers against the rulers of the world of this darkness..."

They reacted as though a great force had pushed against them. Each held up their hands to shield themselves. They turned without a sound and continued toward the wood line, with the man in black following them, continuing his recitation. The line followed close behind as if to ensure they continued heading toward their destination, wherever that might be.

The duo and the glowing flashlights of those following them disappeared among the dense woods that surrounded Edward's family farm, leaving him standing in the damp cool night, confused and terrified, with the sounds of crickets replacing the voices and wails that had filled the air. He stood there for a few moments more, listening and watching for any signs of them before he turned and took several terrifying steps back toward the house, looking back at the woods over his shoulder with every sound he heard.

Back in his house, Edward securely closed the front door and double checked each lock. He settled back onto the sofa and turned on the TV. Edward did not try to lie down, instead, he sat there thinking about what he saw over and over. The sounds of the night stayed firmly stuck in his head. There would be no sleeping for Edward for the rest of the night.

7

The alarm on Edward's phone went off at 6:30 the next morning, but he didn't need it, he was awake. Of all times to deal with only a few hours of sleep, his first day at work was the worst possible day. Not feeling the caffeine of his second cup of coffee kicking in, Edward headed upstairs. He hoped a hot shower would help.

As Edward crested the top of the stairs, he heard the bathroom door close. One of the kids beat him to it. Now all the soap and shampoo in the house was behind a closed door. He was forced to stand there and wait. Following the sound of a flush, Sarah opened the door and sleepwalked past him. Edward was unsure if all the commotion outside woke her up at some point last night, or this was the normal teenage state for that time of the morning, so he inquired, "Sarah, did you have any problems sleeping last night? Did you hear anything?"

She never even stopped, just yawned as she closed her door. He muttered to himself, "Teenagers."

After his shower, he felt more human than he did before, but he still couldn't shake the sights and sounds of the previous night. Edward mostly kept things to himself. He spent some time in college trying to research the meaning and cause of his visions, even going as far as talking to a parapsychologist once. He realized there were two schools of thought: those that didn't believe in the ability to see spirits or visions of people like that, and those that did. Each person who believed in the ability had a different theory around why. None of the theories had anything scientific backing them. Several of them theorized that a person could see the spirit or afterimage of a person they had a connection with before their death. That was the one theory Edward could dismiss without question. Over the years, the only images he'd had a prior connection with were his parents and his wife, the other thousands were just random strangers. The remaining theories, the several dozen he read about, all differed from a connection to a location, to a spiritual time vortex—which Edward could never understand—to just a random combination of events, which to him seemed more likely. What Edward knew for sure was that what he saw last night was real and not some sort of hallucination, and at least one other person saw them too. Now, what to do with that knowledge?

That would have to wait, though. He needed to focus on his first day at work. Ready to head out the door, he poked his head into Sarah's room to give her some instructions for the day. "Are you awake?"

She did not respond, so he repeated the question, louder this time, "I am heading to work. Are you awake?"

There was a single groan from the direction of the mass of covers clumped on her bed.

"Remember to make sure Jacob eats breakfast and see if you guys can do more unpacking. I want to get these boxes out of here. I should be home just after three, OK?" He waited for a response, which finally came in the form of a single hand thrust out of the covers giving a thumbs up and then a quick wave goodbye.

He closed her door, knowing they would both be asleep until ten o'clock, and headed out. The drive to work brought back tons of memories, just like the drive in. Of course, the difference was now he was driving, and, in his memories, he was a passenger sitting next to one of his parents. Edward's thoughts distracted him so much he nearly missed the turn into the high school, another place he had been many times before. For the first time though, he took a slight veer to the right into the faculty parking lot. Once parked, he sat there for a few moments in his quiet car before heading in. He needed to clear his mind.

Walking up the front walk, he realized he had never been inside the high school before. Plenty of trips to the football stadium with his parents, but never inside, so this really was a first for him. He followed the signs that directed him to the office, feeling a tad nervous about meeting with the principal, a something he found no one ever shook from their days as a student.

Edward walked into the office as two other teachers exited. They greeted him with a friendly good morning as they passed by him. To him, it felt rather welcoming, and it helped to calm his first-day nerves. So much so that he felt rather confident as he walked up to the counter that separated the office into the traditional two halves, student, and faculty. He waited there for a few seconds before a woman on the other side of the counter acknowledged him. Small picture frames covered her desk. She turned and flashed him a big smile across her cherub face and, in the most welcoming and sweetest voice, asked, "Can I help you, sir?"

"Yes, ma'am." Edward never stopped addressing people with the polite *ma'am, miss, missus,* or *mister* no matter what his or their age. "I am Edward Meyer. I am here to see Principal Stephens."

"Oh, the new English teacher. Welcome." She grabbed a stack of folders and a brown envelope from her desk and brought them over to the counter. She told Edward what was inside each as she slid them across the countertop to him. "Here is your class schedule and rosters, and of course your key. Robert is yelling at the painters in the gym; they were supposed to have the gym floor completed before today. He will be back shortly. Just have a seat. Oh, and welcome." She motioned toward a few chairs lined against the wall on his side of the counter.

Edward took a seat and looked through his schedule and class roster. He'd have five English classes each day, and it looked like each class would have just under thirty students, both a surprise and a relief. Where he taught in the past, the class sizes approached forty, and one year he had forty-three in one class. In his opinion, a class of that size hindered his abilities as a teacher and limited open class discussion and the learning of the students.

A single unfamiliar voice shot through the constant ringing of phones and chatter of people coming in and out. "Eddie?"

Edward scanned the room for the source of the voice. Having no idea what Principal Stephens looked like, and assuming no one would recognize him, he assumed that was who called him; even though he never called him Eddie during any of their prior conversations. As Edward stood up, he extended the hand toward the middle-aged man who stood before him with a big smile on his bearded face. "It is great to meet you, Principal Stephens."

A full-bodied laugh met his introduction. Edward felt a lump form in his stomach.

"Now that is a good one. I am not Robert. You don't recognize me?"

Edward studied his face. "I'm sorry, but not really."

"I'm Mark Grier. We were in the same class from kindergarten until you left in the second grade. We were even on the same baseball team twice. I heard you were coming back to Miller's Crossing. I wasn't sure I could recognize you, but with how much you look like your dad, it was easy." Mark looked at the woman behind the counter and asked, "Ms. Adams, you remember Eddie Meyer, don't you?"

She looked up from her computer monitor and for a brief second looked like she had seen a ghost. It was a face that Edward had seen himself make in the mirror a few times. The color returned to her face as a smile grew. "Oh, wow. I didn't even recognize you. I can't believe you're so grown up. I remember when you and Mark both came in and were registered for your first day of school. Welcome home, Eddie."

Edward examined her closer and a brief memory crossed his eyes: the older woman now standing behind the counter was the same young woman that basically ran the elementary school while he was there. "Ms. Adams?"

"Yes, Eddie. It's me."

"I am so sorry. I didn't recognize you either. When did you leave the elementary school?"

"It's OK, Eddie. I guess I should call you Mr. Meyer now since you are a teacher. I came over here some twenty years ago when the position opened up. I needed a change of scenery, so I drove the three hundred feet down the road for that change." She gave him a wry smile that matched the dry humor of her statement, one trait he remembered about her.

Mark asked, "So, Eddie, where is your classroom?"

"I'm not sure yet." Which was true, Edward still hasn't opened the envelope with his key in it.

Ms. Adams remembered, though. "He is in 343, just down the hall from you, Mr. Grier." She pushed her glasses down to the tip of her nose and looked at them with a sinister look. "This isn't going to be a mistake, is it? I seem to remember you two getting into a lot of trouble together when you were younger."

"Of course not. We have long outgrown putting a potato in your car's tailpipe or a whoopie cushion in your chair. I will say toilet papering your rose bushes is still not out of the question though." Mark gave Edward a light slap on the back. "Do you think Robert will mind if I take him up?"

"Not at all. I will send him up to see you as soon as he returns… and you two, stay away from my rose bushes." Ms. Adams issued that warning with a rather humorous shaking of the fingers at the two nearly forty-year-olds like they were still the same mischievous kids they were back then.

"Let's go. It is so good to see you Eddie…" and with that, Mark walked Edward out of the office and up to his classroom. The walk turned into a dizzying fast trip down memory lane, some of the memories were just as if they were yesterday, others he didn't remember at all. As Mark continued to recount their childhood, Edward took in the school and looked for any other friendly faces he might recognize. It has been thirty years since he saw any of his old friends, but there may be a chance he might recognize a few. Mark recognized him, even though he didn't recognize Mark. When he accepted the job and moved back home, he knew running into his history would be something he could not avoid. The thought both excited and terrified him.

"So where are you living?"

"Back at my parents' old farm with my kids."

Edward's response caused Mark to pause for the first time since he greeted him in the office. The thought of someone moving back into the home where their parents were murdered may be disturbing, but Edward couldn't see any other option.

Mark broke the awkward silence and asked, "Back home with your kids. Wow, you are all grown up. How old are they?"

"My daughter Sarah is sixteen and Jacob is seven."

"Sixteen, huh? So, going to school here? My son Chase is seventeen, he's the tight end on the football team, even has a few schools looking at him for a scholarship. Mostly just Division II schools, nothing like your dad, the legend, did back in his day. But hey, you can get a great education at those places and that's what matters, right?"

"Absolutely… and yes, Sarah thinks she is going to die a million deaths going to the same school I'm teaching at. This would be the first time that has happened."

A wide evil grin stretched across Mark's face. "Oh, really? Then you, my old friend, are in for a treat. First, there is the seeing each other in the hallway and they turn and go the other way. Then there are the crazy looks at home followed by the random accusations of embarrassing them by doing absolutely nothing. But the best of all... you ready for this? The looks you get from your fellow teachers for something they did."

"I see what I've been missing out on for all these years."

Mark stopped at a door and turned toward Edward. Assuming this was his classroom, he looked up and saw the "343" on the sloppily painted around room number plate. He now saw why Principal Stephens might be yelling at the painters. Edward tore open the envelope with the key but stopped as Mark reached forward and opened the door.

"Too much time in the big city. We don't lock anything around here."

He was right, Edward had spent too much time away from the small-town environment. The thought of not locking everything up from the front door at home, his car, and even the door to his classroom was completely foreign and unnerving. "I guess there is a lot I have to get used to, Mark. I spent most of my life in places where they locked everything." Edward decided not to elaborate on the last part of that statement. He was not sure how anyone would react to hearing he was locked away in a mental facility for a while.

Before he stepped into the classroom, a voice echoed from down the hallway. "Mr. Meyer, I see you found your classroom."

A mid-fifties, balding man wearing a buttoned up white shirt, black slacks, and black-rimmed glasses walked toward them. He extended his hand toward Edward, who returned the gesture. He had a firm grip, evident by the twitching muscles exposed below his rolled-up sleeves.

Going out on a limb, "Principal Stephens, it is great to meet you." Inside, Edward hoped he had guessed correctly. One moment of embarrassment today was enough.

"Call me Robert. I insist."

With confidence brimming from being right, he said, "Alright, then. You can call me Edward."

"I will unless students are around. I see Mark showed you to your classroom. So, what do you think? Not the same as what you are used to?"

With a sheepish tone to his voice, Edward confessed, "Well, actually, I haven't been in yet."

"Don't let me stop you. Let's have a look."

Edward stepped inside and returned to a simpler time. The walls were painted cinderblocks, not drywall or paneling like he was used to. Lights hung from a dropped ceiling. A real blackboard with chalk hung on the front wall. No dry erase board here. The student desks were single unit metal seats with wooden backs and desk surfaces. One detail made Edward go wide-eyed. All along the back wall and continuing along the side of the classroom under the windows were bookshelves with what looked like complete classroom sets of the classics. Melville, Wells, Bradbury, Steinbeck, Bronte, and others. He hadn't seen such a display since he was in school and even then, it was only a book or two. At his last school, a handout listing where to obtain the books at a discount was the closest he came to this.

Edward stood speechless a few feet away from his desk, next to his own overhead projector. He took it all in before uttering a single, simple word: "Perfect."

He saw a sense of surprise at his remark on the faces of Robert and Mark, so he explained. "I'm serious. This is perfect. The newer schools with all their technology and perfect modern classrooms are rather... institutional." *Not really*, Edward thought to himself, but he could not think of another word at the moment. "There are times you feel disconnected from the students in those environments. The simple experience of reading from a proper book and not some e-reader creates a more lasting memory and experience. The feel and smell of the old papers that have been flipped through by scores of students before you. And the desks, proper desks. Most of the classes I have been in had tables and chairs where many students would have their back to me. I would have to either remind them to turn around or walk around the class as I lectured and talk to make eye contact with them while losing the connection with others. This is perfect."

Principal Stephens looked rather pleased with the explanation. "Great. We still do a lot of things here the older ways. We find they still work. I will let you get settled in. The first faculty meeting of the year is at ten in the auditorium. See you there."

With the principal gone, Mark closed the door behind him. "Eddie, I need to show you one trick. Don't let Robert's nice guy act fool you too much. He has a few quirks." Mark walked to the back of the room, where a clear box hung on the wall. "He wants all classrooms kept at seventy-two degrees, but on this side of the school the sun can make things warm in the afternoon."

Mark fished a bent paperclip out of his pocket as Edward moved in for a closer view. Holding it up on display with one hand and pointing out the shape with the other. "If you bend it just right, you can push it into one of these vents on top of the box and slide the lever slightly, kind of like that." Edward heard a click followed by the sounds of the overhead air conditioner starting. A few seconds later, a slight breeze of cooler air moved around him.

Feeling there was an obvious question hanging in the air, Edward asked it. "Wait, there is a lock on the box. We don't get a key?"

"Nope, not at all. Robert has one, each of the custodians have one so they can reset them each night, and that is it." Mark held up the bent paperclip. "I have my special key. I will show you how to make one."

"Appreciate it."

Mark hung around and helped Edward set up his classroom, even though it was basically ready when he walked in. They moved the desks into neat rows. Edward's desk was in the center of the room, but he preferred to stand there during lectures, so they pushed it toward the side of the room. Edward half expected to clean most of his first day, but he found himself astonished at the cleanliness of the classroom.

While they moved things around, Mark and Edward continued catching up. Edward told him about his wife, how they met, and how he lost her, which was the catalyst to moving back to Miller's Crossing. Mark felt bad and gave Edward his heartfelt condolences. He married his high school sweetheart, someone Edward remembered as Skipping Sharon. She skipped everywhere. Down the hallway. Across the schoolyard, hell, he even remembered seeing Sharon skip across the classroom once when the teacher called her up to her desk. Skipping without a care in the world with her long brown pigtails bouncing behind her. Edward was tempted to ask Mark if she skipped through the house, but decided to leave the past in the past. Mark told Edward she sold real estate across the three towns that made up their county seat. To Edward, it sounded like Mark had a very happy and stable life with a good job, loving wife, great kid, the complete package. *Lucky bastard.*

Just before ten, they headed down to the faculty meeting. During the walk, Mark addressed Edward with a hint of cautiousness in his voice. "Eddie?"

"Yes?"

"Been meaning to ask but wasn't sure how. How are things back in the old home?"

"It has been good. I hired someone to keep up the maintenance on it while I was gone, and he did an excellent job. Need to do a little cleaning. Not too much. The kids will do more of it today, I hope. We should be able to finish the rest tonight."

"That is not what I meant."

Edward suspected that, but hoped he was wrong. He knew someone would eventually ask about it, considering the tragic circumstances that surround the last time he was in that house. "Oh, you mean...."

"Yeah, any ghosts from the past?"

Surprised by the choice of words, he hesitated before replying, "I won't lie. It felt pretty weird the first time I walked in. A little flood of memories, both good and bad. Took me a bit to work up the nerve to walk into the kitchen. Part of me was afraid they would still be lying there, but having the kids there helps. We have been busy getting settled in." Edward left it at that. No need to bring up what he saw the night before. No need to give anyone a reason to think he was odd, yet.

8

Edward stood at his front door, arms full of books and notebooks, beads of sweat on his brow. The stifling heat of the summer afternoon hit him like a blast furnace when he exited his car and walked the twenty feet to the front door, but the sweat could also be from the stress he felt. He had just under two days to plan out the entire year and review with the head of the language department. He usually used the lesson plan from the previous year as a basis to start from. Now, teaching twelfth grade English at a new school, he had to start over from scratch.

He tried several times to balance the books in one arm and open the door, to no avail. While he considered putting the books down, he took a chance and used his foot to gently kick the door three times. He stood there hoping to hear the signs of someone coming to open the door, but there was just silence. He shifted his balance to his left side one more time so he could try to knock on the door with his foot once more as the door opened.

"Not even the first day of school and you already have homework," Sarah cracked from inside.

"Let's see if you think it's funny when this is you next week. HA!"

With an unamused eye roll, Sarah walked back toward the kitchen while Edward unloaded the books on the dining room table. The table served as a makeshift office for him, much as it did for his father growing up. Edward only remembered his family using the table to eat for special occasions like Thanksgiving. The large kitchen eat-in nook served his family fine growing up. It would work fine for the three of them.

"Did you guys finish unpacking?" he asked.

"Yep, well, everything but your stuff. I even cleaned a bit more. How did you live here with all this dust?"

Hearing his daughter complain about the dust reminded him of her mother, Karen. She was a major clean freak. The sight of their first house together almost caused heart failure. When they moved in, a layer of dust covered everything. She cleaned for close to sixteen straight hours, refusing to sit down until everything was spotless.

"It wasn't this dusty when I lived here. Remember, no one has lived here for over thirty years." Overall, Edward was impressed with how well everything looked, a combination of how well Mr. Morris took care of it and Sarah's cleaning.

"Go get cleaned up. We are going over to an old friend of mine's for dinner tonight." Sarah let out a frustrated sigh, another trait she got from her mother, and stormed upstairs. Edward followed her to the bottom of the staircase and, just as he imagined his parents must have several hundred times, he yelled upstairs, "Jacob, get ready. We are going to dinner. You guys have thirty minutes."

A groan echoed down the stairs from Sarah. Edward realized he didn't tell her how long she had to get ready before that moment. *Oops.*

Just after 7:00, they pulled into the driveway of Mark and Sharon's house. Mark must have heard them drive up. He was outside to greet them. Mark waved welcomingly from the porch as Edward and his children got out of their car.

"Hey Mark, did you hear us driving up?"

"Nah, it's a great time of night. We spend a lot of time out here on the front porch."

He remembered back to all the time spent on the porch in his younger days on nights just like this, something he would never do in the city. Too much traffic noise, smog, and any other of several things that made the experience unpleasant.

Edward herded his children toward the porch and introduced them to Mark. "This is Sarah and Jacob. Guys, this is Mark, we are friends from way back, well... when I was your age, Jacob. And now we teach together at the high school."

Mark flashed a smile. "It's nice to meet both of you. Come on, come on in." He opened the front door and invited them all inside. "Sharon, Chase, our guests are here."

A few seconds later a middle-aged woman in short pigtails skipped around the corner and through the dining room. The display produced a huge laugh from Mark, and a nervous one from Edward.

"Sorry, I couldn't resist," she said. She took the hair ties out of her hair and let braids fall free; then walked up to Edward and gave him a big old country style hug. "Hi, Edward, great to see you again. Mark was right. You really haven't changed that much."

"Hi, Sharon, you haven't either." Which was the truth. Edward was usually bad with faces, but he recognized her right off.

Sharon turned toward Edward's children, extending a hand to each. "And you must be Sarah and Jacob. Sorry about that earlier. Your father gave me a nickname back in elementary school. I couldn't resist."

"Wait now." Edward thought for a minute. He didn't remember being the original source of that name. "I may have used that name, but I don't think I created it."

"Oh please, I remember. I was seven and tripped in front of everyone while skipping down the hallway..." Sharon paused as she noticed the smile forming on Edward's face.

Sheepishly, he confessed. "Guilty. I remember. You tripped, and I yelled, DOWN GOES SKIPPING SHARON."

"Yep, and I didn't care. I got right up and kept skipping."

The three adults in the room had a great laugh while Edward's two kids stared at them like each of them had three heads.

"Ah, Chase. This is Edward Meyer and his daughter Sarah and son Jacob. Edward and I were friends when we were kids, and he will be teaching twelfth grade English this year."

A specimen of a young man extended a hand and greeted him with a firm handshake, "Hi, Mr. Meyer. So, you replaced Mrs. Henson this year."

"Uh yeah, I guess so. Nice to meet you, Chase. I hear you are quite the football player."

Chase modestly explained. "I play some ball, but nowhere near what your father was. We still see his name and records posted in the locker room and around the stadium."

Chase turned his attention to Edward's children "Hi. Welcome to Miller's Crossing. Our um... little town."

The normally not shy Sarah was wide eyed in his presence and shook his hand without saying a word. Edward had seen that expression on her face before. The father in him knew exactly what it was for. *Oh boy, here we go again.*

Sharon ushered everyone into the dining room where a great spread awaited them. Edward hadn't seen a display of comfort food like this since his mother used to cook large lunches for all of their friends after church on Sundays. His mother and her friends took turns hosting these. The women would each cook a dish and the families would gather at someone's house. After everyone ate to the point of being stuffed, the wives cleaned up and sat inside gossiping while the kids went outside to play a pickup game of baseball or football. The men were always out on a porch or in a barn of some type talking privately. When the kids ran through the house, the mothers kept on talking and acknowledged the kids as they passed through, but it was not the same with the men. If you came within earshot of the porch they were talking on or into the barn, they stopped talking and urged you to move along. They were always nice about it, but it was eerie how they watched you and didn't start talking again until you were away from them.

After a great dinner, things proceeded much like those gatherings back in the day, but with a modern twist. While Sharon cleaned up, Mark and Ed were out back talking and Jacob was trying to play basketball with Chase; Sarah was just watching, well, watching Chase. Mark and Ed both tried to help Sharon clean up, but she insisted they go on outside. She even took a few dishes out of their hands. She said she had just a few things to put away and would be right out, which must have been the truth, as she joined their conversation just a few moments later. "Mark said you are living in your folks' old place."

"Yep. I never got rid of it, so it just seemed right."

"Did you have to do a lot of work to get it ready?"

"Nah, I hired someone to act as a caretaker for it. He went by every few months and checked on it and made repairs as needed."

Sharon was taken aback at the thought of someone taking care of it. Her voice quivered as she asked, "He didn't mind?"

Edward replied reassuringly, "Not at all." Mr. Morris said nothing to Edward that gave any indication he had any apprehensions about going to the house. Just like Mark's response earlier, Edward doubted that would be the last person to react to the thought. "Mr. Morris never said anything or asked questions. Not even sure he was completely aware of the circumstances around the house."

"Jim Morris? Old Man Morris?" asked Sharon.

"Yes, he was recommended by a realtor in the area."

"Oh, he knows all about what happens- I... I... mean what happened there."

"She means the tragedy around your parents." Mark shot his wife a look as he stepped in to save her from the uncomfortable conversation she wandered into.

"Mr. Morris just likes to fix things." Mark's expression changed into a youthful, devilish half smile. "Do you remember that time when we were six and playing summer ball? Tim Wischter overthrew you at first base by twenty feet and broke the window in the side of the school building."

"Oh god, I remember that. I watched it go over my head and right into the glass. Shattered it into hundreds of pieces." Edward tried to remember if Tim ever made the throw from shortstop to first that summer.

"Mr. Morris fixed that. Tim's father offered to pay him, but Mr. Morris said he was just happy to see someone on the team had an arm on him."

Edward spit out the sip of sweet tea he just took and said, "Come on, we weren't that bad."

"Ummm, we were. All year we played round robin against the other three teams, and we had more ties than wins or losses. No one could hit anything." It would appear Mark's memory of their baseball days was not as rosy as Edward's. Edward thought they were all future all-stars.

From across the way, a brief cheer erupted from the pickup game between Chase and Jacob. Jacob made his first bucket of the game. Of course, Edward believed the six-foot-three teen went easy on the seven-year-old and let him score, but to Jacob, it was still a victory.

The conversations and reminiscing moved to a lighter tone and turned into a game of "whatever happened to" with various people from Edward's past. He was not that surprised to hear that most of his old friends and classmates still lived in town. Most of those that left for college came back to settle down.

As the evening moved along, the kids tired of the basketball game and sat on the deck and talked among themselves. Well, Chase talked about football. Jacob hung on every word. Sarah hadn't stopped staring into his eyes. Edward doubted she heard anything Chase had said. A smile crept onto Edward's face. For the first time since Karen's passing, his kids looked happy and were just being kids.

Sharon leaned over, saying something to Mark, the expressions on each of their faces unpleasant. Sharon gave Edward a hug. "It's late, and I have an early morning tomorrow. It was great seeing you. We will be seeing you around." She then walked over to the kids and told them it was nice meeting them before heading back inside. Edward felt embarrassed and pulled out his phone to check the time. It was just after nine. In the city that was considered early, but this was a different world.

"Sorry about that, Mark. I didn't realize how late it was."

"Oh, it is fine. Not that late at all. You just don't want to be on the road out toward your place any later than this. It isn't safe." Mark caught himself before he finished his statement.

Hearing the warning as more than just something related to overstaying one's welcome, Edward inquired, "Why is that?"

"The roads are dark and pretty winding."

While that was true, Edward's car had headlights, and it wasn't that dangerous of a drive. Not wanting to question his friend, he called to his kids to get ready and thanked Mark for the great night. They talked about doing it again and Mark agreed. "Absolutely."

"See you at work tomorrow, Mark."

"Yep. See you tomorrow. Drive straight home and be safe."

Edward backed out of the driveway and onto the road. An uneasy feeling came over him. He was not sure if it was what Mark said to him, or how Mark watched them intently as they backed out and headed down the road.

9

During the drive home, Edward had to admit, Mark was right, it was quite dark. Streetlights created small islands of light at the intersections. The rest of the road was only illuminated by the moonlight glowing through the trees or his own headlights. Edward kept the high-beams on the entire time, having not passed a single car the whole way home. He slowed down as he passed the last intersection before his driveway; he didn't want to drive right past the opening.

Edward pulled in and through the trees and within seconds they emerged into the open pasture of the farm which was fully lit by the moon. A slight layer of fog hovered above the ground as the cool night air settled in.

Edward pulled to a stop at the back of the house. He and his kids exited the car and headed toward the house. A few steps away from the back steps, something made him stop. A familiar cold and empty chill filled his lungs and radiated throughout his body. Then something caught his attention out of the corner of his eye. A movement, not that far away from them in the fog. Edward paused for a moment to look in that direction and saw nothing at first, but then it was there again for only a second before it disappeared. It was not clear enough for him to make out what it was. He tried to convince his mind it was just a denser area of fog flowing in the air, but several aspects of that story fell flat on the logical side of his brain. First, there was no wind of any type. Second, there were no other areas in the fog that looked or behaved like that. But the most important factual detail was that there was a shape to it. With his past and what he saw the first night, he would be naïve to not consider other possibilities.

When Edward turned around to follow his kids inside, he nearly ran into Sarah standing there, fixated on the same area. "Sarah, honey. What is it?"

She did not break her gaze.

With no response, he took a step closer and grabbed her by the shoulders. "Sarah, are you OK?"

Sarah snapped out of the trance and looked at her father with a fearful expression. "Yes, daddy, I'm fine."

Her tone of voice and a term she hasn't used since she was nine alerted him to the possibility she saw the same object.

"Are you sure?"

"Yes, just tired. I am going to go in and get ready for bed." Her voice was more resolute, but still not convincing to her father.

Sarah headed inside and Edward followed her as far as the top of the stairs leading up to the porch. He stood there, looking back at the same spot for several minutes, to convince himself he either saw a spirit or something else. Unconvinced either way, Edward headed inside disturbed, confused, and feeling helpless. As a father, Edward wanted to create a safe and happy environment here. With everything they'd been through over the last year or so, his children deserved that.

At the top of the stairs, he noticed Sarah's door open. He looked inside, wanting to check on her to make sure she was OK, and found her in bed all covered up and fast asleep. Edward could be jumping to conclusions. Was it possible he misinterpreted her being tired for something else?

Maybe she saw him and turned to look too. He was not sure. He had been through a lot with his daughter and had seen that look before. That was the same expression he saw on her face the night Karen told them all enough was enough, that she wanted to stop trying. None of the four of them shed a tear at that moment. Each of them knew it was coming, even the kids who were mature beyond their years in such matters. He remembered the looks on everyone's face and the feeling of being exhausted like it was yesterday. They had been through a war. Every day was a new battle through the raw emotions. It was as much physically draining as it was emotionally heartbreaking.

Edward looked in on his daughter one last time, then flipped off the light and pulled the door shut before walking down the hall to his room.

The sounds of laser fire emerged from Jacob's room. Edward poked his head inside and found his son in an all too familiar position. Headphones on, controller in hand, and attention focused on the flashing screen of his video game. Edward thought about telling him it was bedtime, but they had just a few more days of summer vacation and let it slide and closed the door.

Feeling rather tired himself, Edward knew there was one last ghost to confront tonight. One he had put off since returning home. He stood in the doorway of his parents old bedroom holding a box and knew there was no sense in avoiding it anymore and stepped inside. Much like the seven-year-old he used to be, he stood right inside the door for a few moments before taking another step. Back then the pause was to look for his parents. Now it was to absorb the memories. All the times his father sat in the chair in the corner lacing up his shoes. Seeing his mother sitting at her make-up table; the same table still covered with assorted cosmetics. The closet still full of their clothes. After one last look around, Edward took his second and then his third step into the room and placed the box on his father's chair.

Edward stripped the bed and put on a new set of sheets and folded a corner back. Before he climbed in, he took one final look out the window. The fog had settled in thick, obscuring the pasture and the tree line from his view. There were no mysterious lights dancing in the fog tonight, No voices or haunting sounds. Just a cool night with the occasional cricket chirping its delight. The scene was peaceful. Edward cracked the window to allow in the cool night air and the rich fragrance from the wildflowers and lavender growing in the pasture. There was many a night in his youth he fell asleep just like this. Those were some of the best nights of sleep he ever had. Tonight, he could use one of those.

Edward climbed in and pulled up the covers and, as he had done every night since her passing, he thought of his wife until he fell asleep. The five clouds of vapor that circled him did not seem offended when he forgot to bid them a good night before falling asleep.

10

Edward focused on adjusting his lesson plans for the first nine weeks. He sat down the day before with Madeline Smith, the head of the English department, and reviewed his plans. He entered rather confident, hoping to impress her with how he organized his classes. Much to Edward's surprise, the lesson plans were not what she desired. Instead of criticizing and destroying his confidence, she provided feedback and suggestions, feedback that Edward was more than enthusiastic to receive.

His lessons followed the same pattern he had used throughout the years in Oregon. Lecture about a specific period of literature, then read one to two pieces from the period. All reading occurred at home, with discussion and a few quizzes about what was read each day in class to gauge comprehension. Once the assigned reading was completed, there was a multiple-choice test. Edward never liked using multiple-choice to test the comprehension and knowledge of a piece of literature. He would much rather allow the students to write an essay; so he could hear their interpretation of what they read in a form that allowed them to express an opinion and defend it. Edward was not a teacher that subscribed to the "there is only one right interpretation" school of thought. How a person viewed a piece of literature was personal, it depended a lot on their past and viewpoints. No matter how strong his belief was in that, he was forced into the multiple-choice format because of the heavy reliance on standardized tests in the larger school districts. Every test given in every class had to mimic the standardized tests that were given several times each year to allow for plenty of opportunities to practice.

Hearing Mrs. Smith voice her concerns about the value of multiple-choice tests was music to Edward's ears. She preferred the old methods of reading aloud in class and discussing as you go, followed up with essay at the end, allowing the student to voice their opinion. If her personality were friendlier, he would have run across to the other side of the table and given her a hug and a big kiss, but Edward restrained himself.

Edward opened up his lesson planner and began striking things out and writing in his adjustments. They would review his plans again today at 1:00 pm. No computer-based plans here, this was the old-fashioned lesson binder he remembered seeing teachers use when he was in school. He found the whole throwback nature of the school refreshing and energizing.

He was elbow deep in corrections for week three when there was a light knock on the door frame. Edward looked up, and after his eyes adjusted, he saw Mark leaning into his classroom door. "Hey, a group of us are heading to lunch at eleven. You should join us."

Edward quickly glanced at his cell phone and realized the time. It was 10:45. "Crap. I appreciate the offer, Mark, but I need to pass. I have to finish up these changes."

Mark responded with an exaggerated sad face.

Edward explained, "I'm way behind. I still thought it was nine something."

Mark looked up at the old-fashioned clock hanging up above the chalkboard in the classroom, a feature Edward had yet to notice, and accepted his explanation with a quick reply of "Next time," before disappearing down the hallway.

Edward called after him before he was out of earshot, "Mark, wait."

Just seconds later, his head reappeared in the door. "Changed your mind?"

"Nah, I want to apologize about overstaying our welcome last night. Just like now, I didn't realize how late it had gotten."

Mark looked bewildered by Edward's statement, so Edward tried to explain "The comments about how late it was last night."

"Oh." Mark's expression changed from bewildered to one of apprehension. He shifted back and forth in the doorframe, looking for something to focus on that was not Edward. "You guys were fine. Sharon had an early morning, and I was just worried about you guys driving back on the dark roads. Deer like to run out in front of cars in the dark and such."

"Ah, good thinking." Edward gave Mark a reluctant thumbs up, and off to lunch Mark went.

Mark just lied, and Edward knew it. During the years he spent in the hospital, he honed his human lie detector skills. After only a year, Edward could tell when a nurse, orderly, or doctor lied or withheld something. Whether it was the wandering eyes, awkward pauses, or fidgeting, the telltale signs are the same for everyone. That was a great skillset to have when teaching teenagers, and even better for being the parent of one.

He buried his nose back in his lesson plans and updated them based on the guidance he received yesterday. The next few hours sped by with a flurry of strikeouts and notes. Edward leaned back in his swivel chair, which let out a slight squeak. He folded his hands behind his head and smiled. The thirty minutes left until his meeting was just enough time to walk down and scrounge up some nourishment in the teacher's lounge's vending machines. He never liked to go into battle on an empty stomach, not that Edward expected a battle during his meeting. It was quite the opposite. He looked forward to it and to the first day with students tomorrow.

His enthusiasm turned into a semi-strut as he walked out of his classroom in the direction of the vending machines.

"Edward?" echoed a voice from behind, stopping him mid-strut.

Edward turned. Upon seeing who it was he thought to himself, *only in small-town America. This would have never been allowed in Portland.* He walked back toward the visitor and extended his hand. "Father. What brings you to the school today?"

Father Murray, dressed in full black with a white collar and a crucifix dangling around his neck, took Edward's hand firmly. "Walking around before the madness starts." Father Murray's face lit up. "Nah. Actually, I just blessed the football team downstairs. I do it each year. You know... for the safety of the players. Plus, any divine guidance will help. Competition is stronger these days. Coach Holmes told me you had come home. Thought I would stop by to say hello and invite you and your family back to the church." He looked warmly at Edward. "We would love to have you. Your mother and father were very active members of our congregation." His voice dropped slightly to a more somber tone. "God rest their souls. We miss them terribly."

Of everyone Edward had run into since returning, this was the one person he truly recognized and remembered. Of course, he was in his late thirties back then, but the eyes are the same kind eyes which provided him comfort when his parents were laid to rest. The voice sounded the same, maybe a few more years on it. Now in his seventies, he still tended to his flock in the very same community.

Edward and Karen struggled to find a church that felt inviting in Portland. Both of them were from small towns and in the big city, they found the churches had an antiseptic feeling. There was no sense of community. You came, prayed, listened to a sermon, and then everyone went home. They eventually found one, but did not find it to their liking. When Karen became sick their attendance waned. Between hospital stays and all the times Edward could not leave her alone, going to church took a backseat. Not to mention the period in which Edward frequently lashed out toward God. He could not understand why HE let this happen to Karen. He even cursed Him a few times.

Without hesitation, Edward agreed. "Absolutely Father, we'll be there."

Father Murray's face lit up. "I look forward to meeting your wife and children as well, and bringing them into our extended family. Your family has been missing from our congregation for far too long."

"Oh, Father, it will just be me and my kids. My wife, Karen, passed away earlier this year."

Father Murray placed his hand on Edward's shoulder and said, "Oh, Edward, I am so sorry to hear that. We know the Lord will call our name one day, we just never know when. It is always tragic when it is so young, but I am sure he has a greater purpose for her, even if we do not understand it. We are not really meant to."

"Yes, Father, I agree. And thank you for the kind words." Just hearing that was rather comforting, more so than what Edward experienced back in Portland. The priest that presided over her funeral told him he was sorry for his loss and then said a generic prayer with the family. After the service, Edward and the kids never heard from him again.

"My office is always open for you and your children anytime you need to talk. Welcome home. I look forward to you stepping into shoes vacated by your father's tragic loss."

Edward stood there for a few seconds, watching the familiar form of Father Murray disappear down the hall and around the corner. He wondered what he might have stepped into. His stomach rumbled sending him sprinting to the lounge. He had just a few moments left to down some junk food before his meeting.

11

The school year started full of optimism. Of course, that described Edward, not his children. He had to wake Sarah up three separate times so they would not be late. Jacob was up on time, but took his ever-loving time to get ready. As Edward got ready himself, he found it necessary to walk up and down the hall like an old-fashioned barker every five minutes to shout encouragement and reminders of how much time they had left. Just as he expected, at the last minute, both of his pride and joys exited their rooms and headed downstairs.

The ride to school was completely silent. Jacob's nose was stuck in a video game on his phone; Sarah's was buried in her bookbag for a few more moments of sleep. When they arrived at the elementary school, Edward veered right out of the drop off lane and into the parking lot. He parked his car in the first visitor spot next to the walkway. Jacob slammed the door as he got out, and watched with delight as his sister jerked awake.

As Edward walked him in, Jacob seemed nervous at first about starting at a new school, but all that went away when one of his classmates walked up and introduced himself before they were even in the classroom. Edward took just a few minutes to talk to the teacher before heading off. With a final look at Jacob, a smile grew on his face as he saw his son already making new friends. Jacob took after his mother in that respect. She could walk into a room of strangers and have four or five new best friends in just a matter of moments.

When Edward opened the car door to finish the drive to the high school, Sarah greeted him with the largest over-exaggerated smile he had ever seen. It went from cute to eerie in moments. "What?"

"I was just thinking. It is such a WONDERFUL morning outside. How about you drop me off a little way before we get to the school and let me walk the rest of the way in?"

Knowing Sarah hated mornings more than anything else in existence instantly tipped her hat and he called her on it. "You just don't want to be seen getting out of the car with me, dear old dad, a teacher. Huh?"

"Oh, Dad, that's not it." She tried to give him those big eyes that usually cause him to say yes to anything.

There are bigger battles to be had, so he gave in. "Alright. I will let you out just before we get there."

"Thanks, Dad, you're the best." She threw her arm around him and gave him a half hug.

He dropped Sarah off about a quarter mile from the school with instructions to walk straight there and text him when she got there. Edward pulled into the faculty parking lot and took a spot. He grabbed his brown satchel and headed inside among the crowd of rather cheerful teenagers all arriving for the first day of the new school year. Walking into a school that didn't have metal detectors at the front, seeing students walk around being friendly and polite to the teachers and each other, and hearing the magical words "Mister" and "Missus" echo everywhere was a stark contrast to the "Yo, teach" he had heard for the last several years. The refreshing and energizing environment engulfed Edward. He stood outside his door to welcome in his first class instead of waiting at his desk, using it as a shield, as he usually did.

Students filed by him down the hallway with polite and cheerful "good morning's." He checked the time on his phone. Just a few moments left until the bell rang. Sarah walked down the hallway as close to the other wall as she could, doing everything to look straight ahead while cutting her eyes in his direction. Feeling the urge to be the annoying father, he considered yelling something across the hallway such as, "Have a great first day, sweetie." But the disruption to the now peaceful home life wasn't worth the bit of ill-timed humor it would bring him, and he let her pass peacefully.

The bell rang, a real bell sound, not some electronic tone signaling the start of class. The last time Edward heard a real school bell, he was a student in elementary school. A few students made a mad dash toward their classrooms as the doors closed. Back in Portland, half the students treated the bell as a couple minute warning, and it took an assigned member of the faculty to walk the halls and send the students to their classrooms. The hallway beyond Edward's closing door resembled a ghost town. The inside of his classroom was a picture from Norman Rockwell himself.

Edward walked to the front of his class and leaned back on his desk. Every set of eyes in the classroom focused on him. He felt a quick shiver, followed a pressing feeling on every inch of his body. He did not expect to feel nervous about addressing his classes.

He dipped his head and took a deep breath to collect himself before he addressed the class. When he looked back out, he noticed a visitor walking toward the back along the chalkboard to his left. He appeared to be a cheery older gentleman just out for a stroll, wearing a tweed jacket and a Doctor Doolittle hat.

Not now, Edward thought to himself. There was never a good time for this to happen, but a moment like this was the worst. Edward watched as the man disappeared through the back wall and then returned his focus back to his class. As he did, he caught a few students turning around as well. Their expressions were normal, not showing any fear or surprise, maybe a hint of confusion. They were probably all wondering what the weird new teacher looked at.

"Good morning. I'm Mr. Meyer. Welcome to twelfth-grade literature." Edward picked up a stack of papers and took a few shaky steps to the first row of desks, giving several pages to the student sitting in each desk. "This is the syllabus for the class. Please take one and pass the rest back. If there are any left over, please just put them on the table in the back. While we hand these out, let's go around the room and introduce ourselves." The papers disbursed backward, and he noticed students looking at them and reading them.

"Let's start here." Edward stood in front of the first desk on the left side of the room. The occupant of the desk, a curly-haired blonde wearing glasses and a simple t-shirt and jeans, laid her syllabus flat and sat up straight, and said with a tremble in her voice, "I'm Susan Parker."

Edward looked back to the gentleman sitting behind her and without hesitation, said, "Robert Lewis, nice to meet you."

The rest of the class picked up the pattern and each of the other twenty-four students took turns introducing themselves.

"I am usually pretty good with names, so there will be no need for any name cards or anything. I should remember each of your names after the next few days, but now let's get to a more important topic. Why are we here?" Edward saw many students looking down at the syllabus, expecting a read-through or review of what was handed out. "It's a more general topic than even what is on the syllabus, so you can put those down for the moment."

Edward felt enthusiastic and a bit idealistic. "We are here to learn about literature. Now, that is a very broad topic. More specifically, we will talk about the types and styles of the American classics. We will read some of those classics and talk about the styles of each author and what they try to convey to the reader with their story. But there is something else…"

The English teacher in Edward forced a pause in his speech.

"Let me try that again, using proper English." A few students in the class laughed. "We will be reading several of the American classics and talk about their style and content, BUT," he over emphasized that word on purpose, "I am after an even bigger goal. I hope to share and instill with you a love for reading like I have. So, before we begin, who reads for fun?"

Not a hand entered the air, to which Edward was not surprised. "Oh, come on, reading can be fun. Let's try this again, ignoring what you have been forced… I mean, assigned to read for school, who has read something in the last year?"

That time, about half of the hands jumped into the air. "Good. Umm… Lisa, what did you read?" Edward asked, pointing to a girl sitting in the back of the third row.

"*Origins* by Dan Brown."

"Good, and have you read any of his other books?"

"Yes, all of them."

"You enjoyed it, right?"

Lisa nodded yes, as a voice from the back commented, "Not like there is anything else we can do when the sun goes down around here."

"Well Michael, thank you for volunteering to go next. I saw your hand up earlier, what was the last book you read and enjoyed."

Without hesitation, Michael responded, "*Relentless*."

Edward clarified, "The book by Tim Grover?"

"Yes."

"Excellent choice. I have read it myself. You enjoyed it, right?"

Michael's eyes perked up when he heard his teacher had read the same book as well. He straightened up in his seat before responding, "Absolutely."

"Why?" Edward asked, looking for him to clarify with more context.

"I like sports and have always been curious about that edge that some athletes have. How someone who is as talented as everyone else find that extra something to excel further? That book gave me a look into how their minds work."

Feeling his point was made, Edward did quick summary before continuing with his plans for today's class. "See, everyone? Lisa is reading what many think of as one of the best authors of our time, at least one of the most popular, and she enjoyed it. On the other side, Michael read a self-help book. A type of book that many think can be very boring, and he found enjoyment in the topic. There really is something for everyone. I hope you each find something enjoyable in what we read this year."

Looking around the classroom, Edward felt he had the class fully engaged. "OK, so let's look at your syllabus and see where we are going to start..."

Each of his remaining five classes followed suit the rest of the day. Introductions, a quick discussion about what he hoped they get out of the class, and then into the syllabus and preparing for the first selection of the year. Well, almost. By the third class, he started noticing a look. Not a look, perhaps, but a feeling coming from the students. Not one of disrespect, but like he was an animal on display at the zoo. The feeling grew from class to class until it finally came to the surface with his last class of the day.

During the introductions and open discussion, Edward asked, "Does anyone have any more questions?" A timid hand appeared from the middle of the room. A student who was outspoken during the open discussion now appeared hesitant about asking a question.

"Mr. Meyer?"

"Yes, Jeff?"

"Is it true you live in that eerie old house at the edge of town?"

Every town had that one house that everyone tells tales about. In this town, like it or not, it was Edward's home. He had no doubt the story had grown to the level of town folklore. Probably at some point, some school-aged kids stood at the end of the driveway, just outside the tree line that separates the property from the road, daring each other to run up toward the house. The dare, of course, was accompanied with some fable about an old man that lives there that eats any child that comes close to the house.

"Well, if you mean my old family home. Yes. My family and I have moved back to it. Rest assured, none of the stories," more exaggerated than before, "no matter what you have heard..." Edward paused and leaned his head forward slightly, and looked at his class humorously out of the top of his eyes under his furrowed brow, "it is not true. The house is the same as it was when I grew up there."

There was an audible murmur circulating through the classroom as they realize their teacher was that little boy from the story they heard about.

"It isn't haunted?" a voice inquired amongst the murmur.

Edward chuckled and with a straight face replied, "Well no, Robin, I can absolutely guarantee it is not haunted."

When the school day ended, Edward packed up his things, locked his classroom, and headed out to the parking lot. His daughter, who was too cool for anyone to see her driving into school with "dear old dad," now leaned against the car waiting for her ride home.

"So how was school?" he asked as he opened the driver's side door.

"Not bad."

Edward felt fortunate. He received a two-word answer instead of a half-hearted "fine" or something to that effect. "Well, glad you survived. How are your classes?"

"Not bad. Seems I am a bit of a celebrity."

"How so?"

"I... am the girl that lives in the haunted house." She looked at him with that satirical smile he saw when she was being a smartass.

"Yeah, I got a little of that, too. Let's go pick up your brother."

12

Friday afternoon arrived, providing a quiet and normal end to the first few days back at school. Both Edward and his children settled into the rhythm of the school year, and even though they continued to complain about going to school, as all kids do, they both enjoyed it. Of course, they would never admit it.

As they pulled into the driveway, they headed inside for a quick change of clothes and then back to school for the Friday Night Football game. Edward missed that part of his life. His high school education came from teachers the State sent in to conduct classes in the hospital. Having experienced the games with his mother and father, he always felt a longing for it. Now as a father, he wanted to make sure his children did not miss out.

Sarah zipped down the hall toward the bathroom she shared with Jacob. In the breeze caused by her brisk movement he heard, "A few friends want to pick me up for the game."

Sarah appeared to have forgotten how the whole parent and child thing worked. "Is that a question asking for permission?"

Doing her best impression of a whining teenager, "Dad! It's just a few people I met at school. We'll be at the same game."

Edward knew it was safe and said, "OK, al..."

Sarah blurred past him in the hallway, interrupting his answer. The glimpse Edward caught caused a quick change of his answer. "... absolutely not."

The answer stopped Sarah in her tracks at her bedroom door. "Why not?"

"You are not wearing that out. You still have to follow the school dress code." Sarah stood in her bedroom door wearing a skirt that barely covered her butt and tube top that was missing its midriff.

Sarah slammed the door. "If I change, THEN can I go to the game with my friends?"

Settling for one victory, Edward conceded. "Sure, just text me when you get there and when you leave."

Edward took a few moments to get himself ready.

The sound of someone running down the stairs was followed by a quick yell of, "Bye, Dad," and punctuated by the slamming of the front door. Edward glanced at the clock and realized he and Jacob needed to get going, too. Unlike the games in Portland which started at 7:30 PM, the games here had always started at 5:00 PM.

Even the away games. He remembered hearing someone ask his father about the start time once. "It was a tradition."

Edward and Jacob headed to the school and joined the parade of cars and trucks lined up to turn into the football stadium parking. Surrounded by cars blasting music, pickup trucks loaded with people in the back waving pompoms, and scores of others walking past them, they inched their way toward the stadium. He rolled down the windows and the smell of hot dogs on the grill, popcorn, and the sound of two marching bands playing various tunes from their positions in the stands wafted in with a flood of memories that brought a smile to his face.

Once parked, Edward and Jacob walked toward the source of the sweet smells and growing sound. Neighboring Valley Ridge was that night's opponent. Their fans created a sea of gold and crimson walking among the blue- and white-clad Miller's fans.

They parked, bought tickets, and went inside. No large police presence or wanding here.

Knowing what was on Jacob's mind, and his too, their first stop was the concession stand. There was a small line, but not too long. It gave them a moment to look at the simple menu board with the Coca-Cola red wave emblem on it as a sponsor. He felt a quick vibration in his pocket and pulled out his phone. There was a simple message from Sarah's number that just said, "here." He took a quick glance back toward the gate and saw his daughter walking in with a group of students, smiling and laughing. That image took away any doubt he had about coming back here to start fresh. He'd made the right decision.

He and Jacob placed their order, two hot dogs with extra mustard and relish, two Cokes, a popcorn, and a pack of M&Ms. The concession workers made a few trips to bring their food to the counter and Edward handed them a ten-dollar bill and donated the change back to the football boosters. With the food in hand and the popcorn pinned to Edward's chest by the arm supporting his hotdog, they headed to the bleachers and found a seat. Both teams were out on the field warming up.

* * *

The game itself was great. Miller's Crossing won 14-10, but what stuck out to Edward was how right Mark was about his son. Chase had five catches for 120 yards and was an absolute beast out there blocking. Edward tried to find Mark after the game to send Chase congratulations on such a great game, but something else drew his attention. Within minutes, the stands and parking lot were almost empty. Except for the Valley Ridge fans, it was a virtual ghost town. Thinking he might have more luck over at the gym, where the locker rooms were, he and Jacob headed that direction, but found more, or less, of the same. Less than fifteen minutes after the final whistle, the Miller's Crossing players had left with their families. The only folks roaming around were the families of the opposing players, who waited to see their sons emerge from the locker room before they boarded the buses and headed home. He and Jacob gave up and headed back to the parking lot where they found a handful of cars left, all but his adorned with the yellow and crimson colors of Valley Ridge.

There was a quick vibration from his cell phone, and he reached into his pocket to pull it out. Sarah had messaged him she was already home. Edward and Jacob headed home themselves. The drive was filled with the sounds of a father and son reliving the highlights of a great high school football game.

When they walked inside, Sarah was perched on the sofa watching television and mockingly scolded them for taking so long.

"Surprised you were home so soon."

"Yeah, me too. I thought there would be a party or something after the game like back home... but everyone said we had to get home."

13

"Daaddd!!! Do we have to go to church?"

"Yes, Jacob. We used to go all the time, and you liked it." Edward leered at both of his children via the rearview mirror. "You both did." The family was dressed in their Sunday best as they drove along beautiful country roads on the way to Miller's Crossing Catholic Church.

"But that was when Mom was with us."

Sarah was right, they had not been back to church since Karen became too sick to go, but Edward knew this would be great for them. "Come on. This will be great. This is the church I attended when I was little."

"It's the only church in town. Everyone goes here." Sarah had a knack for pointing out the obvious.

"Yes, it is the only one," Edward confessed with a somewhat irritated smile as they pull along the gravel-lined driveway leading up to the single-building country church. The white building had a high-pitched roof. The traditional steeple contained a century-old bell that Edward could hear ringing even with the windows rolled up. The rooster weathervane on top showed a slight breeze blowing out of the north.

The family walked together up the stairs and entered the traditionally styled church, with high ceilings, exposed rafters, and stained-glass windows lining each wall. There was a large stained-glass scene behind a simple aged-wood altar. The sunlight coming through the windows created a myriad of dancing spots of color on every surface. Edward studied the scenes depicted in each of the windows. In all the churches he had been in before, the glass depicted a biblical scene. As he looked at each of these, he realized none of them represented a traditional Bible scene. None of the pictures depicted a child in a manger, wise men, or Moses leading the Jews. The imagery was more contemporary, showing faceless figures walking toward a cross with light emanating from it, pictures of what looked like a Catholic priest confronting a group of the same faceless figures. He didn't remember seeing those when he was there as a child.

Music from the pipe organ in the front interrupted his study. The procession filed down the aisle from the back. A minute into the intro of the song, Father Murray and the choir walked in. The congregation stood as the processional passed them and, once everyone was up front and in place, Father Murray led a quick prayer. He then instructed his flock to be seated. The service had hymns, prayers, and two readings, one each from the Old and New Testaments.

After one more hymn, Father Murray walked over to the pulpit and climbed up the small set of stairs to his perch that overlooked the congregation.

"Good morning."

The congregation returned Father Murray's greeting. "Good morning."

"It is great to see everyone here this morning. It truly warms my heart. Today is a very special day, my friends. I was and am going to give you a sermon about helping others find their way, a topic we talk about often and exercise daily. Now, right here in our congregation, we have an example of someone finding their way back to where they belong. I would like to welcome Edward Meyer, son of Robert and Laura Meyer, and his children back to our flock. Your family has been missing from our house for far too long. It is great to see you back." A brief applause followed the many heads that turned around and looked toward Edward and his children. Each face warm and welcoming. Edward felt Jacob squirm a little in the pew next to him.

Father Murray continued his sermon. "These are trying times, but I don't have to tell you that. The world is full of pain and suffering and they don't do enough to help ease the pain. We, the faithful, have taken it upon ourselves to help ease that pain. To help guide those that are misguided to find their way in the world, and it is not an easy task. It is a calling of pain and suffering that follows the example Jesus Christ, our Lord and Savior, set for us. He suffered on the cross as a penance for the sins of man. We have suffered as our penance for our sins and the sins of all men. Like the great Benedictine monk Peter Damian, this is our path toward our own glorious salvation. Also like our Brother Damian, our pain and battle are not only one of the spirit, but one of the flesh, and it takes a toll on each of us. We should not let that toll cause us to become derelict in our duty. Any lapse, even the smallest lapse, can have life or death consequences. Consequences we have already witnessed and suffered."

Father Murray paused for a second before continuing with a lower and more compassionate tone of voice. "Consequences we do not want to repeat. It is our solemn duty to help these poor souls, both good and bad, evil and innocent, contrite and hurtful, everyone without judgment. Help them down the path of their destination, no matter the cost. By doing this task, we will bask in the light of our Lord and Savior in the afterlife."

Father Murray walked off the pulpit and stood before the congregation with his arms outstretched. "The sacrifice is yours as His was for us."

Without prompt, the voices of the congregation echoed in the rafters. "We help others find their way as he helped us."

A hymn started, and the congregation stood up and joined the choir in song. Edward looked down at the hymnal to find the right page and then looked at both

Sarah and Jacob as he attempted to share the book with them. Each had a fearful look on their face, and neither tried to sing.

Following the hymn, there was a final prayer before Father Murray dismissed his flock. Even though they were seated toward the back, it took twenty minutes or more for them to reach the door. Scores of individuals stopped by to welcome each of them back to Miller's Crossing and back to the church. Most talked of how they remembered Edward when he attended with his parents and how much he looked like his father. Several of the older women gushed over Jacob and how much he also resembled Edward's father. Finally, a familiar arm draped over his shoulder and helped guide him through the crowd and out the door.

"Thanks, Mark."

"Someone had to save you from the chat gaggle. Once they grab you, you're stuck for hours."

Based on his little exposure to them, Edward didn't doubt Mark one bit.

"Glad to see you guys joining the church."

"Yeah, Father Murray stopped by the school and invited me back the other day. I thought it would be good for the kids. We went often before Karen died." Edward paused and thought for a second before making the next comment. He was concerned it may seem inappropriate, but that had never stopped him from speaking his mind before. "Mark, I need to ask you a question."

"Sure bud, what is it?"

"What was up with that sermon?"

"Oh that. Kind of intense, huh? I think Father Murray is losing it a little in his old age. The last few years the sermons have taken a more 'fire and brimstone' approach. Maybe he sees his own mortality coming, not sure. All I know is he is comforting."

No argument from Edward on that point. A honk in the distance prompted Mark to wave in its direction. "Well, Sharon is waiting in the car. We have a bunch of chores to do around the house today. I need to get going. See you at work tomorrow."

"See ya tomorrow, Mark."

Edward and his still-stunned kids found their car in the parking lot of the church and headed home. Edward was the first to break the uncomfortable and abnormal silence between the three. "So, what did you two think about church?"

Jacob said, "It's not like the one back home with Pastor Mike. His sermons used comic strips and television shows to make his point."

Sarah said, "Yeah, no Marmaduke in this one."

14

Another normal week of school, Edward and Jacob headed into the stadium for another Friday night football game. The opponents this week were the Arendtsville Hornets, the two-time defending state champions. It should be a stiff test for the hometown Lions. With their less-than-healthy food choices in tow, Jacob and his father settled in for a good game. Sarah, like the week before, came with a group of friends.

The game was as they expected, a real back-and-forth tussle between two evenly matched teams. It appeared the Hornets were just bigger and stronger, overpowering the Lions on both sides of the ball. After the first quarter, they were down by seven. Midway through the second quarter, they were down by fourteen and the groans in the crowd started as it appeared there was no answer to the power running attack of the Hornets. The other side was full of cheers, and the marching band played their fight song for any reason, not just scores. Edward even heard a few parents above him wonder aloud if they play the fight song when the starting quarterback goes to the bathroom.

Just before halftime, the coaches stopped lining up man on man and try a different tactic: speed. When the whistle blew ending the first half, the Lions were on the board with a field goal cutting the lead to eleven. The Hornets spent the second half trying to adjust to the Lions' fast paced passing and outside running attack. Their size advantage worked against them and appeared to be a step behind the rest of the game. When the final gun sounded, the final score was Lions 24 and Hornets 21.

That would be considered a signature win for the Lions in most communities, prompting hours of celebration afterward, but not here.

Just like the week before, the stands and parking lot cleared out moments after the game. Edward received a quick but surprising text from Sarah. It simply stated, "Won't be home right after the game. They want to show me something. Is it OK?" Edward agreed. A nagging second thought about being naïve, but he dismissed it.

The drive home was just like the one the prior week. Full of discussion recapping the highlights of the game and the strategy of how the Lions came back. Once home, not having had enough football for one night, Jacob and his father cooked microwave popcorn and settled in on the couch, switching back and forth between two professional preseason games on that night.

Around 10:30, Jacob fell asleep. He looked comfortable there, so Edward let him lay there until the game was over. Once it was over, he took him upstairs and tucked him into his bed. With Sarah still out, Edward wanted to stay up until she came home, so he settled down on the couch and looked for a movie to watch. With few enjoyable choices, he left it on the eighth edition of an action film he loved. He paid no attention to everyone else who joked they should have stopped after the first movie.

At 11:00 pm he texted Sarah but received no reply.

11:30 pm arrived, and still no reply.

At midnight, the text messages progressed to phone calls that were neither answered, nor went straight to voicemail. His level of worry jumped from nothing to concerned in an instant. Edward wanted to jump in the car and go look for her, but he had no idea where to start. Also, not knowing who she was out with gnawed at him, making him feel like a negligent parent.

Six more calls resulted in the same response, adding to his panic. Eventually he gave into his concern, grabbed his keys to head out and look for her, but a knock on the door stopped him before he even put his shoes on. He rushed to the door and slung it open. Edward's heart skipped a beat when he saw Sarah standing there, tears running down her face, and a blanket draped around her shoulders. His mind jumped to the absolute worst as he pulled her inside.

"Are you all right?"

She wrapped her arms around him and buried her face into his chest.

"She's fine, Eddie." The voice of Sheriff Lewis Tillingsly startled him. The sheriff walked in through the door while taking off his black wide-brim hat.

"Relax. She isn't in any trouble. None at all. I gave her a ride home, but I think we should talk privately."

Edward felt beyond confused. His sixteen-year-old daughter was just brought home after midnight by the Sheriff, but she was not in any trouble.

"Sarah, why don't you go on to your room? Your dad and I need to have a talk."

Sarah headed upstairs to her room while her father stood there with his mouth gaping wide open.

"Why don't we go into the kitchen and talk? I will try to explain everything." The Sheriff knew his way around the house and walked through the living room and into the kitchen. When Edward pushed through the door, he found the Sheriff searching through the cabinets. "Where do you keep your coffee? Your ma kept it in this cabinet."

He was right, she always kept it in the cabinet next to the refrigerator and above the coffee maker. Edward, however, had things organized a little different. "It's in the pantry. There's a box of k-cups."

"I should have asked. You don't mind, do you?"

Feeling too much in a fog to even care, Edward said, "Not at all." Then he had a seat at the breakfast table in the nook surrounded by windows.

The Sheriff walked over to the pantry and pulled out two k-cups. He then retrieved two coffee cups from the cabinet. Edward sat at the table holding his head in his hands, trying to process everything. The Sheriff made two cups of coffee and joined Edward at the table, sliding one cup over to him. "You'll need this."

There was a knock at the back door and Edward jumped, but the Sheriff put him at ease. "It's okay. Let me get it. I called him." The Sheriff opened the back door and Father Murray walked in, adding to Edward's feeling of complete bewilderment.

"I'm not sure you remember, but your father and the two of us sat at this same table many times talking when you were younger." Edward had not thought about that before now, but now that he mentioned it, it was one of the more common memories he had of his childhood. The three of them, and maybe a few others, sitting at the table drinking coffee, talking about many things from the town gossip, to sports, and politics. Edward also remembers other times they would talk, and he would walk into the kitchen. They would all go silent, and his father would ask him to move along, that they were talking about adult things.

"Father, would you like some coffee?" Sheriff Tillingsly offered.

"No thanks, Lewis. If I have any now, I'll never get to sleep." Father Murray turned his attention to Edward. He was quiet on the outside, but anything but on the inside. "Evening, Edward, how are you doing?"

Edward did not answer as Father Murray placed a comforting hand on his shoulder and took the old wooden seat next to him in the alcove It was a chair he had occupied many times in the past. It gave a familiar by haunting squeak on the floor as he slid it back from the table.

With a high level of exacerbation in his voice, Edward demanded, "Will someone tell me what is going on?"

Father Murray was first to speak. "Eddie, how much did your father ever tell you about this place?"

"What do you mean? This house? This town?"

"The town. Miller's Crossing."

"He and my mother told me lots of stories about their childhood here and I heard a lot about his high school days..."

"No, not that," interrupted Father Murray.

"Father, let me try a different question." The Sheriff took his seat at the table again and looked across at Edward. "Do you remember when I came by to pick your father up late at night?"

"I remember that happening several times."

"Did he ever talk to you about where he went and what we did?"

Edward remembered asking a few times. "He just said it was adult things."

"Lewis, he was too young. Robert would have never talked to him about any of this."

"Eddie, not to play twenty questions with you, but can you tell me if you see things?"

"Things?"

"Do you see ghosts? Spirits? Images of people and creatures you can't explain?"

This question more than stunned Edward. It was a fact he had hidden from everyone for years. The last time he told anyone about the visions, they sent him for a mental evaluation. He wondered if they knew of his past, his stay in a mental hospital, and wanted to use it. Maybe Sarah got into some trouble, and they were using this to show he was an unfit parent.

The mental argument going on within Edward was visible to both of his guests. "Eddie, you can tell us the truth. We both see them too. Most everyone in Miller's Crossing does. It is a gift and a curse of sorts."

Staring at the old priest with a blank gaze, Edward tried to make sense of what he had just heard. The Sheriff added, "Your father did as well. So did your mother."

"This town is a very important place in the spiritual world. There is no natural explanation for why or how, but this town is surrounded by a very strong energy field that attracts spirits. There are other places all around the world like Miller's Crossing. Some are more obvious once you know what they are, like Stonehenge and Peak Kailash in Tibet. Others are just towns, like here, and lakes, like Rila Lake in Bulgaria. Most of the other places are rather remote, with not that many people around them. We are the lucky exception."

He understood what Father Murray said. "So, this energy, some kind of electromagnetic field, makes you think you are seeing things? If so, I am familiar with that. I read about several studies that pointed to EM fields causing most paranormal experiences."

"Well, not exactly Edward. You don't think you see them. You really see them. They are really there. The energy attracts lost souls and simply put; we have to help them find their way."

Edward thought for a moment. Something Father Murray just said brought clarity to his confusion a week ago in church. He asked, "The sermon?"

"Yes, last week's sermon was about this responsibility we have. Those that live here. We have that responsibility to the souls that are lost to help them move along and find their way. It is a responsibility we have not been as diligent about as we should. If we don't help them, they will continue to search for all eternity at best, and terrorize us all at worst. Not all spirits are kind and gentle. Those that are kind and gentle pass through our world and do no harm. Those that aren't can be more dangerous than you can ever imagine."

"Wait." Edward shook his head while he rubbed his eyes, remembering back to the first night back in his family's home. "This isn't just a prayer-type thing, right? This is really confronting the spirits and moving them?"

"Oh yes, this is a lot more than prayer."

"Did you have to move any about two weeks ago out here?"

Father Murray looked over at Sheriff Tillingsly, who answered for the both of them. "Yes, we had two spirits that didn't want to cooperate. I thought I saw a light turn on in the house when we were out in the field. We tried not to wake you."

"So that is what I saw that night? You were helping lost souls?"

"We were there, along with others to make sure everyone in Miller's Crossing was safe that night and to ensure these souls moved on. The group you saw that night is known as the town elders. Each sworn to take this responsibility, no matter the sacrifice. Your father was one. So was your grandfather. Even your great grandfather was one. Your family is one of our town's founding members going back almost two hundred years."

"That's why my father left those nights."

Sheriff Tillingsly finished taking a sip of coffee. "Yes, Edward. Each of those nights, your father was out helping us. Tonight, we were out following a group of the less kind, but not very evil type when we ran into a group of teenagers. Your daughter was with them. Her friends assumed, because of her age and who you were, that she knew our little secret. So, they took her out hunting spirits. She wasn't ready for it. Not all female descendants are born with the gift."

Edward was about to ask a question when the Sheriff stopped him. "I don't know what or if she saw anything. It is possible she just freaked out sitting in the woods as all of her friends tried to tell her there were ghosts out there with them. I tried to talk to her a little on the ride back, but she didn't say much."

Father Murray said, "I can talk to her if you want."

"No, Father, I can handle it. I need to be the one." Edward sat back in his chair and mouthed the word "WOW."

"It is a lot to take in, and I admit it may be hard for you to believe."

"Actually, Sheriff, it is not as hard for me to believe as you think. I spent years thinking I was crazy."

Father Murray patted Edward on the shoulder. "That is my fault, my son. The sheriff and others wanted to tell you, but I thought you were too young. In most children, the gift doesn't show until the early teen years, and you were only seven. I am sorry. If I could go back and change the past, that is one of several things I would change from that night."

"It's late. I'm sure your daughter feels very confused right now. If you'd like, we can talk to her."

Edward insisted. "No, let me. Even though I still need to understand things myself, I am her father. It should be from me."

Father Murray stood up and slid past Edward while Tillingsly rinsed out his coffee cup in the sink. While grabbing his hat off the counter, Tillingsly remarked, "We should go, so you can get to that conversation."

Edward only nodded. He wanted to seem confident in his ability to speak to his daughter about this, but inside, the butterflies and self-doubt created a hurricane of nerves.

"One more thing. I would like for you to come out with us tomorrow night. Take your father's place with us."

"Lewis!!!" exclaimed Father Murray.

"No, it's OK." Edward was curious about all this and felt a strong need to understand. "I'm in."

Edward bided the two of them a good night and closed the back door behind them before going upstairs to talk to Sarah. He noticed her bedroom door was closed, and it appeared her light was off. He cracked the door open and let out a little sigh of relief when he saw her sleeping. Feeling exhausted, he headed to his room and collapsed on the bed but did not sleep much. A few minutes here and there, but that was all.

Throughout the night, his mind raced between the hundreds of visions he had seen over his life. He saw his parents several times, both trying to comfort and assure him. As he fell to sleep, he heard Father Murray's words from earlier mixed with his sermon from the previous Sunday. Words like "responsibility," "duty," and "salvation." Edward woke, sitting straight up after a few hours of restlessness and stared at the clock on the table next to his bed. It was just 3:30 A.M. and still dark outside his window. He got up and walked downstairs for a quick drink of water to soothe his dry mouth. Feeling the cool water slide down the back of his throat was very pleasurable. The only feeling more pleasurable at that moment would be drifting into a deep slumber with a calm mind, which he knows won't be possible tonight. He was so sure of that, he even uttered "yeah right" out loud. What he didn't expect was the reply.

From behind him, he heard the stable and supportive voice of his mother say to him, "No need to panic, son. This is who you are." Edward spun around. He expected to catch an image of the vision he had seen throughout the years, but he only caught a glimpse out of the corner of his eye as she disappeared.

"What do you mean?" Edward asked the empty room.

He knew asking was pointless. Through the years, he tried many times to talk to or communicate with them. Each time resulted in no response. No sign they heard him, or were even aware he was there. This was also not the first time a vision had spoken to him, but this time there was a warm emotion in her words. A feeling that stirred emotions Edward locked up years ago and now emerged as a single tear building in the corner of his left eye.

Edward stood there, focused on where her image was just a few moments ago, hoping she would reappear again. He did not say a word. For several moments, he didn't move. With no reappearance, he crossed his arms and leaned back against the countertop, still not taking his eyes off that spot. After another ten minutes, the area was still void of any presence. Edward headed off to bed feeling a touch of heartbreak, now with something new to ponder.

15

Edward awoke to the light of a new morning sneaking in around the outside edge of his window shade. Laying across his bed instead of tucked under the covers, he was unsure if he was just that tired or that restless in his sleep. He sat up on the edge of the bed to wake up. His mind raced through the events of the last twelve hours. The feeling one had when a dream lingered beyond the world of sleep consumed him.

When he pushed himself out of bed, the face of the clock showed 9:00. He opened his bedroom door, allowing in the sounds of his son and daughter talking and fixing breakfast down in the kitchen. Edward headed down to join them and, when he pushed through the door to the kitchen, he saw what appeared to be a normal morning. One look in Sarah's eyes told him it was not. The play bickering between his two children was an act by Sarah. Even the way she greeted him was forced and unnatural. Jacob may not have picked up on it, but her father did.

"Morning, sleepy head. Did you stay up watching a late movie?"

Edward knew Sarah knew what kept him up so late. Her efforts to avoid any direct eye contact with him confirmed it. Edward went along with this for now. He would need to talk to his daughter alone at some point.

Edward fixed his coffee and headed upstairs to take a shower and attempted to wash the cobwebs out of his head. When he emerged from the steam-filled bathroom, his body felt more refreshed, but his mind was more occupied than ever. While in the shower, he thought about everything he needed to get done that day. That was when the agreement he made with Sheriff Tillingsly and Father Murray came running to the front of the list. Even though he had many encounters with spirits, he had no idea of what to expect. It frightened him a touch.

The rest of the morning took on the normal routine. Edward cleaned while his children watched television or engaged in other non-cleaning-related tasks around the house. Through the entire morning, he noticed that Sarah was rather clingy around her brother, and did not want to be alone. On a normal day, she would be in her room on her laptop with the door closed or out walking the field, on her phone. He continued to look for an opening to talk to her, but so far there hadn't been one.

Around noon, Jacob headed upstairs, leaving Sarah downstairs watching the last few minutes of a movie alone. When Edward saw her sitting there alone, a lump developed in the back of his throat. Before he could open his mouth and talk, she sprung up from the sofa and headed for the stairs.

"Dad, a group of friends from school want to go walk around the town center today and look in the shops. They'll be here in a few. Is it OK?" she asked.

"That's fine. Do you have a minute?"

"Not really. I need to get ready." She continued up another step on the stairs.

"Hold up for just a second," Edward insisted with a tone of voice that caused Sarah to stop in her tracks. She did not turn around. "What happened last night?"

"It was nothing, really. I know it seemed like something because the sheriff drove me home, but it wasn't. He said he was heading this way and offered to give me a ride."

Edward had seen snowstorms in the past, but nothing like what his daughter just unloaded on him. He pulled out his mental shovel and tried to shovel through it. "You know I wasn't born yesterday. Sheriff Tillingsly may have been heading this way, and he is an old family friend, but when you came home, something really upset you. What was it?" Edward needed to hear it from her.

Her shoulders dropped a little as she sighed. "You grew up around here. They have areas out in the woods that can be really spooky. That's all." She turned around, looking at her father from the fourth step. "I got a little scared and a few of the people, instead of stopping there, they kept going and I kind of freaked out and got embarrassed." She stared into his eyes to convince him, but it did not work. "The Sheriff pulled up on us to make sure we weren't up to any trouble, and he saw me in tears. That's it."

Her eyes studied his face to see if he believed her. "Now can I go get ready?"

He did not believe her, not one bit, but didn't want to push things. If she saw what Father Murray and the Sheriff said, she had to be confused. "Sure, but be home early. I have something to do tonight." Before Edward could finish his request, Sarah sprinted upstairs to avoid any further questioning.

Edward tried to have as normal a Saturday as possible, not wanting to dwell on last night or the night ahead of him. He spent a few hours grading papers, which required complete mental focus, but a part of his mind drifted through what he had learned and events that now made sense. Later on, he and Jacob went outside to toss the pigskin out in their expansive pasture. In between throws, Edward caught himself looking over at the area where he'd seen the group weeks ago. Luckily for him, he looked back just in time to avoid being beamed in the nose like Marcia Brady.

Sarah's friends dropped her off just before dinner. She appeared to be more relaxed and more herself now, but not entirely. Edward knew he still needed to sit her down and explain things. Of course, he needed to understand things himself first. He decided it would be best to wait until tomorrow when he understood more.

The kids were watching a movie when Father Murray arrived just before ten o'clock. Edward explained that Father Murray was hosting a poker game with his friends from the old days, and that he wouldn't be back too late. At that moment, he flashed back to the times his father had made a similar excuse and walked out the door with Father Murray or then Officer Tillingsly.

16

Edward did not ask where they were headed, but the path taken by Father Murray transported him back into the mind and body of a stunned seven-year-old. They pulled into the parking lot of the Miller's Crossing police station. Edward got out and stood there for a minute, looking around. The building itself looked the same as it did the last time he was there. The sign was different, instead of an old blue painted piece of wood with white letters suspended between two four by four posts, there was a blue sheet of plastic with white illuminated letters: 'POLICE'.

He followed Father Murray inside. The station was quiet and empty this time of night except for a few men sitting on the couches in the waiting room. Each of them nodded toward or extended a greeting to their priest.

"Gentlemen, you remember Edward Meyer, Robert's boy."

An older white-haired man wearing denim overalls and a presence that matched his girth stood up and extended his hand. "Hey, Eddie. John Sawyer. I was a good friend of your pop's."

Edward looked at the man's weathered face and suppressed his shock. He remembered John Sawyer, but the man in front of him did not resemble him. The John Sawyer he remembered was an in-shape, blonde, outgoing man who always acted like a big kid.

A second man stood up and welcomed Edward as Sheriff Tillingsly walked in announcing, "Mount up boys. That was Larry Mixon. He spotted a group causing a ruckus out around mile marker 23 on route 471."

In mere moments, the room emptied, leaving Edward standing in the center. The Sheriff patted Edward on the shoulder as he walked out. "You can ride with me. You ready for this?"

Edward gave a single nod and followed him out to the patrol car.

The convoy of three workhorse pickup trucks, Father Murray's old Caddy, and a patrol car snaked down the old dark road, surrounded on both sides by old growth oak and pine trees. Edward watched as the various mile markers passed by outside the passenger window of the patrol car. Moments after they passed mile marker 22, blinding red brake lights illuminated from the back of each of the cars and trucks in front. The vehicles pulled off the side of the road and parked.

Edward took a quick look into the woods on both sides and saw nothing. The rest of the men gathered around Father Murray and the sheriff. Standing on the roadside,

Father Murray stared out into the woods. At that moment, Edward felt a familiar impulse to turn and look to his right, but when he did, he saw nothing.

"Where to, Father?" one man asked.

"This way," Father Murray said as he headed in the direction that pulled at Edward seconds ago.

With Father Murray leading the way, the group that reminded Edward of an old-time posse you'd see in the Western movies followed, pushing through the deep and thick woods and underbrush. Edward felt that impulse again, stronger and colder now. To him, he felt it came from farther right of their path. Father Murray turned right as well, leading the group in that direction. What Edward felt differed from anything he had felt before. It usually felt familiar, like the arrival of an old friend. This time, there was a feeling of dread when it arrived, and the feeling grew the further in they walked.

Father Murray stopped, letting the rest of the posse close ranks behind him. Among the sounds of crickets and the occasional croak of a frog, in the distance there was something that resembled the same sound Edward heard out in his pasture that night. A sound that no animal he knew of could make. Father Murray prayed under his breath and the rest of the posse crossed themselves in unison. Edward did the same. As Father Murray took a step forward, he snatched Edward by the arm, pulling him up by his side. Above a whisper he said, "Stand by me the whole time, Eddie. Remember, this is your calling."

A few steps forward and they finally came into view. There were four of them intermingled in the forest. Unlike their pursuers, these creatures moved with ease through the dense forest and underbrush. They were unaware of the group of men until Father Murray recited Proverbs 28:9 out loud.

"Whoever turns his ear away from hearing the law, even his prayer is detestable."

All four stopped and turned toward Father Murray. He reached under his robe, searching for something. When he found it, he pulled it out and handed the rosary to Edward. "This was your father's. Hold on to it and repeat after me."

Edward took the rosary in his left hand as Father Murray grabbed him by both shoulders. The old priest glared into his eyes from under his black wide-brimmed hat. "And Edward, you must repeat with conviction. Do not let your faith wane, or it will put us in a very dangerous situation."

The old priest held up his own rosary and recited, "Glorious St. Michael, Prince of the heavenly hosts."

Father Murray paused and looked at Edward who, with a quiver in his voice, repeated the line. "Glorious St. Michael, Prince of the heavenly hosts."

"Be strong and repeat what I say, immediately after me," ordered Father Murray. He continued, "who standest always ready to give assistance to the people of God."

Edward repeated, staring straight ahead, "who standest always ready to give assistance to the people of God."

"Who didst fight with the dragon, the old serpent, and didst cast him out of heaven."

As Edward was about to repeat the line, the four visions disappeared and then reappeared inches from Father Murray. The old priest's conviction and determination did not waver. "Edward! Repeat the line."

Edward repeated, "who didst fight with the drag..." but stopped as one of them left Father Murray and appeared inches from his own face. The hollow eyes locked on him, as if Edward was his prey. Frozen with fear, Edward heard Father Murray command, "Edward! Do not give in!"

Edward started over, with fear dripping in his voice, "who didst fight with the dragon, the old serpent, and didst cast him out of heaven." As soon as Edward uttered the last word, the creature thrust its hand into Edward's chest, producing a cold and squeezing pain deep inside. The pain sent Edward to his knees. He grasped at his chest and fell over, the creature maintaining its grasp.

It climbed on top of Edward and glared while twisting its hand back and forth. Edward tried to grab its arm in defense, but his hands passed right through. With a primeval scream, it twisted its arm, increasing the pain to a level that caused Edward to grasp at his chest with both hands. The look on his face told of the agonizing pain. He looked straight up through the creature and saw visions of his parents looking down at him as his thoughts shifted to his kids.

"Thrust this up into its heart." The voice of Father Murray cut through all the thoughts.

The priest stood over Edward with something in his hand and then dropped it. It passed straight through the vision and landed on Edward's chest. Using both hands, he reached for the object and gripped the bottom arm of it. He felt an electric jolt run through his arms and into his body. The feelings of fear and despair disappeared. The agonizing pain was no more. He still sensed the four spirits, but the cold and dread he felt before became something different. He was not afraid. With both hands, he thrusted the object, a simple wooden cross, up into the heart of the spirit on top of him. The creature screamed in pain as it disappeared into a cloud of mist, only to reappear a few feet away.

Sheriff Tillingsly helped Father Murray pull Edward up. He held onto that cross with a death grip. Edward searched for answers in the men's faces.

Father Murray again grabbed him by both shoulders and said, "Focus. This is what you were meant to do. The power is inside you. Here." The old priest took his left hand off the cross and shoved a book in it. The book was already opened to a page marked by a simple red rope. "Read from here."

Edward's eyes followed Father Murray's finger to a spot on the page. He heard his voice once more. "Go on."

Edward read, "and now valiantly defendest the Church of God that the gates of Hell may never prevail against her, I earnestly entreat thee to assist me also, in the painful and dangerous conflict which I have to sustain against the same formidable foe. Be with me, O mighty Prince! that I may courageously fight and wholly vanquish that proud spirit, whom thou hast by the Divine Power so gloriously overthrown, and whom our powerful King, Jesus Christ, has, in our nature, so completely overcome; to the end that having triumphed over the enemy of my salvation, I may with thee and the holy angels, praise the clemency of God who, having refused mercy to the rebellious angels after their fall, has granted repentance and forgiveness to fallen man. Amen."

Edward's reading of St. Michael's prayer caused the creatures to scream and howl. Fixated and fearful of the cross in his right hand, they kept their distance.

Father Murray held his rosary up and walked toward the visions. "Come with me." Edward followed the priest step by step.

"With the glory and love of Christ as my sword, I command you unclean spirits to leave this world and to be condemned to the fire of Hell for all eternity."

The creatures were focused on the cross and moved backward as Edward brought it closer to them.

Father Murray spoke again. "I command you to leave this place. In the glory of God and Christ our savior, I command you. In the glory of God and Christ our savior, I command you."

The creatures faded as Father Murray continued to recite the phrase repeatedly. A blue colored haze floated where the creatures were. It descended to the ground, disappearing among the fog and cool moist night air.

"Where did they go?" Edward asked.

"Where they should be. To Hell, I hope. They were pure evil."

"How did you know?"

Father Murray explained rather calmly, "It's pretty easy. It has nothing to do with how they react to us. Even the best spirits can act like that. It is the confusion they feel. It clouds their judgement. The evil ones, you feel without question. Don't tell me you didn't feel that when we first got out of the car."

He was right. Edward felt dread the first time he sensed them.

"Let's get out of here. The bugs are biting." Father Murray turned and walked out of the woods, swatting at the swarm of mosquitoes around them. Edward didn't notice the mosquitoes until now. He followed Father Murray and the rest of the men out of the woods. His body shook with each step. When the group emerged, they were about a hundred yards away from where they parked.

John Sawyer called back at the sheriff, "Any more reports?"

"A couple of friendlies, John, but it sounds like those are all handled."

"If it's all right with you and the Father, me and the boys are going home."

Sheriff Tillingsly passed the question off to Father Murray. "Father?"

"That is fine with me, Lewis. Thank you much, John."

"See you in church tomorrow."

John and the others loaded up in their trucks and headed off. Edward quick stepped a few times to catch up with the priest. "Here," Edward said as he tried to return the cross and book to him.

The priest put his hands around Edward's and the objects. "Keep them. They were your father's, and we have a lot of training to do." With a creak, Father Murray opened the door of his Caddy. "Lewis, see you tomorrow?"

"Yes, Father."

"Good. Make sure Edward gets home safely. He has had a long night." The old priest smirked.

"Yes, Father."

Neither Edward nor Sheriff Tillingsly said much to each other on the entire ride home. Mostly just chit-chat like "the football team looks great this year" and such from the Sheriff. Edward gave simple one- and two-word answers. His mind was too occupied for normal conversation, but he recognized what the Sheriff was doing. This was the second time in his life he had tried to distract him.

Edward got out of the car and walked toward the house as the Sheriff sped off behind him. When he approached the door, a familiar chill and tingling started at the base of his neck. Instinctually he looked around. The sight he saw took his breath away. It wasn't one or two. Not even five to ten. In the layer of fog that hung above the ground, a group of glowing individuals made of vapor and soulless eyes encircled his house. There was no sound or movement. They just hovered there.

Edward thought to himself, *well, this is new,* before he headed inside.

17

Edward sat in a church pew alone after the Sunday morning service. He sent his children out to the car for a few minutes so he could talk to Father Murray alone. The events of the past few days had rolled through his mind, leading to sleepless nights. Safely tucked into his coat pocket were the book and the cross. He hadn't allowed either to leave his possession since Father Murray handed them to him the night before. He laid in his bed after returning home and studied each of them, but never felt the same confidence and power surging through his body as he did in the woods. The cross was a simple wooden cross. Nothing ornate about it. The book was a simple brown leather-bound book of aged handwritten prayers and notes. There was nothing special about either item. Had he imagined the feeling? Edward dismissed that. What he felt was real, but how? Did Father Murray have anything to do with it? He needed to find answers.

"How are you doing, Eddie?"

"Oh, I am just hunky-dory, Father. And you?"

Father Murray motioned with his hands for him to slide over and make room. "I am good."

"Last night was kind of intense."

Father Murray chuckled. "Last night was nothing. They were evil, but we were never in any danger. I knew it as soon as I felt them. That is why I had you take the lead with me. Most of what we encounter is way beyond that."

Edward questioned, "Way beyond that? No danger? That one tried to kill me."

"He felt threatened and responded, but you were never in any danger. It felt that way because of how sensitive you are to them. Many we encounter, not only can, but want to harm you."

Edward tried to wrap his head around that. The pain he felt was real to him, and he'd thought he was moments from death.

Father Murray could see the self-doubt and worry rush into Edward. He attempted to reassure him, "Don't worry, we won't take the training wheels off until you are ready. The power to do all this is inside you. You were born with it. We just have to show you how to use it. We have a lot of training to do."

"Training?" Edward questioned. An image of some mythical magical school popped into his mind.

"This ability is like a muscle. You have to train to use it properly. Last night was just... a push up. Just meant to make you believe in your capability. Before last night, how much of what Lewis and I told you did you believe?"

"Well..." Edward thought about it for just a moment, "... probably more than you will believe. I have seen them since I was a kid. So, hearing that others do didn't surprise me. What you told me about Miller's Crossing and what I saw last night, I still need to make sense of."

Edward leaned down and held his head in his hands. "So, my father and mother were like me?"

"You mean able to see spirits?" Father Murray asked.

Edward nodded.

"Yes. They were just like you," Father Murray answered.

At that moment, Edward realized how different his life could have been. "I'm not sure you know this. I don't tell most people about it and need you to keep this between us."

"Of course. I am a priest, you know."

"I was put in a crazy home when I was fourteen because of what I could see. My foster parents didn't understand me and didn't know how to deal with me. I don't fault them. If my parents had been alive, they would have understood and could have helped me understand."

"I know. There are many things that would be better if your parents were still alive. I knew about what you were going through."

"You knew?" Edward asked, surprised.

"Lewis and I kept tabs on you. We tried to help, hon- "

Edward interrupted. "You tried? I spent years, drugged every day. They treated me like I was crazy. Hell, after enough of the medication I thought they were right."

"We tried." Father Murray attempted to console Edward. "Because of who you were, Lewis and I kept track of you. Lewis attempted to talk to the doctors at your facility to help explain what you had been through, to see if that would give them some perspective. We both tried to talk to your foster parents, but they sent us away and asked us to never attempt to contact you or them again." The old priest held up a hand to stop Edward. "... and, I don't blame them. They were trying to protect you. We even talked to Tony Yates to see if there was some legal avenue we could use. There was nothing."

Edward sat speechless.

"You would have had been about sixteen when Lewis said he wanted to tell your doctors the truth. Can you imagine what would have happened then?" A wide grin stretched across Father Murray's weathered face.

Edward thought about how Doctor Law would have responded. "It's a good thing he didn't. I already had a roommate. He would have been assigned to a different room."

"Those without the gift can't understand. We tried. We owed that to your parents. When you turned eighteen, we lost track of you until about ten years ago. Thank you, social media." Father Murray looked up to the heavens with his hands pressed together in prayer.

"Social media?"

"What? You think because I'm old, I don't know about such things? I post, tweet, share pictures. This church has its own page. I may be old, but I'm not dead." Father Murray bumped Edward with his shoulder and joked, "or am I? Would you know the difference?"

"Yep. You're talking," Edward said through a slight laugh.

"Ah, well... I will teach you how you can talk to them, just like I am talking to you now."

The surprised look on Edward's face said it all.

"You just don't know how yet. It is on one of the many pages of your family's book I gave you last night. I think your great-grandfather added it. Your grandfather added a few pages, as did your father. You will too, in time."

The old priest groaned as he stood up and walked toward the front of the church. His voice echoed in the empty sanctuary. "When we found you, I came out to Portland to see you. I planned to give you the cross and book, but when I sat in my car outside your house you and your family came walking by. You seemed so happy and adjusted. I debated with myself for the next few days. On one side, you needed to know. On the other, you had been through so much. To see you happy and with a family of your own. Do I risk interrupting that? I decided then to let you live your life. You were too young to understand how important your family is in this town."

"I knew how respected my father was, but nothing else," said Edward.

"Oh, your father was special. A great man, intellectually and spiritually. Never one to turn down the opportunity to help someone, but you knew that."

Father Murray was right. Edward remembered many a weekend his father and he finished their chores on their property, only to head out to help someone on theirs.

"He was a brother to me, as was your grandfather. How much do you remember of him?"

"Not too much." Edward was only seven when he passed away. He had a few memories of his father and grandfather out working in the pasture together while he ran around helping with his plastic tools.

"For you to understand all this, you need to understand your history. Are you ready to take that journey?"

His past was a mystery to Edward. He knew more about his foster family than his real family. What memories he had, were vanishing with time.

"Dad, can we go now? It's hot in the car," Sarah demanded from the church's front door.

Walking back toward Edward, Father Murray said, "Go ahead. Take them home. Do me a favor though."

"Of course."

"Think of your home as a museum. We left everything just as you left it. Look around. Discover yourself."

"I will."

Father Murray shook Edward's hand. "I will be in touch soon. Keep those items safe. They are more powerful than you can imagine."

Edward bowed and said, "Yes, master."

"Oh, I am no master. You are. You just don't know it yet."

That thought landed the weight of the world on Edward's shoulders.

18

When Edward and his children arrived home, Sarah and Jacob ran inside to avoid melting in the heat. Edward took his time and looked at the thunderheads developing. As a kid, he would ask his father, "How long do we have today?" Meaning, how long could he play outside before the storms would force him inside. There was no such conversation with his kids. They were inside turning down the air conditioning.

Edward walked in with the ancient Greek aphorism "Know Thyself" echoing in his mind. The pile of photo albums and old books in the dining room bookcases called to him. These were off limits when he was a child. Any time his mother saw him close to them or looking at them she admonished him, "Sweetie, you can look at them, but don't touch. They are old." Those books and that one antique chair in the corner were off limits. The devious seven-year-old inside him came up with an idea. He should sit in that chair while he looked through the books.

First, Edward headed upstairs to change into something comfortable. Once changed, he found himself standing in front of the bookshelf. "Where to start?" he wondered aloud. The obvious answer was the top. He pulled the first album off, a red covered, drugstore bought photo album loaded with instant pictures pressed between the pages. Edward's younger self was the main subject in most pictures. Christmas morning, candid school shots, and him in a few Halloween costumes. He didn't remember ever dressing up as a dog. That was one picture he'd never let his kids see.

He found one picture his eyes lingered on while emotions stirred inside. It was one of a younger version of himself flanked by both his mom and dad, probably the best picture he'd seen of the three of them. Carefully he removed it from the film covered page and put if off to the side. He was sure his mom would forgive him.

Edward returned that book and retrieved a larger dust covered book. Carefully prying it open, he sensed the age of it. The pictures weathered to shades of brown, grays, and hints of faded colors. They were of his father, grandfather, and various other men. Sides of the house and the old barn appeared in several of the images. One picture showed a fresh coat of red paint on the side of the barn. His father was maybe eleven years old in that photo. Someone probably wrote a date on the back, but he did not dare attempt to check.

Page by page he flipped through. Several of the pictures showed a woman with his father. He assumed that was his grandmother. He never had the opportunity to meet or even see a picture of her before. The next picture caused a pause. His father and grandfather were standing on either side of another older man. The mystery man was holding the cross and the book, and both his father and grandfather had their hands on the objects. He studied the men in the photo. His father was only a teen, and his grandfather was maybe in his early forties. The other man could've been in his sixties or seventies. Even with the discrepancy in age, there was something familiar in all of them. They shared the same eyes. He had to be Edward's great grandfather.

He tried to pry it from its page, but the aged adhesive maintained its hold. To avoid damaging it, he used a nearby piece of junk mail as a makeshift bookmark. A few pages deeper there he was again, with his father and a large group of men sitting on hay bales the barn. The image reminded Edward of a scene he walked in on several times when he was younger. It always ended with his father ushering him out.

Edward picked up the next album. The photos were more of the same, but they took on a whole new meaning. Picture after picture of men gathered together in some sort of commune. The cross and book only appeared in a few pictures each with his father, grandfather, and who he assumed was his great grandfather.

He stacked that album off to his side on top of the others. The stack in the bookshelf appeared to be more of the same, except one book. The book on the bottom had a brown leather cover and was much thicker, about the size of four albums. He pried it from its home of the last several decades and blew off the layer of dust covering it. The cover was cracked brown leather, with a single gold leaf cross on it. He remembered the book: the family bible. When he was five, his mother sat him in her lap and showed him their family tree inside it. He opened it, and sitting folded in the inside cover just like he remembered was the family tree.

The last entry at the bottom of the tree was his name, Edward Meyer, with his birthdate July 27th, 1974. Above that appeared his father's name, Robert Carl Meyer, and his birth date, February 11th, 1951 with his mother's name written next to and the date they married. The next one was his grandfather, Carl Edward Meyer, born August 13th, 1924, with his grandmother's name written next to it. Edward continued working up the family tree. It was a single tree, with each generation only having one child, which he thought was odd until he ran into something even more peculiar. There was a line drawn across the tree two-thirds of the way up. Just below the line written on the left edge of the page was "Miller's Crossing–1719". Above the line on the same side was the text "Saint Margaret's Hope, Scotland–1719". *That must be where we settled from,* Edward thought to himself. The mystery around the line only lasted a second. The next name up replaced it with even more questions. William Miller, born December 21, 1694.

Edward let the paper fall to his lap. His family's real name was Miller, like the town. Looking back up the tree, he confirmed the name below the line was Jacob Allen Meyer. *They changed their name when they moved here, but why?*

"Dad, are you ok?" Sarah asked while looking at him perplexed.

"Yeah, why?" Edward said from his position on the floor.

"Well, you're sitting in the floor, surround by old books, and looking out into nowhere, looking all weird."

"Just looking through some old family things."

"Okay," she said with a hint of a question, and then headed toward the kitchen.

Edward called after her, "Hey Sarah, wait up." Now was as good a time as any to have that conversation.

19

Edward followed Sarah into the kitchen. She grabbed a soda from the fridge and started back toward the door.

"Come have a seat with me for a second?" Edward said and sat down at the table.

She rolled her eyes and offered the mild protest, "Why?"

"Because I want to talk to you."

Her shoulders slumped as she dragged her presence over to the table and fell into the chair across from him. Edward knew if he asked her what happened Friday night, she'd give him some other excuse besides the truth. There was one way to do it, and Edward decided to lay his cards on the table, even if it meant she might think he'd lost his mind.

"How long have you been seeing..." he took a moment to choose his word, "things?"

Sarah stopped taking a drink from the bottle of soda mid-sip. Her eyes exploded wide open, and she stared at him over the bottle pressed to her lips.

He tried to reassure his daughter. "It's OK. It doesn't mean you're crazy. Quite the opposite."

Her glare had not moved, and neither had the bottle.

"You saw something Friday night, didn't you?"

The bottle dropped, and she gave a silent yet defiant, "No."

"You have nothing to hide. The Sheriff told me what happened." Edward then threw her a life preserver. "I see things. I have since I was ten."

"You see things? What do you see?"

"Well, I see spirits." Edward searched her eyes and expression for any reaction. Her body language relaxed. The bottle lowered to the table, and she leaned forward. Her eyes blinked for the first time in moments.

"You see spirits. What do they look like when you see them?"

"It is hard to describe. They look like people, but people who are there and at the same time are not there. Does that make sense?"

"The ones you see flash?"

"The ones? So, you *did* see something?"

She leaned back in the chair, looking around the kitchen. "I didn't say that. I don't know what I saw. Whatever it was didn't flash."

"They disappear and reappear in a different spot... but you can see through them."

"Like they're made up of light?"

"Yes, exactly. Some of them have a blue hue, some white. I have even seen a few that were reddish."

"Oh god, I thought they spiked my coke with something at the game or maybe used a projector to play a cruel joke on me. When the sheriff showed up, he yelled at a few of my friends for a while before he offered to take me home. I thought we were in trouble, and that was why he wanted to talk to you."

"He wanted to explain what happened and to help me understand. It took him a while to help me believe it myself. I used to think I was the only one that could see them. You have inherited something of a family trait that is tied to this town. My father had it and his father had it. I don't know how far back it goes. I was looking through our old pictures and family tree when you saw me earlier."

"Are you sure this isn't a trick or something?"

"Trust me. I wish it were. When it first happened to me, no one believed it. They thought it was the emotional stress from losing my parents. To say I had a rough time of it would be saying it lightly."

He motioned for her bottle of soda, which she slid across the table to him. He took a quick swig and continued. "Hell, I didn't understand things until the last few days. I still don't, but I know more now than I did before. Back then I learned to accept it."

"That has to be hard to just accept," Sarah replied with a sigh.

"You ain't kidding, but it was what I had to do to stop it from creeping me out and running my life."

"So, we are the ghost whispering family. Now what?"

"Not sure. Sheriff Tillingsly and Father Murray are trying to help me figure that out."

"Figures that old creepy priest would be invol..."

Edward cut her off. "Hey, wait, he's a nice man and a long-time family friend. Yes, his sermon and ways are a little... off... but the more I learn about this, the more it makes sense."

"So, they see spirits too?"

"Yes." Edward answered.

Surprised by her father's answer, Sarah asked, "Who else? Does the whole town?"

"Some do. I'm not sure who else. What I understand is much of the town sees them, but we have something beyond just seeing. We can interact with them."

Edward slid the soda bottle back to Sarah. Her eyes were wide open, and mouth hung agape. The soda bottle came to rest next to her hand, which did not try to catch it. "What do you mean interact? Can we talk with them?"

Sarah's question was one Edward had given a lot of thought. "Well, Father Murray said we can. I don't know yet? I'm still learning. There is also a chance your abilities may stop at just being able to see them. Father Murray said something about it only passing to male members of the family. So, I am not sure yet, but we can find out together."

"Good god, I was joking earlier. WE ARE the ghost whispering family," Sarah said with a half-hearted laugh. "What about Jacob? He is probably scared shitless... I mean scared to death."

Edward gave her a look at her choice of phrase, but let it slide. "He would be scared shitless, I agree with that, but no he doesn't. At least not that I know of. Father Murray said the ability doesn't develop in anyone that young." Edward realized he was making himself sound like an expert on the subject, when at that moment he was anything but. He had learned to live with it, yes, but was still learning what IT was. "When did you first see something? Was it Friday night?"

"That is something I have thought about a lot." She took a sip from the bottle and slid it to her dad as an offer, but it stopped halfway. "For a while I have had what I would call 'eerie feelings.' I would feel cold and tingly, but saw nothing. A few nights after we moved here, I felt it again and thought I saw something when I was outside. Since then, I have felt it off and on."

"A cold sweat followed by pin pricks from the top of your neck down your spine and the feeling of something heavy pushing down on you?"

"Exactly." She was stunned that he described it so aptly.

"I know it well. I feel it every time one or more of them appear. You get used to it. I have. It doesn't faze me one bit anymore. Neither does the group of them that circle my bed when I sleep."

"No way! You're just messing with me now."

"I wish I were. Every night since the first time I saw one when I was ten."

"Did Mom know?"

"Nope. I never told her."

"That is creepy. A group of them standing there watching you two sleep."

"Yep, and they watched you and Jacob too."

"What? You saw them around our beds?"

"Oh no. I mean the times you guys slept with us. They were there then."

She shivered at the thought and then stopped. "Can they harm us?"

"So, I've been told. Father Murray will teach me how to protect everyone."

"He's getting you a proton pack and traps?"

"No. Wait here." Edward went back to the dining room to retrieve two important objects. He returned to the kitchen and said, "with these," as he displayed the cross and book to Sarah. "They told me these have been in my family for years. They ward off these spirits and send them where they are supposed to go. That is all I know at the moment."

He left the kitchen again and returned carrying the photo album. Sarah was flipping through the pages of the small book he'd left on the kitchen table. Edward laid the photo album down and opened it to the page marked by the junk mail. "Look at this picture. That is my father, and I believe this is my grandfather. The man seated must be my great-grandfather. Look at what he's holding." He pointed to the object in his hands, the object that all three men were touching.

Sarah's eyes grew wide when she recognized it. She reached over and picked up the cross. She studied it as if comparing it to the photograph and uttered, "What the…"

"I don't know. It all seems unbelievable. Father Murray said he knows the story behind all this and will help me understand. This is a part of our family's past I know nothing about."

A loud rumble of thunder rolled across the pasture and rain pelted the tin roof. Sarah got up from the table. "I need to go close my window." She headed toward the kitchen door and stopped short. "I guess we're that one family every town has that is considered weird."

"I guess we are, kiddo."

"Damn, and I was just hoping to inherit something like a fortune, not a freaky ability. Just don't go changing our phone number and buying a white hearse with flashing lights Dad."

He gave her a smirk. "I'm not making any promises."

20

"Cream and sugar?" Edward asked Father Murray.

"Just black, thank you," he answered from the kitchen table.

"Here you go. This should take the chill out of your bones." Edward put a cup of black coffee down in front of Father Murray. The rain was still falling outside, along with the temperatures.

"Say goodbye to summer, my friend. It won't be long until there is snow on the ground."

Edward remembered a few heavy storms growing up that created snowdrifts out around the barn that he could get lost in. He and several friends shoveled all day to create a snow fort. It took a week until the temperatures warmed up enough to melt it. When he moved to Portland, there was just a slight dusting of snow there once. Everyone acted like it was such a big deal, but he brushed it off and went on about his business. That was until he received the fine notice in the mail for not shoveling his walk. He had never heard of such a thing, plus the snow melted by the next day anyway.

"I talked to Sarah."

"Oh, and how did that go?"

"She admitted she saw them."

"Good. I would hate for her to keep it to herself and stay confused. Nothing good can come from that."

"She was scared when the Sheriff showed up. Said he gave her friends a good tongue lashing. She thought they were in trouble for slipping her some kind of drug or something that caused her to hallucinate."

Father Murray let out phlegm-filled chuckle. "That would be an easier explanation, now wouldn't it?" he said. "Her friends are good kids, no reason to worry when she is with them. Lewis was getting on to them for taking her out there with no warning." He sipped at his coffee. "Tony McDaniel, you remember his dad, Robbie, don't you?"

Edward sure did. His father ran the local hardware store, and every time Edward and his father went Robbie and Edward ran around, to borrow his father's term, like two chickens with their heads cut off.

"Tony assumed because of your family, she already knew."

"That brings up an interesting question that Sarah asked. How many people are like us?"

"Well, nobody else is like you. Not even close." Father Murray took another sip. "But most everyone here can see or sense the spirits passing through. Let me be more specific. The original families can. Outsiders that have moved here can't. We keep things our little secret around them." Father Murray held a single finger up to his mouth. "That is why Lewis was so upset with Tony on Friday night. He thought he was showing things to an outsider. Luckily for Tony he only took her out there because he knew who you guys were. Once Lewis realized who she was, he let them off easy and brought her home."

"They knew who we are?" Edward asked. It seemed everyone knew more about his family than he did.

"Your family is one of the founding members of this town. Back in the day, when town elders saw to the day-to-day business of the town, your family had a large seat at that table. Everyone knows who you are and what you can do."

Father Murray's answer reminded him of the family tree and photographs he saw earlier. "I want to show you something." Edward sprinted from the kitchen to retrieve both books from the other room. He returned just as quick and placed them on the table.

"You heeded my words, I see," Father Murray said with a look of approval.

Edward pulled out the family tree and opened it up. "You say my family is one of the original families. Is it possible we were the founding family?" Pointing at the line drawn across the tree, "We changed our name when we moved here. Our last name was Miller, but when we moved here, we became Meyer." Edward searched Father Murray's face for answers. Answers he was more than happy to provide.

"It's true. They named this town after your family."

"OK. Why did we change our name then? Why not just keep it Miller?"

"To protect your family's identity."

"Whoa, wait." Edward sat back in his chair. He broke the silence. "What identity?"

Father Murray grabbed the family Bible and turned it toward him. He flipped in two pages and turned it back toward Edward. "I guess you didn't find the inscription in the Bible yet."

Edward stared at the page Father Murray was showing him. There was in fact an inscription written in deep dark ink. He imagined someone wrote it with a quill and old-fashioned ink well.

This sacred Bible has been blessed and given as a gift to the family assigned to the holiest of duties. May God Bless and guide your family in its duty.

−Pope Clement XI

1718

"This Bible was a gift from the Pope?" Edward asked.

"I presume. I may be old, but not that old. That is not what I wanted you to see, though. Read it again and pay attention to the words."

Edward read it again silently and then paused on one particular word. He looked up from the book and said, "Assigned?"

"Yes. The Vatican assigned your family to this location. Assigned to do a job. Do you remember what I said about this being a sacred site?"

"Yes."

"When the early settlers arrived in the New World, they identified this site. The Vatican picked, trained, and then assigned your family as guardians over it. Each of the other sites have a similar family. Your assigned responsibility is to protect the living while serving the dead. At the time, the United Kingdom and the Vatican were not on speaking terms. So, they changed your name to avoid any chance the Crown or the local British Army regiments could discover who you are."

"Why would the British have cared?"

"I am guessing they never taught you American history in that place did they, old boy?" Father Murray said as he stood up, stretching his old bones made tighter by the cool wet weather. He reached into his jacket pocket and pulled out a tin flask. He said, "I hope you don't mind," while pouring liquid warmth into his coffee.

Edward not only did not mind, but he pushed his own toward Father Murray, who obliged.

"Protestants searching for religious freedom established the colonies. They were Puritans, Quakers, Calvinists, and Presbyterians. Not a lot of Catholics or love for the Vatican. The thought the Pope was handpicking settlers and governors of those settlements would not be looked upon kindly. It could be seen as interference, and with the wrong tempers involved, it could have started the next chapter in the many wars England had with the Vatican, along with the other countries that supported it."

He took a sip of his reinforced coffee before continuing. "Luckily, the church had sympathizers everywhere. When word got around about this place, a few of them were smart enough to get word back to the Vatican through safer channels. Mind you, back then it was not as simple as emailing under a different name or anything. They had to know who to trust. If they chose wrong, their life could be at risk. When word got back, the Pope prepared the artifacts you would need and sent a dispatch for your family."

Edward's stunned look stopped the priest mid-thought.

"Yes, the Vatican knew about your family. How? I am not sure, but I assume their local priest learned of their abilities and reported to his arch diocese, and they reported up and so on and so on... anyway, where was I? Oh yes, they sent for William and trained him on the use of the artifacts, but also how to adapt and expand them. The story your grandfather told me is that the original book only had five prayers in it. Over the last however many generations, pages have been added as new prayers were created. The skills, 'the how's and what's,' were passed down from generation to generation through extensive training that begins as soon as a child shows the ability to 'see', or what your grandfather called 'ascension'."

Father Murray took his seat across from the wide-eyed Edward. "Since your father never had the chance to pass this on to you, I will have to fill in. I will not claim to replace how he would have taught you, but upon his passing I had to take up the cause, and I think I know enough to help point you in the right direction. Now if you can fix us both another cup of coffee, I can fortify it a little and we can get started."

21

Edward prepared another cup of coffee for Father Murray and himself. The cool rain outside and the events of the last several days created an air of discomfort. The warmth of the coffee helped Edward feel a little better.

Appreciative of the second cup, Father Murray added a little of his special sauce to both and asked, "Have you read any in the book?"

"A little. It looks like a book of random prayers."

"Well, you aren't wrong. They are prayers. and they are in there in a random order," said Father Murray. "Added to for over 300 years. Tell me. Is there one tool I can give you that will do everything you need no matter what it is you have to fix?"

Edward looked back at him with a quizzical expression.

"Humor me. I have a point."

Edward considered the question. His humorous side wanted to say, "Yes, a hammer. You can bang anything into shape or destroy it to the point no one cares," but he knew what Father Murray was getting at. "No. For most jobs you need a few."

He nodded in agreement and said, "And others you need specialized tools. Now consider this: are there problems that exist today the tools of a long time ago cannot solve?"

The answer was obvious to Edward, but he lets his smart-ass answer escape. "Well, I wanted to answer the first question with... a hammer. You can use a hammer to bang anything into shape and if that doesn't work you can destroy what you are trying to fix to where you don't care anymore. Same answer could apply now. If a piece of modern technology gives you a problem, you could use a hammer to destroy it and not worry about it anymore."

Father Murray showed an amused smile. The same smile he would make at a child asking if Santa Claus visited Jesus during the Christmas Day Mass. "Well yes, I guess you could, but that isn't fixing things, is it? But I assume you got my point. Things change, and you need new solutions or... eh... new tools to solve these new problems. Just like that book. Think of that book as your toolbox. It has a prayer in there for every unique problem you face. Those before you have created new prayers and added to it when they faced problems the old ones did not handle."

Edward flipped through the book. When he looked through it on Saturday, he saw page after page of prayers in various handwritings, not one labeled with the author or purpose. That begged the question. "How do I know what prayer to use for what?"

"That's what you have me for. I think first we need to go over some rules. And these are extremely important." The stern look on the normally cheerful man drove the seriousness of the message home.

"First, never let either the cross or the book out of your sight.

"Second, never damage either of them, especially the cross. I am not sure which object is the source of most power, but I can tell you they do not work without the other. With the story of the origin of the cross, I believe it holds most of the power." Father Murray paused when he realized he omitted a detail. "I haven't told you about that yet, have I?"

"Told me what?" asked Edward.

"Where the cross came from."

"No." Edward looked at the cross while taking a guess. "Let me guess. It's made from the cross Christ was crucified on?"

Father Murray replied, "That is what they say."

Edward's body language became nervous as he placed the cross on the table with great care.

"I don't know if it's true or not. There have been rumors around for centuries that they found the cross during one of the many Crusades and the church acquired it. What your grandfather told me is they created twelve identical crosses from the wood of the crucifix and sent one to each spiritual site.

"Third, when you read from the book you must do so with purpose. Believe in what you are doing and read with conviction. That is what I was trying to force you to do last night. Just reading the words will do nothing. You must believe with your heart and spirit.

"The last rule is the most important. Edward. I cannot emphasize this enough. Not every prayer in the book worked. Some completely backfired." Father Murray opened the book and then turned it around. With the conviction of God himself Father Murray looked up at Edward and said, "Never read it turned like this."

Edward looked down at the book and realized it was upside down to him, but there was text on the opposing page right side up. He asked, "What are these prayers father?"

"These are dangerous. Not only did they not work, but they also had dangerous outcomes. We logged them in here this way, so we know what not to do." Before Edward could say anything, Father Murray said, "And yes. I made a mistake once with horrible consequences. I logged it, so I would never repeat it."

Father Murray saw Edward's eyes scanning across the lines of the prayer facing him and slammed the book shut with a slap. He reissued his warning, "You can't even read them to yourself. They are not to be messed with. Understand?"

Edward wanted to ask why again, but he saw the serious expression on Father Murray's face and answered with a simple, "Yes, Father."

"Good. Are you ready for homework?"

22

"All right. All right, everyone. Let's settle down. Who did the reading last night?" Edward scanned the class and saw many attentive faces.

"Good. Who has questions?" A few hands sprung up throughout the class. Edward picked one. "Laura."

"Is it me or is everyone insane?" Laura Robinson asked from the middle of the room.

"I hope you are talking about the book and not your classmates. Care to expand on that observation for the rest of us?"

A smattering of laughter filled the room.

"Ahab, Pip, Gabriel. Ishmael describes them as being insane," Laura explained.

"Oh, that." Edward pondered how to explain that without spoiling the entire book. Melville was not the most complicated read, but can confuse someone if they only read the words.

"Let me give a simple answer. The true answer will explain itself when you read more, but I will remind you of one thing. When you read a book told through the eyes of a single person, a narrator, you are seeing their perception. As the reader, take that into account with everything else you read as you form your opinion." Edward walked towards his desk, but turned back to the class to add, "... and no, they are not all crazy. Some are brilliant. Any more questions?"

Silence filled the classroom. No hands raised or inquisitive looks adorning the scholarly faces. Edward pulled a stack of papers from his brown cracked leather satchel and announced, "Good, then you won't mind taking this quiz, now will you?"

The hush turned into a collective groan as Edward handed the front row copies of the dreaded quiz. As many things that are different in this school, the groans were a familiar sound. He resisted the smile which tried to sprout upon his face. "You know the drill. Take one and pass the rest back. Put any extras on the back table."

Edward watched the students consider the questions his quiz posed to them. Each student was quietly focused on their own paper. No sneaky attempts to look at another student's paper. Through his career he had seen many attempts. They ranged from the covert quick glance to the obvious swapping of tests. Edward remembered one creative try that took rather sophisticated planning. Someone paid the smartest kid in class to tap his foot in code for each question. One tap for A, two for B, and so on. Another reason he hated standardized multiple-choice tests. After the fourth question he noticed the tapping, but listened for a little longer. When he noticed the pattern, he put a stop to it and collected the test. The class had an old-fashioned fill-in-the-blanks style test the next day. What always struck him about that attempt was, if they put the effort it took to come up with this into studying, they would have been able to pass the test on their own.

Several students completed their tests and place them face down on the desk. The image invoked a curious thought about the conversation he'd had with Father Murray the prior day. *I wonder if he will give me a test?* Before he'd left, Father Murray retrieved three books from his car and instructed Edward to study them.

The first book was *Spiritual Exercises of St. Ignatius of Loyola*. Father Murray said that would give him the spiritual conviction to do God's will.

The second was *The Catholic Treasury and Prayers*. Father Murray said that would be the most difficult to study. Edward was not to memorize the prayers. Instead, he was to learn their meaning and understand the why and how of the prayer. The mechanics. That would teach him the proper way to develop his own when the time came.

The third was the most surprising. Instead of an official church-endorsed text, it was just the common *Encyclopedia of Saints* that you could find in any storefront or online bookstore. Edward asked Father Murray about it, but he explained that they declared new saints all the time. He needed to keep an updated guide. Father Murray told him every saint had a purpose. He needed Edward to understand and believe in that purpose.

Edward promised Father Murray he would study every night. The intensity of his voice during the request matched the glare of his eyes. That was no ordinary or casual request. When Edward agreed, Father Murray reiterated one last time, "This is a responsibility you cannot take lightly. Too much depends on it. More than you can understand at this point."

The last student turned over their quiz. Edward walked through the rows collecting the papers. To him, quizzes were both a way to measure how much his students were retaining, but also a teaching aid. "How does everyone think they did?"

A small groan, smaller than the one that accompanied the announcement of the quiz itself, radiated around the room. He stacked them on his desk for grading later at home. "Let's see how you did," he said, and quizzed the class. The reactions he saw from some students identified questions they believe they missed, while an air of confidence grew around others realizing questions they answered correctly.

They did a quick reading of a section he picked out to reinforce the topic he planned to cover for the next few days. The whole class took part. The first few days, there were a few quiet students in each class. Eventually everyone became acclimated to his interactive approach. That was a goal of Edward's. He found everyone learned better when asking questions and talking about the topic than just listening. He hated the thought of anyone afraid to ask questions, but could honestly say that did not exist here.

He assigned that night's reading just in time for the bell to ring. The students packed up with haste and headed to their next class. Well, most of the students did. A small group of three meandered in the back. Once most of the students had left, they made their way forward with a question. "Mr. Meyer?"

"Yes, Daniel. What is it?"

"Can we ask you a question?"

"You just did." Edward's try at humor only received a half smile. "But of course. What is it?"

"We heard about the other night. So, you are the guy?"

Edward expected a question on something discussed in class or the reading. It only took him a second or two to recognize Daniel's last name, Ruten. Martin Ruten was one of the group that went out with Sheriff Tillingsly that night. Daniel must be his son.

The three boys stared at him with an idolizing gaze that made Edward uncomfortable. "Look guys. I am not sure what you heard. I'm just your teacher. That's it."

"Oh, come on, Mr. Meyer. We heard how you took care of those creatures."

A small town was a breeding ground for gossip that can build up legends or tear them down. Edward knew that and tried to temper any aggrandizing of the events. "I was there, that is all. Father Murray told me what to do. It was really all him."

Students for his next class started to come in, causing the three to take a panicked glance at the clock. They hurried for the door, but not before Christopher said, "Embrace it Mr. Meyer. Your family is famous around here."

Famous was not something Edward wanted to be. He wanted to be normal.

Once home, Edward fixed his famous hotdog surprise for dinner. It was nothing fancy, just hotdogs in oversized buns. The surprise part was just the name Sarah gave it when she was eight years old. Edward was rushing to get home one night and stopped at the store for hotdog buns. In a hurry and not paying attention, he grabbed hoagie rolls. He didn't notice until Karen announced she'd lost the hot dog in the bun when she fixed one for Sarah. They had a good laugh. Sarah said, "Surprised there is a hot dog in there," and it stuck from that point forward.

After dinner he took a moment to clean the kitchen and then settled down at his makeshift office desk. To his right, the stack of quizzes that needed to be graded. To his left, the books he promised an old friend he would learn. He picked the quizzes and worked through the repetitive task of reading the answers to the same five questions over and over.

Occasionally he heard the words of Father Murray echoing through his head as he read an answer. He forced his way through the stack. He felt both a sense of accomplishment and heavy fatigue when he checked the clock. It read just after one in the morning. He should head upstairs for bed, but he'd made a promise. He reached over and grabbed *Spiritual Exercises of St. Ignatius of Loyola* and opened to the page he'd left off reading.

23

The ringing of Edward's phone startled him, and he jerked awake, grasping at the book falling from his lap, grabbing it before it reached the floor. He slapped around on the desk for his phone and pulled it to his ear. His groggy voice answered, "H... ello?"

An agitated Father Murray responded from the other side of the call. "Edward, thank god I got you. I need you to come with me."

"What? What are you talking about Father? It's..." Edward looked at his phone. "Father, it is 2:13 in the morning."

"Yes, I know. It is an emergency. I will be there in a few minutes." The call ended before Edward could respond.

Edward got up and headed out the porch to wait on Father Murray to see what that urgency was all about. The damp chill of the night cut straight through to his bones. He turned to go inside for a jacket when Father Murray pulled up behind him.

"Get in quick!" Father Murray called through the open passenger window.

Edward jogged down the steps toward the side of the car. His children were upstairs sleeping, and he didn't want to yell back-and-forth and chance waking them.

"What is going on?

"Come, come quick. We need to get to the Kirkland farm." Father Murray reached over and pushed the passenger door open.

"Wait, Father. Please explain what is going on," Edward insisted. The old priest was moving and talking rapidly. He ignored each plea Edward made for an explanation.

"Get in," Father Murray said while leaning across the seat of his road yacht Cadillac. He looked up at Edward and asked, "Do you have the cross and book?"

Edward answered, "No."

"Never let them out of sight! Go fetch them, right now."

He did as he was ordered and sprinted up the steps and back inside. He grabbed both objects from the dining room table where they sat next to the books he was studying when he fell asleep.

The trip into the house gave him the moment he needed. If Father Murray was here at this hour asking about the cross and book, it must be one of those kinds of emergencies. He pulled the door closed behind and locked it, then hopped into the passenger side of the Caddy. Without a word, Father Murray accelerated down the dirt drive.

24

Either the old suspension or Father Murray's ability behind the wheel caused the oversized car to wander from side to side, maybe it was both. Edward hoped his driving would improve once they reached the paved road, but that hope faded when it became more of a swerve at higher speeds.

"This will be difficult. You need to follow my lead." Father Murray's cell phone rang and interrupted him.

"Yes... yes... We are on our way. Should be there in just a few minutes. Try to stay calm." Father Murray slammed his old flip phone closed and dropped it on the seat beside him.

"The Kirklands are scared shitless. Pardon my language."

"What are we walking into?"

"Remember the other night? I said some spirits are more dangerous and malicious than others. The one we are going to fight is absolutely more dangerous. It's not lost. Oh no. This one is a type who is here to just cause trouble. Evil's little helpers is what your grandfather called them. It is ok to feel afraid when you see them for the first time. The first time your grandfather took me to go deal with one my knees almost buckled on me."

The level of concern in Edward spiked to an all-time high. Other than the first few times he saw a spirit, he had experienced nothing that struck fear into him.

"Father..." Edward started a question, but was cut off with more information.

"You cannot let the fear weaken your convictions tonight. These creatures will test you, but hold fast."

Edward pondered what he meant by "test" as they pulled into the driveway of the farm just four roads from his own. There was a group gathered outside, along with Sheriff Tillingsly.

Father Murray slid his Caddy to stop and appeared to be out the door before it even stopped moving. He instantly took control of the scene.

"Lewis, where are they?" he asked the sheriff.

In a tone showing wear from both his age and the late hour of the evening, he answered. "It's still inside."

"Just one?"

"Yes, Father. Last we saw it was in the hall. Had their youngest, Kevin, trapped in his bedroom. We tried to open his window, but... Father... it interfered." The sheriff showed great disappointment at failing to secure the child.

"It is ok, Lewis."

Father Murray made a beeline over toward the sobbing mother and father doing their best to keep their other two children calm. "Calm" at that point was just lower than hysterical crying. He was saying something to them, but Edward was too far away to hear it. They all crossed themselves and he led them in a prayer before giving a final embrace to the parents.

He started toward the front door with conviction. The town elders gathered outside took a few steps, but he stopped them. "Y'all stay out here. We need to handle this alone. It is too dangerous for everyone." He motioned toward Edward and called, "Come on. We need to hurry." Father Murray did not wait, and rushed up the steps and in through the front door. Edward followed reluctantly.

Edward stepped through the door and almost ran into the back of Father Murray, who had stopped at a table just inside the doorway. The priest removed his coat and silently blessed a red stole before putting it around his neck. He crossed Edward and then himself. He placed his right hand on Edward's shoulder and said, "In the Name of the Father and of the Son and of the Holy Ghost, Amen. Let God arise and let His enemies be scattered: and let them that hate Him flee from before His Face! As smoke vanisheth, so let them vanish away: as wax melteth before the fire, so let the wicked perish at the presence of God." He released Edward and turned toward the hallway that ran through the center of the house.

"Get the book and cross out. We will need them for this battle."

Father Murray stepped through the doorway that separated the front room from the hall. When his first foot hit the worn wood floor of the hall, the entire house gave a mighty shake that knocked Edward against the wall. In his attempt to regain his balance, he looked down to see large white particles of dust dancing across the floor. A glance forward revealed the source. There was a line of salt on the floor in the doorway.

The duo proceeded further down the hallway. Rumblings of the floor accompanied every step. Edward felt his heartbeat in his throat, and even though he was not claustrophobic, the walls appeared to be closing in on him as his breathing became shallow. A heavy darkness settled on him.

A growl emerged from behind the closed door at the end of the hallway.

Father Murray yelled at the door, "Kevin, we are coming. Just try to stay calm."

The panicking voice of a child emerged from behind the door: "Ok."

Edward asked, "Was the growl him?"

"Don't be silly. That was the creature in there with him."

As they got closer, the growling and scratching of a great beast continued. Father Murray reached for the door handle and quickly withdrew his hand. He retrieved a large vial of water from his robe and poured it over the door handle. The water sizzled on contact, producing steam. "Holy water is good for many things. Even cooling off a hot door handle." He covered his hand with his robe and gripped the door handle. A grimace of pain exploded on his face. The heat from the door handle was still hot enough to sear his hand through its covering, but he fought through the pain and turned the handle, opening the door.

At first glance, Edward only saw a crying child sitting on his bed, holding up a sheet as protection.

"Where is it?" Father Murray asked the child. Kevin pointed up above the door.

"Edward, push the cross in through the door. That should force it to move back."

Edward adjusted his grip on the crucifix and extended his arm. Before it crossed the threshold of the door, a voice entered his head. *You are not a priest. You don't belong here.*

Edward stopped and Father Murray noticed. "Ignore whatever it is. Push the cross through the doorway."

Edward heard what he said, but no longer saw a doorway. In front of him was the pasture that ran alongside his home. It was a nice spring day. He felt the warmth of the sun on his face and the smell of wildflowers wafted in the breeze. The sound of his children's laughter approached him from behind. A dog chased a butterfly among the tall grass. Edward did not remember ever getting a dog, especially with Jacob's allergies to pet dander. The dog almost caught the butterfly that time. He felt a hand grab his, but before he could look down to see which of his children was holding it, the image, the smell of wildflowers, the warmth of the sun, and the dog disappeared. Father Murray gripped his hand, forcing the cross into the bedroom.

The still calm that was the bedroom became a swirling tempest of wind and debris. The child was screaming, but the sound did not escape the room.

With no sign of fear, Father Murray entered, scanning each of the corners. His hand urgently waved for Edward to join him. With the cross still firmly extended at the end of his outstretched arm he stepped in. Edward scanned the surroundings and froze in place when he saw the mass of glowing red steam hovering just above the floor.

"Open the book." Without even looking at it, Edward opened the book, and the priest flipped through the pages. When he found the one he was looking for, he pointed to the page, like he did that night in the woods, and ordered him to read. Edward looked down at the page and recited: "O most glorious Prince of the Heavenly Armies, St. Michael the Archangel, defend us in the battle and in our wrestling against the principalities and powers, against the rulers of the world of this darkness, against the spirits of wickedness in the high places."

"You don't believe this shit, do you little Eddie?" the voice in his head asked. The voice felt personal and strange all at the same time.

Edward ignored the voice and continued. "Come to the aid of men, whom God created incorruptible, and to the image of His own Likeness He made them, and from the tyranny of the devil He bought them at a great price."

"Come now Eddie. You have always been one of my favorites. Why are you doing this? I kept you company all of those nights God and his many disciples ignored you while they locked you away."

Edward shook his head to clear the voice out. Father Murray took notice. "Are you ok?"

"I'm fine," Edward snapped back at the Priest. A memory stirred inside him of a recurring dream he had as a teen, but he pushed it to the back of his mind and continued reading. "Fight the battles of the Lord today with the Army of the Blessed Angels."

"Angels are just a viewpoint. They are eternal good to some and demons to others. To some I am an angel. Why resist me?" At that moment, his mother appeared before him. Not the spirit of his mother that he had seen many times throughout his life. The full living breathing version of his mother. She hugged him warmly. "Oh Eddie," she said in the voice he remembered as a child. "This is too much for you. Why don't you go outside with the others and relax? You look so tired."

For a moment he felt very comforted, but the distant voice of Father Murray reminded him of where he was. Edward pushed her back and exclaimed, "You are not my mother." The figure morphed into a mass of red steam again. Edward looked closer and saw a humanlike form inside the mass of steam. The cold voice echoed in his head. "No, I am not your mother. But I knew her very well. I was there the day she died. I remember when you came running into the kitchen to find them."

Edward gasped. A flood of emotions sent him alternating between now and the seven-year-old who found his parents. "You were not there. Stop talking about my parents," he screamed.

"I was. Kevin reminds me of you that day. A wide-eyed child full of fear. You left too soon for me to introduce myself."

Father Murray rushed over and yanked the book out of Edward's hands. Edward could see Father Murray talking to him, but could barely hear him. He sounded like he was yelling at him from miles away. The only voice he heard clearly was the cold one in his mind.

Muffled in the background, Edward heard the Priest read, "As once thou didst fight against Lucifer, the first in pride, and his apostate angels; and they prevailed not: neither was their place found anymore in Heaven. But that great dragon was cast out, the old serpent, who is called the devil and Satan, who seduces the whole world. And he was cast unto the earth, and his angels were thrown down with him."

Edward felt stuck between the here and now and the past. His mind's eye only saw darkness. A dark void that the voice echoed from.

"Behold, the ancient enemy and murderer strongly raises his head! Transformed into an angel of light, with the entire horde of wicked spirits he goes about everywhere and takes possession of the earth, so that therein he may blot out the Name of God and of His Christ and steal away, afflict and ruin unto everlasting destruction the souls destined for a crown of eternal glory.

"On men depraved in mind…"

"Speaking of depraved in mind. Ever wonder what a child looks like burned from the inside out?"

The dark void Edward was entrapped in was replaced by a ball of fire. "Leave him alone," he commanded.

"Why should I?"

"Why shouldn't you? Why harm the child?"

"It is simple." The presence circled around his body like a great snake wrapping around a prey. "I have to remind you of your place and me of my place in this world. It ensures balance and fights off chaos. You wouldn't want to put the world into chaos, would you?"

In a strange way that made sense to Edward.

He felt two hands on his back give him a great shove forward, breaking him from the trance, returning him to the bedroom where he now lay face down on the floor. The push forced the cross in Edward's hand through the spirit, sending it retreating to the corner of the room. Edward forced himself to his feet as papers and toys flew into everyone in the room.

He looked at the child on the bed and saw a translucent fire engulfing him.

"Father! The boy!" he screamed.

"He is fine. I need you here with me."

Edward exclaimed, "The flames!"

"What flames?"

Through the wind, Father Murray struggled to take the two steps needed to bring him alongside Edward. He held the book in front of him. "Follow me."

"Behold the Cross of the Lord, flee away ye hostile forces," Father Murray declared in the room.

Edward followed. "The Lion of the tribe of Judah, the root of David hath conquered."

"May Thy mercy, O Lord, be upon us,"

Edward responded, "Because we have hoped in Thee."

"O Lord, hear my prayer."

"And let my cry come unto Thee."

"The Lord be with you,"

"And with thy spirit."

"You need to chase it into that corner and shove the cross right in its heart."

Edward felt a surge from within and moved toward the corner.

The voice appeared again. "Do you really want to do this? Do you really want to follow the directions of the person who released me and let me kill your parents?"

"What does that mean?"

"Now Edward! Don't stop--" A huge explosion sent Father Murray flying backwards. Edward felt himself impacting the cold wet dirt outside the house. He looked over to see terrified parents running toward their child covered in flames.

Edward felt paralyzed on the ground until a few of the elders came over to help him up. Sheriff Tillingsly helped the Kirklands' tend to Kevin while they waited for the ambulance to arrive. He suffered burns on his hands, feet, and face. The only wounds Edward suffered were mental and emotional.

Father Murray emerged from the wreckage that was once the child's bedroom. He talked to Lewis and the Kirklands first, then he approached Edward, who sat on the ground where he landed.

"You lost focus. This is serious. We are lucky that the worst that happened are the burns. People could have lost their lives tonight. This is one of those spirits I told you about. An evil demon." He threw his hands up. "You cannot lose focus while we are doing this. It is a war. And no, I am not using that word lightly. It is a war."

He walked back over to the Kirklands as the ambulance pulled up. Kevin was quickly loaded up, and it headed off with full lights and sirens, with Sheriff Tillingsly's car following behind it. The silence around Edward was a stark contrast to the debris field radiating from the shattered house.

Edward had not moved since they helped him up. He sat there pondering what the creature meant by preventing Chaos, and helping the person who killed his parents. It reminded him of the question he pondered for years: why God let something so horrible happen to his parents, people who were so good.

He stood up and walked toward Father Murray, who was leaning next to his Caddy. "I'm sorry Father. I failed."

"It's all right. We all fail. I lost count how many times I have in this life. Kevin will be fine. The burns have already started to fade. They are something the creature did to scare us, but they are not real, and will be gone in the next day or so." Father Murray pointed to the house. "Now this on the other hand. Insurance companies won't understand an explosion caused by a failed spiritual saving. Lewis will help document a gas explosion to get the house repaired. For now, they will stay with me, which is fine. I need to counsel them on what they have gone through anyway."

He opened the car door. "Come on. Let's go home. We have a lot of work to do, and you need your rest."

Edward pondered the many questions on the ride home. The mental, physical, and emotional exhaustion took a toll. He just needed sleep.

When Father Murray dropped him off, Edward walked through the spirits that encircled his home. There appeared to be more now, and they were standing closer, all facing his house as if it were a religious shrine. He passed through them on the way inside, feeling the cool chill and the familiar tingle of their presence, but paying no bother. He was too tired to and discouraged to even care.

Once inside, he locked the door and threw everything in his hands on the dining room table. Cell phone, book, cross and all.

25

Edward's walk into the school the next morning resembled the trek of a zombie. He was both physically and mentally exhausted. To say the night before took it out of him would be an understatement. His path was strangely solitary. The normal greetings he heard from students and faculty were now replaced by glares, as people move to either side of the hall, clearing his path.

His talkative classes were silent and slightly clinical. They answered the questions Edward asked during class. A few asked questions on their own, but the warmth and idle conversation he had enjoyed was gone. Instead, the students looked at him as though he had a large hairy growth on the side of his face.

Lunch in the teacher's lounge was even worse. Edward was one of the first in the lounge for that lunch period. He set up at the same table he had for the last few weeks. As others came in, they barely acknowledged him. They gathered at other tables or stood at the counter at the back. Edward could hear the murmurs of their conversations, but couldn't make out any specific words.

"Is this seat taken?"

"Sorry Mark, they're all taken," Edward responded, dripping with sarcasm.

Mark pulled out a chair at Edward's table and set out his lunch.

"Are you expecting others for lunch?" Edward eyed the multiple wrappers and containers Mark pulled out of his bag.

"Sharon hosted a bridge party for her friends last night. Tons of leftovers. Hell, I don't even know what's in some of these." Mark opened one container to reveal wings, another with potato salad, and then unwrapped an aluminum foil log with ham in it. Mark pulled out a paper plate and an extra fork and handed it to his table mate. "Dig in."

Edward looked at the spread, and then back at his sandwich. The decision was not a hard one. His sandwich found its way back into the bag it came in. He took the fork and stabbed a piece of the honeyed ham and then dolloped out a lump of potato salad.

"Thanks. You sure you want to be sitting here with me?" Edward said with a mouth half full of ham.

"The back counter is full. Nowhere else for me to sit with all this food." Mark needled his friend with his elbow. "Relax. It will pass in a few days."

"How did everyone find out so fast?"

"Simple. Small town. Just don't fart during the moment of silence anymore." Mark dug in on the wings, leaving Edward to wonder what that meant, and then it hit him.

"Oh stop. I was six." That event was a perfect example of the speed of news in a small town. He farted rather loudly during the moment of silence once in the first grade. There was a mild embarrassment at the moment caused by the half-muffled giggles, by midday nobody remembered it. When his mom picked him up that afternoon, she welcomed him with, "Hey there big guy. Heard you had a rough day." He always wondered how she found out so fast.

"To some of these people you were a superhero the minute you stepped back into town. You took a little hit last night. You will recover."

"All this still seems so strange to me."

"I bet. You haven't lived through it for over thirty years like the rest of us." Mark shoveled potato salad in his mouth. "... W... When I saw my first ghost, I was afraid to tell my parents, but it was at home and they saw it too, so they knew. The explanation they gave seemed like something out of a corny horror film. I didn't believe them at first. A few of my friends thought the town elders were putting something in the water to make us hallucinate. It took years of sighting and experiences before I got it."

Edward thought how lucky Mark was to have parents that understood. "Took me a few years in a mental institution to understand what I was seeing."

Mark stopped chewing on the piece of ham and gawked at Edward. "You're serious?"

"Absolutely. My foster parents thought I was nuts."

"I could see that. How was the looney bin?"

"Crazy."

"I bet. Seriously, how was it?"

"I spent a while trying to convince everyone I was not crazy. Then I spent time convincing myself I wasn't crazy. Eventually I learned how to play the game to make them think I was all better, so I could get out. At that point I didn't care who was crazy or not."

"Maybe we are crazy. Maybe this whole town is crazy, or something is in the water making us all see things. Could be a big government conspiracy."

"Explains why the water is a little green."

"Yes, it would." Mark chuckled. "Know you aren't crazy, and others can see them too. Don't let the weight of your family's role in this wear on you. It took me long enough to accept what my eyes saw. I never had to deal with what you are. By the way, how should I address you? My Savior? Should I bow?" Mark gave a mini bow with both hands over his head.

"You can call me a failure," Edward said, looking down at his plate.

Mark patted him on the shoulder to reassure him. "Just be Edward and take things one day at a time. You have a great support system here. Father Murray, Lewis, and others like me and Sharon."

"I feel like I failed big time last night." The image of the hysterical family circled around the child screaming in agony hadn't left Edward's mind. He wondered if he should have talked to them, instead of just sitting there on the ground. He can't help feeling responsible for what happened to their son and home, but he didn't understand what he could have done differently.

"Think of it as more of a stumble. I hear the boy is fine now and enjoying all the attention in the hospital. Larry and his family will stay with Father Murray until they repair the house. Should only take a few weeks. There is a crew out there now."

Edward was unsure if Mark was just trying to make him feel better or telling him the truth. The bell for the end of the lunch period sounded and Edward helped Mark snap the covers back on the containers scattered across the table. They filed out with the mass of other teachers out of the lounge and down the hallway to their classrooms.

26

Edward tried to keep his yawn quiet, but failed. The sound echoed through the cavernous church. Luckily, it was empty at the time.

"Keeping you up?" asked Father Murray. He had entered through a door on the left of the transept. "It's alright. I still feel last night a bit too." He motioned for Edward to join him up at the front of the church.

He'd taken a pew in the back of the church. His mood and performance made him feel unworthy of sitting any closer to the altar. He only moved because his friend insisted.

"Kevin just came back from the hospital. He is fine. They all are."

"They are? But his burns?"

"They are over in the house watching TV, waiting on pizza to arrive. His burns were not real." Father Murray walked around the front of the church, picking up some bulletins discarded on the floor by the prayer service that just left. "They were more for our benefit, or should I say yours. The creature was trying to scare you, not harm the boy."

If that's the case, it succeeded, thought Edward. Just the thought of the images he saw struck fear in him.

"Did you hear voices?" asked Father Murray.

"Yes, I heard voices. The creature spoke to me."

"He was playing a psychological game with you."

Edward thought back to the images and places the creature took him. They seemed very real, not just a psychological trick. He explained, "It was more than voices. He took me to another place. I was not in the bedroom at times. I was in a field with my kids with a warm fresh breeze blowing around us."

"Trust me. You were there standing next to me the whole time. These beings are crafty." In a tone that echoed his sermons, Father Murray explained, "Like the Devil himself, these creatures will whisper rose colored promises and produce images of deception to bend our will in their direction. We, everyone, not just you and I, must be strong in our conviction and trust in the Lord. If we give in just once, that is the door that pure evil will walk through. Look at the root of all evil in this world and you will find someone that has accepted one of those promises."

The words Father Murray said struck a chord inside Edward. It was a sermon he heard him give when he was a child. It was also a sermon he heard repeated in every church he and Karen attended in Portland. His mind struggled with the literal thought of a creature like they encountered being behind all the evil in the world. It could be an example of the eternal battle of good versus evil. It could also just be a philosophical statement, that true evil comes from acceptance of a promise that was unearned or undeserved. Like a bank robber looking for the promise of riches without working for them.

"Are you coming?" Edward looked around for the Father and saw him standing in the back of the Church, heading out the door.

"Yes, ummm. Where are we going? Edward asked, following him down the aisle.

"More training. You didn't hear a word I said, did you?"

"I did."

Father Murray didn't buy that response. He knew he didn't.

27

After an uncomfortable day of isolation at school, Edward found himself yet again in the passenger seat of Father Murray's Caddy, driving to an unknown location. The trip was more relaxed than others. Father Murray even turned on the radio which was pre-tuned to an oldies station. He hummed along to the Animals singing about "The House of the Rising Sun."

They drove through the center of town, which was still rather active despite darkness setting in.

"If you want a great apple pie, go to Ruthie's right there," Father Murray pointed out. "Have you checked Dan's newsstand? He has several shelves in the back where he keeps paperbacks of the new best sellers. That is the closest you will find to a bookstore here. The next is one of those huge things a couple of towns over. If there is a book you really want, Dan can order it for you."

Edward confessed, "I haven't had much of a chance to explore downtown yet. I've shopped a few times in the corner store for groceries and a few dinners at Len's. I remembered his fried chicken from when I was a kid."

"Doc said I have to watch that stuff for my cholesterol and my gall bladder." A mischievous look spread across his face. "Don't tell him I visit or get takeout from Len's a couple times a week."

Edward smiled. "Your secret is safe with me."

The lights of town disappeared behind them as they continued to drive for a few more minutes, then pull into a driveway of an old farmhouse. There was a single light on over the front door. A man emerged when the Caddy creaked to a stop just even with the front porch.

"Evening, Paul."

"Evening, Father."

"Is it still here?"

"Yep, o'er yonder. Just past the pump house."

"All right, go on inside. We will take care of it. Tell Molly I said hello."

"Will do. Night," the man said, and disappeared back in the house without acknowledging Edward.

Father Murray started down the driveway toward the barn at the back of the property with Edward in tow. "Paul is a good man. His wife is from a neighboring town. She doesn't see the spirits, but the thought of them being anywhere near her scares her to death. I still am not sure why they haven't moved yet."

Edward asked, "If she can't see them, how does she know they are there?"

"Paul tells her when they are around."

The two rounded the barn and Edward saw their destination, a small shed about fifty feet away. "Remember how people treated you when you told them what you saw? Imagine the reverse. You see nothing but are living in a town where everyone else does. It took a while before she accepted this was not a huge joke we were all playing on her. When she did, her fear set in. I think the fear comes from not being able to see and understand like the rest of us can."

A cold shiver traveled down Edward's neck and through his back. "Father..."

"I feel it too. That's why we're here, and I want you to take the lead."

"Are you sure?"

"Absolutely. Show me what you got."

Father Murray stopped short and to the side of the shed. Edward felt timid as he walked around the shed and came face to face with a single spirit, a man, standing there. He fumbled through his pocket for the book and cross. He found them, but while pulling the cross out he dropped it in the high grass at his feet. The spirit continued to look at the back wall of the pump shed.

Edward reached down and searched for a few moments in the damp grass until he found the cross. He held it out with his right hand toward the creature and opened the book with his left. Both objects shook from his nerves.

"Relax and breathe," Father Murray coached from the side.

Edward tried to take a deep breath, but his hands continued to shake. His voice quivered as much as the cross. He recited the prayer on the page. "Holy Michael, the Archangel, defend us in..."

Father Murray cut him off. "You can't use the same prayer every time. Feel your way through this and pick the right one."

Edward stood there, dumbfounded, and unsure.

"What do you feel?"

"I feel the same cold shiver I always do."

"Go deeper."

"I don't understand."

Father Murray asked, "Do you feel fear, Edward?"

"I am afraid to fail."

"Not that. Do you fear the spirit? Do you feel any malevolent intent from this spirit.?"

Edward took a moment. "No, not like last night."

"Reach out with your feelings and tell me."

Edward closed his eyes and searched through his thoughts and sensations. He sensed the spirit. Its presence combined with an overwhelming feeling of being lost. At first Edward thought that feeling was associated with his own lack of confidence, but he soon realized it was different. "I feel unsure of what I'm doing, but I also feel something else. Someone is lost."

"That feels foreign to you, like what you feel when you become attached to a character in a movie or book, doesn't it?"

"Yes. Exactly."

"That is the spirit in front of you. He is lost, not a threat. St. Michael's prayer is used when we go to battle. There is no reason to take hostilities against a peaceful spirit that needs help. Now look through the book. Find the right prayer."

Edward flipped through the pages and searched. All the while, he hoped Father Murray would come point out the right page to him. With his hands no longer shaking, Edward found a prayer on the sixth page that he believed to be the correct one. "I think I found one." He turned to show him. "Is this the right one?"

Father Murray held up a hand to stop him. "That is for you to decide. Go ahead and read it."

"O God, the bestower of forgiveness and the lover of human salvation, we beseech Thee, of Thy tender love, to grant that the brethren of our congregation, with their relatives and benefactors, who have passed out of this life, may, by the intercession of Blessed Mary, ever Virgin, and all thy saints, come to the fellowship of eternal bliss. Through Christ our Lord. Amen."

The spirit disappeared in front of their eyes.

Father Murray gave a light applause. "Good. This spirit was just lost. You gave him the rites needed to pass on. Come now. Let's get out of here, it's getting cold."

Curious about the scenario Father Murray just described, Edward asked, "Is that a guess?"

"Yes and no." Father Murray pulled his coat collar up to shield from the cold. "Call it experience." Father Murray turned. "Over the years I have felt many spirits and tried many prayers. Over time you hone your sense to what you feel. With the non-violent spirits you can try multiple prayers until you find the right one. With violent ones, mistakes empower them, so you must be careful. I cannot emphasize that enough." His words and expression landed on Edward with a fright. "So, what caused you to pick that prayer?"

Edward told him, "I read through the words and recognized a few terms and phrases in what you have me studying. They are ones used for redemption and reunification. It seemed like one that could reunite one with their loved ones."

"Perfect. Good use of information and judgement. Come now. Let's get out of here before we catch death and become spirits ourselves."

The normally quiet drive back was filled with story after story by Father Murray. Some involved Edward's grandfather or father. Others didn't. Each talked about what Father Murray sensed going into each scenario. All knowledge he was trying to impart on his new student.

He asked if it was the same feeling for everyone.

"I asked your grandfather that when I first arrived, and he explained that it is. Based on my experience, it is the same mostly. I felt everything like he described it, more or less. There are slight differences, but the sensations were close enough that I knew. It just takes time to learn and recognize it." Father Murray explained only stopping to laugh.

"What?"

Father Murray pointed ahead of them. "Look up yonder."

Edward looked up the crushed stone driveway of the church. A group of spirits circled both the church and his own car. "The cross draws lost souls. They can sense where it is, and where it has been."

"That would be why they circle the farmhouse now."

"They mean no harm. Kind of like a moth to a flame."

"Why don't they follow me when I carry it?"

"I don't know. Suppose they take a while to sense it. Maybe if you stand in once place long enough with it, they will."

The thought of being the pied piper for spirits tickled Edward's sense of humor. "As if any of this could get any odder."

28

Edward walked through the door and into a parallel universe. Jacob sat at the dining room table doing his homework. Sarah stood over his shoulder, helping. She wore an apron he hadn't seen in years. The sound of the front door closing caused both kids to turn around and look at him.

Sarah put her hands on her hips and attempted to tap her foot while asking, "Where have you been, mister?"

"I had a school meeting. Remember? We talked about it this morning and you agreed to start dinner." Edward did not make a habit of lying to his children, but at that moment he felt he needed to.

"Yes, and dinner is in there covered in foil. Jacob is almost done with his homework." Sarah took off the apron. She handed it to her father.

"Nice apron." He noticed her very non-school-dress-code-compliant-outfit and asked, "Going somewhere?"

"I found it hung on a nail on the backside of the pantry door. I didn't want to mess up my outfit. And yes, Charlotte will be by to pick me up soon. She wanted me to come over to watch a movie together and... before you ask, I won't be out late. I know it's a school night."

Sarah gave him a quick kiss on the cheek and a "Thanks Dad" on her way up stairs.

Edward took over her position behind Jacob, looking at his homework. She was right. He was almost done. With a quick glance it appeared Jacob had answered them correctly. No modern math here, everything just as he learned it years ago.

"Is it good?" Jacob asked while looking up at him.

Edward picked up the page. "Yep, everything looks right. Exceptionally good."

"Are you sure? Mom was always better at math."

"I am sure." Edward then pulled out the chair next to him and had a seat. "You miss her, don't you?"

"Yeah. Sometimes more than others."

"Like now?"

"She always helped me with my homework.

"I know. I miss her too. Just know she is looking down on us."

"Like an angel?" asked the precocious seven-year-old.

"Exactly. She watches over us."

"Even here? Does she know we moved?"

"Especially here. She came with us. We take her everywhere we go in our heart."

"Cool."

He handed the page back to Jacob, who put it in his math folder and slid it into his backpack. "Thanks," Jacob said and then headed upstairs. Edward knew he was off to declare war on a mythical world in the digital universe. The rule in the house was homework first and then video games.

That was more Karen's rule, and one he helped Jacob break a few times. His video game habit was actually Edward's fault. During college, Edward got his first exposure to video games, and he was hooked. When he and Karen started living together, she gave him a little grief about his childish hobby. When she walked in and found Jacob sitting in Edward's lap being taught how to play, she rolled her eyes and walked out. Edward still enjoyed them with his son from time to time. Some fathers and son play catch, some build things, not Edward and Jacob. They bond while hunting people down in a digital playground. The aromatic smell coming from the kitchen reminded Edward he was hungry.

Edward yelled up the stairs, "Hey Jacob, let me eat something and I will be up."

"You will just die a lot."

Edward conceded, "That's fine." Inside though he had other plans.

He placed his bag on the dining room table, along with the book and cross, and made his way to the kitchen. Sarah had a plate on the table in his spot covered with foil. He was impressed. She cleaned up afterwards too.

Edward looked at the balled-up apron in his hand. His mother wore that apron every time they cooked cookies together. Briefly he held it to his nose hoping to detect a familiar smell. To his surprise, even after all the years, a hint of it still existed. Edward un-balled the apron and straightened it out. Feeling like the seven-year-old he was the last time he opened the pantry door, he neatly hung it back on its nail.

The front door slammed. Edward sat down to enjoy his dinner. A smile and a warm feeling came over him. Despite everything that had happened to him and his family, moments like that one made him realize life was good.

29

"H... ello?" Edward said. He was not sure if he was awake or dreaming. His body had acted on instinct, reaching for his phone when he heard it ring, like Pavlov's dog. There was no answer coming from the phone, so Edward said, "Hello, Father?" The entire room was still and silent. There was no vibration from the old boiler fan. The wind blowing outside when he went to bed was now calm.

"Hi, Edward," the creature responded, not from the phone, but from the foot of his bed. Edward sat up in bed confronted by the same red steam he saw in Kevin Kirklands' bedroom. The steam slowly morphed into a form that was both human and not human. There were arms and legs and a head, but the proportions were off. Its legs were too long, and its arms were too short. They ended with hands made up of fingers that appeared to be three times too long. Its head was round, with two dark orbs where eyes should be, and no mouth.

"I like what you have done with this place."

Edward glanced quickly at his night table, but remembered the cross and book were sitting on the dining room table downstairs.

"They are not there. It is just us. Let's have a talk."

"What is your name?"

"You have been watching too many movies. Oh no. I tell you my name and disappear. Like the wicked witch when Dorothy threw water on her." The creature appeared to grow larger on its perch as the dark soulless eyes showed a hint of flames. "It doesn't work that way. Father Murray should have told you that. There is much he should tell you."

"What do you want?" Edward asked.

The creature leaned back, appearing almost relaxed. "I want to be your friend. I am not the enemy here. Not by a long shot."

"I have read about your type. You make promises to convert people."

"More propaganda from a guy that walks around wearing a robe and a white hat. I know, I am supposed to promise you love, success, knowledge of the future, money... all that jazz, or you could listen to your favorite song backwards and hear my best hits. Let me ask you this question."

Edward tried to get out of bed, but his covers pulled against and restrained him. "Sit still. We will be done soon. I have no promises to make you. No fortunes to throw your way. What I can offer you is the truth."

"I don't want your version of the truth," Edward yelled at the creature.

"Now, now. There is no reason to raise your voice at me. I know that they have brainwashed you, and I will not battle that. I offer you a more personal type of truth. One that Father Murray is hiding from you. One you need to know."

The creature, glowing with a reddish hue, got up and strolled toward the bedroom door. "You should ask Father Murray to tell you the truth about him, about you, and about me. We go way back." As it faded into nothing, Edward heard the haunting voice come from above his bed: "He is still on the phone for you..."

30

"Are you there?" Father Murray's voice screamed through Edward's cell phone. The creature that was there a moment ago was nowhere to be seen. His covers released him. A stiff breeze blew at his window and the heater vent chattered as air passed through it.

Edward answered, his voice shaking. "Yes, Father. What is it?"

"I am on the way to get you. We must hurry." Father Murray, irritated, mumbled, "Lewis should have come straight away to get you and not wait for me in this case. There is no time to waste. No matter…" His voice trailed off as he hung up. Edward believed the last bit was a rant Father Murray was making out loud, and not meant for him to hear.

Edward got out of bed and looked around the room for any sign of his visitor before moving about. There was nothing. The bed covers didn't even show signs of anyone sitting on them.

He threw on some clothes and, recalling how cool it was outside earlier, he grabbed his coat before heading into the hall. A quick check on both Sarah and Jacob, who were both sound asleep, put his mind at ease before he headed downstairs.

He stepped off the stairs as the lights of Father Murray's car flashed through the windows. Edward fetched his wallet and keys, expecting the cross and book to be right there. He placed them together on the table earlier. A quick search located them on the other side of the table, by his books. A fleeting thought of the creature moving them ran through his head as he hurried out to Father Murray's car.

Father Murray was on the phone when Edward got in. He sped off, steering with one hand when Edward closed the door. Without a seatbelt on yet to secure him, Edward was tossed around as they speed down the dirt and rock driveway.

Father Murray yelled, "No Lewis! Don't go in yet. We will be there in five minutes at the most." He hung up the phone, dropping it to the seat beside him. It bounced to the floorboard.

"We are heading to the Reynold's farm on the other side of town. This is bad."

"You told the Sheriff we would be there in five minutes at the most."

"I lied. Sue me. I had to keep him from going in," Father Murray said, annoyed.

He drove his oversized car with reckless abandon down the deserted country roads. His speed was only matched by the fire engine and two ambulances that passed them just before the edge of town. Edward noticed red lights flashing on top of the light poles as they darted through town. The original thought was these were to alert aircraft to the poles. The realization that no aircraft would be that low caused him to search for another purpose.

"Father, what are those flashing red lights?"

"What lights?"

Edward pointed one out as they sped by. Father Murray uttered, "Oh my god" and rolled down the windows on both the driver and passenger doors. The nerve shattering sound of a klaxon horn flooded into the car with the cold evening air.

Edward had heard that sound in the movies and asked, "Is that what I think it is? A tornado warning?"

"In most towns, yes. Here it's for something different. Those sirens have only sounded a few times since you were born." Father Murray reached around blindly on the seat beside him.

"It bounced into the floorboard."

The level of annoyance in Father Murray's face increased. "Agh... we will be there soon enough."

He was right. In just a few minutes they pulled into a scene more chaotic than the other night. It appeared every police car in town was there blocking the roads. Lights from the fire trucks and ambulances created blinding flashes. The doors of the ambulances were open. Several people sat on their tailgates, being tended to by the paramedics.

John Sawyer ran up to the Caddy as it slid to a stop. "Father, you need to come quick. Lewis took the boys in back."

"Damn it. I told him to wait," Father Murray exclaimed as he got out.

"A couple of the boys have come back. They are being tended to. Nothing serious."

"I heard the sirens coming through town. Is it what I think it is?"

Edward joined Father Murray on the driver's side of the car and saw the fear in John Sawyer's eyes as he said, "Yes. It is the worst I have ever seen."

Father Murray turned to Edward. "Did you read anything from the book tonight?"

"No. Not since we were together earlier," Edward replied.

"Are you absolutely sure? Not even just to yourself."

Edward confirmed. "Yes. I am sure."

Father Murray's stared sternly at Edward and then asked, "John, which way did they head?"

"Back around the house."

Father Murray took off running into the darkness and summoned Edward to follow.

They rounded the house and entered a dark empty field. The lights and sound of the hectic scene were replaced by the sounds of crickets and frogs and their own movements through tall grass. As they walked further into the darkness, an eerie silence replaced the crickets and frogs. A silence that was only pierced by men yelling and something howling and screeching.

Three forms, backlit by the creatures they were trying to hold at bay, came into view. Father Murray chastised the Sheriff. "Lewis, I told you to wait."

"Sorry, no can-do, Father. People were getting hurt."

"You're not equipped to handle this. Where is it?"

The Sheriff looked confused at the question. There were many spectral beings right in front of them, but at his request, he gave him a situation report, "Three out over there to the right. They have been quiet. Another four or five over to the left over here. They are the troublesome group. I think the one that bit the girl is in that group."

"No. Where is it?" Father Murray demanded while peering into the darkness.

"That depends on which IT you mean. I haven't seen your old friend, but I suspect he is out here. If you are talking about the other, you are right. There is one open. Follow me. I will get you as close as we can get."

The sheriff moved deliberately through the tall grass, watching every step.

"Edward, get up there with the sheriff and hold out the cross. That should keep the path clear."

Edward moved up next to the sheriff and held the cross out at the end of his stiff right arm. He took timid steps in the darkness, unsure where they were heading and what was out there.

Sheriff Tillingsly asked him, "You don't believe that piece of wood will protect us, do you?"

Edward answered without hesitation, "Yes."

"Good, I wouldn't want you out here unless you believed it. Too dangerous for all of us if you don't."

"Lewis wasn't much of a believer when he was..." Father Murray struggled with a memory of yesteryear. "How old were you the first time you went out with Carl?"

"Twenty-two."

"That is right... still wet behind the ears. Ronald was tending to a crash out on Maple Crook Road, I think. You responded to what they called in as a trespassing."

"Yeah, the old days where we used code words over the radio to avoid scaring anyone listening in."

"When Carl and I got there, Keith Lloyd told us you wouldn't wait and headed on back. We got back there, and you were frozen stiff..."

"Is this the best time for a story?" Sheriff Tillingsly said, sounding both annoyed and embarrassed.

"I don't know what he was trying to do. She was just a lost little girl. Carl took out the cross and Lewis kind of scoffed at it. I think he said something like, 'what is a piece of wood going to do?' He saw what it did. The girl settled down and let Carl kneel next to her. I still remember your eyes when you watched him whisper the prayer into her ear and she disappeared."

Still sounding embarrassed, "It's not much farther."

Edward felt the familiar chill and tingles, then the repressive weight settled in. His ears filled with a vibration that resembled static. It grew louder with each step, disorienting at first, and then painful.

"Brace yourself," Father Murray said from behind.

Then it came into view. A spinning black void, darker than the night sky. The cyclonic motion created a ring of distortion around the edge.

Edward asked, "What the hell is that?"

"You used a proper word there. It is a portal."

"To where?"

Father Murray took a few steps closer to the void. "Now that is the good question. They say to hell, but we don't know for sure. What I know is nothing good has ever come through one of those things."

"Now Father, that is not nice," echoed a voice Edward was all too familiar with. All three men tensed up and become alert. Each searched the darkness for the creature. Edward spun around, pointing the Cross in all directions.

Father Murray demanded, "Show yourself, vile creature."

"Is that anyway to speak to an old friend? Hi, Edward. I see you have your little cross now."

"Face us," Father Murray demanded again.

"I wasn't born yesterday," replied the creature. Its voice boomed among the static and vibrations, everywhere and nowhere all at once.

"Behind you," said Sheriff Tillingsly. Father Murray turned around in time to avoid a demonic creature charging at him. It caught his long peacoat in its jaw as it ran by, ripping it off.

Father Murray pulled a vial of holy water from a chain that hung around his neck. He prepared for another charge, but the creature just stood there.

Sheriff Tillingsly let out a painful shriek. Edward spun in his direction and saw a ghastly arm extending through the front of Lewis's chest. Agony on his face as he struggled to breathe. Instinctually, Edward pulled the book out of his pocket and searched through the pages. A sudden silence appeared in his head. There was no static, no vibration, just emptiness. Or so he thought. He sensed there was someone there in the silence with him. A presence he felt and could almost sense its thoughts. Not wanting to wait, Edward seized control.

"I know you are there. You can't hide from me," Edward yelled.

"You are right. I can't hide from you, but then again, why would I want to?"

"You're scared of me. You know…"

A maniacal laughter echoed in Edward's head. "Scared of you? I am here to help you. You keep placing your trust in the wrong people."

"You are pure evil," Edward retorted.

"Am I? I am truth. Face it. I am the only one who will tell you the truth. Father Murray is lying to you. The honorable Lewis Tillingsly is lying to you. You don't want to accept that."

"What truth are you talking about?"

"Oh Edward, Edward, Edward. It is right in front of you. You were handed a piece of wood and an old book and told to go save the world. They sent you out into the world ill-prepared, and to be honest, dangerous."

"I am not dangerous. I am not the one out here hurting people. That would be you."

"Are you so sure? Do you know what page to flip open to make me go away? I think not. You have no idea how dangerous it is for you to pretend you know what you are doing. You are messing with a power you can't understand, and you aren't the first, and won't be the last. You need to stop before someone else gets hurt."

"You are just trying to trick me into stopping," Edward challenged.

"Stop yes, but not by tricking you. I am trying to help you realize you are not prepared for this. One mistake can have horrible results. It happened tonight, and it happened about forty years ago."

Edward asked, "What happened tonight?"

"Oh, come now. The portal was opened. Something I cannot do. Only someone reading the wrong page from the book. Maybe a child experimenting with friends, as they might with a Ouija board."

A hazy image of a kitchen, his kitchen, replaced the darkness. Edward was floating in the air above the scene, as a small boy walked in and screamed. Edward looked at what the child saw, and there was his mother lying in a pool of her own blood. Multiple stab wounds covered her body. Each appeared to have come from the inside. His father's body was on the other side of the island lying in a similar pool. His head separated from his body.

"Wait…" Edward exclaimed as a realization hit him like lightning. "You said a something about a child experimenting. I didn't read from the book. I didn't even know about the book. You are wrong there."

"I said a child was behind tonight. Look closer," the voice said. Edward didn't want to, but he had no choice. That scene was burned into his head. It now rotated below him as a young Lewis Tillingsly burst through the door and quickly scooped Edward up. It paused for just a second and zoomed in on his face. Before he left with Edward, Lewis stopped and glared at something or someone that was outside of

Edward's view. Edward tried to turn to see more, but the scene did not respond to his movement. The creature controlled the scene. Now it rotated below him, bringing in to view a figure dressed in black, weeping on his knees, with a familiar cross and book on the floor in front of him. Edward's mind couldn't believe what it was seeing. He whispered, "Father Murray."

"Yes. Your trusted family priest."

Edward didn't remember him being there that night, but he also didn't remember looking anywhere but at his parents. Edward asked, "What is he doing there?"

"Search for the truth, and be careful who you trust," the voice said, now sounding distant.

The scene faded, and the vibration returned to Edward's ears. The chill he felt from panic was replaced by the coolness of the evening air. His eyes cleared and a new scene appeared before him. Sheriff Tillingsly was lying face down on the ground. Father Murray was on his side in the grass. The dark void was closing, and in the distance behind it Edward saw a dozen or more figures disappear into the darkness of the night. As the final glimpse of the void disappeared Edward heard the familiar voice: "Be careful who you trust."

31

Father Murray rolled up to his knees. Edward rushed over and helped him to his feet. Without saying a word, they both ran to Sheriff Tillingsly's side. He was unresponsive, and Edward could only find a weak pulse. The two men picked him up and carried him back in the direction of the house, screaming for help the whole way. It took several minutes before anyone heard them, and a few more before two paramedics and another deputy reached them.

Edward stood there helpless over his lifeless body as the paramedics administered aid. He heard one of them mention it appeared he suffered a severe cardiac event before one of them began CPR. The other took off and returned with a gurney. Edward helped them load him on the gurney and then rush to the ambulance.

The sirens wailed as Sheriff Tillingsly was rushed to the hospital. The last remaining paramedic crew was tending to the many people injured. They attempted to check Father Murray several times, but he brushed them off each time.

Edward stood in the middle of the chaotic scene of light and sounds as people rushed around. He felt numb to all of it though, like he was watching it all from the outside.

Father Murray brushed off another try to tend to several scratches across his face. He approached Edward very agitated. "You can't just freeze like that. Lewis could have died. We both could have." His tone of voice snapped Edward back to the here and now. A heavy disdain for himself settled on his shoulders. It was fueled by the disappointment he felt in himself and that coming from everyone else that passed him. He was supposed to know how to handle these situations. Or was he? Edward tried to explain. "I had no control over it. That thing took me someplace else. It took me back to the day someone killed my parents."

"Took you some place? What the hell are you talking about?" He turned and walked away from him.

"I couldn't see you or the sheriff. I was some place dark and silent. It was just me and it."

"I told you this the first day. You have to be strong in your convictions. It detected weakness in you and took advantage of it. That is why he went after you and not Lewis or me. You were the weak link he could exploit, and he did." He walked away again, shaking his head. "This is my fault. You are not ready for this."

"That is what it said, too," Edward said.

"See, that is what I am talking about. It knows."

Following a few feet behind the Father, Edward said, "It was more than that. Something about trying to tell me the truth." Edward struggled to remember the details. Like a dream he woke up in the middle of, he remembered a few feelings and words, but specific details dissipated from his mind.

"What truth can that thing possibly offer you? Think about it. The Devil and his minions are creatures of lies and promises. Scripture teaches us that. I don't want to hear anything else about it. WE have a disaster to clean up."

Edward remembered one vague detail he felt compelled to share. "It said something about a child opening something."

At first Father Murray ignored what Edward said, but hesitated for a second and asked, "What did it say about a child?"

Edward tried to remember more details, but he could only come up with disjointed phrases. "Something about an opening and a child playing with something like a Ouija board."

Father Murray looked around at the people leaning against cars and sitting on the ground. His attention focused on Charlotte Reynolds, sitting on the back step of the remaining ambulance. The medics were tending to what looked like a bite wound on her face. Father Murray walked toward her, quicker than before. He approached Carol Reynolds, her mother, who was standing beside her, and placed his reassuring hand on her shoulder. "How is everyone doing over here?" he asked.

Carol turned toward the Father and Edward, tears streaming down her face. "We are ok. Once they are done here, we will head to the hospital, so they can stitch her up."

"How are you holding up Carol?" Father Murray asked.

"I am a mess. What happened here? I have never seen so many, and they were aggressive. They chased us down." At that moment, Edward ignored the fearful look in her eyes and caught sight of the claw marks on her arms. These were all real injuries, not like the flames that engulfed Kevin Kirkland. There was real pain and damage here.

"I am not sure Carol, but trust in me. We will protect you," Father Murray said in that consoling tone of voice he had used many times to comfort people in times of need for the last several decades. Edward thought there must be magic in that tone. They did not protect anyone tonight, but Carol ignored all the pain her and her family had suffered and accepted his promise. "Thank you, Father."

"Before you take Charlotte, I need to talk to her for a few minutes, if that is ok?"

Carol did not question why and agreed. "Of course."

Father Murray took off his large black brimmed hat and settled on the step next to Charlotte. "I thought you would have given it a good upper cut before it got you."

A smirk showed on the young girls face as she replied, "I got a few good blows in."

"That's my girl. Can you tell me what happened?"

"I was asleep when they appeared. These are not like the ones we usually see. Those pay no attention to us. These were here, in our world... and they ran after us, yelling and growling the whole time."

Not finding any helpful details, Father Murray probed further. "What about before you went to sleep? Did you notice anything, or did something happen?"

The girl's body language changed, and she stared at a spot on the ground in front of her.

"Come on, Charlotte. Can you tell us anything that might help us?" Father Murray said as he looked at Edward.

"We just watched a movie. She went home, and I went to bed."

Father Murray had the look of a man who knew he was just lied to. Before he could try another question, Edward jumped in. "Sarah, my daughter. Is that who you were watching a movie with?"

"Yes, Mr. Meyer. We were just watching a movie. We didn't mean to cause any problems," Charlotte said with a quiver in her voice.

"What did you do?" her mother asked.

"Sarah showed me a book. She said it was THE book. We didn't read anything out loud."

Father Murray mouthed "the book," in Edward's direction. "It is important that you answer me truthfully. Did you read anything at all? Even just to yourself?"

"No. I just looked at the outside and flipped through it."

Father Murray looked up at her mother as he said, "Thank you. Everything is going to be ok."

He got up and put his hat back on.

"Come, Edward. We need to go talk to your daughter." Father Murray sprinted toward his Caddy.

32

Father Murray sped down the dark country roads with reckless abandon. Edward's mind raced just as fast, searching for answers. Sarah had never had the book or the cross. Even if she did, how would she even know what to do? Then he remembered. When he rushed out to meet Father Murray, the book and cross were not where he left them. Had she taken them when she went to Charlotte's? That was the only explanation.

"Edward, what is it?"

"Huh?"

"What's wrong? You yelled 'Jesus'."

Edward was unaware of the utterance. It must have been a subconscious reaction to the realization. "Sarah must have grabbed the book before heading to Charlotte's. I noticed when I came to meet you it was not where I left it." Edward was not sure if he could let his priest down any more than he already did, but he had now proven that wrong. "I am sorry. I know I shouldn't have let it out of my sight."

"Don't be silly. You were at home. How could you have known?" His words were meant to reassure Edward, but his tone told a different story. "The important thing now is to find out which page she read from." Edward then heard Father Murray say under his breath, "I think I already know."

As they sped through town, the streets were vacant. The siren wailed and the red lights flashed. Edward struggled with his thoughts, trying to piece together what he was shown and what he saw. The line separating both was rather fuzzy. The word "portal" repeated in his head several times.

"It said someone opened a portal. A portal to where?" Edward asked.

"Where? I don't know. No one does. Here is a way to think of it... or how I think of it. The common thought in the church about possession is you have to invite and accept the demonic spirit. The portal is a doorway opened to accept or invite them in. Whether it is a doorway to some spiritual place..." Father Murray yanked the wheel to the left and then back again. The tires squealed in response, trying to maintain traction on the road surface. "Damn deer, the spirits must be spooking them. Anyways... we are not sure if it's specific to some realm or just a general doorway to all spirits. What I know is every time one is opened, nothing good comes through, and we need to close it."

"There is a page for that?" Edward asked. He hoped for a simple "yes."

"More than one page. We will have to try many things and we may need help. Until then we will have our hands full."

"Wait, help? Help from who?" Edward asked.

"The Church has people I can call who specialize in this kind of thing. But I am hoping we can act quickly enough that won't be necessary. We have to close the portal, and fast. That will limit how many creatures come through. GOD knows, we will have our hands full dealing with what already has."

Edward's mind pictured the swirling disk of black with creatures coming through it. "Why don't we force them back through or open another portal to push them back through?"

Father Murray glared at Edward and said, "No! Clear that thought out of your mind."

Father Murray swerved his Caddy onto Edward's driveway. In just moments it came to a stop in front of the door. Both men exited and raced through the spirits encircling the farmhouse. Edward noticed a few red entities in the grouping, but continued in without a word to Father Murray. He continued up the stairs to wake Sarah, while Father Murray stayed in the living room. Edward returned moments later with a sleepy teenager following behind him asking, "Dad, why did you wake me?"

Father Murray spoke before Edward could answer his daughter. "Sarah darling, we need to talk to you, and you need to be very truthful. You are not in any trouble. Tonight, when you were with Charlotte, what did you guys do?"

The look of someone wide awake and trapped replaced the sleepy look in Sarah's eyes. "We watched a movie, why?" she said.

"Sarah, you need to tell us the truth," Edward pleaded. Father Murray waved his hand in Edward's direction. Edward gave him a curt node.

"Sarah, a demonic portal opened behind Charlotte's house tonight. Several creatures came through. One bit her on the face. Others attacked her mother. I need you to tell me what page you read from tonight when you were there."

Sarah dropped and sat on the bottom step of the stairs. She buried her head in her knees and sobbed.

Father Murray stepped forward and sternly, as if giving a sermon, said, "Everyone will be ok, and you aren't in any trouble. You had no way of knowing what could happen, but I need to know what page you read from so your father and I can stop it before someone else is hurt."

"I am sorry. I did not know. Everyone at school knows who I am, and they have all heard the legend of the cross and book. I get asked everyday if I have ever seen it. I didn't mean any harm. Just wanted to show it off."

"That is fine, but the page. I need to know the page."

Father Murray extended his hand toward Edward. Edward pulled the book out of his pocket and gave it to Father Murray. He knelt in front of Sarah and presented the book. "The page, Sarah. Please?"

She took the book and flipped through several pages. About two thirds through the book, she spun it around and pointed to a page.

Father Murray glanced the page and dipped his head. Without moving he said, "Thank you. You can go back upstairs. Your father and I will handle this."

Sarah stood up, tears streaming down her cheeks. Guilt filled her eyes. In between sobs, she said "Daddy, I am sorry. I am really sorry."

Edward said, "It's ok. Go on back to bed." Edward was not sure if everything was ok. He was trying to shield his daughter from what that was. From the body language of Father Murray, he sensed things were a long way from being ok.

After a few moments of silence between them, Father Murray stood up and walked toward the kitchen. "I will need some coffee," he said while pulling a familiar flask out of his pocket. "I suggest you have some too."

Edward followed him into the kitchen. He took his familiar seat at the table while Edward prepared the base for their liquid courage. Edward delivered the steaming hot cups of caffeine to the table and Father Murray opened the flask and poured a generous amount into his coffee. Father Murray extended it over Edward's cup and paused for Edward to nod permission.

"So now what?" Edward asked.

"It is not Sarah's fault. What she read was in Latin. I am sure it sounded fancy and impressive to her, but she didn't know what the words meant."

"What did they mean?"

"She asked Satan to grant her the power to open a doorway for his army of darkness."

Edward had just picked up his coffee cup when Father Murray explained the prayer. He dropped it the inch back to the table. It landed with a thud. Coffee sloshed over the edge and onto the table. "Why would a prayer like that be in the book?" he asked.

Father Murray sighed and sat back. "Well, do you want to hear the complex answer or the simple answer?"

"Just an answer."

"In all conflicts, there are two sides. The dark and the light. Good and Evil. At some point someone on the side of the light always considers trying to harness the powers of the dark to aid them. There are several prayers or readings in the book that attempt to do that. They were enticed by the power they perceived to exist."

Edward bluntly asked, "My relatives were Devil worshipers?"

"Absolutely not. Your family is one of the most prestigious and religious families in the world. They tried to use these dark passages to aid them in their duties. How can I explain it? It is like someone who is against violence and guns, resorting to violence to further their cause." Father Murray thought about it for a second and then said, "That didn't help clear it up, did it? Just understand your family is an honorable family. They understand the responsibility of their duty and the power that exists on both sides. Along the way, they made a few bad decisions about how to use those powers to fulfill their duties."

"So, what do we do? I assume there is a page that counters this spell."

"Not exactly. I need to call someone. This is above both you and me. I tried once before and failed. I won't take that chance again."

Father Murray's final word crossed into Edward's ears as a loud vibration built inside. The room around him faded to black. There was no chill or tingling forewarning him of the presence, but in just moments he was back in a familiar vacant place, and he was not alone. That same presence was in there with him.

A voice boomed through the blackness. "Remember what I showed you."

The black void gave way to the scene of his parents lying on the floor in the kitchen. Their arms were moving, pointing toward the table, pointing toward Father Murray. He was on his knees weeping.

"Search for the truth, Edward. Search for the truth."

"Edward. Edward, can you hear me?" The image of his kitchen cleared, and he was once again sitting at the table across from Father Murray.

Edward responded, "Yes, Father. I can now. It was here again."

"You must block him out of your mind. Strengthen the conviction of your faith. I will help you learn to battle it."

As Father Murray explained, Edward's mind pondered what it was just shown. The phrase still echoing deep in his thoughts forced a question to the surface. Edward exploded, interrupting Father Murray. "Why were you here the night my parents were killed?"

Father Murray was taken aback by the question. Edward considered the possibility he wasn't there, and the creature was showing him a false story. The expression in the eyes of the person sitting across from him said something different.

"That was the worst day of my life, in so many ways." He took a tentative sip of coffee, his hands shaking the entire time. "I didn't know you saw me."

"Why were you here?"

"We were trying to save you and your mother, but were too late. Your father... your father rushed in before I got there."

Father Murray's words contradicted the story he'd been told. They told him it was a break in, and the cops believed his parents heard a sound and went downstairs to check it out. When they walked into the kitchen, they startled the burglar and he killed them before they had a chance. There was obviously more to the story, and

Edward wanted to know it all. He demanded, "Tell me what happened. Not the story you all told me about a burglar. Tell me the truth."

Father Murray swallowed and took a deep breath. "You should know the truth, but let me say I am so sorry. I didn't understand as much as I do now. We were in the middle of an extremely bad and violent period of spiritual activities. Your father and I were trying everything we could to keep things under control and some days we did, and others were not so good. We were desperate and tried something. Just once. We thought we could keep it controlled, but it got away from us."

"What did?"

"We were out in the pasture just on the edge of your property. One of the creatures took off toward the house. Remember I told you they're drawn by the energy of the book and cross. Your father left the cross inside, and that one was going for it. I heard your mother scream before your father reached the porch. Then I heard your father screaming prayers and commands. I entered the backdoor just as your father fell to the floor. The book and cross both crashed on the floor and slid toward me."

"What did Father?" Edward questioned again, louder, insisting on an answer.

"Before I could do anything it was gone. Your parents were dead, and you were standing in the kitchen doorway. We called Lewis earlier when we headed out into the pasture to deal with it."

Edward slammed his fist on the table, causing coffee to spill from both cups. "Father, you said something got away from you. What did?"

"You have to understand. We were running out of options."

"Tell me. Tell me the truth."

"Your father and I discussed it over and over and we agreed." The expression and body language of the old priest became defeated by a great weight he had carried for decades. Edward felt his temper growing inside and opened his mouth to unleash on his friend.

Before Edward could utter a sound, Father Murray confessed. "We... or I, tried to use a dark prayer to battle the demons." He looked straight at Edward and tried to explain. "It was something we discussed over and over. Things were out of control, and people were getting hurt. We thought if we could gain control of it, we could send them back to where they belong. I even consulted a fellow priest on the matter. We both agreed under the circumstances. I made a mistake. I used one I didn't fully understand. The same one Sarah read tonight. A portal opened outside, letting in several creatures. We had it controlled. Your father tried to force one back through the portal, but a creature emerged. The creature you have encountered several times. It took control and turned everything against us."

Edward's temper had control of his senses. His mind stopped hearing the words coming out of Father Murray's mouth after he admitted to using a dark prayer to battle the demons. He leapt to the next logical conclusion. A conclusion that had shattered his confidence in the man sitting before him and brought the tragedy from so many years ago back front and center. He stood up and walked away, Father Murray still pleading at table behind him.

In a moment of anger and clarity, Edward turned and walked back to the table. Father Murray was still talking, but Edward did not hear him. Instead, he slammed both the cross and the book on the table in front of the old priest. He jumped in shock. "Father, your actions killed my parents. You destroyed my life in so many ways... and you hid the truth from me. You created this problem. YOU released these monsters. This is your problem. I came here with my family for a fresh start, not to continue a tragedy. I will protect my family, but as for this great responsibility you speak of. It is yours to deal with."

"But Edward..." pleaded Father Murray.

"There is no 'but' anything. I am done. You created this. You have done fine without me for so long. Now take those things and get out of my home."

Edward walked over and opened the backdoor. "You will be leaving now, and will not return."

Father Murray reluctantly stood up and paused for a second, searching for the words to say, but nothing came to him. He walked to the door and left.

Neither man said a word to each other as Edward closed the door. Edward took a seat back at the table and had a few more sips of his coffee. His mind and heart bled at the realization of what really happened to his parents. There was no robbery or aggressor. It was a careless mistake by someone his father trusted, the cruelest crime of all.

33

Edward slept little the rest of the night. There were no disturbances or interruptions. At least not outside of his own mind. The scene of his parents in the kitchen played over and over in his head, much like it did when he was younger. There was just one difference now. He had filled in the missing pieces. The more he saw, the more his anger developed toward Father Murray. He wondered who else was involved. Was the sheriff? Was his father aware of the danger? He responded to each question with the same answer. His focus was his family and kids and that was it. The others were all on their own.

He turned over in the bed, trying to get comfortable and clear his mind. He needed to get some rest. Instead, he spied the time on the alarm clock on the bedside table. One minute before his alarm was scheduled to go off, the cruelest trick of all.

Edward forced his tired body and exhausted mind out of the bed and toward the shower. He was hoping the hot water would wake him up. It only took a few minutes for him to realize that hope was full of hot air. He dressed and finished getting ready before he started down the hallway to make sure his children were up and getting ready for school. There was a brief consideration of letting Sarah stay home from school, but he heard her up and heading into the bathroom to get ready.

Jacob met his father downstairs sitting at the table, already showered, and dressed for school. It looked like it would be one of the easy mornings, and Edward was thankful for that. "What'll you have for breakfast, champ?" he asked his son.

"Cereal."

With a choice of four varieties in the pantry, Edward gave his son a look that asked for clarification. Jacob's reply was also non-verbal, as he pointed in the air, directing his father's hand until it hovered in front of the right box. Edward pulled down the box of sugar covered morsels and poured Jacob a bowl and then covered it with milk.

Edward leaned back against the countertop while he downed a cup of coffee. He wanted to get two in him before he went to work. Sarah emerged through the door and walked over and gave her father a hug. She whispered "Sorry" in his ear and then fixed herself a cup of coffee. He wanted to let some of his anger loose on her and tell her that sorry didn't come close to even covering it, but he stopped. She did not understand what she was doing or even how bad things were. Edward wanted to keep it that way and protect his family.

He started on his second cup and wondered if there would be any reaction at work today to what happened last night. He remembered how surprised he was at how fast things got around after the first time. It was almost a guarantee people would know. The last drop of his second cup hit his lips and he checked the time on his watch. They should have left five minutes ago, but he was too tired to panic. He said, "Let's go. We're late." Neither kid resisted nor hesitated. They grabbed their things and headed straight for the door.

Jacob hopped out of the car at his school and shut the door. Edward pulled off and headed toward the high school. His drive was mostly on auto pilot. He sat there looking straight forward. Sarah was too. She broke the silence. "Charlotte texted me earlier. She is all stitched up and feeling much better, but won't be back to school for a few days."

"That is understandable. How is her mom doing?"

Sarah said nothing. Instead, she looked down at her phone and typed feverishly. About a minute later there was a ding. "Her mom is doing fine. Father Murray is with them now."

Edward wanted to say, "Tell them not to trust that old goat. He is more dangerous than helpful," but he held it to himself. Instead, he said, "Ok, good."

Sarah said nothing and appeared to be waiting for her Father to start a lecture about what happened last night, but he didn't. He left the tension sitting there above them both and pulled into the parking lot at the school. He parked and turned off the car. She sat there, still waiting for the lecture of a lifetime. Edward opened his door, exited, closed the door, and walked into the school, leaving his daughter sitting there bewildered.

Edward felt the looks and glares of others as he walked down the hallway. The level of disappointment hanging in the air was heavier than before. He half wanted to respond, but also half didn't care what anyone else thought. Luckily for everyone, the second half won.

He walked into his classroom, which was half full of his students. It was quieter than normal. No pre-start of class chatting going on. Each student was sitting at their desk, staring at him.

These kids are too young to understand, thought Edward. Instead of saying anything, he returned the same cold welcome back to them and unpacked his bag to prepare for the day.

Each class took a few minutes to warm up, but eventually the discussion on the lessons picked up to close to the normal level. That was all Edward could ask for. He didn't know what people thought of him or his actions, and he didn't want it to affect his effectiveness as a teacher. The discussion also helped him stay awake through the first few classes.

After his fourth class, he packed up a few things and prepared to pull out his lunch. He did not feel he would be welcomed in the teacher's lounge today. A voice from the door called him. "Mr. Meyer." He turned, expecting to see a student with a question, but saw a young man in a deputy uniform standing in his doorway with his hat in his hands. Tillingsly introduced him once, but Edward was currently drawing a blank trying to remember his name. He thinks it is Mike, but he is not sure of his last name.

"Mike?"

"No. Marcus, Marcus Thompson," the deputy said.

"Oh, that's right. We met at the Kirklands' farm last week. I am so sorry."

"Yes sir, we did. It is ok. We only met once. Do you have a moment?" he asked.

Edward motioned for him to come in. "The sheriff asked me to check in on you and make sure you are all right."

"I am just fine, Deputy Thompson. How is the sheriff? He is the one I am worried about."

"Well, he is not doing too well. The doctors said he had a pretty serious heart attack. He will be out for a few weeks."

Edward's remorse hit him tenfold. As much as he tried to convince himself he was not totally responsible for what happened, it didn't work. "Next time you see him, tell him I am sorry. Will you do that for me?" Edward asked. He wanted to go see him, but felt now was the wrong time.

"He said you would say that, and asked me to tell you not to worry about it. None of this was your fault. He also gave me a list of things to tell you. If you know the sheriff, you know he may be out of service for a while, but he will still run the department from the hospital bed. There was this one time he stepped in a hole out possum hunting with old man Rickers out on route 142. He snapped his ankle in two, but that didn't stop him, oh no..." The deputy looked at Edward and cut his story off. Either the mood in the room or the look on Edward's face told him this was the wrong time for a story. "The sheriff asked me to tell you to not be too hard on Father Murray. You three need each other. He also said to tell you that I am at your disposal while he is out."

It seemed the deputy was correct. Sheriff Tillingsly was still trying to control and manage things right from the hospital bed, and had named someone to be his eyes and ears. That made Edward wonder something, so he asked, "Deputy Thompson, do you know what that last bit means?"

The deputy looked around and fidgeted. "Yes, sir."

"Are you sure?" Edward asked while walking toward the deputy. "You are ready to go to war with the supernatural. To fight against an evil as old as the world itself. One we cannot physically fight against, but can only use mystical blessed relics and words. Are you really ready for that?"

"I am ready to do what you need me to do."

Edward was less than convinced by the deputy's tone, so he asked, "Have you seen a spirit before?"

"Not up close, but a few out in a field or across the road," he said.

"Have you heard the sound they make when you fight them?"

He did not respond. Edward pressed again, "Have you felt their cold touch as they reach in and squeeze your heart? Or how about when they enter your mind and play with your thoughts?"

The visibly shaken deputy swallowed deep and answered, "Mr. Meyer, I am here to do whatever you and Father Murray need me to do."

The deputy's reaction confirmed Edward's assumption. "Let's be honest, Marcus. You aren't. None of us are. We can say we are ready for this, but we aren't. I know the sheriff trusts you, or he wouldn't have sent you here to see me. If I need anything, I will call you. You are the sheriff now."

"No sir, he is the Sheriff. Only an election can change that. I am just standing in for now."

"My mistake. I thank you for stopping by. Please give the sheriff my best."

"I will, and you take care. Call me if you need anything." The deputy donned his hat on his way out of the door.

Edward had no intention of taking him up on his offer. Deputy Thompson had no clue what they asked him to step into. It was bad enough with neither Father Murray nor himself knowing what they were doing. Taking him out with them would only put him in danger.

No matter. Edward was out of all this anyway. His children were his only focus. A glance at the clock changed that focus for just a second. He was starved, and only had a few minutes before students would file in for his next class.

34

Edward settled in at his dining table turned desk. Exhausted but determined to grade at least two classes' worth of essays, he pulled the stack from his bag and started to read. The quiet calm of the house wasn't helping his fight against exhaustion. Thinking some background music might do the trick, he reached for his phone to start up the music app. The phone vibrated and danced across the table before he could grab it. The display listed the familiar number of Father Murray.

He checked the clock on his phone; it was just after eleven at night. That was not a social call, not at this hour. Not that he would have answered a social call from that man at the moment. He must need help. Out of both fear and anger, he used his thumb and swiped left to reject the call.

The display changed to his screen saver and Edward unlocked the phone and opened his music app. He selected his favorite eighties playlist and dove back into the essays. Thirty seconds into the first song a ding interrupted the music. Edward had no intention of stopping to listen to the message. At least not yet. The music started again, and Edward found where he left off in the essay.

Two essays in and the music stopped, again alerting Edward to a new text message. At this hour it could be only one person. His hand reached for the phone in reaction to the tone, but he stopped it halfway. There was a small voice in his head telling him to read the text. The hurt and anger yelled that voice down.

He graded another five essays before the phone rang again. Edward threw his hands up and let out a frustrated sigh. He gave up and stacked the papers back in his desk, declined the call, and headed upstairs to bed.

The next day Edward encountered the same looks and avoidance as he walked into school, but he didn't care. There was a slight feeling of being an outcast, but his subconscious combated every look or glare with the thought, *you don't understand anything.* His students were still standoffish, but not as much as yesterday. They engaged during classwork-related discussions. There were no such casual talks or students coming in early or after class to say "hi."

At lunch he ventured into the lounge to get a drink from the vending machine. As he walked through the door, conversations stopped, and everyone looked at him. Their eyes watched him as he crossed the room toward the machine. As he turned his back to them to make his choice, he felt their gaze burning a hole through him. He wanted to turn around and yell something like, "go ahead and hate me, not like I care." But he didn't care enough to cause a career limiting scene. This was where he worked. He needed to work past this.

He made the perp walk back across the lounge and out the door. Mark got up and followed him out. Edward heard footsteps following him, but did not stop. He continued to his classroom.

"Edward," Mark called when he walked through the door of his classroom.

"Hi, Mark. Aren't you worried what the others will think if they saw you talking to me?"

"Not really. See, they elected me to talk to you," Mark responded with a wry smile.

Edward was not in the mood to take the humorous bait. "That so?"

"Yea, it is. Most of us know about what happened. We don't know all the details, just pieces of what is going around. What happened in that field that night would have shaken anyone up. To be honest, I don't know how you do it. I still get scared when I see them. It must be something in your DNA. You have to know what happened to Lewis was not your fault, and none of this is your daughter's fault either. She didn't know. Neither did Charlotte. Hell, that creature has been running around for years."

Edward sat there at his desk, listening to his friend's impassioned plea.

Mark changed his approach.

"What I am trying to say is, you can't give up. We, everyone, need you and what your family does. Times have been rough here for a long time. Many of our old friends left because of it. I can't blame them. I thought about it myself a few times. We need you. Don't lose confidence."

Mark stopped and looked at his friend for a reply. Edward sat in silence for several moments, calculating his response. His mind stewed on how out of touch everyone was. He was not sure how much to say, but the built-up frustration got the better of his judgement and he unloaded. "Confidence? Is that what you guys think this is about? I lost confidence?"

"Well maybe not confidence. What happened would have shaken anyone."

"Stop right there." He stood up and walked to the end of his desk and leaned against it. "That is not it. There is so much more to it. Did you know the great Father Murray is only guessing at what to do? There is no science to this stuff."

Mark looked at Edward with a confused look.

"Oh yea. You didn't know THAT, did you? The magic book is just a bunch of prayers with no explanation of when or how to use them. You have to," Edward made air quotes, "'feel your way through things.' You can just as easily make a mistake than make the right choice. Oh, and these mistakes can kill. I should know. Father Murray made a mistake years ago that killed my parents. You didn't know THAT either, did you?"

A look of unspeakable shock crossed Mark's face. Edward had just exposed one of Mark's heroes as a fraud.

"His guesswork, his mistake, killed my parents. He wasn't even man enough to own up to it. He only admitted it after I asked. That... that thing roaming around out there... that thing he released, told me. I will protect my family, but I am not doing it anymore Mark. I am not going out there with him and making another mistake that will cost someone else their life. Nope. That will not happen."

Mark remained standing there stunned, looking at his friend.

"You can hate me, but I have my reasons. I am a father first. This stuff cost me my parents. I won't risk my kids or let them go through what I did. I don't care if anyone understands."

"That makes sense. I understand, and I might do the same in your shoes. Not sure how many others will. Things have been rough here for a while. You were a sign of hope."

The last statement Mark said rubbed Edward the wrong way, but he stayed silent. He was no sign of hope. Everyone was on their own.

"You and the kids should come over to dinner again," Mark offered.

Edward's first reaction was to decline, but he realized Mark may be the only person in town that didn't hate him, so he answered in a non-committal fashion. "We'll see. Right now, I want to stay at home."

35

The next few days at school were the same. Edward felt isolated, like a leper, but the urge to respond or make a scene had been diminishing. The interaction in his classes was mostly back to normal. It was not as social as they had been before, but it was a good learning environment.

That day was exam day, so the classes were silent. He'd spend the weekend grading each exam in the five rubber banded stacks, one stack for each class. In fact, he'd start tonight. He was skipping the football game. No reason to expose himself to the ire of the entire town.

As he gathered up the stacks of exams, his phone rang from inside his bag. His first instinct was to dismiss it, like he had most calls recently. Those calls had been at night, and he knew who they were from. It was just after three in the afternoon, and odd time for Father Murray to call him. Edward retrieved the phone to check. The number was not one he recognized. He answered. "Hello."

"Hey Edward, hope I caught you at a good time," Sheriff Tillingsly said.

"Sheriff, how are you feeling?"

"Not too bad. The doctors are still poking around on me. They are trying to tell me I need to cut back on the greasy food, red meat, and alcohol. I just say yes sir every time they read me a list of things I can't have anymore. I also need to exercise more, they say. I think I will take up walking. You can walk with me since you put me here."

The sheriff laughed loudly, but Edward did not feel the humor. "Sheriff, I feel just horrible."

The sheriff cut Edward off before he could continue apologizing. "You stop that. I was joking. I intend those walks to be times to catch up while I smoke a big cigar, something else I am not supposed to have anymore. This is not your fault. This could have happened whether you were there or not."

Edward was not sure how to respond, creating an awkward silence on the call.

"The Father told me what happened between you and him."

"I am not in the mood for a lecture. I feel everyone's disappointment in me, so you can save that talk," Edward said.

"Oh, you misunderstand me. I am not calling to give you a lecture. That is all between you and him, but I have to think about what is best for the rest of Miller's Crossing. If you don't want to put yourself and your family at any risk, not that they aren't already, that is your choice. I won't try to convince you otherwise, but... I do need to ask you a favor. There is a gentleman heading over to your home with Father Murray. I need you to meet with him."

"This is not a good night. I have exams to grade, and I am not in the mood to talk to anyone else that will try to sway or convince me to change my mind."

"This is not that. This is someone from the Vatican that will try to help Father Murray close the portal and try to restore order to things here. He wants to interview you about your encounters. Can you do that for me?"

"Yes," Edward begrudgingly agreed. He might as well get it over with.

"I thank you. I will be in touch about those walks, though. Would like to catch up with you."

The call disconnected before Edward could convey the same sentiment. Edward still had much to learn about his family. The sheriff could help fill in the gaps for him.

36

When Sarah, Jacob, and Edward arrived home, they found Father Murray's Cadillac parked in front. Next to the car stood two men, Father Murray, and another, both dressed all in black. Both men watched as Edward drove up and parked.

"Who is that?" Sarah asked.

"That is a friend of Father Murray's that I need to talk to for a few minutes."

Sarah looked concerned and asked, "Is it about Charlotte?"

Not wanting to lie to his daughter, Edward said, "Sort of. He wants me to talk to him about what I saw there so he can help Father Murray with it. Why don't you two go on inside? See if your brother needs help with his homework while I talk to them."

Sarah ran past the two men, only pausing to say, "Good afternoon, Father."

Father Murray returned the pleasantry. "Afternoon, Sarah."

Jacob just smiled as he bounced up the front steps.

Edward walked over to the two men and politely nodded and greeted Father Murray.

Father Murray nodded back.

Edward extended his hand to the stranger, who was wearing a black overcoat over his black pants, black shirt, and white collar. The man looked at him from under the brim of his black hat and greeted him while firmly taking his hand. "Mr. Meyer. I am Father Lucian. It is a pleasure to meet you." Father Lucian spoke with a very strong Italian accent, catching Edward off guard.

"Thanks for agreeing to meet with us," Father Murray said.

Edward snapped back, "I wasn't given much of a choice. I was told you were heading here before I was even told you were coming."

"Um... yea... sorry about that. Time is of the essence. Father Lucian has come a long way to speak with you. Can we go inside?"

"You know the way," Edward said, and all three headed toward his front steps. Father Murray walked through the spirits that still encircled Edward's house, but as Father Lucian approached them, they parted and allowed him through. Edward watched as they closed ranks behind him again before walking through himself.

Once inside, Father Murray continued on into the kitchen. Edward resisted asking him how it felt to return to the scene of the crime. Father Murray took his familiar seat at the table and Edward leaned back against the counter next to the sink. Father Lucian remained standing, holding his hat in his hands before him. His posture was upright and proper. He turned and spoke directly to Edward. "Mr. Meyer, they sent here me to assist Father Murray with the situation."

Edward was quick to interrupt and looked straight at Father Murray. "So, you brought another priest in to convince me to help you again." Father Murray shook his hands in denial the whole time.

"No, Mr. Meyer. That is not why I am here. Father Murray has explained the issue between him and yourself. That is not my concern. I want to know about the creature. Father Murray said you had direct contact with it."

Feeling foolish about his earlier outburst, Edward responded to the visitor, "Yes, a few times."

"Can you tell me about them?"

"Well, the first time would be at the Kirklands.' It took me out of the room, showed me images of this room from when I was a child and the dead bodies of my parents, and said he was trying to show me the truth. That is pretty much all I remember."

"He took you from the room? Where did he take you?" Father Lucian asked.

"First it was someplace empty, dark. It was just him and I, but I couldn't see him. I could only hear his voice." Edward suddenly remembered a field with his children and mumbled, "Then a field with warm sunlight." He paused for a minute, trying to remember more before continuing. "I am sorry. A lot of the details escape me, like a dream after you wake up. It seemed we kept alternating between the dark space to other places he wanted to show me, like the field, and my kitchen."

"You keep saying 'he,' but you said you never saw it."

"His voice was masculine, plus I saw it once. Not that night, another time."

Father Murray asked, "How many times have you encountered it?"

"Three. At the Kirklands,' and the other night at the Reynolds'. Both times were similar. The black empty space and showing me this kitchen. The whole time he offered to tell me the truth, which he showed me." Edward glared past his visitor at Father Murray. "Then, just before you called me to help at the Reynolds,' he appeared in my bedroom."

Father Murray and Father Lucian both appeared shocked at the revelation that the creature appeared to Edward. "Can you be more specific?" asked Father Lucian.

"The phone rang. I thought it was Father Murray. When I tried to answer it, he or it was sitting there at the foot of my bed."

"What did he look like?"

Edward described the creature for the two men. They exchange a few interested looks while Edward gave his description.

"You say it kept talking of truth. Did it tell you what truth?"

Edward looked past Father Lucian and straight at Father Murray seated behind him. "No, he never told it to me directly. He kept telling me Father Murray was lying or hiding things from me. Told me I was putting my trust in the wrong person. But every image it showed me led me back here to the part Father Murray played in the death of my parents." Edward looked Father Lucian in the eyes. "I am sure your friend told you about that."

"He did. Was there anything else? Did he try to get you to harm anyone or join him?"

"No, he said he was trying to help me find the truth and avoid committing similar mistakes."

Father Lucian turned to Father Murray. "Abaddon? Did you release him?"

"I don't know who I released, but it sounds like him. It would explain his more leadership type of actions. He tries to manipulate us and sends other spirits to do his work."

"Will someone tell me what you are talking about?" Edward demanded, feeling more than a little confused.

"You hadn't taught him yet?" Father Lucian asked Father Murray.

"We were starting on prayers and their meaning first. I thought I might have more time before he needed to know demonology."

Father Lucian appeared to disapprove of his fellow priest's method. "The sower of discord. The angel of the abyss, or as Revelation 9:11 says, 'whose name in Hebrew is Abaddon, The Angel of Death'. In other religions they call him 'The Destroyer.' It would appear he is building an army. What better place to do it than one of the most spiritually sensitive sites in the world?"

He turned his attention back to Father Murray. "You should have called sooner. Not waited a day, a month, and definitely not decades. You have put everyone at risk."

"Wait a minute. An army?" Edward asked. The explanation provided by Father Lucian both confused and frightened him.

"Mr. Meyer, take a walk with me please."

37

The two men strolled together, one next to the other, out into the pasture beside the main house. Father Lucian looked around and took in the fresh cool air and the lasting orange glow of the setting sun. Edward watched two geese flying to the south. That was the peacefulness he sought when he returned home. So far it came only in fleeting moments.

Father Lucian said, "Beautiful home you have."

"Thanks."

"It is not uncommon for nature to use true beauty to hide significant dangers."

"I don't catch your meaning."

"Nature often disguises the dangerous creatures and places. To the uneducated eye, no one would ever guess what really goes on here."

"If you tried to explain it to a true outsider, they would think you're nuts."

"Ah, true. There are many non-believers out there. Truly faithful believers would know they are being told the truth."

Edward's common sense disagreed on the surface, but considered there maybe deeper meaning to his statement.

"I didn't come here to talk to you about this..." Father Lucian said as he gestured toward the horizon line. "Mr. Meyer, can I speak completely freely... honestly to you?"

"Of course, Father."

"Father Murray means well, but he is not able to deal with what goes on here. His training does not cover this. The Vatican hand selects, trains, and assigns the priests for these sites. None, and I mean none, of the training involves how to handle the demons or spirits. We look for priests with a certain level of faith and personality. They are to be trusted allies and confidants to the Primaries assigned. To help sure up and deal with their spiritual and mental health. He has had none of the training your family has."

"Is the training you are talking about knowledge handed down through our family?" asked Edward.

"Yes and no. That is part, but once a child in the Primary family ascends, they undergo formal training at the Vatican."

Edward looked at Father Lucian with a quizzical expression. "Ascend?"

"Oh yes, you were probably too young to have heard that term. Think of it as a coming of age when a child first shows an ability. You lost your parents and disappeared from our view before you ascended. Your father was seventeen when he ascended, and like all before him, he came to the Vatican for one year for training." Father Lucian's stoic expression now showed a hint of a smile. "He was an inquisitive one."

"You knew my father?" Edward asked.

"Yes, very much so. His training was my responsibility."

"So, you taught him which prayers to use and when."

"We talked about the prayers a little, but I left that to his father. He was more familiar with the book than I. Actually, until Father Murray showed it to me earlier today, I had never seen it. My training was more around an ability. Do you know why the church selected your family as the Primary for this location?"

Edward answered with confidence. "Because we can see the spirits."

"Wrong. Most every family here can see spirits. Father Murray can see them. I can see them. Not that unique of an ability. Most can, they just need to accept it. There is something more to your family. You were too young for anyone to tell you about it, but you have felt it. You felt the surge flowing through you before, haven't you?"

Edward remembered the conversations he and Father Murray had about the importance of his faith and conviction. That must be what Father Lucian was talking about, so Edward guessed, "The surge? You mean a feeling of faith?"

Father Lucian shook his head. "No, my son. Not everything I speak of is about faith. It is a power flowing through you. A strength from within you."

"Wait!" Edward exclaimed wide-eyed.

"So, you have?" Father Lucian asked.

"I think once. The first-time Father Murray took me out. A spirit was on top of me. He had me thrust the cross up into it while reciting a prayer."

"What did you feel?"

"It is hard to explain."

"Try."

"Power. Confidence. Strength."

"You felt it coming from within you and projecting out, right?"

"Yes. Have you felt it before?"

"No. It is not something I nor Father Murray would ever experience. It is something deep inside you, your family, and the few families like yours around the world."

That left Edward speechless.

"If that is surprising, what I am about to tell you will be... well, the relic is just a prop."

Edward tried to ask a question, but Father Lucian continued before he had the chance.

"Don't get me wrong. It works through the Cross of Christ's crucifixion, but that is not where the power comes from. The prayer book is just a book passed down from generation to generation. The power..." Father Lucian stopped walking and turned toward Edward. With his right hand he made a cross in the air and then touched the center of Edward's chest. "It is within you. It is that power, that ability that is your weapon in this war. It is that which can drive these creatures back from where they came. I can help you learn to control it, in time. But first I need your help to deal with this. Things are far worse than you know. This creature has been running loose for almost thirty years. Father Murray tells me it has killed seventeen and terrorized hundreds. I need your help to end it."

Remorse overtook Edward. He had failed to deal with that creature twice. Maybe he didn't have the true capability, or not in the way his father and the others did. "Father Lucian, I would love to help, but I don't know how. Whatever you think I can do, maybe it skipped a generation or something. I have failed now twice."

"Mr. Meyer, you do. You need help to find it and use it. What you felt that day with Father Murray was just a fraction of what you are capable of. I know you have had bad experiences and doubt things now, but that was not your fault."

"Father Lucian!!! Come quick," Father Murray yelled while running toward the two men. "It showed up at the high school and has attacked two people. We must go."

"Mr. Meyer, you must come with us. We need your help," Father Lucian pleaded.

Still full of self-doubt, Edward said, "I can't help you. I am not who or what you think I am. I am sorry."

Father Lucian passionately pleaded again, "You are. Let me show you."

Father Murray exclaimed, "Father Lucian, we must go!"

Edward once again tried to explain. "I am sorry Father. I would only put more in danger."

Father Murray exclaimed again as he reached them, "Father!"

Father Lucian looked dismayed and disheartened at Edward's refusal to help. Without further delay, he hurried with Father Murray toward his car and they both sped away.

38

Edward sat in the living room for a few moments to gather his thoughts before trying to have a normal Friday night. The thought that a special power ran through his family should've been strangely humorous to him, but living in a world of ghosts and demons opened a world of possibilities. He knew he was no superhero, and other than that one time, he had felt nothing. That moment could have been adrenaline kicking in from the stress, and the pure fear of the moment. That had to be it. "Well superhero, time to grade exams," he said to himself.

A blood-curdling scream echoed down the stairs from Sarah's room. Edward leapt off the sofa and sprinted up the stairs, taking two at a time. He knocked through the door without even turning the door handle. Standing on her bed was the creature, holding Sarah above its head. She appeared to be unconscious.

"Hello, Edward," it said to him.

Edward commanded, "Put her down."

Defiantly, it shook its head, and then spun it all the way around. "Not going to happen. Seems she has inherited the same ability you have. Can't let this continue."

The creature forced Sarah's back into an unnatural arch above its head. The sight of his daughter being broken in half caused something to snap inside of Edward. Fear, anger, or something deeper surfaced and his voice boomed through the house, "Put her down!"

The creature took notice and stopped. "I didn't think you had it in you. You don't know what to do with it, though." It bent Sarah again.

Edward felt a warmth flowing through his body. He lunged for the creature. It jumped away, dropping Sarah down on her bed. When she hit the mattress, she woke up and screamed. She clawed her way to the headboard of her bed, as far away from the creature as she could get. Edward had it trapped in the corner.

Edward wished he had the book in his hands. With no option at all, he attempted to create his own prayer. "Foul creature, you have invaded my home and my realm. I condemn you back to the depths of hell you came from. In the name of God Almighty, the protector of heaven, earth, and all that is just, I command you out." At that moment, Edward made a cross with his right hand in front of the creature. While finishing the cross, a fingertip contacted its torso, creating a burning singe they both felt. The contact created a mark on the creature. It fell to the floor writhing in pain, making the most inhuman sound Edward had ever heard, like a thousand souls screaming all at once.

"Out with you, Abaddon. Back to the bowels of hell with you." Edward pressed his right hand on the creature. Its skin felt like worn leather. In appearance it looked hot, but it felt freezing cold at first and then sizzled under his palm. The smell of burnt flesh permeated from the corner of the room and a cloud of steam developed around it. Edward continued to press while he repeated, "I command you to leave this world. I command you to leave this world."

The cloud of steam grew large and dense, obscuring the creature for a second. When it cleared, the creature was gone. Deep down Edward knew it was not gone from this world. Just gone from his daughter's room. This was not over.

Edward turned his attention to his daughter sitting at the head of her bed, still screaming hysterically. He embraced her warmly and told her she was ok. She stopped screaming, but he did not let go. He sat there holding her, rocking back and forth for several moments, telling her it was ok. Then he stopped and whispered, "I need to go. You will be safe now." She said nothing. She let go and watched him walk out of the room.

Edward pulled out his cellphone and dialed. "Father Murray, where are you?"

Over the sounds of screams and howls, Father Murray screamed, "At the high school, hurry," and the call disconnected.

Close to the school, Edward passed groups of frightened people running away. They had abandoned their cars in the road, making it unpassable. He drove as close as he could get and then stopped and ran toward the school, weaving his way through the masses.

Edward fought through the crowds and finally reached the gate of the football field. He ran through and emerged out on the field. From there he could survey the scene. There were people injured and bloodied laying on various spots of the field and surrounding track. There was a circle of red spirits and demons about thirty feet away. Father Lucian was on the ground in the center. Father Murray stood over him holding the cross. They had not noticed Edward yet.

He crossed himself quickly and silently prayed, "GOD as my protector, guide me tonight in the protection of others." He felt what he felt in Sarah's bedroom, but this time it was stronger, much stronger. There was a pulsating glow around his hands.

Edward walked toward the circle and yelled, "Leave them alone." His voice appeared to echo as if it came from above. The creatures all stopped and looked at him.

Father Murray finally saw him and pleaded for Edward to stop. "You are not ready!"

Edward ran toward the group of spirits. He felt a strength building within him. Something unlike anything he had felt before. The power surged through every fiber of his body, while inside he had doubts about how to use it. The bodies littering the ground were all he needed to convince him he had to try. Which one should he go for first? The time to think was at an end. The time to act was now. They were on top of him.

Edward ran through the horde, throwing his hands at as many as he could. Each one he contacted staggered backward. He felt a slash on his shoulder and a quick stabbing blow to his lower back. The adrenaline of the moment blocked the pain. The cold touch of a spirit trying to grab his neck caused him to leap out of the way. A demon wildly swung at Edward's head. Its claw grazed his left temple, sending a trickle of blood across his vision and down his face.

"O Father..." he started a prayer, but stopped to dodge another attack. The demon's claw ripped across his right thigh, digging into the tissue, sending Edward down to one knee. As the creature passed him, Edward hit him with his right hand, causing it to howl in pain while it retreated to the circle that had formed around him.

"Edward, here!" Father Murray yelled with both the book and cross in hand. Edward held up his hand to tell him to wait, but Father Murray threw them anyway. Edward reached to catch them, but a creature covered in scars jumped up and used its body to knock them away. It fell to the ground, limp, with a thud following the contact.

The circle closed in on Edward. Outnumbered and injured, he was running out of options. But as hopeless as he felt, the confidence and strength inside him built to a level of that made Edward want to scream and jump out of his own skin. He held up a hand and prayed, but couldn't get a word out before a small four-legged creature ripped into his forearm with a claw. Edward yanked his injured arm back and held it close to his chest. When he looked down at it, he took notice of his other hand, now on the ground supporting him. The glowing he saw coming from his hands was now radiating out along the ground. Father Lucian told him the power to deal with all of this was inside of him. Maybe he was right.

Out of options, and now a wounded prey being circled by predators, Edward placed both hands firmly on the ground. The ground below his feet and knees shook. He began, "O Divine Eternal Father, I, your humble warrior, beg your strength to cast out the forces of your greatest enemy. Send them to the darkest depths of hell, where they will be imprisoned for all eternity. Use my body as your weapon against them."

The glowing circle on the ground shot out away from him across the field. The creatures and spirits reacted violently as they came into contact with it and then froze, unable to move. Edward pushed through the pain in his right thigh and stood up. He walked through the frozen beings and touched each, one at a time, repeating "In the name of God and Christ Almighty, I condemn you to hell, foul creature." One by one they disappeared in a puff of fog.

Edward left one for last, one he knew intimately. First, he retrieved the cross from off the ground. Then he walked over to the frozen creature. Its soulless eyes watched him the whole time. Edward pressed the cross against its cold leathery flesh. Flames emerged at contact. "Abaddon, in the name of the son, the father, and the holy spirit, I condemn you to the darkest depths of hell for all eternity."

The creature did not howl or make any sounds of pain as it disappeared. From the darkness its voice made one last proclamation. "I always return. The seed has been sown."

Edward limped over to Father Murray, who was helping Father Lucian to his feet. "Everyone ok?" he asked.

Father Lucian picked up his black wide-brimmed hat and put it back on. "I am ok."

Edward and Father Murray looked around the ground. Paramedics rushed in to help many of the injured. Others were being covered in sheets, as they had succumbed to their injuries. Father Murray lamented, "Not everyone was so lucky."

A great sadness and feeling of guilt came over Edward. He looked at both Father Murray and Father Lucian. "I am sorry. I could have prevented all this."

"No, you couldn't. This started long ago. You stopped it from getting worse," Father Murray said. "There is hope now that this darkness that has shrouded our community is coming to an end. We have you to thank for that."

Father Lucian cautioned, "Father Murray, don't be lulled into believing this. This is not over. It never is. Abaddon gave up too easy. This may be just the beginning."

Ready for what is next for the Meyer's Family?

Dear Reader,

Thank you for taking a chance on this book. I hope you enjoyed it. If you did, I'd be more than grateful if you could leave a review on Amazon (even if it is just a rating and a sentence or two). Every review makes a difference to an author and helps other readers discover the book.

As for what's next for the Meyer's family, you can keep reading with book 2—The Demon of Miller's Crossing. I have included the first chapter below.

As always, thank you for reading,
David

P.S. Signup for my readers list and I'll send you my monthly list of free offerings from other authors and notifications of my new releases: www.authordavidclark.com. You will receive the Miller's Crossing prequel—The Origins of Miller's Crossing—for free, just for joining.

DAVID CLARK

THE DEMON OF MILLER'S CROSSING

1

"What are you guys doing back here in this dark corner, huh?" Sarah asked the two flickering figures in the back of old man Tyson's barn. He saw them run in there just before sunset and immediately called for help. There had been problems on his property for the last several days. The chickens were spooked, his cows were so upset they wouldn't produce any milk, and his wife went on and on about not feeling right. At first, he blew it off as his wife just being her odd self, but the chickens and cows were something different. If they weren't acting right, then something was wrong. The night before he had caught a glimpse of something running through his farm, but he thought it had left. Today it was back, and it had a friend.

The two flickering vapors paid no attention to her as she inched closer. She held her hand out as if trying to lure a leery puppy out from under the bed with a treat. Inch by inch, she moved closer. With each step she ignored the chill that ran up her spine, and the cold sweat that gathered on the back of her neck. Those were feelings she felt almost every day, and was used to them by now. The dark pit she felt in her stomach was a less frequent sensation, but unfortunately it had become more frequent than it should. She felt the evil within these things and knew just how dangerous they could be. Her first experience was with another very dangerous demon. These two were far weaker than that one, but her training taught her you never let your guard down, any of these entities can be deadly, to her, and everyone around.

"Come on. Can I show you what I have in my hand?" she asked, holding her right hand out further. Both entities were still ignoring her presence, or were they? One glanced in her general direction a few times, with the beady black orbs he had for eyes. They felt it, and she knew it. They always felt it, and the closer they were to it, the feeling, the fear, became stronger.

The barn door behind her opened with a loud creak and squeal of the rusty metal wheel and hinge. Sarah looked back at the door, as did both entities. Father Murray poked his head through the door and asked, "Sarah, " he stopped and coughed twice, "do you need any –."

Both entities screeched and howled as they turned and rushed toward the door.

"God dammit!" Sarah exclaimed. She opened the palm of her hand, exposing the old wooden cross she had hidden in it. As the entities reached her, she swung it out at the end of a cord she had looped around the cross and exclaimed, "Be gone, foul beast. You are not the image of God and not permitted in his realm." The cross made contact, sending the creature away in a cloud of vapor. She pulled the rope in just as the second entity took a swipe at her. A quick duck and forward roll kept her from being hit. The creature moved past her and headed to the door. She pulled the cross into her hand and then threw her own punch, connecting with the side of the great beast. Flames burst from its side, and it fell to the ground in pain. It screamed and howled with a sound that raped the silence of the night air.

Sarah circled around it. The cross was in her right hand, and extended inward, toward the beast at all times. "You need to go, too. Go follow your friend to the bowels of hell. Never to return to this realm." Her voice was forceful, not a tad of fear in it, as her left hand retrieved a small vial of water from her pocket. With her thumb she flipped the top off and splashed it on the beast in the shape of a cross. The water froze on contact with the beast. "With this, I seal your fate. You are banished from this world, never to return."

The creature shuddered and moaned on the floor. The flickering sped up until it was not there, more than it was. Eventually, it disappeared altogether, with just a layer of red fog where it had originally laid. The fog soon dissipated, and Sarah walked toward the door.

"I said I had it," she said as she passed Father Murray standing at the door.

Father Murray wiped his nose with the red paisley handkerchief he had tucked tightly in his left hand. He pulled his collar up to guard against the damp night air and followed Sarah. "Oh, I know," he said. "Just was there in case you needed some help."

"I don't need any help. As you saw, I had it under control until you antagonized them."

"Well.. um.. yeah..," responded Father Murray. "Why did you banish him for all eternity? You can't use that kind of prayer haphazardly. We still don't know enough about the afterlife. Maybe we are reincarnated, and that poor soul will never be allowed back."

Sarah kept walking, now ten feet in front of Father Murray. "Nothing to worry about there. Neither of them were human. Even you should have been able to see that. They were not one of God's creatures. At least not ones he'd planned for this world."

Father Murray struggled to keep up with her pace as she trounced through the high grass, out toward the driveway and her car. The severe cold he had didn't make things any easier. "Sarah, you can't play God," he pointed out. "Some of those decisions are not yours to make."

Sarah stopped and spun around, startling the old priest. "You are the wrong person to lecture me about playing God. Those two were one of your doings. Not ones I released. I can feel how long they have been in this world, and those had been here a while." Her words where harsh, but her tone was harsher, which she realized and stopped to wait for him. Father Murray was a well-meaning family friend, and they both shared a bond, which some might consider a scar or branding. "Look, we both have enough blood on our hands from our mistakes. I am committed to fixing mine." She threw an arm around the old priest's shoulder's and said, "Now, let's get you out of here before this night air makes a ghost out of you. I don't want to have to send you out of here."

Sarah helped Father Murray to her two seat hatchback. She threw the car in reverse and sped down the driveway. Once out on the road, her pace didn't slow down at all. Even when she passed Sheriff Thompson's patrol car. Her foot didn't even twitch to come off the gas. He never went after her anyway, so what was the point? She hung a left, without slowing down an iota, and flew through the opening in the trees, down the dirt covered drive, up and over the rise to her dad's family farm. They slid to a stop in front. She got out and went around to the back, opening the hatch.

"Need any help?" Father Murray asked, halfway to the house.

"Nah," she said. The hatch sprang open, and she reached in and grabbed the Tupperware bowl of homemade chicken noodle soup that Mrs. Leonard had made for them earlier. She said it was an old family recipe, perfect for getting rid of the creepy crud. "Go on inside and to the kitchen. I will have this warmed up quickly."

She was carrying the bowl inside, marching toward the kitchen, when she heard the shuffling of papers off to her side. "Dad, what are you doing?"

Her father, dripping with sweat, but wearing a sweater and a jacket, was positioned behind two stacks of papers, at the old family dining table. Dark circles had made a home under his eyes, and several coughs interfered with his attempt to respond. He took a sip from his cup of hot tea and lemon, to clear his throat, before he was able to finally explain, "I have papers to grade. I feel fine."

"You look like shit."

"Sarah, language please," Edward said , trying to sound parental in between coughs and sneezes.

"Oh, she has been a real sailor tonight. Don't think I didn't notice you took the lord's name in vain back at the farm. Oh, I noticed, " said Father Murray, from the kitchen.

Sarah stuck her tongue out at the kitchen door and Edward smirked.

"Come on, Dad. Mrs. Leonard sent this. She said it would have you two right as rain, whatever that means."

Edward got up from the table and followed Sarah into the kitchen. She put the bowl down on the counter and pulled out a large pot that she placed on the largest burner on the stove. She turned the burner on high and poured the contents of the bowl into the pot.

Edward walked past the stove and looked inside the pot on his way to the table. "What's in it?"

"Chicken, chicken broth, vegetables, noodles, and something green. Maybe that is the special ingredient she talked about."

"Sounds good, I wonder what that ingredient is," said her father. He took another sip of his tea, not prepared for Sarah's answer.

"Probably pot."

Edward almost choked on his tea when he heard that answer. He was about to scold his daughter when Father Murray spoke up. "Eh, that wouldn't surprise me. She always has been a little too happy."

The three of them had a good chuckle at that. Sarah watched the pot and once it started to steam, she spooned out two bowlfuls of the soup and delivered them to the table. "Okay, you two eat up. And no more chasing things when it is pouring rain and thirty degrees out. Do that a few more times and you guys will be ghosts, yourselves." She stood over the two men for a few seconds with her arms crossed, both felt her gaze and responded with, "Yes ma'am."

"Okay, good. I am going to go talk to Jacob about ordering a pizza or something. There probably is pot in that stuff."

Sarah walked out, leaving the two old men to their soup. Both were studying spoonfuls of it. Each pondering if there could be some truth in what she said. Eventually both hit the same 'what the heck' moment and took a bite.

"She has grown up to be something else, Edward. You should be proud."

"She came back from training a different person that is for sure, and I am," said Edward. The combination of soup and how proud he was of his daughter, made him all warm and fuzzy on the inside.

Click the links below to keep reading "The Demon of Miller's Crossing."
For the US Store, tap here.
UK, tap here.
Canada, tap here.
Australia, tap here.
Everywhere else, tap here.

Want more Miller's Crossing? Check out the Miller's Crossing series?

The Origins of Miller's Crossing
Amazon US
Amazon UK

There are six known places in the world that are more "paranormal" than anywhere else. The Vatican has taken care to assign "sensitives" and "keepers" to each of those to protect the realm of the living from the realm of the dead. With the colonization of the New World, a seventh location has been found, and time for a new recruit.

William Miller is a simple farmer in the 18th century coastal town of St. Margaret's Hope Scotland. His life is ordinary and mundane, mostly. He does possess one unique skill. He sees ghosts.

A chance discovery of his special ability exposes him to an organization that needs people like him. An offer is made, he can stay an ordinary farmer, or come to the Vatican for training to join a league of "sensitives" and "keepers" to watch over and care for the areas where the realm of the living and the dead interaction. Will he turn it down, or will he accept and prove he has what it takes to become one of the true legends of their order? It is a decision that can't be made lightly, as there is a cost to pay for generations to come.

The Ghosts of Miller's Crossing
Amazon US
Amazon UK

Ghosts and demons openly wander around the small town of Miller's Crossing. Over 250 years ago, the Vatican assigned a family to be this town's "keeper" to protect the realm of the living from their "visitors". There is just one problem. Edward Meyer doesn't know that is his family, yet.

Tragedy struck Edward twice. The first robbed him of his childhood and the truth behind who and what he is. The second, cost him his wife, sending him back to Miller's Crossing to start over with his two children.

What he finds when he returns is anything but what he expected. He is thrust into a world that is shocking and mysterious, while also answering and great many questions. With the help of two old friends, he rediscovers who and what he is, but he also discovers another truth, a dark truth. The truth behind the very tragedy that took so much from him. Edward faces a choice. Stay, and take his place in what destiny had planned for him, or run, leaving it and his family's legacy behind.

The Demon of Miller's Crossing
Amazon US
Amazon UK

The people of Miller's Crossing believed the worst of the "Dark Period" they had suffered through was behind them, and life had returned to normal. Or, as normal as life can be in a place where it is normal to see ghosts walking around. What they didn't know was the evil entity that tormented them was merely lying in wait.

After a period of thirty dark years, Miller's Crossing had now enjoyed eight years of peace and calm, allowing the scars of the past to heal. What no one realizes is under the surface the evil entity that caused their pain and suffering is just waiting to rip those wounds open again. Its instrument for destruction will be an unexpected, familiar, and powerful force in the community.

The Exorcism of Miller's Crossing
Amazon US
Amazon UK

The "Dark Period" the people of Miller's Crossing suffered through before was nothing compared to life as a hostage to a malevolent demon that is after revenge. Worst of all, those assigned to protect them from such evils are not only helpless, but they are tools in the creatures plan. Extreme measures will be needed, but at what cost.

The rest of the "keepers" from the remaining 6 paranormal places in the world are called in to help free the people of Miller's Crossing from a demon that has exacted its revenge on the very family assigned to protect them. Action must be taken to avoid losing the town, and allowing the world of the dead to roam free to take over the dominion of the living. This demon took Edward's parents from him while he was a child. What will it take now?

ALSO BY DAVID CLARK

The Dark Angel Mysteries

The Blood Dahlia (The Dark Angel Mysteries Book #1)

Amazon US

Amazon UK

Meet Lynch, he is a private detective that is a bit of a jerk. Okay, let's face it he is a big jerk who is despised by most, feared by those who cross him, and barely tolerated by those who really know him. He smokes, drinks, cusses, and could care less what anyone else thinks about him, and that is exactly how the metropolis of New Metro needs him as their protector against the supernatural scum that lurk around in the shadows. He is "The Dark Angel."

The year is 2053, and the daughters of the town's well-to-do families are disappearing without a trace. No witnesses. No evidence. No ransom notes. No leads at all until they find a few, dead and drained of all their blood by an unknown, but seemingly unnatural assailant. The only person suited for this investigation is Lynch, a surly ex-cop turned private detective with an on-again-off-again 'its complicated' girlfriend, and a secret. He can't die, he can't feel pain, and he sees the world in a way no one ever should. He sees all that is there, both natural and supernatural. His exploits have earned him the name Dark Angel among those that have crossed him. His only problem, no one told him how to truly use this *ability*. Time is running out for missing girls, and Lynch is the only one who can find and save them. Will he figure out the mystery in time and will he know what to do when he finds them?

Ghost Storm—Available Now

Amazon US

Amazon UK

There is nothing natural about this hurricane. An evil shaman unleashes a super-storm powered by an ancient Amazon spirit to enslave to humanity. Can one man realize what is important in time to protect his family from this danger?

Successful attorney Jim Preston hates living in his late father's shadow. Eager to leave his stress behind and validate his hard work, he takes his family on a lavish Florida vacation. But his plan turns to dust when a malicious shaman summons a hurricane of soul-stealing spirits.

Though his skeptical lawyer mind disbelieves at first, Jim can't ignore the warnings when the violent wraiths forge a path of destruction. But after numerous unsuccessful escape attempts, his only hope of protecting his wife and children is to confront an ancient demonic force head-on... or become its prisoner.

Can Jim prove he's worth more than a fancy house or car and stop a brutal spectral horde from killing everything he holds dear?

Game Master Series

Book One - Game Master—Game On

This fast-paced adrenaline filled series follows Robert Deluiz and his friends behind the veil of 1's and 0's and into the underbelly of the online universe where they are trapped as pawns in a sadistic game show for their very lives. Lose a challenge, and you die a horrible death to the cheers and profit of the viewers. Win them all, and you are changed forever.

Can Robert out play, outsmart, and outlast his friends to survive and be crowned Game Master?

Buy book one, Game Master: Game On and see if you have what it takes to be the Game Master.

Book Two - Game Master—Playing for Keeps

The fast-paced horror for Robert and his new wife, Amy, continue. They think they have the game mastered when new players enter with their own set of rules, and they have no intention of playing fair. Motivated by anger and money, the root of all evil, these individuals devise a plan a for the Robert and his friends to repay them. The price... is their lives.

Game Master Play On is a fast-paced sequel ripped from today's headlines. If you like thriller stories with a touch of realism and a stunning twist that goes back to the origins of the Game Master show itself, then you will love this entry in David Clark's dark web trilogy, Game Master.

Buy book two, Game Master: Playing for Keeps to find out if the SanSquad survives.

Book Three - Game Master—Reboot

With one of their own in danger, Robert and Doug reach out to a few of the games earliest players to mount a rescue. During their efforts, Robert finds himself immersed in a Cold War battle to save their friend. Their adversary... an ex-KGB super spy, now turned arms dealer, who is considered one of the most dangerous men walking the planet. Will the skills Robert has learned playing the game help him in this real world raid? There is no trick CGI or trap doors here, the threats are all real.

Buy book three, Game Master: Reboot to read the thrilling conclusion of the Game Master series.

Highway 666 Series

Book One—Highway 666

A collection of four tales straight from the depths of hell itself. These four tales will take you on a high-speed chase down Highway 666, rip your heart out, burn you in a hell, and then leave you feeling lonely and cold at the end.

Stories Include:

- Highway 666 - The fate of three teenagers hooked into a demonic ride-share.
- Till Death—A new spin on the wedding vows
- Demon Apocalypse - It is the end of days, but not how the Bible described it.
- Eternal Journey - A young girl is forever condemned to her last walk, her journey will never end

Book Two—The Splurge

A collection of short stories that follows one family through a dysfunctional Holiday Season that makes the Griswold's look like a Norman Rockwell painting.

Stories included:

- Trick or Treat—The annual neighborhood Halloween decorating contest is taken a bit too far and elicits some unwilling volunteers.

- Family Dinner—When your immediate family abandons you on Thanksgiving, what do you do? Well, you dig down deep on the family tree.
- The Splurge—This is a "Purge" parody focused around the First Black Friday Sale.
- Christmas Eve Nightmare—The family finds more than a Yule log in the fireplace on Christmas Eve

Available now on Amazon and Kindle Unlimited

ABOUT THE AUTHOR

David Clark is an author of multiple self-published thriller novellas and horror anthologies (amazon genre top 100) and can be found in 3 published horror anthologies. His writing focuses on the thriller and suspense genre with shades toward horror and science fiction. His writing style takes a story based on reality, develops characters the reader can connect with and pull for, and then sends the reader on a roller-coaster journey the best fortune teller could not predict. He feels his job is done if the reader either gasps, makes a verbal reaction out loud, throws the book across the room, or hopefully all three.

You can follow him on social media.
Facebook – https://www.facebook.com/DavidClarkHorror
Twitter – @davidclark6208

Cover designed by Milan Jovanovic

This book is a work of fiction. Names, characters, places, and incidents either are products of the author's imagination or are used fictitiously. Any resemblance to actual persons, living or dead, events, or locales is entirely coincidental.

David Clark
Visit my website at www.facebook.com/davidclarkhorror

Printed in the United States of America

First Printing: Aug 2019
Frightening Future Publishing

ISBN-13 9781096895640

This book is dedicated to my buddy, my friend, my dog Chip. He was always there to listen to me, no matter what I was talking about and never complained. Instead, he gave unconditional love. Your loss has affected me more than I ever expected, but your life has enriched mine in ways I will never be able to explain. I will never forget you.

Printed in Great Britain
by Amazon

86114515R10092